Dying Swans and Madmen

Dying Swans and Madmen

Ballet, the Body, and Narrative Cinema

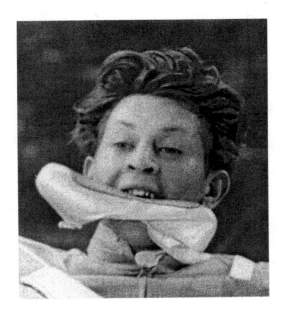

ADRIENNE L. McLEAN

RUTGERS UNIVERSITY PRESS

NEW BRUNSWICK, NEW JERSEY, AND LONDON

LIBRARY OF CONGRESS CATALOGING-IN-PUBLICATION DATA

McLean, Adrienne L.
Dying swans and madmen : ballet, the body, and narrative cinema / Adrienne L.
McLean.
    p.   cm.
Includes bibliographical references, filmography, and index.
ISBN 978–0-8135–4279–9 (hardcover : alk. paper)—ISBN 978–0-8135–4280–5
(pbk. : alk. paper)
    I. Ballet in motion pictures, television, etc.   I. Title.
GV1779.M35   2008
792.8—dc22   2007024986

A British Cataloging-in-Publication record for this book is available
from the British Library.

Visit our Web site: http://rutgerspress.rutgers.edu

Manufactured in the United States of America

Frontispiece
Moira Shearer dancing *Swan Lake* in *The Red Shoes* (1948).
Collection of the author.

Donald O'Connor in *Something in the Wind* (1947) (detail).
Copyright 1947 Universal Pictures.

For Larry and my parents,
and
in memory of
Moira Shearer (1926–2006)

CONTENTS

ACKNOWLEDGMENTS

I suppose my first awareness of ballet as something I wanted to do occurred when I saw a performance of *Swan Lake* in Cairo, Egypt, in the mid-1960s; my English teacher's daughter was a member of the corps de ballet, and soon afterward I began to listen compulsively to ballet music, especially anything by Tchaikovsky, and to demand ballet lessons. My first lessons took place at the Mary Nick School of Ballet in Dallas, Texas, and although I did not stick with it through my teenage years, I returned to dance in college and have never been very far away from it since. So I am grateful to everyone in the Dance Division, Southern Methodist University, Dallas, Texas, including faculty—especially Toni Beck, Karen Kriete, and Betty Ferguson—as well as staff and fellow students; and to the Meadows Foundation at SMU, for enabling me to pursue graduate study as a Meadows Fellow in Dance. In turn, my interest in film, especially classical Hollywood cinema, was, from childhood, always related to the dancers and dancing that I saw there, and I am grateful to the Graduate Institute of the Liberal Arts at Emory University in Atlanta, Georgia, and its interdisciplinary focus for helping me to learn how to merge the study of film, American history, and dance. I would particularly like to thank Amy Schrager Lang, my mentor in the ILA; Robin Blaetz (to whom I owe particular thanks for inviting me to Mount Holyoke to do a presentation on some of the work in this book); and Matthew Bernstein, Director of Graduate Studies in Emory's Film Studies Program, for their help and encouragement over the years.

Libraries, archives, and institutions on whose help and superlative staffs this project has relied include the Cinema-Television Library, University of Southern California, especially the wonderful Ned Comstock and Constance McCormick Van Wyck of the Constance McCormick Collection; the Margaret Herrick Library, Academy of Motion Picture Arts and Sciences, Los Angeles, with special thanks to Barbara Hall; Elaine Burrows and the British Film Institute, London; everyone at the Dance Collection, New

York Public Library of the Performing Arts; and the library and staff of the University of Texas at Dallas. I am grateful also to John Hart, C.B.E., formerly of the Sadler's Wells and Royal Ballets, for his fascinating stories about the companies and their visits to America; Barbara Peterson, director of the Conrad Veidt Society (American Branch), for making a copy of *The Men in Her Life* available to me; Steve Crook and his fount of documents relating to Powell and Pressburger; Andrew Moor for having me on his Powell and Pressburger panel in Warwick; Drid Williams, both for her anthropological work on dance and for conversations about dance and film on numerous occasions; and Naima Prevots for her superlative study of theatrical dance in cold war America and for answering all sorts of questions relating to the topic. I am also grateful to Cosmas Demetriou for giving me a place to stay while doing research in Los Angeles. A special thanks to my uncle Jim McLean, who always supported my love for movies and who once, in pre-home video days, provided me with a typed blow-by-blow account, as it were, of Red Skelton's ballet class in *Bathing Beauty* when I thought I would never get to see the film on my own.

Other colleagues and friends whom I would like to thank include Michael Wilson, Deborah Stott, Erin A. Smith, Susan Branson, R. David Edmunds, Dan Wickberg, Marilyn Waligore, and finally Dennis Kratz, Dean of the School of Arts and Humanities at the University of Texas at Dallas. I am grateful also to George Dorris and Jack Anderson, editors of *Dance Chronicle*, who published my very first article, on *The Red Shoes*; to Steven Cohan, Mary Desjardins, Ina Rae Hark, David Lugowski, Ann Martin, and especially Murray Pomerance and Richard Dyer for their kindness and conference conviviality; and to my great friends Judy V. Jones and Scott Belville and Charley and Annie Morgan. I also want to thank Larry Thomas again, one of the people to whom this book is dedicated, for keeping an eye out for weird ballet stuff during his travels all over the world and for being my best friend for more than twenty-five years.

And, as always, I offer my warmest thanks to everyone at Rutgers University Press, especially Joe Abbott for his typically expert copyediting; Alicia Nadkarni for her assistance and kindness; Marilyn Campbell for all of her logistical help and guidance; and of course Leslie Mitchner, for her continued enthusiasm and commitment to this project over the years and for her wisdom, patience, and generosity in all things.

Finally, I always meant to dedicate this book to Moira Shearer, with whom I became acquainted in the late 1980s when I was working on that article about *The Red Shoes*. We first met for lunch at Claridge's and became prolific pen pals for many years thereafter; and whenever I visited London, we got together for long meals (which always included many glasses of wine for both of us). I looked forward to our meetings, and to her letters, with the utmost pleasure and anticipation. Moira was not only a great source of information, but she was also always encouraging about and interested in my own work, incredibly generous and kind, and simply wonderful fun to be around. I hope she would have enjoyed reading this book—even the parts about *The Red Shoes*.

Dying Swans and Madmen

Introduction

Ballet in Tin Cans

I have never yet given a lecture on ballet, especially in the provinces, when someone has not asked me if the films could not make an important contribution to ballet. It is a natural question since there is more demand than supply, and ballet in tin cans could reach the smallest village. . . .

This is not a question that can be answered very easily.

—Arnold Haskell, 1951

Ballet stands like a colossus bestriding the world of dance.

—Wendy Buonaventura, 2003

[I]n general, people don't know about ballet from seeing it. . . . People know about ballet from the movies.

—Joan Acocella, 2004

The 1953 MGM musical *The Band Wagon* stars Fred Astaire and Cyd Charisse as professional dancers named Tony Hunter and Gabrielle Gerard. He is an aging hoofer, she a young ballerina, and it has been decided that they must dance together, perform together, in a new Broadway show. The idea is mutually terrifying: each thinks the other the more brilliant, the greater artist; each thinks the other opposed to the partnership; each believes that they will look ridiculous together. He is afraid that at the very least she is much too tall for him. So when they meet for the first time, at a cocktail party, he covertly examines her feet and says, "Pretty shoes—do you always wear high heels?" To which she responds, "No, not always. Sometimes toe shoes." He mutters under his breath and changes the subject.

I am a big fan of *The Band Wagon* as a classical Hollywood musical, as a Fred Astaire film, or as part of the oeuvre of auteur-director Vincente Minnelli, but this scene has always made me cringe. Partly it is just because I know something about ballet, was trained extensively in it as a young adult, know what can plausibly be attributed to it or claimed about it and what cannot. No less than anyone else who happens to possess knowledge of an arcane or specialized subject, I have to bracket out my "real-life" experiences to accept Hollywood's conventionalized versions of them. At the same time, I am sure that *The Band Wagon* does not really mean us to believe that female ballet dancers spend their entire lives with their feet encased *only* in toe shoes or stiletto heels. Betty Comden and Adolph Green, the film's writers, doubtless intended simply to play up the height situation and to wring an easy laugh out of an absurd image, a common enough ploy in a genre as defined by fantasy as was the musical film. But given Cyd Charisse's own background and training in classical ballet—the field in which she began her performing career—one wonders what she thought about the line or of the even more egregious or bizarre claims made about ballet and, most particularly, ballet dancers in the numerous other Hollywood films in which she appeared.

In fact, *The Band Wagon* is otherwise relatively well informed on the subject of dance and dancers, and by the mid-1950s "the world of the ballet" had become a rich source of subject matter for commercial cinema. Anyone who pays attention to movie box-office trends now probably has noted the number of films appearing in the twenty-first century that feature budding or professional ballet dancers as protagonists, among them *Center Stage* (2000), *Billy Elliot* (2000), *Save the Last Dance* (2001), *The Company* (2003), and *Step Up* (2006). And anyone who studies the history of popular cinema, whether of Hollywood or its overseas equivalents, likely could, if pressed, also come up with the names of other commercially or critically successful films in which ballet and ballet dancers have played some key role in the plot. The tragic heroines of films from *Grand Hotel* (1932) to *Waterloo Bridge* (1940) to *The Red Shoes* (1948) were ballerinas, and several might remember, and even admit to, *The Turning Point* (1977), *Fame* (1980), or *Flashdance* (1983) as more or less guilty pleasures from their youth. Partisans of the film musical are familiar not only with *The Band Wagon*, of course, but also with the big ballets in Hollywood musicals from the 1930s on, or the ballet set pieces typically included in film adaptations of operas and operettas; revues frequently featured "toe dance" numbers too. Even May McAvoy wore a tutu and toe shoes in the first feature film with synchronized sound, *The Jazz Singer* (1927), and performed a few simple steps in them in front of a chorus line of similarly clad dancing girls.

There are still other interesting and significant ways in which ballet and film have interacted over the years. The well-known Americanization of ballet as a theatrical art in the twentieth century occurred in tandem with, and demonstrably as one result of, its representation in and by Hollywood

Posed still of May McAvoy, *The Jazz Singer* (1927).
Courtesy National Film Archive, London.

cinema. In fact, so necessary were dancers to Hollywood and its studios and genres that at various times from the 1920s to the 1950s Los Angeles was proclaimed the "dance capital" of America.[1] Conversely, European as well as American theatrical ballets of the 1920s and 1930s featured characters—the flapper, the cowboy, the gangster and his moll, Charlie Chaplin's little tramp—drawn from Hollywood movies. George Balanchine was famously lured to New York by Lincoln Kirstein in 1933 partly by America's potential to produce girls "as wonderful as the movie star Ginger Rogers" and by Balanchine's sense, also derived from American films, that a "country that had all those beautiful girls would be a good place for ballet."[2] In turn, in 1948 the success of the first seasons of the fledgling New York City Ballet, the permanent American company that Balanchine and Lincoln Kirstein had been working to establish since the 1930s, was greatly enhanced by the concomitant popularity of the British film *The Red Shoes,* showing only a few blocks away in a Manhattan movie theater. And in yet another turn, some dance scholars have posited that the attenuation of the ballet line visually in the past several decades, such that professional male and particularly female dancers are now much thinner and longer-limbed, is itself partly the result of how ballet and its bodies have appeared in various forms of photographic media, including commercial cinema.

These sorts of anecdotes begin to suggest the complex intertextuality of ballet and popular film, but to date only ballet's deployment in the generic film musical has received sustained critical attention. In her influential 1977 essay "The Self-Reflexive Musical and the Myth of Entertainment," Jane Feuer discusses the ways in which the backstage musical (musicals in which putting on a show organizes the narrative action) affirms its own value for popular audiences by positioning entertainment against the "stiff, formal, classical art of ballet."[3] Feuer reiterates the importance of classical ballet as set against popular and populist entertainment in the musical's syntax in her book *The Hollywood Musical* (1982/1993), where she describes the numerous parodies of the high-art form in musical comedies, as well as the film "wars" between ballet and tap dancing that took place beginning in the 1930s (and in which *The Band Wagon* certainly participates).[4] At the same time, what Feuer calls ballet's "narrative style" became the preferred performance mode of the musical's problem-solving "dream" or "wish" sequences, such that what came to be commonly referred to as the dream ballet in musicals of the 1940s and 1950s stands in a parallel escapist or imaginary relationship to the film's dreamer as the movie musical itself does to the film's viewer. Jerome Delamater's *Dance in the Hollywood Musical* (1981) and Rick Altman's *The American Film Musical* (1987) also note the importance to the film musical of ballet in the general senses described above: it could be employed to raise the prestige or class value of a film, although it was often lampooned or criticized in the process; or it was featured in highly stylized fantasy sequences.[5]

As valuable as the work of Feuer, Altman, and Delamater is, it does concentrate on the generic musical and attends primarily to the structural meanings of ballet in the context of the musical's dual-focus couple-forming romantic narrative (in Altman's study) or drive toward the platonic ideal of romantic, narrative, and stylistic integration (in Delamater's). Thus, there

An American in Paris (1951) contains one of the most famous and lauded of Hollywood's "dream ballets."

is a tendency toward what dance critic John Chapman calls an "aesthetic interpretation" of ballet's history in film scholarship: that is, ballet is meaningful in the musical as it signifies in relation to the musical's "progress" toward an end, whether that end is utopia, integration, self-reflexivity, or affirming the musical's own value as cultural capital.[6] But ballet has been ubiquitous in American cinema, appearing over and over again in film after film, decade after decade, across one century and into another. And not just in musicals. American audiences have therefore learned a lot about ballet from the way it has been employed and the functions it has served in such films—about what ballet dancing is and what ballet dancers are supposed to be and to do.

Yet what does it really mean to say, as Joan Acocella does, that people know what they know about ballet "from the movies"? (She draws on a 1977 survey by the National Endowment for the Arts and the U.S. Census Bureau, which found that only about 6 percent of the population had seen at least one live theatrical ballet, including The Nutcracker, in the preceding twelve months.)[7] Why did British ballet critic Arnold Haskell find it so difficult, even in the 1950s, to answer questions about the significance or usefulness of what he called "ballet in tin cans" (and what accounts for his sneering tone)?[8] These issues are the broad subject of this book, and in addition to considering ballet in musicals, and what and how it is that we learn to think about art and the performing aestheticized body from this generic mode and its offshoots, I also investigate the sizable number of arguably more profoundly affecting *non*musical films that depend on ballet, that use it and its practitioners to say something interesting, and frequently dire, about the lived relationship of the artist to his or her work and life. In short, this book engages ballet in tin cans as a set of complex and intertextual relationships: the historical, aesthetic, and ideological meanings of ballet, as *dancer* as well as *dancing,* in narrative cinema—ballet not only as a mode of theatrical performance but as an embodied and lived relationship to personal identity and fate; as a mood or affect; and, finally, as an enduring and ubiquitous representation and arbiter of mass-cultural ambivalence about the place of art in American life. Whether ballet and ballet dancers are depicted "realistically" is not the major issue (although such questions become points of passionate contention in many critical discussions of ballet in and on film and must be addressed). Rather, what narrative films show and define as ballet is important because of the politics of representation as such—because, as film theory has so well elucidated, mass-mediated versions of "reality" shape expectations and ideas about real-world experiences rather than simply depict more or less truthful renderings of them.

Although the relationship of ballet and film involves virtually the whole of cinema's history, I focus primarily on classical Hollywood cinema, with a few European films released in the United States serving as points of comparison and because of their demonstrable interaction with American films and filmmakers. *Narrative cinema,* of course, refers to films that tell stories, often but not always (or else ambiguously) fictional, in which actors play roles and speak lines. There is an enormous number of films in which ballet dancing is featured in one or more set pieces; but I am less interested in these films than those in which the dancing—if there is any—is supported by people who are *playing, acting as,* some sort of ballet personage as well (dancer, teacher, impresario, and the like). For the sake of economy, these are the films I will often refer to throughout the rest of this book as *ballet films,* a term employed by some film reviewers, too, from at least the 1940s on.

There have also been points in cinema's history when the power and meaning of film as a medium was located precisely in its mechanical abilities to record reality objectively, to preserve time and space. Much of the earliest theorizing about film centered on such ontological questions, with Rudolf Arnheim famously arguing in the 1930s that the motion picture camera did *not* merely mechanically record the real world because the real world was not silent, black and white, two-dimensional, and so on.[9] It should

Loretta Young warming up on the set of *The Men in Her Life* (1941).
Photo by A. L. "Whitey" Schafer. Collection of the author.

not be surprising, therefore, that much of the literature about the relationship of dance and film, and ballet and film specifically, seems to focus most
on what might be called documentary issues, on how well film (and, more
recently, video) records, reproduces, represents, or creates dance and dance
movements. What, for example, is the best or most true or most effective way
to film a ballet work? How does the movement of any dance interact with the
movement that film itself can imitate or insinuate through its own formal
characteristics, such as editing and cinematography? Cannot film itself, as a
kinetic, time-based medium that creates its own rhythmic, patterned, and
expressive movements, "dance" in new and previously unimagined ways?
Essentially concerned with issues of adaptation on the one hand and the
creation of "new" experimental forms on the other, the dance-film debate
(as it is sometimes called) continues to this day. More germane to my project

is the role that commercial cinema plays in the debate, for these questions were often being asked not about films made as documentaries or for a few cognoscenti but about narrative feature films produced by a profit-driven mass-entertainment industry. Indeed, because many of the previous critical discussions of the interaction of ballet and film in narrative cinema are framed as participating in the dance-film debate, I would like to consider it a bit more at this point, to help set up both what has already been done and, conversely, what I will and will not be doing here.

A Warped and Pitifully Fragmentary Picture

In 1929 the Russian choreographer Michel Fokine, who had settled in New York in 1923, was called to Hollywood to record his dance oeuvre on film—including the famous ballets he had choreographed for Serge Diaghilev's Ballets Russes—and to establish a connection with movie studios to stage ballets for the screen. According to the contract Fokine signed with a producer, Morris Gest, Fokine had to abandon his New York studio, sever all connections with other ballet companies, and contribute his services exclusively to Gest. But Gest went bankrupt, and all of the proposed film projects were cancelled. Disappointed, frustrated, and more than a little angry, Fokine wrote to his son in 1930: "I felt now, in Hollywood, with the perfection of sound and color in motion pictures, there were tremendous possibilities for filming ballets. . . . It is impossible to describe all the advantages the screen has over the theatre, all the technical means which offer the director the opportunity to create an important artistic tie between the music and the picture. But alas! I learned in Hollywood that the time for the musical pictures about which I was dreaming had not yet arrived."[10]

At about the same time, however, other dance critics were beginning to ponder the effects of "ballet in tin cans" on the theatrical form's meanings, traditions, and future, and their prognosis was somewhat different from Fokine's. Although his suggestion that film sound and color had been "perfected" in 1930 makes Fokine seem inordinately naive now, in fact what was being debated, and what would continue to be a point of contention among dance historians and critics in the ensuing decades, was an enormously important issue: how film and its "technical means" would affect the living tradition of an art form that had heretofore had no permanent physical presence beyond its moment of performance.

Unlike music, plays, or operas, Western theatrical dance forms like ballet have no widely used "language" in which they are written. Film's capacity to preserve time and space could result in immortality—a new means of protection from the depredations of time—but it also might surrender "classic" or "timeless" meanings to the dictates of fashion. Would film, in short, benefit a traditional elite dance art like ballet by preserving its past and by promulgating more widely the performances of its present, or would the medium destroy that art for exactly the same reasons, preservation and commercialism? This debate was carried out most widely and vociferously from the late 1920s through the 1970s in English-language editorials, articles, books, and encyclopedias by dance critics, historians, choreographers, and archivists.[11] On the one hand, there was perceived to be, as dance critic and theorist John Martin wrote in 1945, a "natural affinity" between film and dance generally: dance is an art of movement, and film's "essential nature" is to record movement.[12] But on the other hand, it was impossible not to notice that film, especially commercial cinema, often produced "a warped and pitifully fragmentary picture" of many of the dance artists who had "helped to shape an epoch," and thus dance's history (especially that of the longest-lived theatrical form, classical ballet) was being distorted even as it was being preserved. (That dance could be archived, and how museums and film clubs and dance fans employed both professional and amateur dance records for their own uses, deserves its own study.) As will come up again and again in these pages, the related class and gender politics, and the differences between European and American viewpoints on art and popular culture more broadly, mark the most contentious debates about commercial cinema's potential to turn classical ballet especially into, in Haskell's scornful words, a "boom like miniature golf."[13]

At the same time, the burgeoning of terms like *cinedance* (or *cine-dance*), *choreocinema, cineballet, choreophotography, cinechoreography*—all irregularly applied but synonymous appellations used in Hollywood, as well as by avant-garde dance artists and filmmakers—from the 1940s through the 1970s points to the desire among many to produce an entirely "new" medium, one created from the symbiosis of film and theatrical dance in which results could be achieved not possible on the stage. In contrast, television, even in the 1930s, was being touted for its ability to show "an actual thing at the moment it is happening," as Haskell put it, thus bypassing the problems of preservation as well as mediation (television would merely make the spectator "richer by several pairs of eyes from which he can select").[14] But critics became gradually disaffected with television (for, to us, probably obvious reasons), even as video became part of the choreographer's and set designer's creative arsenal.

Now, in an era in which most theatrical performances of ballet or indeed of any form of dance are likely to be mediated mechanically or electronically (or digitally), the dance-film debate (much less its tendentiousness) can seem at once quaint and moot; but it really is neither. Much dance history now depends on film and video records, whose transparency is seldom questioned by the historians who rely on it. Equally significant, that we have film records of some dance but not others has affected the historiography of dance itself. For example, in her 1998 book *Dancing Women: Female Bodies on Stage,* Sally Banes notes in passing that her analyses are "limited . . . to dances I could study, through motion picture documentation, in order to be able to base my interpretations on close studies of choreography."[15] This problem is no less true of my own project; I can only really study that which is available for me to see. Thus, revisiting the changes in the dance-film debate over time—from Fokine's and others' initial euphoria about the possibility of rendering one's work and reputation inviolate for all time; to Arthur Franks's 1950 book *Ballet for Film and Television,* in which the film and television discussed is predominantly commercial, and often from Hollywood; to Arthur Knight's laments in the 1960s that dance and film's now "*vague* affinity" (italics mine) had never been led out of a "blind alley"; and on to many other discussions, through the present day—suggests, as we will see, that the theoretical concerns that it once engaged remain relevant not only to the historiography of dance but to issues of representation and (and *as*) history generally in an ever more mass-mediated age.[16]

The dance-film debate also, however, involves many other narrative films that I do not attend to in depth, if at all: again, movies that simply contain ballet performances of some kind, whether as a generic convention (operettas, for example) or as incidental performances. Even though many historically significant figures in theatrical ballet show up performing this or that set piece—often truncated, heavily edited, or badly accompanied musically—this book is *not* a compendium of films in which a ballet "number" is simply performed as a species of spectacle.[17] I am interested in how and what ballet dancing *signifies* in narrative cinema, and I investigate the sorts of dancing that commercial cinema *defines* as ballet; in addition, by the 1940s films had begun to appropriate ballet that was not overtly named or characterized as such, recognizable as ballet through its technique rather than its repertoire or costuming. But ultimately I am more concerned with how and what commercial cinema imagines about ballet's *people*—its choreographers and dancers and their work but also their lives, families, relationships, fates. I cannot pretend to discuss or even to name all of these films either, but I believe that I have been as comprehensive as I need to be. More detailed information about the films to which I devote extended attention can be found in the filmography at the end of the book.

Defining Terms

So far, I have been using terms like *ballet* and *ballet dancer, musical* (and by implication *nonmusical*), and even *the body* as though their meanings are well understood and self-evident. The dying swans and madmen of the book's title certainly require a bit more discussion. Yet in many ways, one of the points of this book is to show that Hollywood *did* define ballet, and its practitioners, quite narrowly at times and without much regard for the complexities of ballet's status as a performing art that has a long history and that required (and requires still) trained choreographers and dancers, a codified but flexible vocabulary of movements and steps, and, when performed in a theatrical setting, all of the apparatuses and personnel of stagecraft and mise-en-scène (staging and blocking, lighting, sets and props, costuming and makeup and hairdressing), music and musicians and conductors, and so on. The image of the dying swan and of the madman are meant to invoke well-known and ill-fated historical figures like *prima ballerina assoluta* Anna Pavlova, whose most popular solo was *The Dying Swan*, choreographed for her by Fokine around 1905, or legendary dancer Vaslav Nijinsky, who died after years of incarceration in an insane asylum (and who had once been the lover of impresario Serge Diaghilev). The terms also allude, of course, to the doomed winged women and tormented lovers of familiar classic ballets such as *La Sylphide* (1832), in which a nobleman falls in love with a beautiful winged dream-creature, a sylph, and accidentally kills her; *Giselle* (1841), in which a nobleman betrays the love of a peasant girl, who dies of a broken heart and becomes a wili, one of a sisterhood of spirits who every night prey on wandering men; and, finally, *Swan Lake* (1877/1895), in which a nobleman vows love for and then betrays an enchanted princess/swan, who is thus doomed either to remain a swan or to die.[18] As I show here, ballet's popular history and its romantic narratives—especially the ballerina's image as an inhuman, delicate, and dangerous creature with wings, at once victim and wielder of supernatural power—are what end up most frequently employed by commercial cinema as representative of a mode of living, dying, and artistic creation whose meanings always already reside in the hyperbolically or, conversely, ambiguously gendered and nationalized body.

It is not that Hollywood *only* made films featuring dying swans and madmen, however, and I also chose the title in order to play around with it. That is, many movie swans *do* die, but sometimes they are replaced, maybe even killed off, by ordinary healthy people who dance in different roles entirely, perhaps dressed in gingham and jeans rather than tutus and feathers. Sometimes the movie madmen are perfectly sane; they are merely mad about dance as opposed to being tragically flawed and diseased or abnormal (in a few cases they are just plain angry). I will not push this already tortured metaphor too much further, but the plastic relationship of ballet and film, the interdependence of each form on the other, and, of course, the social and cultural contexts in which both occur mean that I will not simply proffer discussions of films in which ballet and being a ballet dancer are equated with tragedy and death.

Anna Pavlova as a dragonfly, c. 1911.
Photo by Herbert Mishkin. Collection of the author.

As for *ballet* itself as a term: what does it mean, given that Hollywood has called so many different things ballet, so many women dancers ballerinas, so many danced set pieces ballets, even when they are performed in cowboy boots or tap shoes? What is a ballet artist—a dancer, or a choreographer, or an impresario? And what is the possible or determining gender of each? Ballet's history in America and its intersection with other forms of performance-based art and popular entertainment (opera, burlesque, vaudeville, Broadway theater) are the topics of the next chapter. But as the references above to Pavlova and Nijinsky, or to *Giselle* and *Swan Lake,* indicate, I use the

Tamara Toumanova playing Anna Pavlova as a dragonfly in *Tonight We Sing* (1953).
Courtesy National Film Archive, London.

term in the same way that commercial cinema, although rarely explicitly, does: to refer to the theatrical dance art whose techniques and vocabulary, the *danse d'école*, were codified in France in the early nineteenth century, and which then passed through Imperial Russia and Western Europe in the early twentieth century, and whose repertoire was, and remains, primarily romantic, ballerina-based, and narrative.[19] (The most dependable draws in ballet companies around the world today remain revivals of big romantic nineteenth-century classics like *Swan Lake, The Sleeping Beauty, Giselle,* and, in America especially, *The Nutcracker,* although ballerinas now share star billing with star males.) There was, to be sure, an avant-garde in ballet from 1909 on, mainly associated with Diaghilev's Ballets Russes, but this avant-garde's formal innovations and style (shorter dance works, greater abstraction or obviation of narrative, the rise of the male ballet dancer especially) rarely made it to the movies. What *would* become more commonly seen in films was the increasing interaction of the *danse d'école* with vernacular forms, as shown in the folk ballets and the jazz ballets that dot the Hollywood musical from the 1940s and beyond. But it is the visual iconography picked from the classic full-length ballets that becomes commercial cinema's most economical and effective means of identifying all "high-art" dance forms, even today.

Thus, my overarching goal is to elucidate the way that ballet has historically been associated in narrative cinema with, on the one hand, agency, joy, and fulfillment—an affective version of utopia, as Richard Dyer might call it—and, on the other hand, perversity, melancholy, and death.[20] Indeed, these two apparently opposed visions of ballet sometimes occur in the same film. Generic musicals might use ballet one way in the narrative and another in the musical numbers. Conversely, what *Variety* eventually came to call the "ballet meller" in the 1950s might only deploy ballet as an element of narrative, of characterization, with no danced performance occurring at all. The implications of a split between ballet as an element of identity in a narrative sense and ballet as a mode of expressive performance with its own techniques and vocabulary are profound. In general, my epistemological opposition of character to performance—of dancer to dancing—replicates that adopted by and embodied figuratively in the films themselves.

In fact, I became fascinated by Hollywood's treatment of ballet precisely because of the way films so frequently and compulsively rendered the art in binary terms that oppose what ballet dancers, male as well as female, signify in a narrative context to what ballet dancing signifies in, or as, musical spectacle. In both cases ballet is always a double moment of representation in which bodies at once produce and are produced by wider cultural discourses of gender, nationality, ability, age. More important, what and how ballet means in these binary terms is, I believe, of striking relevance to film theory and its interest in other sorts of binary oppositions, for example narrative versus spectacle, active versus passive, subject versus object, male versus female.

As is well known, *spectacle* in the context of feminist film theory is generally allied with stasis, with objectification, with fetishization, with two-dimensionality—all feminine attributes, all the province of the "not-male."[21] This is in opposition to narrative, which is active, the realm of the masculine subject, change, growth, will. But a few scholars have also begun to consider *danced* spectacle in another light. Angela McRobbie, for example, points to the way that ballet in commercial films like *Fame* or *Flashdance* seems to produce a "fantasy of achievement" for female spectators (especially young women), representing an imagined alternative "separate sphere" of satisfying and enjoyable work and associated familial relationships based on chosen, shared goals that are not linked to marriage and domesticity (although, as McRobbie also notes, the ballet world is not "progressive" in the usual political sense because its "families" also tend to be highly hierarchized and under male domination).[22] Feminist dance scholars, too, are now actively engaged, as Ann Cooper Albright puts it, in "trying to demonstrate how dance can stretch and reinvigorate feminist cultural discussions of the body, representation, social differences, and cultural identity."[23] Rather than reifying the dancing body, in Albright's words, as "a passive surface onto which society inscribes its political and social ideologies," these scholars suggest that consideration of the dancing body—even when it is the "tool" of the choreographer, or performing steps not of its own devising—can help us to understand the "complex negotiations between somatic experience and cultural representation—between the body and identity." Although we may at first see the filmed body as female or male, white or of color, fat or thin, these visual categories can be—and I believe always have been in ways that film theory is only now beginning to acknowledge—"disrupted by the kinesthetic meanings embedded in the dancing itself."

The remaining term in this book's title is perhaps, then, its most loaded one: the *body*. Here it refers, of course, to the human body as it is represented in commercial cinema, but, until recently, it must be said at the outset, only if that body is, or can be made to appear, white. Ironically, *ballet blanc* is a term coined by Théophile Gautier in 1844 in protest against the domination of the ballet stage of the time by white gauze, tulle, and tarlatan, such that "white was almost the only color in use."[24] It can be applied even more literally to the racial politics of ballet as represented in classical Hollywood cinema. Musicals regularly featured astonishing specialty performances of dancers of color (Bill Robinson, the Nicholas Brothers, and Katherine Dunham and her dancers are familiar examples), and some American theatrical ballet companies began to employ a few African American dancers after World War II (Betty Nichols with Balanchine's Ballet Society in the late 1940s and, in the mid-1950s, Raven Wilkinson with the Ballet Russe de Monte Carlo or Arthur Mitchell as principal dancer with the New York City Ballet; Mitchell also founded, with Karel Shook, the Dance Theatre of Harlem in 1969).[25] But only rarely does a classical Hollywood ballet feature a nonwhite ballet body, and even when it does, as we will see, it is likely to be a white body passing as black. Later ballet films, however, like *Fame, Flashdance, Save the Last Dance,* and *Center Stage,* overtly if ambivalently contest the presumed whiteness of the ballet body by making ballet's relevance dependent on the infusion of entertainment values linked to the nonwhite dance performer.

On a different level, because every human does have some kind of body, and because "normal" human bodies are, in an abstract mechanical and biological sense, assumed to be similar and to operate according to more or less well understood physical and biochemical processes to which all human bodies are subject, it seems like the one term that might not need definition in the theoretical sense. And certainly bodies have only rarely, until recently, been discussed theoretically in writing about film and representation, other than as part of a film's mise-en-scène or as objects of the gaze. Cultural studies in a wider sense avoided discussion of the body, although not its race or ethnicity, coverings, adornments, modes of display, stances, performances of gender, and so on, precisely because the body seemed irreducible, inescapable, the locus of "the real" for all of us.

As mentioned, however, dance scholars have always been interested in how bodies, even as basic biological entities, are molded, sculpted, manipulated, and controlled by processes of regulation and the requirements of dance techniques, and they have always also discussed these issues in relation to subjectivity and the self. A dancing body is not only the object of the gaze but also a subject who participates and presents chosen aspects of her self to that gaze, willingly and consciously. Ann Daly's work on Isadora Duncan describes how Duncan worked to bring "the female *dancing* body into feminist and radical discourses," discourses from which that body has never entirely disappeared.[26] Indeed, Ann Cooper Albright discusses the process of "trying to 'talk back'" to some feminist theorizing about the objectification of the body, the time that she spent working to show "that dance, as a representation grounded in live moving bodies, held the potential to disrupt this repressive paradigm. . . . Put more simply," Albright concludes, "dancing bodies simultaneously produce and are produced by their own dancing."[27] And, in an essay entitled "Power and the Dancing Body," Sally Banes writes, "I do not want to deny that dancing bodies may at times reflect the way things are, but I want to emphasize that they *also* have the potential to effect change."[28]

Although cultural studies did undergo a conversion of sorts to a theoretical interest in the body over the past few years that resulted in a rash of books featuring the term somewhere in their titles, it generally took little notice of the way that dance studies and its scholars (and dancers themselves) think about and discuss the meaning of the body in relation to subjectivity, personhood, and self-identity.[29] Some of this work did consider bodies in more nuanced ways than as the inescapable biological ground on which representation is superimposed, as it were, or conversely as objects always already perceived through the hegemony of dominant ideology and its notions of gender and sexuality, race and ethnicity, class, age, or health and illness. But one of the more urgent tasks of this book is to show how commercial cinema, in addition to promulgating "fantasies of achievement," helped to ossify the aestheticized performing body into something from which complex meaning was drained to be replaced by clichéd and teleological cause-and-effect plot divagations, Hollywood's conventional and often rigid approach to gender and its relation to public life, the primacy of marriage and the family as the natural order of things.

Dancing men also participate in these negotiations of gender and identity. Studies of masculinity and queer readings of classical film texts have drawn attention to the complexity of male as well as female identity politics as they are represented and constructed by American commercial cinema. Steven Cohan, for example, writes that the film musicals of Fred Astaire and Gene Kelly "imagined an alternative style of masculinity, one grounded in spectacle and spectatorship," and Cohan, Matthew Tinkcom, and Brett Farmer have also explored the camp sensibilities of certain MGM musicals as an inflection of the gay sensibilities of their production personnel, as well as their relation to fantasy and spectatorial pleasure.[30] Alex Doty's analysis of the "aesthete-and-diva" politics of *The Red Shoes* points to the importance of some ballet films' homosocial, if not homosexual, narrative structures.[31] Although Richard Dyer claims that classical ballet "yearns towards the potentials of the human body, all human bodies, stripped of the specifics of class, gender and sexuality," American ballet culture has always stood out against the background of what Olga Maynard referred to in her 1959 book *The American Ballet* as the audience's "fear" of "the pervert on the stage."[32] Male roles in ballet films thus provide ways to interrogate both the "fear" of the exhibitionist male in American culture and the value of those males as queer and camp discourse within the larger patriarchal dimensions of Hollywood cinema.

Paradoxically, the importance of dance and dancing as a site of such potentially disruptive significance—even, or especially, in historical terms—can perhaps best be argued for through analysis of ballet's film presence outside the confines of the generic musical, in what film studies would now call melodrama. Along with the musical, the "ballet meller" forms an important locus for the circulation of ballet's meaning in American culture, its immense rhetorical power drawn from ballet's fetishistic and fetishized appurtenances—tights, tutus, tiaras, toe shoes—and from the widely circulated meanings of its best known and most notorious performers. In these films ballet signifies as costuming, music, destiny, but not necessarily dancing—an iconographically rendered allegory about the difficulty, if not impossibility, of reconciling art and normal life. Dance critic Arlene Croce has named the way Hollywood typically handled ballet in this tragically inclined fashion a "tradition of morbidity," a useful appellation that I will employ frequently against the musical's utopian dimensions as well as McRobbie's "fantasy of achievement."[33]

Genre Trouble

It would be convenient to be able to map ballet's deployment by commercial cinema according to the genre of each film, attaching the tradition of morbidity to melodrama and fantasies of achievement and utopia to the musical. But the genre situation turns out to be markedly more complex. I have already referenced some of the scholarly studies of the Hollywood musical; among these scholars there has been a bit of quibbling about whether a musical is best identified by the presence of song and dance numbers (its semantic elements) or by a particular relationship of those numbers to the surrounding narrative (its syntactic structure), but musicals have never seemed all that hard to identify as such, and, indeed, much of the work on the musical seems to concern itself with the same quasi-canonical films. Even more academic attention has been paid to classical Hollywood film melodrama, and melodrama, too, has acquired its own canonlike body of films according to the scholarly definitions of the genre: that Hollywood melodrama of the 1930s, 1940s, and 1950s is concerned with domesticity, family and children, and women's lives and relationships (or really crises thereof, which is why the term alternatively refers to films known to their contemporary audiences as women's films, weepies, tearjerkers, three-handkerchief pictures, and so on).[34]

But as Rick Altman, Steve Neale, Ben Singer, and others have shown, Hollywood *itself,* its producers and publicity and promotional materials and reviewers, only rarely thought of melodrama as a distinct or separate genre and then virtually never in the terms that have become generic today through their repeated use in film scholarship.[35] Rather, as Neale notes, the "mark" of what Hollywood termed melodrama "is not pathos, romance, and domesticity but action, adventure, and thrills; not 'feminine' genres and the woman's film but war films, adventure films, horror films, and thrillers, genres traditionally thought of as, if anything, 'male.'"[36] Seldom, then, does one find a now-canonical domestic or maternal melodrama—*Now, Voyager* (1942), for example, or the 1950s films of Douglas Sirk—referred to as such at the time in advertisements or reviews, and this new slipperiness of melodrama as a term has perforce complicated my discussion here. That is, when I began to work on this project, everyone in film studies knew what a melodrama was, *especially* a domestic or maternal melodrama. And many of the films I was going to be discussing in this book fell neatly into that, or those, categories. For with a few notable and interesting exceptions, my films feature women protagonists negotiating the demands of professional work, domesticity, and family, frequently with tragic results, and often with powerful and charismatic male mentors or father figures or husbands placing the women in impossible double binds that replicated the Manichean nature of the melodramatic universe.

As my own archival research continued, however, Hollywood's failure to name many of my subject films melodramas in their press books or advertising campaigns, as well as the term's absence from journalistic reviews, became more apparent and a bit troublesome to the organizational structure I had planned to follow. Yet thinking about melodrama more broadly, especially in terms of action, thrills, and "anything male," helped me to make sense of other, disparate elements in some of the films I was studying. I was less pleased when the contours of a presumably even more basic if not more clearly defined genre, the Hollywood musical, began to shift quite alarmingly during my research as well. I did know that classical Hollywood had categorized musicals in several ways, for example as musical comedies and "serious musicals"; these last could be anything from Broadway adaptations like *Oklahoma!* (1955) to biopics like *Night and Day* (1946, subject Cole Porter), *Till the Clouds Roll By* (1947, Jerome Kern), or *Words and Music* (1948, Rodgers and Hart). But some of the films I had planned to write about as *obviously* musicals, albeit noncanonical ones, turned out to have been publicized and reviewed as dramas with music, dance-and-drama romances, music-and-dancing romances, backstage stories, lavish backstage dramas, stage romances, lively stories of backstage life, romantic musical dramas, and so on. MGM's *The Unfinished Dance* (1947, produced by Joe Pasternak and starring Cyd Charisse and Margaret O'Brien)—clearly a musical, surely, because it gets discussed only in books and compendia of same—turned out to have been publicized simultaneously as "M-G-M's big, new, different Technicolor musical" *and* as "M-G-M's glamorous Technicolor drama of the ballet world," a "thrilling romantic drama," and an "engrossing story of laughter and tragedy backstage."

But if the generic situation is no longer neat, it is all the more interesting for being messy. The shorthand label "ballet meller" was not actually used by *Variety* until 1954, in a review of a little-known British film *Dance Little Lady* (1955). But it can function as shorthand by that time precisely because of the range of meanings the term is able to mobilize in relation to a film's characterizations, narrative details and plot trajectory, and even mise-en-scène. Rick Altman claims that film studies as a field has redefined *melodrama* itself into a shorthand term, such that it *does* now have a clear generic meaning, if only to members of an academic community. Most important, I believe, is that these same meanings can be found, or were given ritualized and conventional form, not only in dramatic films (the aforementioned

Grand Hotel, Waterloo Bridge, and *The Red Shoes,* as well as *The Mad Genius* [1931], *Ballerina/La Mort du Cygne* [1938], *Dance, Girl, Dance* [1940], *The Men in Her Life* [1941], *Specter of the Rose* [1946], *Limelight* [1952], *The Story of Three Loves* [1953], *Gaby* [1956]) but in musicals *(Shall We Dance* [1937], *Gold Diggers in Paris* [1938], *Something in the Wind* [1947], *The Unfinished Dance, Hans Christian Andersen* [1952], *The Band Wagon);* in comedies *(You Can't Take It with You* [1938], *The Dancing Masters* [1943], *Bathing Beauty* [1944]); in war films *(Days of Glory* [1944]) and cold war and espionage films *(The Red Danube* [1949], *Never Let Me Go* [1953]). And this is not a comprehensive list. What are these narrative details? What are these plots? And how did they acquire the power to define ballet as an art form and identify the common characteristics of its practitioners so easily? And while certainly we know that ballet's real-world existence affected its portrayal in films, how did the same films affect real-world ballet's own characterizations, narrative details, and mise-en-scène, and consequently the "post-studio" ballet film of the 1970s and beyond?

These topics will be discussed at length in subsequent chapters; but in brief, and with variations in plot specifics, in virtually all of the noncomic and nonmusical films (but in some of the musicals too) the physical and psychic fates of the protagonists reproduce those of the sylphs and swans (or, in the case of male dancers, fauns, satyrs, fantasy princes and lovers, and the like) they presumably portray on the stage. In some films (as in some ballets, like *Giselle*) the desire "to dance" is itself toxic, whether that desire is simultaneous with or precedes the action of the film's plot. Regardless of whether a dancer actually commits suicide or merely dies young, the implication is typically that she or he has as well effectively extinguished the brightest sparks of life and creativity in the lover or family left behind—with extreme cases suggesting that merely associating with "the world of the ballet," much less a ballet dancer, can prove fatal. When the dancer is depicted as an "offstage icon," in Otis Stuart's useful term,[37] who dances either not at all or in brief bits consisting of heavily edited close-ups, then just what it is that dancers must devote themselves to so religiously, and at such high cost, is mystified, rendered unknown and, more important, unknowable and therefore threatening.

Ballet in commercial cinema, then, is frequently *something other* than a danced performance, and this becomes even more clear when its bodies do not dance or when dancing is a signifier not of what Dyer names as the musical's utopian attributes—energy, transparency, abundance, intensity, community—but of disease, disaster, despair, death. Yet there are also intriguing exceptions, nonmusicals that feature these same utopian elements as well as those of a tradition of morbidity, or musicals that are marked by tragic events. Although *the body* remains a key visual category in all these films, and continues to organize some of the complex negotiations between indi-

Glamour photo of Vivien Leigh in swan costume for her tragic role in *Waterloo Bridge* (1940).

Photo by Laszlo Willinger. Collection of the author.

vidual and cultural identity described above, it is the body of ballet itself, its meaning as a profession, avocation, even religion, that motivates and shapes narrative action. Peter Brooks has famously written about the "moral occult" in theatrical and literary melodrama as a locus of real and intense ethical feelings, carried in other "registers of signs" than the verbal, that seem to be repressed by appearances of reality and by the inadequacies of language.[38] Tom Gunning has enlarged the domain of the "melodramatic tradition" to include its other aspect, "that of the thrill or sensation," and Brooks more recently has suggested the centrality of the body to melodramatic meaning.[39] The moral occult of ballet films—even, occasionally, when they are also musicals—may be, again, the deeply felt ambivalence that marks not only American attitudes about art and artists but also our fear of our own enjoyment of the "thrills and sensations" afforded by the performing or aestheticized body.

Yet when the dancer's body *does* dance, the tradition of morbidity can also become a fantasy of achievement (as *The Red Shoes*, a film that ends with the suicide of its protagonist ballerina, demonstrably was to many of its viewers, male and female). In this, ballet is much like opera, whose presence in commercial cinema has, as opposed to ballet, received significant scholarly attention. Opera has its own traditions of morbidity both in and out of film, and several arguments have been made—most notably by Catherine Clément in *Opera, or, the Undoing of Women*—that many classic operas (like many ballets) are driven by narratives that victimize women and depend on the aestheticization of the dead woman's body.[40] Arguments against Clément's conclusions, however (which Carolyn Abbate has compared in their influence to Laura Mulvey's "male gaze" paradigm of visual pleasure in film studies), neglect not only the frequency with which men die in operatic narratives, or the ones in which no one dies, but what Abbate calls the "unique phenomenal realities of musical performance"—namely the overwhelming power of the female voice to "usurp" authorship in phenomenological terms.[41] As Sally Banes has noted, much of the critical work, like Abbate's, that argues for the importance of "vocal assertiveness" as against narrative logic in opera applies equally as forcefully to dance: "even the realm of ballet, with its patriarchal hierarchies," Banes writes, provides opportunities for women dancers to "'wrest the composing body' away from the choreographer"[42]—or, I will show, from Hollywood's conventional ideologies, and even from certain of the rigidities of film theory.

Thus do Hollywood films not simply "contain" ballet, nor are ballet artists necessarily performing in films the ballet they would perform in a real-world theatrical setting. Conversely, as ballet's popularity increased from the 1930s through the 1970s and its well-known "ballet boom," it was always partly *because* of the concomitant popularity of ballet films. And in the next chapter I will consider why ballet in America has never been as easily categorized in its theatrical existence as it might have been in Europe. Decades ago ballet was most commonly designated a "high-art" or "elite" form that nevertheless somehow functioned as a subculture within a larger context of commercial entertainment, especially film but also vaudeville, burlesque, and

Broadway theater. But it is clear from my research, and that of other scholars recently, that ballet in America was always *also* popular culture, from Mme. Francisque Hutin's 1827 appearances at the Bowery Theater through the present day.[43] Ballet always moved easily and freely between opera house and film set or burlesque house and made use of commercial venues of all types, adjusting its formal requirements to fit the needs of those venues while retaining bits of the aura of its aristocratic and aesthetic or artistic origins. And it happily absorbed and reconfigured technique, stagecraft, and even ideologies from adversary forms, such as modern or jazz dance (or, in the past few years, hip-hop and street dancing), no less than Hollywood easily swallowed and recast the formal characteristics of avant-garde film, Italian neorealism, or the French New Wave at various moments and spit them out as elements of big-budget commercial films.

Aesthetic Interpretations: Commercial Cinema and Dance Scholarship

Despite the association of ballet and film in the senses described so far, it nevertheless is hardly surprising that ballet's formal vocabulary, technique, performance values, and history have received little attention in film theory. What is of more concern, though, is that even dance scholars often dismiss Hollywood ballet that does not conform to their own preferences or to current standards of taste. Arlene Croce, for example, has referred to Harriet Hoctor's dance performances in *The Great Ziegfeld* (1936) and *Shall We Dance* as "gruesome travesties," one of the many examples of "ersatz ballet" that appeared in Hollywood movies in the 1930s.[44] Hoctor wears toe shoes and performs multiple pirouettes and *tours jétés* and often sports feathers yet is a bit chubby and turned-in, her feet too flat and not pointed enough, her arms flabby. Worse, her major virtuosic element is to bend backward from the waist and turn and glide in that position while kicking herself in the head, thus addressing her audience more or less upside-down. In contrast, Croce approves vociferously of Vera Zorina's body, form, and technique, as well as those of Balanchine's American Ballet of the Metropolitan Opera, who were performing at virtually the same time in two ballet sequences in the musical *The Goldwyn Follies* (1938); Zorina was married at the time to Balanchine, too. To us, now, Zorina and cohorts are clearly the superior dancers, with superior bodies and training, and of course they are performing superior (Balanchine) choreography. They are recognizable to us as "good" ballet dancers in a way that Hoctor is not.

Yet there is an enormous amount of primary and secondary evidence that Harriet Hoctor, backbend and all, was widely respected and regarded by her contemporaries—by dance critics, film critics, and audiences—as one

of the best of America's classically trained dancers. Hoctor was regularly
compared to Pavlova and Danish ballerina Adeline Genée and even the
nineteenth century's Marie Taglioni by knowledgeable critics, like Lillian
Moore and Arnold Haskell, for her "delicate and ethereal grace."[45] Zorina
made several films after *The Goldwyn Follies* in which she danced less and less
frequently (but acted more) through the early 1940s; although Hoctor only
appeared in a couple of films that I have ever seen, she continued performing theatrically and teaching ballet in New York and Boston through the
1960s (she died in 1977). Most significant, however, is that not much seems
to have been made at the time, in the 1930s and for some years later, of any
differences between Hoctor and the now "obviously" superior Zorina. Hoctor,
no less than Zorina, was "superb," her dancing "beautiful to watch and a
technical delight."[46]

It is not that easy, then, simply to dismiss Hoctor's brand of dancing as
a travesty of ballet. For Hoctor's (or anyone else's) style of dancing to be a
travesty there must have been some prior correct version standing in place
already, and there was not. Moreover, *The Goldwyn Follies*, although meant
to be the first film in a more or less annual series of *Follies* films à la MGM's
Broadway Melody series, was such a disappointment critically and at the box
office that Goldwyn deserted the franchise after its first entry. To read reviews
of both films, in fact, is to notice how little variation there was in the critical language used to describe the ballet components of each. Croce would
undoubtedly attribute this to the critics' lack of discernment and education,
their *inability* to recognize the true ballet from the travesty. But in fact the
situation is much more knotty: sumptuous ballets with "toe-dancers doing
relevés in strict time and strict formation or fluttering in mothlike droves,"
in Croce's mocking words, continued to be featured in many Hollywood films
through the late 1940s and even 1950s, and if the thinner, longer-limbed
Zorina-style ballerina body came eventually to be accepted as "better" than
the plumper or the shorter-legged version exemplified by Hoctor and several other American ballerinas, it was also because commercial cinema was
training its audiences to do so—not primarily through Zorina or ballet, however, but through the bodies of movie stars themselves. Balanchine's desire
to work with "*American* girls" (or their bodies) came about through seeing
them on movie screens, as movie stars; it was American movie stars' bodies
that Balanchine wanted to train.

The problem, in other words, returns us to the dance-film debate: much
dance historicizing relies extensively on film and video records but does not
always seek to establish the context in which these records were made. In
fact, film's effect—and here I mean commercial cinema—on ballet history
and our understanding of what belongs and does not belong in our versions
of the past (and therefore our understanding of the present) can scarcely be

overestimated. While augmenting film theory with some of the insights of dance theory is one of the tasks I have already described, I also believe that dance historians are not yet fully employing the insights of film-based theories of representation to the historical dance image or the preserved dancing body. Understanding the frameworks in which ballet and its practitioners acquire meaning in film and American culture includes exploring film's effects *on* the ballet body and, in turn, how the ballet body has come over time to represent the "perfect" body for men as well as for women. Indeed, the "startling modern phenomenon" of the prevalence of "ballet postures," in G. B. Strauss's words, in diverse "non-dance" arenas and activities such as sports and fashion incarnates an "aesthetics of dominance" (the "expansion of the body to its most commanding aspect") but also, still, an aesthetics of disorder and disease (particularly, now, eating disorders), as well as visual beauty.[47] Ballet may stand "like a colossus bestriding the world of dance," as Wendy Buonaventura puts it, but as she also claims, "ballet is the most concerted attack on the female body of any dance ever invented," and she ends her discussion with a reference to the devastating price that little girls will pay for "putting on the red shoes."[48]

YEARS AGO I WROTE a short essay about this topic called "The Image of the Ballet Artist in Popular Film," and while I can no longer maintain the same carefree relationship to the notion of the "image" as "reflecting" some prior objective reality, I also feel even more acutely that, when a film's topic has a somewhat or demonstrably tangential relationship to the daily life of large segments of the public, the "image" created by mass-media forms potentially becomes the prior reality against which real-life experience will be measured. We may not all evaluate our friends or cleaning house or walking our dogs according to their representation in the films we see, but, to return to Joan Acocella's words, a lot of people do learn what they know about ballet "from the movies," so it makes sense to investigate what, how, and to what ends these movies teach us. Television may now feature ballet performances more frequently on public-broadcasting or cable and satellite arts channels, but so do the films discussed here continue to circulate as an amorphous presence in the "mediascape," an anthropological term that James Naremore appropriates for the study of film and characterizes as "a loosely related collection of perversely mysterious motifs or scenarios that circulate through all the information technologies."[49] Today, Web sites and message boards abound on the Internet to proffer opinions, reviews, plot summaries, and ratings of most, if not all, of the films discussed in this book, some by their original audience members but many by individuals new to the films in question; debates about an old film's merits (or lack thereof) can at times become heated. And while almost every metropolis of any size has its Christmas *Nutcracker,* and a lot of little girls (though still not so many boys) take ballet lessons, our points of view about what the art form means, especially as a way of life and living, continue in many cases to be derived not from empirical experience but through the "mysterious motifs and scenarios" of popular culture.

Organization

My discussion has already crossed all sorts of obvious disciplinary boundaries (film studies, dance studies, performance studies, American studies, women's studies), and it will continue to do so. The primary and secondary material I consider in the following chapters includes not only films and the stories they tell through mise-en-scène, framing and camerawork, editing, and sound but also studio production files and scripts, press books and other types of promotional and publicity documents, censorship files, star scrapbooks, photographs, amateur or noncommercial films, and reviews. All of this is integrated with analysis of dance itself—its bodies and their visual lines, technical capabilities, costuming, and interaction with other bodies—in the various contexts that constrained the range of its potential meanings. I aim to coordinate film theory's interests in the representation of sexual difference and identity politics with dance theory's articulation not only of the disruptive possibilities of dancing as dancing but of classical ballet's own binary divisions, to borrow Sally Banes's words, of the ballerina as well as the danseur as "expressed in oppositions between active and passive, assertive and yielding, strong and gentle."[50] One might also add that both the ballerina and the danseur are always expressing another opposition, between their own potential as geniuses and their status as the muses or tools of other creative geniuses, such as a choreographer or impresario. Ballet films all express a self-reflexive fear of the evanescence of art, with the treatment of the performing artist a manifestation of the passivity of the master or the master's oeuvre, whether that master is a choreographer or the film industry itself. Without performers, those purportedly powerless objects of the gaze, there would be nothing to prove that the master, the genius, the subject, was ever there, ever wielded power and authority, ever engaged in processes of creation and expression.

And finally, because I know that this book, regardless of my own wishes in the matter, will end up catalogued and shelved as dance studies rather than film studies (perhaps standing right next to Jerome Delamater's *Dance in the Hollywood Musical*), I have tried to make it useful to both camps—to be considerate of readers not as familiar with the terms of film theory and of those who take it up as a book that predominantly discusses Hollywood films but who do not know much about dance. The first chapter is devoted chiefly

to American theatrical ballet history in a cultural-studies context, and all of
the film chapters situate ballet's interaction with commercial cinema within
particular formal and historical parameters (for example, the transition to
sound film in the late 1920s and early 1930s; the relationship of Hollywood's
storytelling practices to the demands of censorship after the "uniform interpretation" by the industry of the Production Code in 1934; the loosening of
such restrictions after World War II and with the importation and influence
of postwar European film styles; and so on).

The first chapter sets the stage, as it were, by tracing ballet's history in
America and its interaction with both elite and popular-culture systems of
representation. I discuss the shifting meanings of *ballet* as a term in a variety
of nonfilm settings and contexts—burlesque, opera house, vaudeville, musical-comedy stage. The often polemical discourses, especially of the early
twentieth century, about what "American ballet" was supposed to be or to
become embody the conflict between those who approved of ballet because
it represented an elite European culture and those who opposed its trans-
plantation to America for the same reasons or who sought to "Americanize"
ballet's subject matter, technique, and style. These conflicts can be seen as
the framework for understanding the interaction between ballet's history
and repertoire and, equally important, its best known stars, such as Pavlova
and Nijinsky.

Pavlova was a mass-media sensation, touring America from 1910 to 1925
and performing in vaudeville theaters as well as opera houses on a self-
styled mission to take ballet to the masses; her effect on the emergence of a
"ballet consciousness" in America can hardly be overestimated. Her melancholy image as a dying swan—her most frequently performed solo—was given
immense staying power by her untimely death in 1931 and the legend that she
died asking for her swan costume. Nijinsky toured America twice with Serge
Diaghilev's Ballets Russes in 1916 and 1917 and was identified with the ballet
avant-garde. His descent into insanity (he was declared schizophrenic) only
months after his American appearances—and the explosive circumstances of
his well-known if unnamed homosexual relationship with Diaghilev—made
the "mad genius" the distaff version of the dying swan in terms of its entertainment value. These images, as at once notorious but also representative
of taste cultures that cinema wished to invoke in order to raise its own status
and respectability, form a key locus for the film industry's eventual quasi-
generic iconography of ballet.

The general meaning of *ballet* as a term from the 1910s through the present as the "art-form" version of theatrical dance is also shaped by nation-
alistic and racist concerns at specific nodal points (the 1920s, world wars,
the cold war). And in this chapter I explore the various claims and treatises,
by Isadora Duncan, Ted Shawn, Lincoln Kirstein, and others, made roughly

over the first half of the century about what American ballet *should* be, in order to introduce how the film industry's treatments of the art narratively and as performance, beginning with silent films like *The Ballet Girl* and *Bobbie of the Ballet* (both 1916) and *The Dancer's Peril* (1917), help negotiate these different meanings.

Because of the multivalent generic nature of many of the films I discuss in the remaining chapters, it would again not make sense to discuss musicals in one chapter and melodramas in another; some of the musicals are morbid, and some of the dramatic films have happy endings. Some of the dramatic films also include dancing, and some do not. I also want to present information more or less chronologically whenever possible. So the second chapter begins a two-part discussion of gender in the ballet film, focusing on women in films from the silent era through the late 1940s (or up to *The Red Shoes*) in terms of several interlocking issues: how the films present the ballet artist's relationship to domesticity and normative versions of family life—romance, marriage, children—in the narrative and how, or if, the films deploy ballet and the performing ballet body as elements of film spectacle. Concerns about the morality and sexuality of the dancer, her devotion to an art that is sometimes shown, sometimes merely alluded to or represented by decor and costuming or in dialogue and musical themes, runs throughout the discussion. Although there is a strong tradition of morbidity in these films, it is not static, nor are the questions and concerns about profession and family or domesticity always addressed and answered in ways that one might expect.

In addition to considering the nonmusical films in the way that Hollywood defines them—which is again rarely overtly as melodramas—it also clearly makes sense to employ recent film scholarship on the melodrama to explore how the "expressionist body," in Peter Brooks's words, can be produced both by the denial of the body's capacity to communicate verbally and by refusing its participation in bodily practices of its own choosing. If, to paraphrase Brooks, anyone who is not allowed to speak will convert affect into somatic form, what happens to a body that seeks to be expressive but is forced to remain "mute" *because it is required to speak,* to talk *instead of* to dance? How and why does the romantic repertoire of classical ballet become iconographic in commercial cinema, and how is bodily performance at once linked to the ballet artist as character, and muted, or foregrounded, as a signifier of corporeal competence, subjectivity, agency?

In chapter 3 I continue the discussion of gender in the ballet film through its "madmen," beginning with *The Mad Genius* in 1931 and concluding with *Specter of the Rose* in 1946, as well as the lampoon films of the era in which men perform in comic ballets or in drag—a different kind of "madness." Although fewer films exist that depend overtly on the male dancer as the agent of narrative meaning, those that do are no less invested with morbidity, on the one hand, through a particular iconography of mental and sexual perversity, and on the other, with a camp interest in feminizing the male ballet dancer through disguise, gender-bending, and cross-dressing. Overall, the dramatic films suggest the dis-ease of Hollywood with the spectacular aestheticized male body. There are also a number of musicals and comedies in which men perform in tutus as well as tights or, although dressed as men, are thrown about by ballet girls, that are at once the misogynistic flip side of this uneasiness and a joyous acknowledgment of the pleasures of gay male camp. These films are considered in conjunction with scholarship on the musical's song-and-dance men as an alternative style of spectacular masculinity.

Chapter 4 focuses on a single but exceedingly influential film, *The Red Shoes*, and interrogates Arlene Croce's claim that it "caps" the tradition of morbidity attached to ballet's presence in commercial cinema. *The Red Shoes* has generated an extensive literature mostly as an auteurist masterpiece from the team of Michael Powell and Emeric Pressburger. I study it in relation to the status of ballet in the United States and Britain during World War II and in terms of other films that were attempting to exploit the growing popularity of theatrical dance on the concert stage. In America, ballet became an element of the box-office success of musical theater following the recognition of choreographer Agnes de Mille's ballet contributions to *Oklahoma!* in 1943. Not surprisingly, several Hollywood films attempted to mimic the success of *Oklahoma!* in the 1940s through the addition of ballets to one or another studio films; and in Britain there had been several ballet films that had not attracted much attention or had failed outright. Although I concentrate most on *The Red Shoes* in an American context, the growing interaction of American and international ballet after World War II, with all that this implies about ballet's relation to stardom, art, and popular culture, is set up as well.

After *The Red Shoes* ballet as ballet was more widely known across the country, and more and more American artists were becoming famous under their own names. In chapter 5 the curious interaction of cold war politics and McCarthyism with ballet's identity as "Russian" is explored at some length, particularly in relation to the gender and sexuality of the male dancing body. While the "pervert on the stage" became a bigger concern for some critics as ballet's popularity increased, the cold war also instantiated a new interest in "cultural diplomacy," with dance companies (along with their "perverts") being employed by the U.S. State Department as envoys of American artistic, social, and political values. At the same time, if Croce's tradition of morbidity had truly been capped by *The Red Shoes*, films of the 1950s might be expected to be more cheerful and straightforward about

Janet Leigh (on left) as a tragic ballerina in the cold war film *The Red Danube* (1949).
Copyright 1949 Loew's.

art's compatibility with life—especially if American dancers were being sent abroad to serve as cultural ambassadors. Certainly some are, but, I argue, it is not until the mid-1950s that several over-the-top and contradictory renderings of the dancer's life and death make the conventional ballet meller all but untenable. After a film such as *The Story of Three Loves* (1953), in which *Red Shoes* star Moira Shearer easily dances difficult choreography, by Frederick Ashton, that she is supposed to have improvised in response to a growling but artistically impotent impresario's need for inspiration, and then, a few minutes after they kiss, falls dead of a bad heart, the tradition of morbidity cannot help but become the subject of self-reflexive parody or satire. Big ballets and ballet set pieces become virtually standard in the integrated musical, and, as a consequence of ballet's increased fame and a higher degree of academic knowledge circulating more widely, trained dancers, often dance doubles, frequently do the performing rather than "hastily tutored" movie actors (to borrow a phrase from one film critic about child star Margaret O'Brien and her wobbling about in toe shoes in *The Unfinished Dance* in 1947). This is no simple record of "progress" or "improvement," however, for uncredited dance doubles appeared in many pre–*Red Shoes* ballet films, too. And paradoxically, as ballet becomes more famous theatrically and appears more frequently as dancing in commercial films, the women in ballet films from the 1950s on often decline in narrative, if not spectacular, stature. No longer geniuses on their own, they serve as inspiration or muse for the male creative genius, redefined as the Balanchine-style balletmaster/choreographer/manager. Conversely, male dancers appear more often, but when they are ballet-dancing men, they have virtually no narrative function at all.

The defection of several spectacular male ballet dancers in the 1960s and 1970s, especially Rudolf Nureyev and Mikhail Baryshnikov, in a sense reversed the dominance of the ballerina in American dance in favor of the star male. Chapter 6 opens with a discussion of the well-known "ballet boom" of the era and continues through the present day. Despite the number of decades covered, though, the chapter is not the longest in the book. Partly this is because, with the nationwide saturation of television after the 1950s and a number of industrial developments (among them the breakup of the classical Hollywood studio system, the decline of Production Code–mandated morality, changing audience demographics, the influence of other national or narrative cinema styles, and the rise of independent film), Hollywood films arguably became, as they remain, less significant as arbiters of a uniform mass-taste culture. There were certainly fewer narrative ballet films made after the 1960s—none to speak of in the decade of the 1960s itself—but this decline was accompanied by a correspondingly greater number of feature-length documentaries that were released into new "art houses" and shown on television.

Yet one of the most popular ballet films ever, The Turning Point (which "introduced" Mikhail Baryshnikov as a dancing film star), was released in 1977. The Turning Point, and the films its success inevitably inspired, are discussed in relation to the shifting gender dynamics of the ballet film toward the end of the twentieth century and, or as stemming from, the final institutionalization of ballet, rather than modern dance, as America's true "art dance." The increasing prominence of New York and its ballet—especially George Balanchine and the New York City Ballet—created an image of the American ballerina and her body that was, and remains, everywhere: the ultrathin, long-legged, and pin-headed "Balanchine ballerina." The ballet body to this day is at once associated with swiftness, precision, speed, and beauty, as well as with the "new" diseases of anorexia, bulimia, and, for men, AIDS. Perhaps not coincidentally, the popular commercial films that employed ballet in the 1980s—there are virtually no ballet films in the 1990s—did so peripherally, using the image or iconography of the ballerina as emblematic of fantasies of achievement—Fame (1980), for example, or Flashdance (1983), both also significant for their reintroduction of dancing bodies whose race and ethnicity need not be white. Other films, however,

Zizi Jeanmaire and Roland Petit demonstrating post–Production Code ballet style in the *Carmen* section of the 1962 French all-dance "art house" film *Black Tights*, which also starred Moira Shearer and Cyd Charisse.

Courtesy National Film Archive, London.

that attempted to revive the tradition of morbidity, or that were unable to conceive of ballet and its bodies except as morbid or diseased, were less successful. Even attempts to capitalize directly on or repeat the success of *The Turning Point*—films like *Nijinsky* (1980) and *Dancers* (1987), made by the same production personnel and starring some of the same performers, a flagrantly womanizing Baryshnikov in the second instance—were box-office failures. That these final two films took male dancers as their subjects suggests the ambivalent status, still, of the male dancer and his body in the cultural imagination.

In the end my choice not to devote a separate chapter to the cluster of ballet films that appeared in the beginning of the new century—*Billy Elliot, Center Stage, Save the Last Dance, The Company*—derives from their remarked-upon nature as pastiches of earlier films and their conventions and iconography. My discussion, therefore, focuses on what is interesting or imaginative or useful about them, for even in their relentless recycling (or perhaps as a consequence of it) they can offer new ways to think about identity politics—race especially—and the relationship of art and life, or art and entertainment, or the performativity of the dancing as well as nondancing body. The final ballet film discussed at length is Robert Altman's *The Company*, which stars Hollywood actors but also purports to avoid the usual conventions and mythology of commercial cinema's treatments of ballet by being "about" a real ballet company, Chicago's Joffrey Ballet, and using "real" dancers and their lives as subject matter. But, as I hope even this introduction has shown, there is no longer, nor has there really ever been, any such thing as "real" ballet or "real" ballet bodies that can be understood as standing, literally or figuratively, outside mediated representations of them. I also make some concluding remarks at the end of the chapter, specifically in relation to what I initially believed this project would tell me and how it ultimately turned out.

A final word on a few practical matters. First, the illustrations in this book are, whenever possible, taken from material that would have been circulating publicly at the time in relation to whatever film or body is under discussion. Rather than frame enlargements (the film-studies gold standard for the study of elements of film form), I employ posed publicity photos, press-book ballyhoo, posters, and other visual culture to help illustrate the ways in which film and ballet were represented to their contemporary audiences. Second, while I do not automatically include directors' names or list the stars of all the films discussed in the text, more detailed information is offered in the filmography that follows the notes at the end of the book. And finally, dates for essentially all historical personages mentioned, regardless of their profession or affiliation, are listed in the book's index. Only when the dates themselves are significant are they listed in the text proper.

1

A Channel for Progress

Theatrical Dance, Popular Culture, and (The) American Ballet

There will always be certain personalities that will be attracted to the ballet as the type of dance that they most like to see. . . . But the ballet as a style is not the channel for progress any longer.

–Ted Shawn, *The American Ballet,* 1926

American dancers have earned the right to be *American* dancers. In the films, on ball-room floors, and on the musical-comedy stage, they are encouraged to be American. . . . But in the realms of the "serious" dance they are not yet permitted to come of age. The old Russian names can still be worked, and it naturally pays better if the Russian monopoly is tightly held.

–Lincoln Kirstein, *Blast at Ballet,* 1938

Our American democracy seems able to produce ballerinas . . . as well as it turns out low-price automobiles.

–Sol Hurok, 1946

When I first began to study dance history several decades ago, most books on the subject presented the history of ballet as a sequence of more or less cause-and-effect events involving various influential people and a few important dance works. From these books I learned that ballet was European, elite, and popular among the aristocracy from at least the time of Louis XIV, who loved to dance himself and who founded his own ballet schools so that ballet could move from being something performed by amateurs in a ballroom to a form of professional theatrical exhibition. Another of ballet's many big steps "forward" occurred in the eighteenth century with the publication of Georges

Noverre's *Lettres sur la danse et sur les ballets* (1760) and Noverre's creation of the *ballet d'action*, which did away with previously conventional spoken or sung interludes and relied on dance and mime entirely for the presentation of story events. The academic vocabulary of ballet, the *danse d'école*, the same French vocabulary of steps and positions and *enchaînements* that are used every day in ballet technique classes, was partially set into place with the publication of *The Code of Terpsichore* (1830), by Carlo Blasis. But despite the omnipresence of the *danse d'école* in the ballet classroom from that time to our own, it was really during the romantic period that "ballet as we know it" seems to have been born, that ballets "still performed today" were created, that the ballerina began truly to reign supreme and to wear tutus, tights, and, most significant, toe shoes.[1] An essential element of *recognizability* thus helped to make study of the romantic period more enjoyable than that of the previous eras, a situation about which I will say more in a moment.

The list of ballerina names alone from the romantic period was extensive and included Marie Taglioni, the first famous dancer to dance *en pointe;* Fanny Elssler, the fiery "pagan" dancer, in Théophile Gautier's famous words, to Taglioni's ethereal "Christian" one; and the Italian Carlotta Grisi, who married dancer and choreographer Jules Perrot. Some ballets of the early nineteenth century, most of them featuring otherworldly doomed women with wings and their tormented but worldly male lovers, were still in the repertoires of many of our contemporary ballet companies—*La Sylphide* (1832), *Giselle* (1841). But somewhere in this history, ballet "began to lose favor in Western Europe, and the center of interest . . . shifted to Russia."[2] The centerpieces of this parallel development were the partnership of ballet master and choreographer Marius Petipa and composer Peter Tchaikovsky, which resulted in several familiar classic ballets—*Swan Lake* (1877/1895, again with a winged and doomed heroine and a tormented prince), *The Sleeping Beauty* (1890), and *The Nutcracker* (1892). While these ballets are often called romantic because of their fantastical subject matter, Imperial Russia was also the birthplace of ballet's classicism, a "clean and noble style" with an emphasis on clarity of shapes in space, an increased use of turnout in the hips and the body's *aplomb,* legible movement quality, and a formal structure for ballet works—three or four acts, with a pas de deux in each.[3]

The categories of romantic and classic confusingly overlapped, however: as one standard text put it, "classicism applies to style and structure only, romanticism to period and contents only, hence a classic ballet can be and often is romantic . . . and a romantic ballet can be and often is classic."[4] The "reforms" of choreographer Michel Fokine around the turn of the twentieth century ushered in yet another "new era" in ballet, the *modern* (especially through Fokine's affiliations with Serge Diaghilev's Ballets Russes beginning in 1909). Fokine's modern ballets were at once classic, romantic, and "organic," in that Fokine demanded an equivalence of dance, music, and decor rather than fealty to the "arbitrary academic limitations" of the three-act ballet and its combination of "ready-made and established steps." Modern ballet was still classic, but much less romantic; new patterns of steps, gestures, and movements were created in support of characterization and of story, and all the components of the production were unified in the service of a work's total effect. No longer could a pas de deux from one ballet be lifted out to serve as a showpiece in another, which was a typical practice with the Imperial Russian warhorses.

Not much was American about any of this, of course; America's contributions, or lack thereof, to romantic or classic or modern ballet do not really begin to be noticed internationally until the 1940s, when the "center of interest" of the concert dance world—as of the art world generally—began to move once again, this time to the United States. The shifting meanings of ballet in America, and of American ballet, prior to and through the exultant years immediately following World War II—or before the advent of the cold war and its cultural controversies, to which we will return later in the book—are the topic of this chapter. For there was ballet in America from the moment of the nation's founding, although the narrative of American dance history always begins with the fact that practically by definition the place had no artistic traditions of its own.[5] Certainly many histories of ballet in America read as chronicles of the acceptance of a preexisting elite art form by an untutored and unruly mass American audience. On the one hand, ballet was something fine and artistic because it came from Europe and its opera houses, and on the other, ballet was suspect and decadent for the same reasons.

Yet the birth of an indigenous ballet tradition, however puny it may initially have been, was also part of the story being traced in the dance-history narrative. There were at least a few American dancers and American choreographers interested in producing something that would be American ballet at the same time that it was technically classical, eventually employing the vocabulary of the danse d'école just as I and my cohorts did (albeit with Texas twangs) when I was a ballet student. The list of names populating this chronicle was long, too, beginning with that of American dancer John Durang, who not only had a lengthy career but produced a dancing dynasty of sorts centered around Philadelphia in the 1700s. More European dancers began to perform, mostly in larger cities, after the Revolutionary War (and the repeal of an antitheater law in 1789).[6] Among the many other important nineteenth-century performers whose names I loved to roll off my tongue were Mme. Hutin, Mlle. Héloise, Mlle. Céleste, M. and Mme. Achille, Mlle. Rosalie, Mlle. Louise, M. Charles and Mme. Ronzi-Vestris, and finally Fanny Elssler.

Mme. Francisque Hutin was notable for performing in the Bowery Theater and provoking a class-based controversy centering on the degree of public exposure of a woman's performing body. Some in the audience railed against ballet as "the public exposure of a naked female" (to quote Samuel F. B. Morse), with others responding that the female in question at least "dance[d] beautifully" and that her bodily display was "no worse than others on the stage" (it helped when Hutin put on a pair of "Turkish trousers" under her ballet skirt).[7] There was also a story that physicians called on Hutin, asking to examine her feet because they wanted to know how she could dance on her toes.[8] Céleste, who performed here in 1827 and 1834, was significant because she danced the first *La Sylphide* in America, thus introducing to theatergoers the narrative and formal conventions of romantic ballet. She was physically small and slight, and she clearly was not interested in nor could she be accused of licentious display of her body; she was an otherworldly creature, not a flesh-and-blood woman. Then comes Elssler in 1840, who stayed here touring for two years, the first true ballet star in America, rival to Marie Taglioni, so popular as well as respected that champagne was drunk out of her slippers, Congress adjourned because so many of its members were out watching her dance, she was received by President Martin Van Buren at the White House, and adoring young men removed the horses from her carriages to pull her through the streets themselves.[9] The general effect of Elssler and the "Elsslermania" she sparked, however, was to leave "a memory of herself, not of ballet."[10] Elssler founded no real ballet tradition in her two years here; she only made it popular for a time and raised its prestige levels.

Some American-born dancers, however, who were working during this period—Augusta Maywood, Mary Ann Lee, George Washington Smith, Julia Turnbull—did become nationally known. Lee began as a singer and dancer who toured with the P. T. Barnum circus and performed in burlesque houses while training with one of Elssler's partners, James Sylvain; she later studied in France and produced the "first authentic *Giselle*" in America, in 1846, in Boston, partnered by Smith.[11] That many of the American dancers burnished their prestige in Europe in order to become acceptable to American audiences as artists set into place a pattern that would return even more forcefully in the twentieth century. And while there were still more well-known European dancers and choreographers who showed up briefly in America in the nineteenth century—Jean Antoine Petipa and his son Marius in 1839, the Italian Cecchettis (including then seven-year-old son Enrico, who would later become one of the most famous and influential teachers in the world), and Hippolyte Monplaisir (who toured as far as California, and was a choreographer at La Scala in Milan) in the mid-1850s—the general conclusion of all of the historical narratives, like that of Elssler, was that none of these individuals provided any academic foundation for American ballet. From Elssler's time through the early twentieth century, as Olga Maynard wrote

in her standard 1959 text *The American Ballet,* "American audiences went to
the ballet theatre with a benevolent Persian attitude toward dancing girls."
There was a lot of native talent, but historical events like the Civil War
(money got tight, Americans were not interested in supporting art during
times of national crisis) were always given as reasons for the failure of this
talent to develop, and to be developed by, academic traditions and schools.

As for early American ballets, the signal work here was *The Black Crook,*
a spectacular 1866 production that was also the first American musical and
the first big blockbuster theatrical extravaganza featuring "vast assemblages
of talent, tons of gorgeous scenery, cartloads of sequined costumes, dozens
of divas, and hundreds of coryphées."[12] Its initial run, at Niblo's Gardens in
New York City, was of close to five hundred performances and it was revived
almost continually for the next forty-three years. Its story was, as George
Freedley put it, "a completely ridiculous melodrama," but the ballet-pantomime that was organized around the ridiculous melodrama was publicized
in ways that made it practically a guaranteed audience draw even in troubled
times: it was rumored, in Freedley's words, that "the chorus girls and dancers
were to be nearly nude." The reasons *The Black Crook* mattered to American
ballet history were that, regardless of its other multifarious attractions, it
also sported a fairy ballet (winged women again) that was performed by
"real" ballet dancers, not mere ad hoc dancing girls, and it stimulated a
tremendous ancillary ballet-training industry of sorts around it. Among
what the *New York Daily Tribune* called at the time "the bewildering forest
of female legs" were those of ballerinas Marie Bonfanti, who had graduated
from the Blasis Academy and danced at the Paris Opéra, and Rita Sangalli,
also from the Opéra. The corps de ballet included thirty-nine American and
twenty-three English girls, and as the run wore on, new ballerinas and dancers were imported from Europe. The "foreign style of dancing" featured in
The Black Crook and numerous other spectaculars of its ilk became deified
everywhere as ballet (with American dancers masquerading as Europeans),
and as Olga Maynard writes, "any *sur les pointes* movement on the part of
the female dancer was ballet"—at first "Parisienne" and, by the end of the
decade, also "Russian Imperial."[13]

At least the "influx of well-trained dancers" sparked by the continuing
success of *The Black Crook* brought, in George Amberg's words, "good talent and good teachers into the country and, if the production was not of
the highest artistic order or the surest taste, it was nevertheless clean and
competent."[14] Here, however, most of the historical accounts, like Amberg's
and Maynard's, end discussion of *The Black Crook*'s influence by concluding
that still there was "no continuous development, no sustained tradition,
in the American ballet during the nineteenth century," and that there was
"little opportunity for aspiring artists to study classic dancing and even less

to see good performances." The "magnificent efforts and accomplishments" of all of the dancers, teachers, and choreographers of the era were "almost totally lost because there was no succession, no provision for handing them on from one generation to another in a perpetual progress of tradition." At this point the historical narratives usually make a few nods toward ballet's continuing affiliations with opera in major American cities through the end of the nineteenth century, but mainly, at least in relation to the *art* of ballet, the general tone was one of lament at opportunities lost: "For several years nothing of note occurred," writes Maynard, except for the formation, in 1909, of a ballet school at the Metropolitan Opera, which for many decades was "the oldest surviving ballet school in the United States."[15] And as represented in all those famous Dégas paintings of little ballet girls, albeit little French ballet girls, women dancers (there were very few men) were also "low on the scale"—even lower than actors—in the American theater, their career prospects "haphazard and depraved."

American philistinism toward the arts and lingering puritanical attitudes toward bodily display were usually blamed for some of the attitudes of American audiences toward ballet in the nineteenth and early twentieth century.[16] As was true of most of Europe (again see Dégas' ballet girls and their leering male patrons), ballet was omnipresent in urban areas, at least, but mainly as a species of spectacular feminine display; even male roles were usually performed *en travestie.* A very early Biograph short, *How the Ballet Girl Was Smuggled into Camp* (1898), consists of a "pretty ballet girl" popping out of a large barrel of sugar rolled onscreen by two soldiers; then "she dances a few steps and proceeds to make herself at home."[17] Occasional mentions were also made of ballet training becoming more common as a way for city girls and young women to learn how to be graceful or to correct "poor posture, knock-knees and flat feet."[18] But discussions of ballet's history in America during the late nineteenth and early twentieth century remain predominantly couched in terms of decline or decay or moribundity—"real" ballet was hibernating everywhere, waiting to be woken by the kiss of a new genius or event.[19] The next historical locus for discussion of such ballet, then, of ballet that adhered to the vocabulary and technique of the *danse d'école,* were the arrivals of Adeline Genée and Anna Pavlova, first, and then Serge Diaghilev's Ballets Russes. Genée, the Danish ballerina, appeared as a guest with the Metropolitan Opera in 1908 but had come to America mainly to appear in a musical, *The Soul Kiss.* She had been in England for several years and is generally credited with providing the ground against which both the classicism of Pavlova and the radical experimentation of Diaghilev's Ballets Russes could be understood and venerated there. Pavlova, with partner and choreographer Mikhail Mordkin, also débuted at the Metropolitan, in a revival of *Coppélia* and a program of *divertissements,* in 1910.

Russia's Poetess of Art in Motion

All American dance-history books allot quite a bit of space to Anna Pavlova. The heading above comes from a *Musical America* review of her first appearances here and exemplifies the sort of response she initially engendered.[20] Pavlova, a product of Petipa-style Russian Imperial training, was apparently no revolutionary in ballet technique. Nor, despite a brief association with Diaghilev's Ballets Russes and with Fokine, who in 1905 choreographed her most famous dance solo, *The Dying Swan,* was she in any way radical or experimental in her choice of choreography, music, or subject matter. Her success was always attributed to her personal genius: "She was great because she was Pavlova," wrote one dance historian, "the sum total of a divine gift, an active mind, a perfect body, superb craftsmanship."[21] Her self-imposed mission became to take ballet, *her* ballet, to every part of the world; and to the majority of those audiences, for example those in the American hinterlands, she was the first contact they were likely to have had with the art form.

When Pavlova began touring America in 1913, doing one-night stands in tiny towns as well as big cities on a nearly annual basis until 1925 (she had scheduled another tour here in 1931, the year of her death), it did not matter whether she performed in an opera house, a music hall, or a high-school auditorium. It all was significant to the development of American appreciation of ballet—to laying the groundwork for that eventual shift of the center of the ballet world from Europe and Russia to America. Pavlova was, following Elssler, the first female ballet mass-media star, her likeness appearing in advertising endorsements and on all sorts of products ranging from face cream, soap, clothing, three different makes of pianos, and the instructions for social dances like "The New Pavlowa Gavotte."[22] (I possess a vintage needlebook with Pavlova's picture on it.) She provided articulate, well-thought-out and educational interviews and articles from her first appearances in which she would lay out her life story, the course of her training, the place of ballet in the European and Russian artistic firmaments. An article titled "The Russian Ballet," ostensibly written by Pavlova for *Good Housekeeping* in 1913, for example, gives a five-page history of classical dancing and begins the process of defining the life of the ballet dancer in terms of self-denial ("I studied dancing for years, and work very hard at it now. One cannot be a great dancer and have much amusement").[23] This image of the ballerina became one of Pavlova's most powerful legacies, a template for other representations of the ballet dancer's life (especially the movies) from the mid-1910s on. At the same time, such devotion to ballet training was hard for Americans to *do,* if not to understand. There were no state-run academies of dance here that trained students from childhood for a theatrical career. Therefore, some dance teachers recast Pavlova's admonitions about childhood training in terms of un-American "subordination": "Imagine our American girls submitting to such an apprenticeship," wrote American teacher Ned Wayburn in a 1925 dance manual; "And fortunately you don't have to, for we've revolutionized all that."[24] Wayburn claimed to have invented a method that could teach one to dance like Pavlova in only a few weeks.

Despite the fact that Pavlova's career was rooted in traditions and training to which few Americans had access, or that far fewer Americans saw Pavlova dance than read about her or pondered her image in pictures, so significant was Pavlova's influence on the emergence of an American ballet consciousness between 1910 and her death in 1931 that it can scarcely be grasped, even now. Her image was ubiquitous because of her canny understanding of the apparatuses of publicity and her ability to control the representation of her private and her public lives. Certainly I was once amazed at the seemingly endless number of photographs available of her, and I tried very hard to see through the much more fragmentary cinematic record of her performing to understand the enormity of her gifts.

In a 1924 "interview" reproduced in full in Keith Money's *Anna Pavlova: Her Life and Art,* Pavlova announced that she would "like to go into the movies."[25] Unlike Isadora Duncan or, later, Vaslav Nijinsky, Pavlova believed that film would "preserve her art" rather than subject it to the dictates and whims of fashion and changing tastes. The films of Pavlova that I saw in the 1970s—I have not seen them since—include *California Poppy,* in which she dances in a flower costume, and *The Dying Swan,* the Fokine piece most identified with her. I remember one film as being shot outdoors, on grass, the other on a stage. And as I watched, I worked desperately to understand why she was the greatest ballerina of the twentieth century, but all I could really admire at the time was the astonishing arch of her feet.[26] I watched all of *The Dumb Girl of Portici* (1916), a big-budget silent version of an opera in which Pavlova was the star but as actress rather than dancer; there are two short dancing sequences, neither of them performed in toe shoes. Her bosom heaved and her eyes rolled no more than those of other early silent film actresses I had seen, and she was strangely mesmerizing, even though I was disappointed not to see her *dance*—as was apparently much of the film's contemporary audience, for *The Dumb Girl of Portici* was not a box-office hit.

In short, despite what I read about the near-mystical power that Pavlova wielded over her audiences (here is Agnes de Mille, for example, on her childhood exposure to Pavlova's dancing: "My life was wholly altered by her"),[27] the filmic records, as well as some of her many photographs, seemed to suggest that, although Pavlova may have been great for "back then," she would never get very far "now," because her technique was nowhere near as good as those of the dancers *I*, and my fellow dance students, venerated. Pavlova and her contemporaries looked "primitive," amateurish, even awkward, while our contemporaries, our own ballet stars—in the 1970s Natalia Makarova, Gelsey Kirkland, Mikhail Baryshnikov—represented progress, achievement, advancement, and any other term relating to evolutionary improvement (more about this in moment). Pavlova did not, after all, perform truly difficult ballets, and she did not really dance for ballet companies. For most of her adult life she had something like a vanity company of which she was the centerpiece. It was impossible not to be attracted to and moved by the legends and mysteries about Pavlova (was she really married to manager Victor Dandré, as he claimed but as she denied?);[28] her special relationship to *The Dying Swan* (her white winged costume featuring a ruby jewel on the breast to represent the fatal wound made by the hunter's shot) and, indeed, to swans and birds generally; her devotion to her art, at the expense of children and a "normal" family life; and the peculiar circumstances of her death (she died asking for her swan costume, and they carried on the performance she was to have appeared in that night with an empty spotlight marking the space that her corporeal body no longer could occupy). I could learn the fact that, but could not fully understand *why,* Pavlova was the only ballerina who mattered to American audiences for some two decades at least. But Pavlova was not the only ballet dancer about whose genius I was confused; my early exposure to Diaghilev's Ballets Russes and to Nijinsky provoked a similar epistemological quandary.

Saisons des Ballets Russes

Integrated into all the accounts of the "Pavlova era" in the United States were the brief but no less resonant effects of the American tours of Diaghilev's Ballets Russes with Vaslav Nijinsky in 1916 and 1917. Diaghilev had introduced Pavlova to Europe, but Pavlova had preceded Diaghilev, and his stars Nijinsky and Tamara Karsavina, to the United States.[29] American intellectuals and artists, especially, who during the period from 1912 to 1917 loved all things Russian, were aware of the importance in Europe of the "impeccable modernity" of Diaghilev's Ballets Russes, but few except the traveling rich could actually have seen the company.[30] Diaghilev's tripartite ballets—made up equally of music, visual art, and dance—allied the traditional form with the idea of progress, each work being meant to provide a *frisson nouveau.* Diaghilev created ballet as fashionable—that is, as a form that responded to the most up-to-date influences in the worlds of art and music. But by the time the Ballets Russes made it to the United States, bowdlerized and uncredited versions of some of its most famous works—the frenzied voluptuousness of Fokine's *Schéhérazade* and *Cléopâtre* (1910), as well as his more genteel *Les Sylphides* (1909)—had already floated around the country, from New York to Los Angeles, thanks to the 1911–1912 "Saison des Ballets Russes"

In Memoriam—Anna Pavlowa

Late Thursday, January twenty-second, the great dancer died of double pleurisy after a three days' illness in the Hague, Holland. The fatal condition was precipitated by exposure following a train wreck while Madame Pavlowa and her company were engaged on a Continental tour. Her death brings to a close a dance career that blazoned her name in every country of the world as the supreme exponent of the dance art

Memorial for Pavlova, "the supreme exponent of the dance art," published in *The Dance*, March 1931, in which she is represented in her most famous role, *The Dying Swan*.

of vaudevillian trouper Gertrude Hoffman and her hundred-plus company of Russian and French dancers, with staging and choreography by former Diaghilev dancer Theodore Kosloff.[31]

The Diaghilev company's most interesting attraction to U.S. audiences, therefore, was undoubtedly Nijinsky himself, who had already left the company but rejoined it for the first American tour in 1916 and led it, sans Diaghilev, on its second during 1916 and 1917. One of the most historically significant features of Diaghilev's Ballets Russes was the shift from the ballerina as the locus of attention to the potency and virtuosity of the male dancer, although Diaghilev's ballerinas were also legendary, beginning with Pavlova and Tamara Karsavina. Nijinsky's dancing was accorded acclaim, although "certain objectionable features" of his ballets—especially *L'Après-midi d'un faun*—often ran afoul of local censorship boards, as did the fact that *Schéhérazade* "mingled whites and blacks on the stage."[32] And the story of Nijinsky's "strange relationship" with Diaghilev had preceded him to the United States and appeared to be of more prurient appeal and enduring resonance than the fact of Nijinsky's marriage in 1913. When Nijinsky appeared in New York in *Narcisse* in 1916, "with his golden curls, white pinafore, and immaculate nether garments, from which a pair of exceedingly healthy legs protrude, he look[ed] like a living advertisement for the best food for infants" *(New York Mail),* or "Mr. Nijinsky . . . succeeded in being offensively effeminate, but at most he succeeded in being nothing else" *(New York Tribune).* One of Nijinsky's new ballets, rehearsed and performed in America only, was *Till Eulenspiegel,* which was very well reviewed. It was seen and admired on the West Coast by Charlie Chaplin; here the rumors began, to this day unsubstantiated, that Chaplin had made a film of Nijinsky dancing. Nijinsky remained in the news after the company left the United States, when in 1918 he was declared insane and incarcerated in an asylum.[33]

The problem with the American reception of the "real" Ballets Russes was not only that audiences had already seen Gertrude Hoffman's fake versions, or liked Pavlova more, or were suspicious about Nijinsky's sexuality (wrote New York's *Evening Post* in 1916, "While the effeminate quality, almost inseparable from the male ballet dancer, is quite visible in Nijinsky, he has at the same time a certain masculinity of strength and rhythm which counteracts the other impression").[34] The problem was not even that feature-length American movies, such as *The Ballet Girl* and *Bobbie of the Ballet* (1916) or *The Dancer's Peril* (1917, which ends with a version of *Schéhérazade* performed by "Alexis Kosloff and a corps of 100 Russian dancers"), were already appearing as a result of the wider fame of ballet but otherwise maintained the prurient interests in the ballet girl's body of *How the Ballet Girl Was Smuggled into Camp.* Rather, as Elizabeth Kendall puts it, "American critics weren't even curious about the mechanisms of their own solo dancers' art." In America, where

Tamara Karsavina and Vaslav Nijinsky, in his costume of pink rose petals, posed in *Le Spectre de la rose* (1911).

Collection of the author.

dance was an art of stars and their vehicles, "people failed to grasp that a dance was a construct in space and time, involving principles of composition as palpable as those in painting or sculpture."[35]

And yet, regardless of how American audiences reacted to Pavlova or the Ballets Russes or to Nijinsky, clearly discussion of them and their work is a discussion of ballet as art, however flawed or old-fashioned or shocking that art was.[36] Pavlova's tours through 1925, and the plans for her return in 1931, are closely followed by the arrival of George Balanchine in America in 1933 in most history books, and once Balanchine's name appears, we are on a straight, fast line through to the glories of the American dominance of theatrical ballet in the latter half of the twentieth century. No more were there references to ballet in vaudeville or variety or burlesque. Even Balanchine's stints as a Broadway choreographer and as a Hollywood dance director could be couched in terms of making money to support his ballet school, founded soon after his arrival here, and the various companies, all of them visions of *the* American ballet, that he and Lincoln Kirstein organized throughout the 1930s and 1940s.[37] Ballet Theatre (it became American Ballet Theatre in 1956), the other big American company that remains in place today, grew out of the U.S. tours of various post-Diaghilev Ballets Russes troupes and the Mordkin Ballet (founded in 1937) and was easily assimilated into the narrative of American ballet's progress, which is discussed further below.[38]

I have been framing this discussion in relation to my own past and dance education not in order to criticize any of the scholarship from which I learned so much but to show how clearly intertwined popular culture and ballet always were, even though this interdependence was rarely acknowledged except as something that would eventually be overcome, if that is the word, by "real" ballet and "real" dancers. The fact that ballet was performed in burlesque and vaudeville and musical comedy theaters was merely a sign that there was not yet a proper appreciation for ballet as ballet rather than as a species of entertainment. As described by Doris Hering in a 1965 article about Harriet Hoctor, the early years of the twentieth century were a "period when the American-trained dancer with serious aspirations had no ballet company to which she could turn. And if she were to get ahead in musical comedy or vaudeville she had constantly to tread a tightrope between the vulgarization expected by the audience and her own attitude toward her art."[39] The historical outline of ballet's forced affiliation with the music hall or variety theater more or less ended once there were American ballet companies, American ballet schools, and American ballet theaters devoted in significant proportion to ballet performances alone. One could begin to recognize ballet as ballet once one started watching not Pavlova flittering about in scratchy silent films but Balanchine ballets on *Dance in America* videotapes.

METROPOLITAN OPERA'S BALLET

DECEMBER 28, 1936 **10** CENTS

Members of George Balanchine's and Lincoln Kirstein's American Ballet, here as the resident company of the Metropolitan Opera. The inside spread is on the growing presence of dance in American culture.

Photo by Alfred Eisenstaedt. Copyright 1936 Time.

As a historian working now, I have to be abashed at how easily I used to be able to think about American ballet history—about any history, really—in such crassly progressive or evolutionary terms. Moreover, I realize now, if I did not then, that once we were in the twentieth century, I was actually learning less from what I was reading than what I was looking at. That is, I was analyzing history through what a quarter of a century ago was less ambiguously an accepted repository of visualized truth: the photographic and motion picture record. I knew what I *saw* in these records: that ballet dancers of the past, even Pavlova, were fatter or lumpier, their turnout was worse, their legs were rarely taut or their bodies pulled up, and their feet were not always pointed. They did only one or two pirouettes, not three or four or five. When they jumped, it was not very high, and their arabesque extensions hardly passed waist-level. But in fact, the much more crucial issue that I was failing to grasp—what was not yet being discussed academically very widely either—was one of historiography as much as history. Namely, that the very records of the past being studied, its extensive visualization through largely photographic means (however altered or retouched some of those photographs were), was *itself* the source of my understanding of the superiority of my present. I could *see* the films of Pavlova; I could *see* at least the photographs of Nijinsky—and while his legendary status remained a bit more firmly in place precisely because there were no films to counter it, all the evidence seemed to prove that his thighs were too big and his turnout bad.

Because so much of ballet history, especially in America, is closely linked to and transmitted by photographic representation, comparisons of the present with the past are easily accommodated: it was all too easy to relate, or equate, the increasing quality of the films, and videos, to the increasing quality of the dancing and the dancers. This accommodation occurred, though, through the obviation of what we now know and of course study more routinely: the intertextuality of all forms of public amusement in a mass-mediated age. There were films of Pavlova because she was a famous ballerina, and she became an even more famous ballerina because she performed in films, especially a big-budget Hollywood film (*The Dumb Girl of Portici*, in which she danced almost not at all). Other films about ballet dancers, seen arguably by a wider audience than was Pavlova herself, drew on the circulating fame of Pavlova and the Ballets Russes. Now, as cultural historians, we are at pains to stress the consequence of the bigger picture, the ways in which the politics of celebrity and stardom have always intersected with the traditional and the artistic, particularly in mass-media representations.

Certainly it was hardly clear or inevitable, even in the 1940s and 1950s, that American ballet was going to turn out to be Balanchine ballet. It was not inevitable that lean, tall, and "pin-headed" would become desirable attributes of women's ballet bodies.[40] Indeed, it was not always clear what type of ballet "American ballet" was or would become—what *American* meant in this locution, and even what *ballet* meant, given the way the term could both refer to concert or "art" dancing generally and to any and all dancing "done on the toes." To a degree that remains astonishing to me, it was commercial film that helped us to define what ballet should look like; who should do it in terms of race, class, and gender; how to think about it in relation to national identity and the place of art in modern society; and also, as will be discussed in subsequent chapters, what could happen to you if you dared make it the center of your life.

The lack of nuanced discussions of gender and sexual identity, or nationality, or race, in the dance history books of several decades ago no longer pertains. And the clear distinctions between ballet as "high" art and ballet as popular culture are not so easily made today either. In the remainder of this chapter I explore the ways that ballet was positioned in American culture from the 1920s through the early 1950s, how it interacted with other forms of art dance (modern dance specifically), and how its Americanness became defined not only through adherence to the formal principles of "traditional classic stage-dancing," in Lincoln Kirstein's 1938 words, but its stylistic basis in "the personal atmosphere of recognizable American types as exemplified by the behavior of movie stars like Ginger Rogers, Carole Lombard, or the late Jean Harlow."[41] That women's names are all that Kirstein lists is not beside the point; femininity, even "frank, open, fresh and friendly" femininity, comes to define American ballet as well in these decades. The treatises and public statements by, first, Isadora Duncan and Ted Shawn and, later, Lincoln Kirstein and others about what should constitute and define American ballet provide a backdrop against which the film industry's treatment of ballet and ballet dancers can be seen to negotiate the different meanings of the term. Rather than placing theatrical ballet and commercial popular culture against each other as two antithetical entities, I draw on the work of several other dance and cultural studies scholars to argue that theatrical ballet in America has always been as much a part of popular culture as it has of an elite art establishment and that commercial cinema itself was, throughout virtually the whole of the twentieth century, strenuously engaged as much in perpetuating as in undermining ballet's high-art status.

The Goddess of Liberty Doesn't Dance Ballet

As already mentioned, ballet in America was a European import in terms of its early stars, its technical basis in the *danse d'école,* and much of its repertoire. This accounted for its stature as well as its triviality. And, as has been implied if not overtly acknowledged in the discussion so far, the dominance of women—the ballerina and her cult of personality, and the generic equivalence in so many cases of the ballet girl and the chorus girl—also helps to explain the form's perceived triviality as well as prestige. Conversely, it is well known that, in America as in Europe, both theatrical and social dancing were frequently associated with the emancipation of women, whether that emancipation was understood as physical, psychological, spiritual, or political. Fashion reform began to promulgate a sort of religiously based hygiene—the body as God's handiwork—and helped to inaugurate a "new aesthetic" of exercise, health, and bodily freedom for women by the 1890s; thinking about the body, writes Deborah Jowitt in her book *Time and the Dancing Image*, became "not only advisable but fashionable" for women across a wide range of classes around the turn of the twentieth century.[42] Fashion reform went hand in hand with the recognition of new movement capabilities for the body that its practical liberation entailed and allowed, and increasing attention was paid to the locomotive and expressive capacities and abilities of the female body in physical culture movements that drew often on the theories of the relationship of gesture, pantomime, and emotion of François Delsarte, as disseminated in America by his pupil Genevieve Stebbins. Physical culture and training also were extolled as ways to work on and potentially to alter one's inner self (a Delsartean principle as well), but it was the new *visibility* of the female body in art and popular culture—a body whose physicality could not help but invoke its sexuality—that continued to produce the most strident responses among critics and public watchdogs of various kinds.

The relationship of physical culture with art and with fashion reform resulted in what is usually thought of as the "early modern" dance movement of women such as Isadora Duncan, Loie Fuller, Maud Allen, and Ruth St. Denis.[43] Duncan, situated historically as the first American dance pioneer and international star, answered the negative responses to her body's overwhelming physical prowess and public presence early in the twentieth century by linking her dancing to philosophy and religion, a noble Greek "ideal of harmony," in Ann Daly's words, as well as to the prestige of the concert hall and opera house, denying any connection of what she did onstage to the commercialized spectacle of the ballet girl or the chorus girl. As Daly further explains in her exploration of Duncan's presence in American culture:

> Americans looked askance at "Culture," at the same time that they longed for it. On the one hand, it appealed to their desire for respectability, but on the other hand, it smacked of European pretentiousness. This ambivalence is evident enough in the early reportage on Duncan: a mixture of admiration and skepticism, alternately poetic and derisive. But by carefully defining her relationship to class, race, and gender, she eventually managed to institutionalize the opera house dance concert: it became as unapologetically American as vaudeville

and yet as tasteful as Shakespeare or Mozart. As Duncan packaged her performances, and as her audiences understood them, her dancing offered all the vigor of the West, tempered with the refinement of a Greek goddess. Her dancing appealed to a growing upper-middle-class desire for social prestige.[44]

As Daly shows, Duncan took all of the negative attributes of dance in America at that time—that it was cheap, mindless, feminine, trivial, profane— and turned them on their heads, associating herself with upper-class audiences and acquiring male mentors and liaisons whose "cultural or economic power accrued, by association, to her."[45] The strategy that Duncan employed, however, to define her dancing as *American,* and as a reflection of American ideals, was predominantly one of exclusion. Her dance art was not ballet, certainly, because until Pavlova's appearances in America in 1910, ballet, to Duncan, was not an art form worthy of the name. (Duncan's performances in Russia, however, were said to have inspired Fokine to reintegrate personal expressiveness and free-form movements with the conventional patterns and repetitive vocabulary of Imperial ballet; and Fokine himself settled in New York to teach in 1923.) Moreover, Duncan wrote, "The real American type can never be a ballet dancer. The legs are too long, the body too supple and the spirit too free for this school of affected grace and toe-walking. . . . A tall finely made woman could never dance the ballet. With the wildest turn of the imagination, you cannot picture the Goddess of Liberty dancing the ballet."[46]

Nor did Duncan's art have anything to do with the newly popular jazz forms of music and dance, because those "African" forms were, to her, primitive, nonwhite, race-based, and innate and therefore illegitimate as forms of personal expression.[47] For Duncan, "African" could not be integrated into "American." While Duncan wanted to be popular, and remembered, her separation of her body and her work from what were quickly becoming the most significant of America's "indigenous" forms—jazz, musical theater, even film, for Duncan refused to be filmed—as well as from the popularity of competing forms like the Imperial Russianness of Anna Pavlova, meant that Duncan's legacy would be limited. By the teens Duncan became something of an embarrassment to the American dance world as technical proficiency began to dominate in critical and evaluative discourses and as personal expression in the arts was supplanted by modernist interests in formal rigor, novelty, and experimentation. Daly quotes Walter Lippmann's retrospective assessment of the era of Duncan's greatest fame and her decline before World War I:

We had vague notions that mankind, liberated from want and drudgery, would spend its energies writing poetry, painting pictures, exploring the stellar spaces, singing folk songs, dancing with Isadora Duncan in the public square, and producing Ibsen in little theaters.

We seem completely to have overlooked the appetite of mankind for the automobile, the moving picture, the radio, bridge parties, tabloids and the stock market.[48]

And, as it turned out, for ballet over modern dance.

We Need Never Borrow Material from Any Nation

Ted Shawn's 1926 book *The American Ballet* is a curiosity that also argues for a particular construction and constitution of American ballet (writ large, with *ballet* serving here as a generic term for concert dance).[49] In the end *The American Ballet* is really a record of Shawn's views on dance and men, dance and religion, dance and nudity, and dancing in church; it is also a chronicle of how the Denishawn branch of modern dance conceived of Americanness in its concert dance forms. Denishawn (the name from that of Shawn and his partner and, for a time, wife, Ruth St. Denis) was an amalgamation of popular conceptions and misconceptions about the free expressiveness of non-Western cultures, especially ancient cultures, as taught in the school the pair founded in Los Angeles in 1915 and essentially franchised to other cities (ironically, Denishawn was often mistaken on tour for the Ballets Russes).[50] Shawn's artistic creed for the school was as follows: "The art of the dance is too big to be encompassed by any one system. On the contrary the dance includes all systems or schools of dance. Every way that any human being of any race or nationality, at any period of human history, has moved rhythmically to express himself, belongs to the dance. We endeavor to recognize and use all contributions of the past to the dance and will continue to include all new contributions in the future."[51]

The works of Shawn and St. Denis are incredible pastiches, invoking ancient Egypt, Greece, India, Japan, China, the Aztecs, Babylon, the Pueblos, and any other antique culture they could learn anything about, whether from touring and studying abroad or from popular representations of them. Nevertheless, Shawn was interested in defining and founding—actually in "fathering," for his nickname was "Papa Shawn"—*the* American Ballet. Again, by *ballet* he usually means art dance generally; but, confusingly, he sometimes uses the term to refer to "toe-dancing."[52] Pavlova, for example, he calls "the greatest ballet or toe-dancer on the stage today," but Shawn also declares that "ballet as a style is not the channel for progress any longer." Regardless of what he means by *ballet*, however, it is more clear what he means by *American*, and he is happy to acknowledge the significance of what he calls "abstract elements of America" in the definitions of its dance: the rhythms of machinery, of "our motor transportation, unique in the world's history," of the "rhythm and emotional expression of business commercialism," of our "sports—football, baseball, tennis, rowing, golf," and of our "unique new architecture." Because of such bounty we "need never borrow material from any nation for we are full to abundance with undeveloped ideas and themes." This is not that far, as we will see, from the way that Lincoln Kirstein later wants to define American ballet too. But while Shawn's American ballet is not quite as exclusionary as Duncan's—Shawn wants to lay claim to the masculine virility of Native American dance as our first "indigenous" forms, for example—it is even more racist in regard to jazz and the contributions to theatrical dance of African American performers.

For Shawn, "jazz as the expression of America in the dance is a lie. Jazz is the scum of the great boiling that is now going on, and the scum will be cleared off and the clear fluid underneath will be revealed."[53] When a "white person" performs dances like the "shimmy" and the "Charleston," writes Shawn, "[i]t is disgusting, because the negro mental and emotional conditions cannot be translated into the white man." Despite Shawn's nods to "American" dance forms, the American ballet must be "Anglo-Saxon," because America is an Anglo-Saxon country with Anglo-Saxon "ideals." Yet the "classic European ballet" is also not adapted to "our American temperament. It is not a style in which our own native point of view will express itself." If there is to be an American ballet, it *cannot be,* according to Shawn, in the form of "a ballet school with imported ballet masters from Europe to teach Americans how to do European ballet dancing." Rather, "if we are going to have a great American Ballet," it will consist of "American born and American trained dancers, dancing to music by American composers, with scenery and costumes designed by American artists, and under the direction and management of American business men of great vision."

Duncan's and Shawn's visions, or versions, of the "American" in American dance are not merely quaint or, from our vantage point, obtuse, exclusionary, and oddly argued. They represent in capsule form what many in American concert dance were seeking: the emancipation of the (white) body from the restrictions of middle-class culture, and a means to represent the American character through dance in ways at once popular and, especially to the innovators of modern dance in the Depression era, politically significant. Working primarily in big cities, Martha Graham, Doris Humphrey, Helen Tamiris, and Charles Weidman were, in Ernestine Stodelle's words, "pioneers, and proud of it—each one an individual artist with an individual technique and approach. And they had no doubts that they were creating an art worthy of twentieth-century America."[54] Ballet had no part in the "moderns'" conception of American dance either. The problem for them was that classical ballet seemed perfectly capable of adapting and borrowing the moderns' new movement vocabularies and themes, and ballet companies and their choreographers were no less interested in making *their* art into the true American dance form.

In 1934 the Ballets Russes de Monte Carlo—one of the several "Ballet Russe" companies competing in Europe and the United States for the legacy of Diaghilev—commissioned an "American" work from Diaghilev's last official company choreographer, Leonide Massine. *Union Pacific*, with a libretto by Archibald MacLeish, had its premiere in Philadelphia but was criticized, in the words of Julia Foulkes, as being an "overly Russian, and therefore an inauthentic and superficial, view of America."[55] But soon other, more successful ballets by American choreographers began to appear, both with the Ballets Russes and American regional companies, including Ruth Page's *An American Pattern* (1938) and *Frankie and Johnnie* (1938); Catherine Littlefield's *Barn Dance* (1937); Lew Christensen's *Pocahontas* (1936) and *Filling Station* (1938); Eugene Loring's *Billy the Kid* (1938), *The Great American Goof* (1940), and *Prairie* (1942); and Agnes de Mille's *Rodeo* (1942). Foulkes continues: "The American subjects of ballet pieces and ballet choreographers' free use of modern dance movements signified the beginnings of an American style of ballet. In the late 1930s and early 1940s the boundaries between ballet and modern dance began to blur, even though distinctions in approach remained. . . . In technique the new ballets rarely focused on delicate pointe work or traditional pas-de-deux partnering. Instead, they featured stylized folk dances and everyday motions to convey character and narrative. Modern dance loosened ballet technique, and both forms shared nationalist themes."[56]

And, as Foulkes shows, even modern dance was not open to all: "Women [in modern dance] held leading roles on stage and off, replacing the common stage image of the sexual ingenue with that of the pioneering individual who moved her own body with disquieting, abrupt force. Gay men, too, recast the effeminate image of the sissy into a hardened, heroic, dancing American athlete. African American dancers, however, did not find an easy place within this new American art form."[57] Moreover, it is relatively common knowledge that the first company actually *named* "The American Ballet" would in fact be founded by a Russian, Balanchine, in conjunction with a highly bred American, Lincoln Kirstein. It is also well known that Balanchine's and Kirstein's School of American Ballet would, starting in the 1930s, become the preeminent training ground of American ballet dancers (and remains so to this day) and was later one of the first mainstream American ballet companies to train and hire African American performers.[58] Ted Shawn might have claimed that Denishawn was the American equivalent of the Russian Ballet, but, in Elizabeth Kendall's words, Denishawn "established nothing as the core of American dance."[59]

Other companies and schools have been important in promulgating versions of ballet throughout America somewhat at odds with Balanchine's often abstract classicism. In dance magazines of the late 1930s, for example, advertisements for Fokine's studio of "modern Russian ballet," on Riverside Drive in New York City, appear right next to advertisements for Balanchine's "School of American Ballet," on Madison Avenue. As mentioned, the Ballets Russes de Monte Carlo, one of the companies spun off from the remnants of Diaghilev's Ballets Russes after Diaghilev's death in 1929, began in Europe with Balanchine and Massine as choreographers and with Alexandra Danilova and three "baby ballerinas" (recruited by Balanchine) as its stars (Irina Baronova, Tamara Toumanova, and Tatiana Riabouchinska).[60] Brought to the United States by impresario Sol Hurok in 1933, the company (becoming simply the Ballet Russe de Monte Carlo after its second American season) returned again and again through the 1930s and 1940s, performing cheerful pastiches of Russian Imperial classics, as well as remarkable new work—de Mille's *Rodeo* was choreographed for the Ballet Russe de Monte Carlo—in all sorts of more or less (often less) suitable venues. Its history is colorful and complicated; the Ballet Russe de Monte Carlo lost all of its major personages to a competing company, but that company was also called the Ballet Russe de Monte Carlo and was also managed by Hurok, so it scarcely mattered here, where American audiences had been trained to think, to Kirstein's consternation, that all ballet was Russian anyway. (Eventually there were two companies, the other being called for a time the Original Ballet Russe.)[61]

The significant fact is that during World War II the Ballet Russe de Monte Carlo became essentially an American company when it was stranded in the United States. This was not only because of its production of major American-theme ballets (like *Rodeo*) but also because of the gradual replacement of its dwindling and underpaid rank of European dancers—many of whom left and settled here to found dancing schools and eventually regional companies—with (still underpaid) Americans, who had themselves been trained by expatriates from Pavlova's and Diaghilev's touring companies or other Europeans (like Fokine and Mordkin) who had established dancing schools across the United States in the 1920s. The first of Balanchine's and Kirstein's several American companies (the American Ballet) was founded in 1934 and had its initial performances in 1935, and Kirstein launched his own performing entity, Ballet Caravan, in 1936, expressly to feature the work of American choreographers, dancers, composers, and designers (among its signal commissioned works was Loring's *Billy the Kid*).[62]

Kirstein's own claim is that he founded Ballet Caravan (American Ballet Caravan by 1938) because Balanchine had departed for Hollywood, along with Vera Zorina and several members of the American Ballet, to make movies.[63] Kirstein and Balanchine rejoined ranks in 1940, but American Ballet Caravan

Vera Zorina and members of the American Ballet of the Metropolitan Opera in *The Goldwyn Follies* (1937), one of several films on which Balanchine and Zorina worked in the late 1930s and early 1940s.

Courtesy National Film Archive, London.

was disbanded a year later. [American] Ballet Theatre was launched in New York in 1939, and among its notable features were a number of American dancers with American names, a number of American-theme ballets (one of the company's three wings was the "American Wing," headed by American Eugene Loring), and a lack of so-called ballerinas and premiers danseurs; one was either a principal dancer or a member of "the company."[64] And for its first season only, Ballet Theatre included a "Negro unit," whose only ballet, *Obeah (Black Ritual)* was choreographed by Agnes de Mille but performed by a cast of sixteen African American women. Although reviewed more positively than many of the other works that first season, *Obeah* soon disappeared from Ballet Theatre's repertory, along with the Negro unit itself.

Russianballet Is Not a Single Word

What should be clear from these cursory but complicated descriptions is that in the first half of the twentieth century ballet's status and identity in America were in flux, a set of potentialities that could have taken the art form in many different directions technically, politically, and aesthetically. Furthermore, however high an art form impresarios like Lincoln Kirstein and Sol Hurok believed ballet to be, they also were happy to sell it as a footloose and perambulating species of spectacular entertainment.[65] Regardless of how often Kirstein invoked ballet's classicism and the "absolute" status of its "timeless" form, the ballets he supported, especially in the 1930s and 1940s, were very much aimed at regular audiences. In fact, as Mark Franko notes in his study of American dance in the 1930s, Kirstein's project was to show that the "average American consumer of popular culture could become a balletomane. If only ballet could be made to reflect the clichéd content of movies and newspapers," Franko writes, "everyday folk would want to see it."[66] But a lot of "everyday folk" *were* enjoying ballet, because the ballet Kirstein was arguing for essentially existed already—in vaudeville, on Broadway, in motion pictures. *The Black Crook* was certainly enjoyed by "everyday folk," and if it was only filmed once (in 1916), this was because its manifold attractions—melodrama, mystery, romance, singing, dancing, scantily clad girls, and so on—quickly became features of much, if not most, of Hollywood's typical film product. The entity Kirstein rages against in 1938, "Russianballet," as though it were "a single word," was hardly at the time "The Great Conspiracy" that Kirstein calls it, a "Russian monopoly" still "tightly held," a "recent drag of Russian blackmail."[67]

Or rather, if there *was* a conspiracy to keep American ballet dancers from "develop[ing] freely in their own personal and national style," a right they had earned in "the films, on ball-room floors, and on the musical-comedy stage" where they were "encouraged to be American,"[68] it was the conspiracy of white Americans against nonwhite. The monopoly that Kirstein describes had already been substantially broken apart in theatrical concert dance. Nevertheless, in terms of "Russianballet," the epithet of "conspirator" could reasonably be leveled at Hollywood films themselves and the increasingly conventionalized view of ballet and ballet artists that *they* were offering in the 1920s, 1930s, and 1940s, the same Hollywood films in which Kirstein sees such a brilliant embodiment of "the personal atmosphere of recognizable American types."[69] Balanchine, according to biographer Bernard Taper, went to America partly because "Europe had become a museum; in America he sensed the promise of new possibilities."[70] But at least as far as ideas about ballet were concerned, American movies were ironically also museums, promulgating outmoded notions about the art and its artists culled from a romantic and imperial dance past.

So while Kirstein was arguing in print with modern-dance enthusiast and "dean of the dance critics" John Martin of the *New York Times* about whether modern dance or ballet was the most authentically American of dance forms, or about whether Martha Graham or George Balanchine was the greater artist, ballet had already become the dominant art dance in the country, as well as one of its most popular theatrical forms.[71] Modern dance had no "four-hundred-year-old tradition" to use as the basis for institutionalizing itself (there were a few individuals, like Graham, who did create pedagogical formats that outlived them) and found itself unable to answer the question that Julia Foulkes names as crucial to its establishment as a mass-cultural form: "How does an art form expressly based on individual vision institutionalize itself?"[72] By 1942, in fact, George Beiswanger could lament that "it is quite possible that the final and only lasting service of the modern dance will be the rejuvenation of ballet."[73]

Even the leftist periodical *New Masses* positively reviewed Jerome Robbins's new work for Ballet Theatre, *Fancy Free,* in 1945, claiming that the piece and other ballets like it were "modern and American" and that each "sparkles, in its own way, with the authentic gleam of our unique national brand of youth, sprightliness and wit."[74] Foulkes argues that the "embrace of ballet by *New Masses* reflected a changed political environment in which ballet choreographers' whimsical Americana dance works ultimately triumphed over modern dance choreographers' more critical visions" and that *Fancy Free* "cemented the end of the Americana era of modern dance and heralded its ascendancy in ballet and musical theater"[75] (and, I would add, film). *Fancy Free,* with music by Leonard Bernstein, was about three sailors who, while on shore leave in a big city, participate in a dance contest. The ballet became the basis for a Broadway show in 1945 and, later, the 1949 Hollywood musical *On the Town,* with Gene Kelly. Agnes de Mille's ballet choreography for another Broadway show, *Oklahoma!* (in 1943), also showed the extent to which ballet—American ballet, with movement vocabulary drawn from ballrooms, sports, stage hoofing, and modern dance itself, as well as from the "four-hundred-year-old tradition" of the *danse d'école*—had become part of the repertoire of popular culture and mass-entertainment forms and, more important, the repository in musicals of expressed character motivation, feeling, emotion. Mark Grant believes that with *Oklahoma!* "movement assumed parity with book, music, and lyrics as a carrier of the dramatic through-line of a show."[76] De Mille "understood," in Grant's words, that musical-comedy styles like tap dancing "couldn't subsume ballet, but ballet could subsume tap. Because of de Mille the typical Broadway hoofer changed from tapper to dancer trained in all forms; those who could only tap-dance were in effect thrown out of employment."

In fact, it is the chorus girl that Mark Franko sees as the liminal figure in all of the debates over American identity and class issues in theatrical dance, the chorus girl who taps but who also sees toe dancing as the special skill that might elevate her status. By 1920 the blocked toe shoe had been "very much improved by American manufacturers—too well improved," in

Ann Barzel's words in 1944, because anybody could "appear in them" before they knew how to dance.[77] As Franko writes:

> Since neither ballet nor modern [dance] were situated unequivocally as "high" or "low," any historically informed comparison between them raises issues of class in relation to performance. Ballet maintained its "high" status by appearing to be "low" (popular), and radical modern dance was perceived as "high" by deprecating the commodifications of popular culture in favor of the working-class audience. Each contained the supplement of the other, a supplementarity within the identity of each genre embodied by the repressed figure of the chorus girl, whose shadowy identity configures her both as ersatz or would-be ballet dancer and as proletarianized entertainment industry worker.[78]

Even by the 1920s and 1930s, then, ballet, and more specifically the ballet dancer, is already a *popular* element of popular culture. But conspicuously absent here is any real discussion of the motion picture, except as an element that could be integrated into ballet *works*. Some American theme ballets, for example, featured characters from the movies. Balanchine choreographed *La Pastorale,* a ballet about a motion picture company, in 1926 for Diaghilev's Ballets Russes. And there were experiments with film projection onto the dance stage in lieu of conventional decor in Massine's 1928 *Ode,* also for Diaghilev. But it was the motion picture that ended up defining ballet *for* Americans, and in ways that often had little to do with how Shawn or Kirstein wanted to define it. American movies were not, with rare exceptions, interested in the kinds of questions Shawn and Kirstein (or John Martin) were asking. Rather, if you were becoming famous, or were noticed and thought to be exploitable by some talent scout, you belonged in the movies no matter what you did, even if it was classical ballet. (Not surprisingly, the glamorous and beautiful "baby ballerinas," none of them American, of the Ballets Russes de Monte Carlo all ended up with Hollywood contracts of one kind or another.)[79] And if Hollywood wanted to add a little prestige to a picture, Russian ballet would serve nicely because it had already become so familiar.

What Kirstein failed to acknowledge (and what Balanchine perhaps did, too, when he choreographed *La Pastorale,* was lured to America by fantasies about Ginger Rogers, or went to Hollywood to put ballets into *The Goldwyn Follies*) was what would happen not when movie stars served as the exemplars of our frank, open, honest American character and thereby as raw material for a frank, open, honest American ballet; nor even what would happen when the Americana ballets of *On Your Toes, Oklahoma!* or *Fancy Free* ended up on the movie screen (*Oklahoma!* did not become a film until 1955).

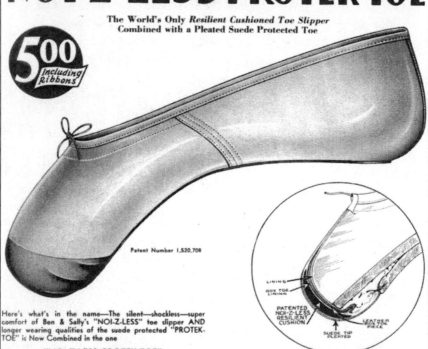
American ingenuity improves the toe shoe.

Ad from *American Dancer*, Sept. 1934.

Rather, the question nobody was yet posing was what ballet would become when movie stars rather than dancers were actually made to *do* ballet, when movie stars started representing it and its meanings, through commercial cinema, to an unimaginably vast American audience. No matter how many times the Ballet Russe de Monte Carlo made it to small towns in the 1930s or 1940s, the average American would already have watched, and learned far more about, "ballet" in motion pictures than in live performance. As we will see in the following chapters, commercial films of the 1930s and 1940s pay lip service to the traditional definitions of ballet as Russianballet, and define the life of the dancer in what they see as an unproblematic fashion: odd, difficult, sometimes painful, and often tragic, just like the lives of Pavlova and Nijinsky or the jinxed characters of the old romantic warhorses—the sylphs, swans, and princes—on which American audiences had been raised.

These generic features, however, repeated with such frequency, easily became clichés too. David Van Leer, writing about "cultural carelessness" on Broadway in the 1950s, points out that cultures are "as interesting for what they think is not a problem as for what they think is," and he locates some of the most provocative features of popular-culture texts as deriving from "the very unanimity on which consensus critics build."[80] The "very absence of anxiety" in consensus culture—which classical Hollywood cinema, governed by the Production Code, certainly was—allows challenges to the normative to emerge because the normative is assumed to be fixed, immutable, conventional; but, of course, it is not. Thus, Hollywood made many films in which the ballet is Russianballet, and ballet artists are crazy or hysterical or have pitiful, doomed existences. But in taking these truths for granted, Hollywood also could make films in which the conventions were lampooned or inverted—having ballet dancers pretend to be Russian in order to gain acceptance as ballet dancers but who were really Americans, or making films that seem bent on reifying the tragic life of the ballet artist but that end happily after all. Or, eventually, making films in which ballet dancing is recognizable not through tutus and tights and toe shoes but through the deployment of dance technique alone. Perhaps most important, many if not all films from Hollywood, and its overseas counterparts, end up embodying and promulgating on their own—in their excellence as cinema, or in their de facto promotion of stardom itself as a worthy achievement—the message that life and art are hardly antithetical but the source together of great pleasure, fulfillment, riches, and even joy.

2

The Lot of a Ballerina Is Indeed Tough

Gender, Genre, and the Ballet Film through 1947, Part I

I always said I'd leave off when the time came—and no trouble about it.
Grusinskaya, who dances no more. What would she do? Grow orchids,
keep white peacocks? Die? That's what it comes to at last. To die.

—*Grand Hotel,* 1932

David, do you know what a ballerina is? A bundle of muscles with a
smile.

—*The Men in Her Life,* 1941

We artists suffer so.

—*Specter of the Rose,* 1946

If a dancer can't dance she just dies, you know that, don't you?

—*The Unfinished Dance,* 1947

What do the following actors have in common: Donald Cook, Greta Garbo, Eleanor Powell, Fred Astaire, Vera Zorina, Ann Miller, Vivien Leigh, Maureen O'Hara, Maria Ouspenskaya, Loretta Young, Cyd Charisse, Stan Laurel, Tamara Toumanova, Ivan Kirov, and Margaret O'Brien? The answer, for the purposes of this book, is naturally that they all played ballet dancers in Hollywood films. Some of the names on the list are those of actual or erstwhile ballet dancers—Vera Zorina, Tamara Toumanova, Cyd Charisse—who had backgrounds in theatrical concert dance. Fred Astaire, Eleanor Powell, and Ann Miller are also dancers, although they are not usually associated with ballet in the public's mind. Most of the other actors on the list, however, have no association with ballet or even with dance. In this regard, the roles they played in what I am calling ballet films would perforce have had to depend less on the performance of dancing than on the acting out of the dancer's life.

There was, however, plenty of recognizable ballet dancing in films from the beginning of the sound era, from *The Jazz Singer* (1927) and *The Broadway Melody* (1929) on. Film versions of operettas virtually always included one or more ballet interludes, usually performed by droves of women in fluffy tutus and spangles. Even revues like *The King of Jazz* (1930) and musical comedies that starred dancers (Marilyn Miller, for example, in *Sally* or *Sunny,* both 1930) included ballet set pieces, with ballet being defined as such mainly through the visual presence of toe shoes. The history of this type of dancing, and of its ubiquity, was introduced in the previous chapter. Here and in the next chapter I concentrate on how commercial cinema, Hollywood specifically, represented the dancer's *existence* in films from the late sound era through 1947, before, that is, the British import *The Red Shoes* (the topic of its own chapter) was released to become arguably the most popular ballet film of the twentieth century. The wide variability of the sorts of actors, and actor-dancers, that populate even the partial list above should give an indication of how wild some of these films are—Donald Cook as a ballet dancer, or Stan Laurel? Who is Ivan Kirov? And Margaret O'Brien, a child star, could hardly portray a professional ballet dancer, could she? Even Fred Astaire and Eleanor Powell seem miscast as ballet dancers; both are better known for their tap dancing and, equally important, for the lightness of tone of their musical-comedy films. They may both *be* artists, but they do not play artists who suffer.

I have alluded already to some of the "genre trouble" plaguing the scholar of classical Hollywood cinema in regard to the study of melodrama, in that what film studies means by *melodrama* has little to do with how Hollywood conceived of the term from at least the 1920s through the 1950s. As Steve Neale outlines the elements of melodrama according to the film studies "standard account," melodrama was a pejorative term; was opposed to the more estimable category of "realism"; and was most consistently associated with pathos, romance, domesticity, the familial, and the "feminine." The woman's film, in particular, led a "lowly" existence as a result.[1] As Neale and others have found, however, melodrama was only very rarely employed to characterize films starring, about, and aimed at women, and the term would not have been applied necessarily to films about suffering ballet artists unless they included "action, adventure, and thrills." Trade journals and reviews, however, frequently used the terms *melodrama* and *meller* (Neale finds them in reviews of more than a thousand different films in *Variety* alone between 1938 and 1959), but when it is not being used "neutrally" to describe an action-packed film or what we might call a film noir (most films noirs were called melodramas in reviews), sometimes it seems to mean pathos-laden, and sometimes it just means overwrought, hackneyed, or clichéd. Part of my project is to trace the accumulation of elements that will come, over time, to constitute the "ballet meller" and to clarify how these elements function to define ballet and its artists generically.

In fact, the promotion and publicity campaigns of Hollywood films clearly wanted most of the time to emphasize the multiplicity rather than the singularity of generic categories to which any individual film text might lay claim. *Dance, Girl, Dance* (1940) is an interesting ballet-film example; it stars Lucille Ball and Maureen O'Hara as a burlesque dancer and a budding ballerina, respectively, and is relatively well known among film scholars because it was one of the very few Hollywood films to be directed by a woman, Dorothy Arzner. While publicity about *Dance, Girl, Dance* does sometimes mention its "feminine touch" ("Written by a woman, directed by a woman, with a cast predominately [sic] women—and with women in many key technical positions"), it more often emphasizes the film's dramatic or sensational features ("Drama stalking the stage where gayety's on parade!" or "Dancing through teardrops on the rocky path to footlight fame," or "The tooth-and-claw battle of a burlesque teaser and a ballet hopeful for love and success!").[2] Musical fans are also addressed and assured that they can expect a "realistic drama of backstage life, interspersed with original music, songs and dance numbers." Finally, for those interested in the high-art credentials of ballet itself, press-book articles proclaim the technical and artistic superiority of the film's "widely-known ballerinas of the concert and opera stage" (which did not, however, include the film's stars), as well as its "noted European dance directors." But nowhere is the film described in its publicity either as a melodrama or as a musical; and in its review of the film, *Variety* called it "a drama with music, rather than a musical comedy."[3]

Yet a film advertising itself as "woman-made" and announcing itself a "feminine hit"—much less a "romantic backstage drama" or a film about "career girls' trials"—is clearly assuming that its primary audience is women. And a film that trumpets the artistic credentials of its ballet dancers and choreographer is clearly aiming to be a "prestige" picture. The repeated use of the terms *drama* and *dramatic* in association with femininity are also signifiers of a desired association with prestige in Hollywood's lexicon. As Steve Neale writes, "[D]rama is, as it were, a classier term (and a classier genre) than western or thriller or horror film—or melodrama. . . . And this would certainly be consonant with the status of the woman's film in Hollywood. . . . Indeed, what were adjudged to be the finest women's films were also consistently regarded (along with . . . social problem films, biopics, biblical epics, and literary adaptations) as exemplifying the industry and its product at their best."[4]

So the very features that identify a film text to a film-studies scholar as a woman's film and, therefore, as a melodrama are precisely those that Hollywood invoked to advertise a film's prestige. At least in the case of *Dance, Girl, Dance*, this has sent us around in a circle: the film can be identified generically as a melodrama now (even if it was not by its producers or its contemporary audiences or critics) because it was characterized as a romantic drama aimed at women. According to Ben Singer, the "more or less stable meaning" of melodrama in film studies is located within a "set of subgenres that remain close to the heart and hearth and emphasize a register of heightened emotionalism and sentimentality," and Neale claims that "the standard account" of melodrama in film studies has "tended to founder on the assumption that the woman's film embodies their quintessence."[5] Whatever Hollywood called a film like *Dance, Girl, Dance,* and however its reviewers characterized it generically, the fact remains that it is, like many if not most Hollywood films, a participant in a hybrid genre. What matters to me are the sorts of things that *Dance, Girl, Dance* and the numerous other films under consideration here say about the compatibility or incompatibility of life and art in relation to normative gender roles, and scholarship about film melodrama still provides the most useful framework within which to discuss these issues. So the genre trouble that the multigeneric or hybrid nature of the ballet film causes comes mainly from the peculiar academic evolution of the term *melodrama* itself or the fact that much of the scholarship I want to engage, specifically with relation to gender and family in the ballet film, assumes that the films in question are domestic melodramas, family melodramas, or maternal melodramas—and that, as such, their most important features cannot possibly be thrills, chills, action, or musical numbers and ballets.

As for the few generic musicals that are also ballet films, Rick Altman claims that the musical as a genre structurally links success as a public performer and as an entertainer with success in love and family life.[6] We would not be speaking of suffering artists and a tradition of morbidity, however, were musical ballet films to follow this model unequivocally, which anyway, as Richard Dyer points out, usually more frequently rewards the male performer than the female (and it is predominantly women who are the protagonists of ballet films, although there are some notable exceptions).[7] In this sense, even the musicals are melodramatic, their narratives virtually always about the intersection or clash of the demands of the dancer's or dance artist's profession with those of her family life. This arguably is true of all Hollywood films, after 1934 especially, when the Production Code prescribed particular interpretations of women's and men's social roles through the mandate that the sanctity of marriage be upheld and so on. But in the ballet film, there is an additional layer of signification added through the shadow presence of the roles the dancer plays and of his or her corporeal authority, an authority that always potentially generates fame, wealth, success, personal satisfaction, and a connection to traditions as large and as rich and as meaningful as those of marriage and domesticity. In this and the next chapter, in short, we will be able to see how the same films can at once be melodramatic and morbid, as well as melodramatic and utopian. There are surprises in these films, and not only on the order of Stan Laurel dancing in a tutu, or of what Hollywood thinks goes on in a ballet studio, or of how many films feature the music from *Swan Lake* (even Universal's first *Dracula* film uses *Swan Lake*'s famous theme as its title music). While artists do "suffer so," they also, sometimes, are only pretending to suffer and are actually quite cheerful, successful, and fulfilled.

Ballet Girls in Peril

The earliest full-length (five reels or more) American ballet films seem to have been quick attempts to capitalize on the tours and newsworthiness of Pavlova and Diaghilev's Ballets Russes in 1916 and 1917 (as, of course, was Pavlova's own feature, *The Dumb Girl of Portici,* in 1916). In some cases these silent films were also adaptations of popular novels or plays that appeared hard on the heels of the early twentieth-century successes of ballet performers and troupes in England and Europe, making them part of what Ben Singer calls the "close cross-medium intertextuality" of the modern era in which movies, novels, short stories, and topical events "were bound together into a larger textual entity."[8] *The Ballet Girl* (1916), made in New York and starring Alice Brady in a dual role, was the first film version of Compton Mackenzie's commercially and critically successful novel *Carnival* (1912, but reprinted regularly through the 1950s). Mackenzie's Scottish parents were both actors, and his mistress was a chorus girl; and *Carnival* follows the life of a young English music-hall ballet dancer, Jenny Raeburn, who refuses to become the mistress of a gentleman and instead marries an unsuitable and brutal Cornishman who kills her out of jealousy when the gentleman reappears at the novel's end. Although the film's story differs substantially from that of the novel—Jenny's mother is made into an "aerial dancer" in a circus and is murdered by her husband, and eventually an orphaned Jenny (sometimes written Jennie) "feels the urge to dance"—the twist ending is noted in reviews of the film. As *Variety* put it, "[U]nless the spectator is familiar with the novel, [he or she] cannot, with any certainty, guess the finish until the very end."[9] And today most descriptions of Mackenzie's novel, which was adapted for several stage versions as well, employ the term *melodramatic,* especially in relation to the unhappy "twist" ending.

    The Dancer's Peril, also starring Alice Brady in another dual role as a Russian prima-ballerina mother and her ballerina daughter, was released in 1917. (Given the film's date, *Variety* was compelled to note that the film's Russian setting was "without any Nihilists and devoid of attempts upon the life of the Czar.")[10] A grand duke secretly marries the prima ballerina of the "St. Petersburg Ballet," but the marriage is discovered. The ballerina is banished to Paris, and her infant daughter remains behind to be raised by the elderly mistress of the Imperial Ballet school. The baby grows up to be a prima ballerina, too, but is abducted by the impresario of the ballet school, Pavloff, who, in *Variety*'s words, "seeks her virtue." The girl's mother shoots the seducer, but the grand duke appears in the nick of time to claim that he shot the man to preserve his wife's honor. Mother, daughter, and father reconcile, and all ends happily. Unlike *The Ballet Girl*, *The Dancer's Peril* contains a considerable amount of danced ballet, including a spectacular and densely populated performance of *Schéhérazade* that takes place in Paris (the film itself was shot on the East Coast of the United States).

There were other early full-length silent films with ballet girls as characters—*Bobbie of the Ballet* (also 1916), for example, a romantic drama with a happy ending in which a parentless ballet girl pretends that she is a widow so that she can take care of her young brother and sister.[11] But in many ways it is *The Ballet Girl* and *The Dancer's Peril,* made so closely together with the same female lead and released by the same company, that end up forming a sort of narrative template for later ballet films, even later silent ballet films. In the first case, this is undoubtedly due to the reliance of *The Ballet Girl* on a literary source that is itself couched as a tragic version of the familiar love story of Harlequin and Columbine. The first chapter of *Carnival* is "The Birth of Columbine," the final "Carni Vale"—more or less literally "farewell to the flesh," as well as a reference, along with the book's title, to the ballet-pantomime of Harlequin and Columbine. I can find no information about the derivation of the plot of *The Dancer's Peril,* which was written by Harriet Morris (she seems to have no other films to her credit), but its Imperial Russian setting as well as its grand duke become semantic staples relatively quickly as well. In *The Midnight Sun* (1926) an American girl, under the name of Olga Balashova, becomes a Russian prima ballerina and falls in love with Alexei, a member of the grand duke's personal guard whose brother is a nihilist who has been sentenced to Siberia for insulting the grand duke.[12] The film ends with a boat chase and Alexei in front of a firing squad for consorting with revolutionaries, but the grand duke eventually gives up his designs on Olga and allows the lovers to reunite.

Ultimately it seems to be the dancer-as-mother trope that appears, or reappears, most frequently. It is manifest in at least one other silent film—*Stage Madness* (1927)—and later in a novel, (Lady) Eleanor Smith's *Ballerina* (1932), as well as a number of Hollywood and post-studio sound features. In *Stage Madness* a French ballet dancer returns to the stage after having a child, but the child is stolen by the husband, who raises her.[13] Years later, the ballet dancer is injured and, jealous of the girl who replaces her, shoots the ballet manager and frames the girl for his murder. The older woman dies when she discovers that the framed girl is her own long-lost daughter. In *Ballerina,* whose film version, *The Men in Her Life,* was released in 1941 and is discussed in more detail below, a dancer gives up her child to be raised by the child's father, because the husband forces her to choose between him and another lover, and the dancer will not give up her ballet career. After the lover is killed in an accident, the husband will bring the child back to her mother, who will also train her to dance.

And finally, while *The Ballet Girl* and *The Dancer's Peril* were categorized by trade papers as dramas, *Midnight Sun* and *Stage Madness*—and others, such as *A Woman's Way* (1928), in which a Parisian ballet dancer in love with a wealthy American is threatened by an escaped criminal—were called, because of their sensational aspects and high degrees of action, *melodramas.*[14] More important, all of these films clearly bear the marks of what Peter Brooks calls "the melodramatic imagination" or of what Ben Singer has more recently identified as five "constitutive elements" in melodrama's identity in popular culture from the early twentieth century through the 1940s and 1950s: strong pathos, overwrought or heightened emotionality, moral polarization, nonclassical narrative structure and mechanics, and sensationalism or spectacular effects.[15] If the meaning of *melodrama* is ambiguous or contentious, Singer claims, it is both because a film so designated might contain all five, just a couple, or "perhaps even just one" of these five elements and because there have been "so many different historical combinations" of them as well.[16] Brooks's early work in some sense forms the basis for all other studies of film melodrama, and his later work is even more concerned with the centrality of the body in modern commercial entertainments. Singer's study of the "serial-queen melodrama," a species of sensational melodrama popular in the early years of the twentieth century that, like most ballet films (or indeed classical ballets), features young women as protagonists, also provides helpful tools for understanding commercial ballet films as part of an extensive intertextual nexus of popular literature and theater, ballets, biography and topical events, and, ultimately, other films.

Modes of Melodrama

Brooks's well-known study *The Melodramatic Imagination* (1976) deals with melodrama as a literary form and as a "mode of excess." For writers such as Balzac and Henry James, melodrama employs the world's surfaces and objects as "indices pointing to hidden forces and truths, latent signifieds."[17] A "form for secularized times," melodrama allows us to "go on entertaining ourselves day after day with the chase, the shoot-out, the open-heart operation" and is "evidence of our need for fully externalized, personalized, and enacted conflict and for its clarifying resolution." Unlike tragedy, in which "pity and terror derive from the sense of communal sacrifice and transformation," melodrama is only the "nearest *approach* to sacred and cosmic values in a world where they no longer have any certain ontology or epistemology." Brooks's famous "moral occult" in melodrama, then, is a locus of real and intense ethical feelings that exceed the capacity of language and that are therefore made manifest in registers of signs other than the verbal—in setting, in costume, in lighting, in music, in cause-and-effect relationships, in battles between villains and heroes. Indeed, melodrama is marked by the "easy identification of villains and heroes (who can often be recognized simply by uniform)." In a later essay, "Melodrama, Body, Revolution" (1994), Brooks writes that the melodramatic body itself is a "body seized by meaning," and since melodrama's simple messages must be made absolutely clear to the audience, the bodies of "victims and villains must unambiguously signify [the body's] status."[18]

Ben Singer, on the other hand, analyzes film melodrama as a "cluster concept," precisely because of the genealogy problems plaguing the use of the term that have already been described. Over the last two hundred years melodrama's "basic features have appeared in so many different combinations" that Singer worked to locate a range of factors that might be emphasized differently across different film texts but whose presence links these films to Brooks's "melodramatic imagination" and to melodrama's literary and popular theatrical antecedents.[19]

Singer's five factors again include *pathos,* a species of empathy that allows spectators to "superimpose their own life (melo)dramas onto the ones being presented in the narrative."[20] *Overwrought emotion* is often related to pathos, but not all scenes that produce the oft-described bodily effects of melodrama—the tears that are jerked, the gasps of surprise or terror, the hisses provoked by villainy—involve pathos. The expression of raw emotion through frenetic and frantic or broad gestures and facial expressions in confrontations with social repression are among the best-known features of melodrama as it is academically defined but are not necessarily pathos-inducing. *Moral polarization,* the clear delineation of good and evil in a modern social environment in which the two are rarely so easily recognized, accounts for the form's continued presence in popular culture; melodrama "express[es] the anxiety of moral disarray and then ameliorat[es] it through utopian moral clarity." At the same time, as Singer himself would likely recognize, most classical Hollywood films are known for their institutionalized insistence that evil must never be rewarded and, as a corollary, most of them feature a ritualized triumph of good guys (often represented physically by the stars of the film) over bad. Melodrama's *nonclassical narrative structure* has a "far greater tolerance, or indeed a preference, for outrageous coincidence, implausibility, convoluted plotting, deus ex machina resolutions, and episodic strings of action that stuff too many events together" to be managed by a logical, cause-and-effect chain (I would argue that these are all familiar features of Hollywood musicals and comedies too). This nonclassical structure helps to produce melodrama's "classic iconography" of *sensationalism*, the locus of the trap door, the "persecuted heroine," the chases and falls and rushing trains and split-second timing that identify the generic mode that Hollywood and its producers recognized as a genre of action rather than of domestic spaces but that also allowed modes like the serial-queen melodrama to become fantasies of female glamour and power. The serial-queen melodrama featured intrepid young women, victimized but ultimately triumphing over adversity and villainy, and offered the spectator "a representational structure that indulged conventionally 'feminine' forms of vanity and exhibitionism while it refused the constraints of decorative femininity through an action-packed depiction of female prowess."

Brooks and Singer give us tools with which to approach the ballet film and to understand it generically as what Singer calls a "parable of modern anxiety."[21] On the one hand, sensational forms of melodrama "external-ized psychology by proclaiming obvious, unequivocal dispositions of vil-lainy, virtue, and valor" while also "*avoiding* the private sphere in favor of an adamantly nondomestic mise-en-scène of criminal dens, submarines, lumber mills, diamond mines, munitions factories, racetracks, abandoned warehouses, gothic mansions, military front lines, rooftops, airfields, high-ways, and railways."[22] And, I would argue, theater stages, rehearsal halls, and ballet classrooms. On the other hand, we will see that what will eventually become routinized enough to be called the ballet meller depends on *both* a domestic and interior mise-en-scène of home and hearth that contrasts with and defines the public space of the theater. But the theater in turn contains its own interior and quasi-domestic spaces (rehearsal hall, classroom), as well as the spectacular and exhibitionistic exterior performance space of the stage itself. If, as Singer claims, at the "heart of the sensationalism of classical melodrama was not simply action and violence but also a peculiar mode of scenic spectacle that tried to combine amazing sights with cred-ible diegetic realism,"[23] then Hollywood's dependence on ballet as a form of spectacle—*even when ballet is not danced*—also helps to make Hollywood ballet films melodramatic.

Thus we arrive back at the films themselves, equipped with theoretical concepts and intertextual references with which to discuss how *all* ballet films and their frequently suffering artists mediate the interaction of pub-lic and private, domestic and nondomestic, male and female, success and failure, pathos and action, spectacle and narrative. We will begin with the women, not only because there are far fewer films of the classical era that feature male ballet artists as protagonists but because one of the points I want to make—and one of the reasons I discuss the women's roles first in their own chapter—is that the men's textual quandaries stem precisely from a problematic relation to spectacle and to the male ballet artist's stature in the American mediascape. In fact, I believe that the men in these films cannot be fully understood except as occupying the usual place of women in the ballet film's syntactic structure. Sometimes this results in camp and comedy, sometimes in disaster and death; but in either case, as we will explore in chapter 3, the men are caught between an often misogynistic uneasiness about the spectacularly aestheticized male body and the conventionalized ways that Hollywood conceives of the relationships among gender, spectacle, and power.

I begin with a discussion of one of the best-known ballerina roles in classical Hollywood sound cinema, that of Grusinskaya, played by Greta Garbo, in *Grand Hotel* (1932). The next cluster of woman-centered ballet films occurs in the early 1940s, when *Waterloo Bridge* and *Dance, Girl, Dance* were released nearly simultaneously in 1940, followed by *The Men in Her Life* in 1941. Finally, I turn to *Days of Glory* (1944), a war film, and *The Unfinished Dance* (1947), a Hollywood remake of a 1938 French film *La Mort du cygne* (American title, *Ballerina*). Most of the films involve tragic events of some kind, but the placement of the events and, more important, their effects on the lives of the films' protagonists differ substantially across time. I do not have equal amounts of information about the production context of all of the films I discuss—the archival resources, including script files and press books, of some studios are extensive, of others nonexistent—but in several cases I am able to trace the process by which ballet came to be included in films whose stories did not initially call for it.

I Can't Dance Tonight!

Grand Hotel is an omnibus "all-star" black-and-white MGM film featuring what were for the time extraordinarily high production values (in addition to Garbo, the film stars John and Lionel Barrymore, Joan Crawford, Wallace Beery, Lewis Stone, and Jean Hersholt). Virtually all of *Grand Hotel* takes place in the eponymous hotel itself, in Berlin; the hotel is its own world, and we learn of all exterior events only through how they affect the film's many protagonists. One of *Grand Hotel*'s interlocking stories—and, according to production notes, meant to be one of the two most significant ones—is that of Russian ballerina Grusinskaya (Garbo), who is tired, fractious, temperamental, and, at least until rejuvenated by the love of a baron and jewel thief, Gaigern (John Barrymore), apparently fading as an artist. Although we see none of this onscreen, the audiences for whom she dances—when she can be wheedled by her maid and manager into making the trip to the theater—are shrinking, the applause dying too early. In her first scene Grusinskaya is so overcome with lassitude and depression that she can barely get out of bed ("I want to be alone. . . . I think, Suzette, I've never been so tired in my life"), and we watch her ballet master and her manager lie to her about the lines at the box office waiting to see Grusinskaya dance (there are none), about how the audience is crying for her (the theater is half-empty), and about the flowers all over her dressing room from admirers (none there either). The lies do work, however, for "Gru" agrees to dance. (In the hall, later, her manager mutters, "After this, no more ballets for me. Jazz, just jazz.") Grusinskaya's car is ordered, her retinue packs up, and they depart.

When next we see Grusinskaya, several scenes later, she has escaped the theater rather than face an audience again; dressed in nothing but a tutu, her toe shoes, and a satin cape, she has rushed back to the hotel. "I want to be alone," she says again; "I just want to be alone." Her hair remains as we have seen it so far, down and curled in a medium bob (no buns for this ballerina). She is again so overcome with despair and fatigue that she can only lurch from one piece of furniture to the next and finally to the floor, where she removes her toe shoes, kissing them as she puts them by ("I always said I'd leave off when the time came—and no trouble about it. Grusinskaya, who dances no more." In the novel a reference follows to "Nijinsky [waiting] in an asylum to die. Poor Nijinsky! Poor Gru!").

Gaigern is hiding in Grusinskaya's room, surprised by her early return from the theater; he had been attempting to steal her famous pearl necklace, the one given to her by her own now-dead grand duke. Grusinskaya is about to swallow an entire bottle of sleeping pills when Gaigern emerges, in turn surprising her, and they begin to talk. They spend the night together—signaled by a discreet fade out—and the next morning Grusinskaya is radiant, bustling about, ready to dance again, full of plans for a new life in ballet as well as new life with "Flix," as Gaigern is now lovingly called by her (it was a childhood name given him by his mother). She is not put off for more than a few minutes by his admission of his attempted thievery, and the baron in turn has been clearly redeemed by her love and trust. He will flirt with but no longer seriously pursue easy sex with the "little stenographer," Flaemmchen (Crawford), who looks up to and fancies him. He will not take Grusinskaya's pearls or her money, but in trying to steal the sums he requires later that night from another hotel guest, the brutal and duplicitous factory owner Preysing (Beery), Gaigern is beaten to death when Preysing discovers him in his room. At the end of the film, Grusinskaya leaves the hotel fearful about Flix, whom she has tried several times unsuccessfully to telephone, but hoping still that he will keep the promise he made to meet her at the train that will take them to her villa in Italy and a new life for them both.

Garbo in a publicity still for *Grand Hotel* (1932), in which we never see her dance. Note the wings on her tutu.

Courtesy National Film Archive, London.

Grand Hotel was adapted from a 1930 Broadway play by Viennese writer Vicki Baum; MGM had helped finance the production in exchange for the film rights.[24] The play in turn was an adaptation of Baum's 1929 German novel, *Menschen im Hotel,* which had been translated into English by 1930 and become an international best-seller (it had also been performed as a play on the Berlin stage). In the novel the character of the Russian prima ballerina Grusinskaya is modeled on Pavlova, who was then still performing, still touring, but nearing the age of fifty and whose zenith as a dancer was clearly past. Baum wrote in her posthumously published memoirs of having once seen "the fading Pavlova and her shabby small troupe of dancers. I came away with an infinitely melancholy impression, a half-empty house, . . . and yet there was the luminous glow of a great, a born, dancer."[25] Pavlova was still considered great in 1929 and 1930 but was no longer the draw in some locations that she once had been; and as her body aged, all of her performances produced journalistic murmurs about how much longer she would go on, public musings about what her life would consist of, what it would mean, when she could no longer perform.[26] Grusinskaya's predicament, as Baum describes it, is similar:

No one knew how old Grusinskaya was. There were old Russian aristocrats in exile . . . who asserted that they had known Grusinskaya for forty years. . . .

Grusinskaya did not alter. She had weighed ninety-six pounds since the age of eighteen and in this lay part of her success and her capabilities. . . . Grusinskaya bent all her force to one aim, to be as she had been. And she did not observe that it was exactly this of which the world began to tire.

Perhaps the world would have loved her as she really was, as she looked now, for example, sitting in her dressing-room—a poor, delicate, tired old woman with worn-out eyes, and a small care-worn human face.[27]

In addition to having black hair that is "drawn down over her cheeks in two smooth black wings," Grusinskaya's big solo number is a dance of a dying *dove,* and, like Pavlova's dying swan, her costume features a "large ruby red drop of blood [that] tremble[s] on her white silk bodice." In public, Grusinskaya is a "work of art"; in private, she wears a rubber bandage under her chin while she sleeps, has two thin hairline scars from plastic surgery, and cannot bear to look at her haggard and ravaged face in the mirror.

Between the publication of Baum's novel and the release of the film version of *Grand Hotel* Pavlova died suddenly in Europe, in 1931, to a huge amount of publicity, publicity that undoubtedly helped to blur even further the boundaries between the fictional Grusinskaya and the legendary Pavlova. Garbo bore more than a passing facial resemblance to Pavlova, too, and had a deep voice and accent that easily fit with Pavlova's image. Pavlova had her dying swan costume (and again, among her final words were reputedly a request that her costume "be prepared");[28] Garbo as Grusinskaya has butterfly wings on her wrists and tutu.

What we do not see Grusinskaya do, however, is dance. In Baum's novel the character is introduced dancing, or rather in the wings *after* dancing: "Grusinskaya, who but a moment before circled as light as a flower among her troupe of girls, crept panting into the nearest wing. . . . Her hands shook and she gasped for breath like a wounded animal. Sweat ran along the wrinkles below her eyes. The clapping made no more noise than distant rain and then it came suddenly near—a sign that the curtain had gone up. . . . Grusinskaya adjusted her smile like a cardboard mask and danced forward to make her curtsey before the footlights."[29] In contrast, Garbo's Grusinskaya is among the first, if not the first, of the sound era's "offstage icons" of ballet. And the success of *Grand Hotel* at the box office and as an award winner could not help but make her one of its most influential. This is a prima ballerina whom we never see doing the work that ballerinas do but whose life is wholly bound up in it, wholly run by whether or not she will "dance tonight" and how many curtain calls she will or will not receive. Because there is no ballet dancing in *Grand Hotel*, what can we learn about it from Grusinskaya and Garbo and the lines they speak, from what happens, from what *else* we see on the screen?

First, when Grusinskaya gets out of the bower of beautiful bed linens in which the camera initially locates her, we see that she is wearing toe shoes, for when she finally gets out of her bed, she rises *en pointe* briefly before collapsing again. There are very few contexts in which a ballet dancer would wear toe shoes in bed, but it certainly serves a fetishistic purpose that is echoed later by her kissing of the shoes she wears home in her escape from the theater. Then, when she and Gaigern talk of their pasts, she recounts to him her training from childhood at the Imperial ballet school, where they were drilled "like little soldiers." And she repeatedly states that she is tired, as tired as she's ever been in her life, and that she wants to be alone—she wants everyone to *leave* her alone. The suspense that is generated from Grusinskaya's refusal to dance, then her capitulation, then her return to the hotel in her tutu is diverting but ultimately confusing. For finally, not only is she treated like a child by all of her employees, but the sumptuousness of the mise-en-scène—the grandeur of her hotel room (rather than the "banal and tawdry elegance" described by Baum), the perfection of Garbo's complexion and makeup, her au courant movie-star hair, the fabulously flattering glamour lighting, the devotion of her maid and, of course, of John Barrymore—belies what we are told about her dwindling audiences and box-office receipts (and, in turn, we do not really know how she earns all of this material wealth, only that rehearsals, toe shoes, and a tutu are involved). Grusinskaya wears a glittering lamé dressing gown and a gorgeous negligee for the early scenes, and she departs the hotel at the end of the film in a full mink coat and glamorous hat and shoes. She has a villa in Italy, and a car, and jewels given to her by a grand duke. Equally important, Grusinskaya, in contrast to her much more detailed characterization in the novel, is *good*, and quite sweet; she helps a little old lady onto the elevator, her servants are devoted to her, and even her displays of temperament are victimless, represented not as signs of the power she can choose to wield arbitrarily over shrinking subordinates but of her insecurity as an artist and a woman.

Spectators of *Grand Hotel* who had also read the novel perhaps chose to fill in the blanks of Grusinskaya's life with the many scenes of onstage and backstage life, her nastiness to other dancers and her partners, and the decaying face and body that Baum describes so well. I myself experience Garbo's Grusinskaya not as the ballerina of Baum's novel (no matter how many times I read it or how many times I see the film) but as a supremely romantic figure whose tragedy has only to do with the death of "Flix." The melodramatic aspects of such a densely plotted film, a film dependent on timing and coincidence as well as overwrought emotion, should be obvious; coincidence brings Gaigern and Grusinskaya together, coincidence places Gaigern in Preysing's room, where—indeed, *so that*—he can be killed and kept from happiness with Grusinskaya. Ballet has held Grusinskaya apart from love until now; her body does not function in the film as an expressive body except when it is *not* dancing—and even then it is expressive primarily as a hysterical body whose fidgets and wild gestures she cannot control. Ballet in the movie version of *Grand Hotel* is hard, but it is labor with no product. Nevertheless, it is Grusinskaya who is the artist here, not her male manager or her ballet master. Ballet is work that is talked about as valuable but also that has gone out of style. What we want for Grusinskaya as she leaves the hotel is to find Flix alive, because without Flix her life will return to the way it was when we met her, beautiful and opulent but empty and meaningless.[30]

Romance and Looniness

Despite the box-office and critical success of *Grand Hotel,* for the next several years following its release few films feature ballet dancers as protagonists who do not also dance, and usually these films are also musical comedies. As mentioned earlier, there *was* plenty of ballet-as-toe-dancing to be found both in operettas and in "serious" musicals. Jeremy Tambling refers to some opera films like *One Night of Love* (1934), for example, with soprano Grace Moore, as belonging to "a whole genre of films that advertise opera as the accompaniment to romance,"[31] and the same thing could be said of the ballet interludes, often choreographed by Albertina Rasch and featuring her troupes of female dancers, that dot any number of films from *Grand Hotel* through the end of the decade.[32]

Vera Zorina plays a sort of all-purpose and vaguely Russian comic diva who acts crazily and dances beautifully in *The Goldwyn Follies* (1938). But the ballets that Zorina performs, choreographed by Balanchine and also featuring his American Ballet (then appearing by permission of the Metropolitan Opera), are, while gems of early "cine-dance," not connected to the plot of the film itself. Zorina's character has no relation to ballet except when she dances it in two big numbers—one a "water-nymph" ballet featuring many special film effects, another that ends with a tap-ballet battle between the American Ballet and the Goldwyn Girls (it ends in a draw). In Frank Capra's screwball comedy *You Can't Take It with You* (also 1938), Ann Miller plays Essie Carmichael, a college football player's young wife who wears a tutu and toe shoes whenever she can and dances all over the house as one of the film's plentiful signs of the genial lunacy and virtuousness of her extended

Tap dancer Eleanor Powell in toe shoes in an Albertina Rasch ballet in *Broadway Melody of 1936* (1936).

Courtesy National Film Archive, London.

family. In the Capra universe, play and fun always beat wealth and stuffiness. But Essie appears to have no real desire to dance professionally; she just likes ballet, and the distance between any Capra heroine's desires and public demeanor is meant to be slight.

Essie is hardly the most bizarre of the lunatics that populate her household, nor is she (nor is Zorina, for that matter) the only "crazy" ballet-film character of 1938 (see chapter 3). What is important is that ballet, specifically ballet *dancing,* had become familiar enough, famous enough, and American enough by 1938 to permeate American musical theater and musical films, yet, in terms of its narrative placement, it remained associated with lunatic behavior or with being Russian most of the time (or comically pretending to be). Ballet set pieces were now functioning as a prestige element, even while ballet dancers as characters remain crazy divas—the men as well—or else were hankering, like Fred Astaire's Petrov in *Shall We Dance* (1937, discussed in the next chapter), to be tap dancers.

Despite the popularity or at least ubiquity of ballet dancing in this sense in commercial films through the 1930s, when next a Hollywood nonmusical featured a woman as a ballet-dancing protagonist, the level of morbidity

The assorted loonies of Frank Capra's *You Can't Take It with You* (1938), with Ann Miller (in tutu and toe shoes) as Essie Carmichael.

Courtesy National Film Archive, London.

was ratcheted back up to *Grand Hotel* level. The interrelationship in Western culture of femininity and death is well known; as Elisabeth Bronfen puts it in *Over Her Dead Body: Death, Femininity, and the Aesthetic,* "[B]ecause the feminine body is culturally constructed as the superlative site of alterity, culture uses art to dream the deaths of beautiful women."[33] The triad of *Waterloo Bridge, Dance, Girl, Dance,* and *The Men in Her Life* is most interesting, however, for how this tradition developed in relation to what was expected of, and allowed for, women who attempted to live "the life of the artist."

A War Is No Excuse for Indecorum

Tchaikovsky's *Swan Lake* provides much of the nondiegetic (and some of the diegetic) music for *Waterloo Bridge,* and there is a brief pastiche of the ballet early in the film, during the performance of which the hero, Roy (Robert Taylor), essentially falls in love with the heroine, Myra (Vivien Leigh, who had just completed filming on *Gone with the Wind*). As we will see, however, no one initially involved in the film knew much at all about *Swan Lake,* either as music or as a narrative ballet. Moreover, *Waterloo Bridge* was the second film version of Robert E. Sherwood's 1930 two-act play, and there was no ballet of any kind in either the first film version or the play from which it was adapted. Sherwood's play is an antiwar drama about a Canadian soldier in World War I who knows he is going off to die and who leaves his money to the equally fatalistic prostitute he loves. The first film version (1931, directed by James Whale) not only kills the prostitute-heroine with a zeppelin attack, but it makes the marriage of the prostitute to an honorable man the moral dilemma of the narrative. No prostitute, no matter how wonderful or loved or forgiven by her fiancé, could be allowed to prosper or to marry happily, not even in "pre-Code" Hollywood.[34]

The 1940 *Waterloo Bridge* retains the earlier film's moral dilemma but gives Myra a much more romantic profession: she becomes a ballerina, meeting Roy, an officer, during a World War I air raid on Waterloo Bridge, where he mistakes her for a schoolgirl. They discuss her training ("We try to combine slenderness with strength"; "I've been dancing since I was twelve") and her ability to do an *entrechat six* (however incorrectly she defines it); her fatalism; and the rigors of life under "Madame" (Maria Ouspenskaya), the director of "Olga Kirowa's International Ballet," the company of which Myra is a member. Roy goes to see Myra in *Swan Lake* later that night; their eyes meet across the footlights, and they fall in love.

More significant, the script of this version attaches the ultimate fate of Myra to a series of much more obviously melodramatic elements, especially pathos and plot twists based on coincidence and bad timing. For example, Roy asks Myra to marry him virtually after their first date, and they attempt to marry before Roy leaves for the front; but because of an unforeseen waiting period and Roy's unexpectedly early departure—she rushes to the station to see him off yet arrives only in time to see the train pull away from the platform—Myra ends up neither married nor employed, for she is fired for missing a ballet performance in order (not) to see Roy off. In another coincidence, Myra learns that Roy has been killed right before her first meeting with his mother, Lady Margaret (Lucile Watson), but in her agony not to reveal the news she antagonizes his mother. Myra tries to return to her job at the ballet, but it has just left for America; Myra and her only friend, Kitty, move, and therefore Lady Margaret, when she realizes what probably accounted for Myra's strange behavior at lunch, is unable to locate her and to take care of her. With nothing to live for, Myra becomes a prostitute rather than be a burden to Kitty, who has been supporting her with what little she has. And in the final coincidence, the most ironic, Myra meets Roy at the train station where she has gone to pick up soldiers; he is not dead after all. Roy wants to take up where they left off and, of course, does not know about her new profession. Myra tries to think of her past as a bad dream and gets Kitty's permission to "go to him." The couple visits Roy's relatives at the family country estate, where Myra realizes that she cannot bring dishonor to such a fine family and ends up confessing privately to Roy's mother why she, Myra, cannot marry him (although the problem cannot be named directly because of Code restrictions) and leaves in the night. Back in London, Myra commits suicide by throwing herself in front of a convoy of trucks.

A World War II framing story is added to the 1940 version of *Waterloo Bridge* as well; the film begins with Roy as an old soldier during World War II (which was then just beginning), back at the place on Waterloo Bridge where he met Myra during World War I and where she died. He fondles a charm that Myra gave him and hears her voice speaking to him. With the bulk of the film told in flashback (although a typically omniscient one), in essence Myra seems to be giving Roy strength from beyond the grave, strength he, and England, needs at this crucial time. She has become, properly, a man's muse, rescued in an odd sense from the inappropriate but quasi-familial relationships of Madame Olga Kirowa's International Ballet.

The question is how ballet came to be featured in the 1940 *Waterloo Bridge* in the first place. Why did Myra become a ballet dancer—was it a throwback to the conjunction of "ballet girl" and "chorus girl" that marked nineteenth- and early twentieth-century popular culture? Or had someone noticed the ubiquity of ballet and toe dancing in musicals of the mid-1930s, both in film and on Broadway? Had a producer or writer seen the French film *La Mort du cygne,* which was in limited American release in the late 1930s, or did he or she remember that another MGM blockbuster, *Grand Hotel,* had had a tragic ballerina in it (MGM was always a studio to repeat its past successes)? Or had someone simply sat through a ballet recently and recognized in it something of use to the new version of the film being prepared? *Waterloo Bridge* was in production from January 1940 through March 1940 and was released in May. Surviving production memos suggest that by late 1939 the decision had been made to use ballet music in the film and that the music was going to be Tchaikovsky's *Swan Lake.* Yet few on the film's production staff had apparently heard the music or seen the ballet, and certainly no one knew very much about either. A letter from an uncredited scriptwriter, Dodie Smith, to one of the film's producers, Sidney Franklin, is a snapshot of ballet's compelling but amorphous presence in popular culture at that time and of what Hollywood deemed to be most significant and, indeed, worrisome about it.

Smith begins her memo as follows:

> You will remember that Tchaikovsky's "Swan Lake" (better known as "Lac de Cygnes") was chosen for our ballet and I was rather anxious to have some research done on it but you felt that as only a glimpse

would be shewn [sic] this was not really necessary. I did, however, make a point of listening to the music and it seemed to me most tuneful and quite admirable for our purpose. So I went ahead and tied "Swan Lake" into the story and, as you will see, the idea has been a great help. Since finishing the work, my husband has brought me a comprehensive book on ballets and I now find that "Swan Lake" includes quite a large number of male dancers as well as girls. I expect we can get over this in one way or another but I think we shall have to look into it all rather carefully. I am not even sure whether the choreography of the ballet and even the title may not be copyright [sic]. I should hate to take it out now and don't know how I could as it is tied into many pieces of dialogue.[35]

Several other memos are concerned with how to obtain the rights to the music, the title, and the choreography of *Swan Lake,* but of course none of these turned out to provide problems on the order of discovering that *Swan Lake* "has men in it." In the finished film the *Swan Lake* theme and music, as arranged by Herbert Stothart, are heard in the overture and under at least six scenes, including Roy's and Myra's first date, when Myra learns (erroneously) that Roy has died, and when she meets Roy at the station (but not when she commits suicide, when the main sounds are the rumblings of the trucks). And, of course, it is the music for the ballet that Myra, as a member of Olga Kirowa's International Ballet, performs.

Swan Lake in *Waterloo Bridge,* in fact, has no men in it, nor a recognizable vocabulary of steps or gestures, nor any story at all. It is a pastiche musically and visually, with all of the many girls in long tutus and with swan feathers framing their faces. Most of the dancing by anyone but Myra takes place on a ludicrously cavernous stage (it is meant to be a variety theater), in long shot, and all is very brightly lit. Again, *why* do we need to see Myra dance, much less in this cheerful pastiche? Myra could easily have been an offstage icon, and Vivien Leigh was not a ballet dancer. An early handwritten script note by Sidney Franklin suggests an answer: "The boy meets the girl, but she is in the chorus, and she has not become a streetwalker yet. . . . We've got to find a personality for her . . . a character for her. . . . She must have a little quality that makes her stand out." Myra's being the most beautiful swan onstage provides that quality—we only see Vivien Leigh in close-up, except when she is exchanging dialogue with Kitty, while they are dancing, about having noticed Roy in the audience ("Kitty! He's here!")—and clearly Roy (the Prince) is mesmerized. That no performer on such a vast stage could possibly see, much less recognize, a particular audience member goes without saying—the lights onstage are blinding, there is a giant orchestra pit, Roy is nowhere near the front row, and so on. Nor do ballet performers usually indulge in large amounts of audible cross-talk during a performance such as occurs here between Kitty and Myra. These Hollywood conventions are not rare, however, and realism is not the issue. Rather, the performance only matters, is only included, to provide a way for Roy to recognize Myra as a beautiful, otherworldly creature with wings and to fall in love with her. He will be unable to possess her ever, and this too is supported by the versions of *Swan Lake* then being performed theatrically around the United States and by the synopses to which Dodie Smith presumably refers.

Equally significant is the character of Madame Kirowa, a small, wizened, severely dressed and pitiless martinet who recognizes nothing of Myra's dilemma, who is presented as knowing nothing about love but only about discipline and the mechanical execution of steps. Ballet, through Madame, becomes, as it is in *Grand Hotel,* something to which fealty must be paid but for reasons that are not named, except by aphorism: "You don't honor ballet by your presence in it; the ballet honors you." All of the girls, except the working-class Kitty (a former chorus girl, we are told), are utterly cowed by Madame. While Madame is indeed frightening, we learn nothing about her own connection to ballet or anything about why it matters. We learn mainly what it prohibits: "I must emphasize," proclaims Madame, "that if you want supper parties, officers, and delight, you shouldn't be here with me but in some other occupation. . . . A war is no excuse for indecorum." She makes Myra write a note rejecting Roy's written invitation to supper. They meet anyway.

But in however truncated or amateurish a fashion (Leigh is photographed primarily from the waist up and waves her arms through basic ballet positions, which she does perfectly convincingly), ballet *is danced* in *Waterloo Bridge,* and it is meant to be a thing of beauty and some respect. It is a species of high art, and it elevates Myra above the level of chorus girl so that her fall can be all the more affecting. In fact, the duke (played by C. Aubrey Smith), Roy's regimental commander and arbiter of his and the film's morals, tells Myra that it is "too bad" that she cannot live up to the idea of a "dancer as someone a little—racy?" It would be "good fun, wouldn't it," if she could. But no, Myra is "sound. And good." The duke's "instinct" tells him what Myra "is."

One of the perverse reasons for the continuing popularity of *Waterloo Bridge,* I believe (it remains a frequent rental at video stores and the like), is the way in which it makes Myra indeed sound, and good, and also a prostitute. The duke's lengthy speech and his quite obvious approval of Myra is "wrong," incorrect, in that he actually *cannot* recognize Myra for what she is; but it is also "right" because she is a good and sound person who happens to have been a prostitute for a few months. Part of the appeal to jaded audiences now, too, is the camp way in which Myra's profession is alluded to but

An exceedingly romantic glamour shot of Vivien Leigh in her swan costume, by Laszlo Willinger, for *Waterloo Bridge* (1940).

Collection of the author.

never named—I know some people who can quote Myra's confession to Lady Margaret, Roy's mother, verbatim:

LADY MARGARET: Has there been someone else?
MYRA: Oh Lady Margaret, you are naive.
LADY MARGARET: Myra!
MYRA: Yes—yes, yes!
LADY MARGARET: Myra!
MYRA: Yes—that thought which is now in your mind, which you are telling
    yourself *can't* be true, *is* true!
LADY MARGARET: Myra!!

Myra's suicide also achieves the status of camp in that it now reads as an ironic comment on the strictly gendered morality of Code-era films and the extravagant waste and misery that adherence to that morality causes. We even see that Roy finds out from Kitty what Myra "was" and that it does not matter to him—he searches for her at every train station and on every bridge but it is "too late."

In her influential study of melodrama and, or as, the Hollywood woman's film, Mary Ann Doane writes that Myra in *Waterloo Bridge* has to die because she is a prostitute, and about the dialogue between Myra and Lady Margaret and the choker close-up of Myra's eyes that precedes her final leap Doane writes: "This empty space, the unsaid, anticipates her death. For prostitution is absolutely irrecuperable. Myra's fiancé, Roy, can cross class lines in order to become engaged to her, but once she slips into prostitution, she is lost, her death inevitable. The woman associated with excessive sexuality resides outside the boundaries of language; she is unrepresentable and must die because, as Claire Johnston points out, death is the 'location of all impossible signs.'"[36]

Leaving aside for a moment all of the prostitutes with hearts of gold that populate Hollywood films and who do not die (they are seldom the protagonists), it is not the boundaries of language or excessive sexuality that make Myra unrepresentable or that condemn her to death but the strictures of the Production Code. And it is hard not to notice that ballet is treated in much the same way as the unrepresentable prostitution in *Waterloo Bridge*. Each has its "Madame," each has its cohorts of girls but no men, each involves the disciplined and codified performance of romance (when the romance is real, tragedy ensues). Moreover, as we will see in chapter 5, the third film adaptation of *Waterloo Bridge* made in Hollywood, *Gaby* (1956), allows its ballet-dancing heroine/prostitute to live.

Dance . . . Dance . . . Dance . . .

Maria Ouspenskaya played another ballet madame in 1940, in Dorothy Arzner's *Dance, Girl, Dance*. Madame Basilova, "formerly Ballerina of the Imperial Russian Ballet," is a much more sympathetic character in *Dance, Girl, Dance*, however, running a troupe of showgirls who perform the gamut from burlesque to ballet. Burlesque, particularly in the form of Bubbles (Lucille Ball), the "hot one," sells better than ballet, with ballet personified by Judy (Maureen O'Hara), a gentle girl who is pretty but unable to be "hot" and who dreams of becoming a "real"—that is, ballet—dancer. Early in the film, Madame wangles an audition for Judy with Steve Adams (Ralph Bellamy), an American impresario who runs "the American Ballet." Just as Madame and Judy arrive at the skyscraper—"We're but a few short steps from destiny"—that houses the American Ballet, Madame proclaims, "Never shall it be said that the great Basilova did not make the last sacrifice for art," and as she steps forward to cross the street, she is hit by a speeding cab. Her last words before she dies are, "Dance . . . Dance . . . Dance," but, as the discussion of the generic features of *Dance, Girl, Dance* at the beginning of this chapter suggest, the film is full of missed opportunities and plot twists (like Basilova's death). Judy misses her first appointment but about a week later returns to the skyscraper to fulfill the destiny Madame planned for her. But she watches part of a ballet rehearsal and is so demoralized by what she sees there that she flees. "At that place today I saw what *real* dancing is," she says later; "I discovered I . . . I just don't know anything!" She meets Adams on the street but, in a series of misunderstandings, thinks he is a "masher." She will meet him again at the end of the film, and he will recognize her talent and dedication ("Dancing means everything to me—I've never *cared* about anything else"), and the film ends with her crying in his arms.

Because so few classical Hollywood films were directed by women, *Dance, Girl, Dance* became a significant text for film feminists in the 1970s and 1980s in search of a woman's cinema or countercinema. Attention has been focused on how Ouspenskaya is costumed to resemble Arzner herself—severe bun, buttoned-up shirt, and man's tie—and on the competing sexualities of Bubbles and Judy in the all-girl milieu of the dance troupe. Bubbles's own rise to success as a burlesque dancer named Tiger Lily occurs at the expense of Judy's dreams; when Judy runs away from her audition at the American Ballet, Bubbles takes her on as a stooge, hiring her to dance ballet before an unappreciative and derisive audience as a warm-up for Bubbles's appearances. Judy achieves some fame herself as the stooge, but the extremely skeletal romantic story line, in which Judy and Bubbles halfheartedly compete for the attention of a married British drunkard who will eventually return to his (also British) wife, pits the two women, heretofore good friends, against each another.

One of the best-known moments in *Dance, Girl, Dance,* a moment that has the power to shock still, is when Judy confronts her audience directly after one of her stooge costume's straps breaks. It happens to be when Adams and "Olmi" (Miss Olmstead), Adams's loyal secretary/Girl Friday/factotum (played by Katharine Alexander), are in the audience to audition Judy informally. In a lengthy, scathing speech, Judy invites the audience to "go ahead and stare—I'm not ashamed." She continues:

> I know you want me to tear my clothes off so's you can look your fifty-cents'-worth. Fifty cents for the privilege of staring at a girl the way your *wives* won't let you. What do you suppose *we* think of you up here—with your silly smirks your mothers would be ashamed of. . . . We'd laugh right back at the lot of you only we're paid to let you sit there. . . .
>
> What's it for? So's you can go home when the show's over and strut before your wives and sweethearts and play at being the stronger sex for a minute? I'm sure they see through you just like we do.

At which point Olmi stands up and applauds, with the applause being taken up by everyone else—the men, the women, and the slumming "suits." Acknowledged by most critics to be a diegetic comment on the nondiegetic audience for *Dance, Girl, Dance,* and by extension all Hollywood films and their displays of women's bodies, the moment's effectiveness is muted, several have noted, by the fact that it ends with Bubbles calling Judy a "jealous little pig" and attacking her in what becomes an all-out hair-pulling, clothes-tearing catfight onstage. The pair ends up in court, whence Adams and Olmi rescue Judy. She will be Adams's "latest discovery"; she has been a "silly child" who has had her "own way long enough" and is from now on going to listen to *him.*

Although we already know that the producers of *Dance, Girl, Dance* assumed it would be a "feminine hit" (the film is based on an original "intimate story" by Vicki Baum, and apparently Arzner replaced Roy del Ruth as director), by far the most intriguing character for anyone interested in American ballet history is Steve Adams. He appears to be a Diaghilev-style impresario wearing American business clothes and speaking with a midwestern accent. He has a foreign ballet master and choreographer, Fitch (Ernö Varebes), who does the training (the film's billed dance director was Ernst Matray, who also directed the dances in *Waterloo Bridge*). He has a prima ballerina, Vivian (Vivian Fay, herself an American dancer who had achieved some fame in New York stage productions and for bits in other films), and he has strong views—as strong as Lincoln Kirstein's, whom he sounds like—on what American ballet should be. After Adams (and we, the film audience) watches about two minutes of what is clearly an "American scene" ballet, he complains to Fitch about an excess of "classical influence." In one of the next scenes he loses his professional demeanor while he is dictating a rejection letter to a dancer who has imitated a bluebird: "Who do you think cares [about bluebirds]?" *He* wants ballets about "telephones, factories, cafeterias." He asks Olmi, who has recast the letter in gentler terms, to read it back: "What we are interested in, . . . is not an interpretation of bird life, however lovely, but an interpretation of American life today—shopkeepers, mechanics, aviators." Adams reacts approvingly, murmuring, "Why is it, Olmi, that you are the only woman who ever understands me?" We then see the ballet *again,* from the beginning, but more of it this time.

Adams's ballet begins with a pair of women, against a curtained backdrop, dancing to a tinkling minor melody. When the curtains are pulled back, Vivian Fay appears in a short, Martha Grahamesque (but sequined) tunic, her hair down in a curly pageboy bob. She is massively muscled in the hard high-contrast light and performs a brief solo in toe shoes. There are several cuts to Judy's face as she watches wide-eyed from behind a curtain. The first time we see the ballet, Adams interrupts this sequence, and we return to narrative action, the dictation of his "bluebird" letter. The second time we move further into the piece, to a city set, actually the New York skyline seen through the enormous office window. It is not clear, in usual Hollywood fashion, where the music is coming from (it is a dress rehearsal but with no orchestra in sight), but now we hear a siren in the score. The ballet is populated by street sweepers, janitors, newsboys, college girls, organ grinders, and an African American couple, or rather a pair of white dancers in blackface. Some of the women are in toe shoes, others in ballet flats. After they dance around a bit, Vivian Fay is surrounded and hidden by all of them and reappears in a sort of constructivist tunic with a wired hem, padded shoulders, and patterned in jagged blocks of black and white, but she is also wearing a bonnet and long gloves. She dances some more with the company; they lift her aloft (suddenly she has a parasol that she holds high), and the ballet ends. Judy is still watching, and, awed by what she has seen, she tells the ballet master she "made a mistake" and runs away in dismay at her own inadequacies. Again, this is named as "real" ballet, as opposed to what Judy performs with Basilova's troupe or even the little dances Judy choreographs in private herself (and dances in toe shoes).[37]

In short, in contrast to *Grand Hotel* and *Waterloo Bridge*, quite a bit of screen time in *Dance, Girl, Dance* is devoted to the performance of ballet that is presented as being "American" and "modern" as well as "classical." In 1938 Lincoln Kirstein was raging in print against the assumption on the part of American audiences and critics that "real" ballet was Russian ballet, even though "Russianballet," in Kirstein's sardonic locution, had "stopped being specifically Russian" when Diaghilev left Russia for Europe in 1909.[38] In all of the films discussed so far—and several yet to come—ballet has never stood apart from its Russianness; but in *Dance, Girl, Dance* its primary Russian exemplar, Madame Basilova, is killed by that most American of inventions, the automobile. Moreover, in contrast to *Waterloo Bridge*, there are at least men in Steve Adams's American Ballet. In one scene we see ballet-master Fitch in the middle of a group of male dancers who are all performing barrel turns around him in a circle. Yet *Dance, Girl, Dance* presents nothing new or innovative or "neoclassical" in terms of dance steps but instead takes costuming and character types, along with an urban street setting and a police siren, as indicative of an updated relevance to American life. The steps that Judy performs in a long tutu as Tiger Lily's stooge are virtually identical to many of the steps that Vivian Fay performs in her more severe tunics or, indeed, to the bits of ballet we glimpse in *Waterloo Bridge*. The "interpretation of American life today" rests on costuming, setting, props, and character stereotypes, not dance technique.

Still, the interest of *Dance, Girl, Dance* in the value of art dance as an avocation is significant. But it remains a profession controlled by men, who "discover" women and turn them into "real" dancers. Judy herself does not have a tragic life, although Madame Basilova's death alludes to the possibility that a life devoted to ballet will end tragically. Several film scholars have argued that Basilova dies because she is coded visually as a lesbian, but she was also a ballet-artist lesbian—surely a double curse. Yet Olmi's line to Steve Adams, when he grimaces on learning that he is going to have to go to a burlesque house if he wants to see Judy dance, is, "That's right, condemn a girl because she has to earn her own living!" And Olmi herself seems to be a perfectly happy single working woman; she is not mooning after Adams. The press book for *Dance, Girl, Dance* alternates references to "hotcha burlesque teasers" and "heartbreak, hate and hope behind the gayety of a girly-girl show!" with references to "career girls' trials" and the film as being "woman-made."

One could read the film's gender politics in the context of the approach of U.S. involvement in World War II and the "media blitzkrieg," in Michael Renov's words, that would be employed to get women out of the home and into munitions factories.[39] A reading of the film's unconscious gender and racial politics might also link the urban setting of the film's big ballet number (among many other things) and the fact that the squabbling married couple is British to a wider World War II context as well. In the end I am persuaded that the film aims truly to be a "feminine hit" and that its continuing fascination for those who love it stems at least partly from its attempts to represent both artists and "burlesque teasers" as valuable, necessary, and honorable human beings.

I Shall Teach Her to Dance If I Have to Kill Her in the Attempt

The final ballet film in the cycle of 1940–1941 is a period piece, *The Men in Her Life,* an adaptation of Eleanor Smith's 1932 novel *Ballerina.*[40] The film is relatively unknown today, but it is extremely interesting as a repository of many of the sentiments and even some of the lines that would resonate so strongly in *The Red Shoes* a few years later. While I have no evidence that Michael Powell and Emeric Pressburger saw *The Men in Her Life,* I would be happy to bet that they did because of the resemblance of the latter film's dialogue to their film in several scenes. *The Men in Her Life* stars Loretta Young as Polly Varley, a circus performer in England who is discovered by Stanislas Rosing (Conrad Veidt), an aging and bitter ballet dancer who now has the chance to redeem himself (when Polly learns his name, she says, "I thought you were dead," to which Rosing replies, "As far as dancing is concerned, I am. And as dancing is my whole life . . ."). At the circus, when a boy begins heckling Polly, Rosing stops him: "Young man, you are in the presence of great beauty. You may not realize it, but that is your misfortune." Rosing goes backstage, as it were, to pose to Polly the crucial question. Standing very close to her, in Veidt's familiar clipped Teutonic tones, he asks, "The question is, how great is your desire, your ambition, to be a dancer?" Polly, a key light glowing on her face, responds breathlessly, "Oh, I think I'd give anything in the world." When Polly shows up at Rosing's house that very night, believing that he has invited her to live there to learn to dance, her first lesson begins within the hour. He "shall teach her to dance if [he] has to kill her in the attempt," and even though his devoted housekeeper, Marie (Eugenie Leontovich), is worried about *his* health—Rosing's doctors have forbidden him ever to dance again—he is ecstatic because through Polly he now has "a chance to *live* again."

Rosing is more developed as a character than either of the two ballet mistresses played earlier by Ouspenskaya; not only does he control Polly Varley's life (one of the first things he does is to rename her Lina Varsavina) and training (we see him beating time with a cane as she does endless *pliés* and *battements*), but he will eventually marry her. He gets many of the best lines, too. When Lina complains about the hard work and repetitions of the same old steps over and over, Rosing cuts her off: "Yes, *plié, battement:* this is what you will hear all your life. Then one day you will be old, and there will be nothing left of you but a memory." After an extended nightmare montage sequence—Lina tossing and turning hearing Rosing's voice shouting "*Plié! Battement!*" over and over again, superimposed over a dancing double's feet—Lina returns to the classroom but that day runs off, still in black practice tutu and toe shoes, for an impromptu afternoon with Roger (John Shepperd), a young man who happens by and sees her practicing. When they get caught in a storm and she returns home late, Rosing is apoplectic: "What have you *done?* Who do you think you are—Polly Varley? You are Lina Varsavina!" He has spent two years creating an "instrument"—"You take the body that *I* have made, and you try to destroy it!" As for the possibility of love, Rosing scoffs: "A dancer has no time for such nonsense, do you hear me?"

Lina, however, does protest against this treatment: "I'm a person, I'm *not* a machine!" But it is another woman who loves Rosing, Marie, who urges Lina to apologize to him. She does, and he forgives "my little girl." He takes her to audition for a well-known prima ballerina—again an uncredited dancing double is used, with shots of her from the back facing a mirror, and with close-ups of her feet and bars of shadow to hide the dancer's upper body—and Lina is next going to be shown onstage, already a dancing star, in Paris. Roger is sitting in the audience, and much like the recognition scene in *Waterloo Bridge* (and, more ambiguously, in *Dance, Girl, Dance,* when Steve Adams watches Judy in the burlesque house), he falls in love with her by watching her dance onstage. Rosing tells Lina that Paris is hers, "and in one

Publicity still of Loretta Young in *The Men in Her Life* (1941).
Photo by A. L. "Whitey" Schafer. Collection of the author.

night." At the opening-night supper party, Roger tells Lina he loves her, out on the balcony. But *Rosing* proposes to Lina, and she, because of all she owes him, accepts and announces the engagement at supper. A *Swan Lake* medley, the only one in the film, plays throughout this scene, which fades out on Roger's disappointed face.

Another montage sequence, time has passed, and now Lina and Rosing are on a ship, and Lina has a scene with David (Dean Jagger), the "first American she has ever met." David has not seen a ballet in ten years, but later, when he sees Lina dancing the ballet Rosing has created for her, "The White Rose" (danced to music from Tchaikovsky's *The Sleeping Beauty* and stealing much from Pavlova's *Dying Swan*), he too falls in love with her. (The choreography of the dancing in *The Men in Her Life* is by Adolph Bolm.) Rosing dies the night of the premiere of "The White Rose," and within a short time David proposes. But no, "Hard work will fill my life, David." And Lina goes on yet another montage-sequence world tour to Vienna, Berlin, Paris.

In Paris Roger is again in the audience, with his fiancée (the fiancée says, watching Lina dance, "If I were a man I'd fall in love with her myself"). When Lina discovers after the performance that Roger has a fiancée, and despite *our* recognition that Roger is still in love with Lina, she cancels all her remaining tours, lets *David* come to her dressing room (he happened to have been in the audience too), and, when David asks her again, this time accepts his proposal of marriage. "David, do you know what a ballerina is? A bundle of muscles with a smile," Lina tells him. David, a businessman, does not want to put Lina on display; he wants to "free" her from "all that" and, in fact, demands that she "give up the ballet. I insist on that. You'd have to sacrifice it." He promises her a "pleasant, peaceful life," to which Lina responds, "I'm almost happy." Again, all of this action takes place on the *same night.*

Lina does not remain almost happy for long, and the gender politics of *The Men in Her Life* are probably the most astonishing thing about it, not only as a woman's film but as a ballet film. Lina is asked to perform in a memorial performance for Rosing, but David, as dour and inexplicably rigid a character as any in Hollywood cinema, says, "No, Lina." He tells her she is *his* wife now and calls her selfish for wanting to do what she wants rather than what he wants. She responds, "All right, perhaps I am [selfish], I don't know. But I'm no more selfish than you are." David wants her only to give him a "home and children," but now, she wants her career back: "I'm not one of your business deals, I'm a dancer! Don't make me a clause in a contract!" David storms out (or rather exits stiffly), and Lina picks up her dance career again. But it is not long before she collapses onstage because, it turns out, she is going to have a baby ("But I can't, Doctor, I'm a dancer!" / "Nature makes no exceptions"). In the next several scenes we see, first, the baby, Rose, in a blanket: Lina will not tell her father that she exists because "He'll want you for his collection." David, then, *the father,* is the villain of this film, because he wants Lina to be other than she is, to give up her career, and because he, no less than Rosing, treats Lina as a possession. Next, the young child (who is growing up fast because of the film's temporal elisions here) also watches her mother dance, recognizing her as the most beautiful thing in the world just as Rosing, Roger (and his fiancée), and David have already.

In perhaps the film's most outrageous set of melodramatic coincidences, a glowing Lina exits the theater in the next scene to find Roger again, who just happens to be passing by. He is without his fiancée, whom of course he never married because he really loves Lina. Another montage sequence of performances and reviews indicates Lina's surpassing greatness as a dancer and ends on a loving family scene, toddler Rose's birthday, with Lina, Rose, and Roger laughing and Lina proclaiming ecstatically that she is "in love!" This happy family, portrayed as a true, loving, supportive, nuclear family, is broken apart by David, who shows up to take Rose: "I want Rose, because I'm lonely," David intones expressionlessly. He then criticizes Lina for her bad mothering, although the evidence with which we have been presented visually belies all of his comments. He calls Rose Lina's "victim," claiming that she will end up a "pale, tortured little girl." And he issues an ultimatum: "Be selfish with your own life, but not with hers. Are you big enough to make a sacrifice—the sacrifice of your child for her own sake?" And Lina does, on a dock, and clearly Rose's happiness is ending too. Rose has been captured by the villain, David, her biological father. And then, *on the way to the theater immediately after giving up Rose,* Lina urges Roger to make the carriage go faster because she is going to be late. Lina is at this point punished by Roger's death in the resulting carriage crash but not before Roger yells, "Jump, Lina!" and saves her life.

But just what it is that Lina is being punished for is not clear—for her happiness with Roger, to whom she was not married, or for giving up her child? After her recovery from the crash Lina falls on hard times; she has nothing to live for, and David will of course not let her see Rose, because he has told Rose her mother is dead. But eventually, a few years later, Rose is allowed to come to the theater to watch Lina Varsavina dance and is transported—"Wasn't she marvelous Daddy? She's so beautiful too!" Rose is taken backstage to meet Lina, whom she does not recognize. Lina, practically hysterical, gives her shoes to the child, who cannot take her eyes off of her mother as she leaves. David returns to the dressing room, alone, and says one word: "Lina." Then there is a cut, and now we are back with a new happy family—David, smiling broadly as he returns home from work to Rose and Lina. Lina has gotten her child back, and the rigid father has conformed to the mother's/woman's/dancer's world, supporting it but not taking part in it. He watches, beaming, as Rose practices to Lina's piano playing and beat counting. "Mommy, how long do I have to do this?" To which Lina replies, "If you want to be a good dancer, all your life. Now, *battement . . .*" and the music swells. The End.

The Men in Her Life was directed by Gregory Ratoff and released in the United States the same week as the attack on Pearl Harbor, but while its treatment of gender is even more protofeminist than the "woman-made" *Dance, Girl, Dance*—women should be able to have careers and children and supportive husbands, as well—it would be hard to argue that it is a film with a wartime *message.* Because it was made at Columbia, archival resources are virtually nonexistent (Production Code Administration file memos suggest that the film began production at RKO, the studio of *Dance, Girl, Dance,* between May and June 1941).[41] The very capable uncredited dancer who doubles in the film's many ballet sequences remains unknown. One review, however, in *Time* magazine, claims that the film was originally scheduled to star Vera Zorina, whose "ballet-conditioned muscles (plus a more inspired script) might have made something out of this old-world period piece. As it is, the picture takes a long time saying that the lot of a ballerina is indeed tough."[42] The *New York Times*'s Bosley Crowther laments the film's lack of "freshness and spontaneity and [even] a moderate amount of common sense," writing that it is "made up of all the old routines that ever were pulled in ballet films."[43] Crowther despises Loretta Young—she is "not a good actress," and her "lack of resemblance to a dancer is almost laughable." The central character leads a "self-centered life," in which all the men are just "shadows." The *Motion Picture Herald* review is subtitled "Ballet vs. Marriage," and at the bottom of the review of the "woman's picture" there is a note that the film was previewed "at the home office before a small crowd of reviewers who greeted the film with no visible enthusiasm."[44]

The *Hollywood Reporter*, however, predicts that the film will "mark a happy meeting" of "great film artistry and boxoffice success, for it is at once a motion picture of rare beauty and finesse, and also a drama of great woman appeal."[45] *Daily Variety* pointed to the film's "lavish production, great performances, direction and music," and to its "many moments of intense feeling," but noted that these moments were "at wide variance with the present-day entertainment mood."[46] *Motion Picture Daily* thought the film would be admired by "music and ballet lovers" and that "women may be expected to shed a few tears at several points."[47]

Neither *Dance, Girl, Dance* nor *The Men in Her Life* were box-office hits on the level of *Waterloo Bridge*, however. And it would arguably have been hard for any period ballet film to appeal to American audiences in the aftermath of Pearl Harbor—*Daily Variety*'s reference to the "present-day entertainment mood" was made two months *before* America's official entry into World War II. Although *The Men in Her Life* was the last American ballet film for several years, ballet itself was entering a period of some sustained glory. On the same New York newspaper pages that advertised *Dance, Girl, Dance* were announcements of Sol Hurok's presentation of the Ballet Russe de Monte Carlo, and ballet numbers, if not ballet stories, were no less common in films of the 1940s than they had been in the 1930s. One must also note the brief comic use of ballet in *The Philadelphia Story* (1940), in which Katharine Hepburn's and Virginia Weidler's characters, sisters, concoct a bizarre and hilarious "horrible child" act of upper-class pretentiousness designed to fool gullible reporters by having Weidler totter around in toe shoes speaking French and then launching into a loud rendition at the piano of the burlesque song "Lydia, the Tattooed Lady."[48] That many of the ballet numbers from the late 1940s on are not performed in toe shoes but in ballet flats and loafers will be discussed later in this book, and, in fact, the recognizability of the ballet dancer, or rather changes in his or her costume, affects the melodrama quotient of later films as well.

Ballet is more than a mood in *Dance, Girl, Dance* and *The Men in Her Life*—it is also dancing—but the price paid for devotion to it in all three films under discussion here remains high. Nevertheless, morbidity is outshone in these two later films by the surprising gestures toward the value of ballet as a profession, with *The Men in Her Life* probably the most unexpected in allowing the woman to transgress sexually as well as socially and yet end up reunited happily with career, husband, and child. In 1944, however, *Days of Glory*, a war film, restored the morbidity to the ballerina's image, and took her off the stage as well.

Why Did They Make Me an Outsider?

Best known today as Gregory Peck's first film role and for pro-Soviet sentiments that would soon be condemned by HUAC-led investigations into communist influence in Hollywood, *Days of Glory* (directed by Jacques Tourneur) stars one of the original baby ballerinas, Russian Tamara Toumanova, *as* a Russian ballerina "from the Moscow Theatre," Nina Ivanova. It was Toumanova's first film, too (she was then married to one of the film's producers, Casey Robinson), and her "thespic abilities" were politely referred to in reviews as having "possibilities." Nina joins a group of Soviet guerilla fighters battling Nazis in the forest, and initially scorn is heaped on her by all but one of her bunker mates ("Just what we need—a dancer"). She wants to be "one of them," but she also abhors killing. As one of the fighters tells her, she is a "person of light" and therefore "out of place in this region of death." Nina eventually takes on some risky tasks and the leader, Vladimir (Peck), falls in love with her and she with him. As the group is overrun by Nazi tanks at the end, she has become "one of them" and dies lobbing hand grenades at the advancing German army.

Despite Toumanova's sterling ballet credentials and her limited acting abilities, she is never called on to dance in *Days of Glory*. Another offstage icon, Nina speaks softly, is coiffed and made up beautifully (in contrast to the few other women in the film), and is set apart by ballet as at once useless and fantastically romantic. In her big solo scene Nina starts to perform an imaginary ballet for a young boy and his sister, neither of whom have ever been in a theater. She creates an ambience by asking them to listen to the beautiful music (music begins to play on the soundtrack), mimes getting dressed ("My tutu—is it fluffy?"), and gestures with her hands to indicate the curtains opening and flooding the stage with light, where she will be revealed standing on one toe ("It is very difficult to do but I can do it for almost one minute"). At that moment, however, a German soldier is sneaking down the stairs, and Nina's distraction almost proves fatal to the little band, as it does several other times in the film. Although certainly it would be a stretch to claim that Nina brings doom to the Soviet fighters—the Nazis do that—her presence is primarily represented as disruptive, an unwelcome intrusion of femininity and elitism in the film's diegesis. Criticized for its talkiness and lack of action, *Days of Glory* uses the ballerina to verify the heterosexual credentials of its leading man and to add "beauty" to the brutalities of war, even as it implies that art has had nothing to do with any of the lives of the film's noble characters until now and that they are none the worse for it.[49] Moreover, one of the film's penultimate moments is when Peck's character says to Nina, "Light your heart, dear, you're a soldier now." Not only ballerinas die in *Days of Glory*—everyone does.

Yet *Days of Glory* is an anomaly in the context of 1940s ballet films only because of the sheer number of deaths it records, a number largely the result of its genre. Its treatment of the ballerina and what she represents is of a piece with Grusinskaya in *Grand Hotel* and with Myra in *Waterloo Bridge*. Ballerinas are, in this sense, hardly out of place in "regions of death"—they are very much associated with death, with dying. The final Hollywood ballet film of the 1940s, however, returns us to a woman-centered universe, one that is even more melodramatic, more implausible, more expensive, and ultimately more startling than any film discussed so far—*The Unfinished Dance*, the only Technicolor Hollywood ballet film prior to *The Red Shoes*.

I'm the Happiest Woman in the World;
I'm the Prima Ballerina Now

Unfortunately for posterity, *The Unfinished Dance* is a remake of the small French masterpiece *La Mort du cygne* (1938; directed by Jean Benôit-Lévy and starring Mia Slavenska, Yvette Chauviré, and Janine Charrat, all dancers in their first film). The problem is not that MGM remade a serious study of the life of a child, a *petit rat* in the Paris Opéra ballet school, as a candy-colored musical. Rather, what is unfortunate is that MGM, in buying the rights to the French film in the early 1940s in order to remake it, removed *La Mort du cygne* from circulation for decades (it was considered a lost film until a 35-mm print of the English subtitled version began to circulate, apparently discovered in a Warner Bros. vault, in 2000).[50] *Ballerina*, as the film was called in the United States, did not have a wide release in 1938 beyond major urban markets, but it earned plaudits everywhere it was shown for its realism, its grittiness, and its feeling for the peculiar dynamics of childhood, although some critics did claim that it had "technical faults" in construction and editing.[51]

The story of *La Mort du cygne,* based on a novel of the same name by Paul Morand, concerns a young dancer who adores a young ballerina, also her ballet teacher. When a rival laughs at her idol, the child, Rose, releases a trapdoor on the stage during a performance and cripples the rival for life. Not only does Rose have to confront the enormity of her crime, but she discovers that the ballerina whose performing career she ended was a great artist, while the dancer whom she idolized and tried to protect was a relatively minor talent who easily gives up her career for marriage. The film was regularly compared to the play *The Children's Hour* "with its sketch of a vicious little school-girl busy as a bee with her malice," in the words of the *New Yorker*'s reviewer, for its "Degas-like tone" *(Cue),* for the skill and truth with which it portrayed "the full cruelty and sweetness of a little girl's soul. . . . The French picture demonstrates that children can be presented as children. If our producers could learn that lesson they would spare us many miles of photographed automatons and falsifications of the child mind" *(The Nation).*

It is not too much to say that *The Unfinished Dance* did not learn the lesson of *La Mort du cygne,* for the children in the updated version are meant to be cute and winsome and, most important, without real malice of any kind. They are jealous of one another, tattle on each other, and respond to material blandishments and bribes. But *The Unfinished Dance* exists to be a star vehicle for Margaret O'Brien, and at no point are we allowed to believe that she has a mean bone in her body. In adapting the story, then, many of its crucial plot points are altered. The film's action is prefaced by a title card that reads, "Long before people sang, they danced. Out of their dancing grew a new world, strange and wonderful—the world of the ballet. This is a story of that world, of those who dance, of those who love and of those who hate, *and of one who loved too much*" (italics in original). Then we see Meg (O'Brien) up in the flies watching her idol, Ariane Bouchet (Cyd Charisse), rehearsing, alone, yet another pastiche version (this one a solo) of *Swan Lake.* Ariane calls Meg "Little Sparrow" and seems to have some special connection to her, making sure she goes to class and so on (later, however, in one of the film's many sloppy plot holes and implausibilities, Ariane will state that she "hardly knows the child"). When the assembled ballet company, supposedly the "Metropolitan Opera Company" but composed almost exclusively of women and young children in pointe shoes (more on this later), is told by its fat rich elderly manager that the great ballerina "La Darina" (Karin Booth) is going to dance with them, Meg worries that she will displace Ariane, who aims to be prima ballerina. Meg tells her best friend Josie (Mary Eleanor Donahue) that she will turn the lights off during Darina's performance—which is *Swan Lake,* of course—because then everybody will laugh at her. Instead, Meg accidentally pulls the wrong lever and Darina plunges through a trapdoor and is crippled. Ariane instantly—in the same scene—is elevated in status and a whole "buildup" planned for her. When Meg asks Ariane whether she is happy, she replies, "I'm the happiest woman in the world; I'm the prima ballerina now."

Meg is a poor orphan being raised by a largely absent showgirl aunt and Mr. Paneros (Danny Thomas), a clockmaker who fills in while the aunt is on the road (and who has asked the aunt to marry him to no avail). Meg tells no one but Josie about what she has done but begins to be consumed by guilt about her action when she finds out that Darina will never dance again. Meg even goes to visit Darina, and dances for her, and Darina discovers that she, Darina, wants to be a teacher—it would be even *better* than being a ballerina. Eventually Meg confesses to having caused Darina's "accident," but no one, even Darina, appears to mind.

When Ariane decides to get married and to leave the ballet, it takes Darina to bring her back to her senses. We see Ariane trying on beautiful clothes, babbling constantly. Darina says, "You're getting married, Mademoiselle? I hadn't heard." Ariane replies, gushing, "I'm giving up the ballet—the young man insists upon it—and I'm glad. I've had enough of the ballet—ever since I was five. I'll be happy to be out of it." When Darina says Bouchet's career is "important," Ariane responds, "Well, it was for me once too." Then Darina delivers the final punch: "Mademoiselle, how can you be so shallow?" When Darina leaves, Ariane bites her knuckles, the theme from *Swan Lake* is heard again on the soundtrack, and the scene fades out. In the next scene Meg—who has been told that Darina wants her to leave town (Mr. Paneros lies freely to everyone throughout the film if it suits his purposes)—sees Darina, who tells Meg that she wants her to dance instead. Meg says, "I love you very much" to Darina, who responds, "I love you too." Meg "didn't mean to hurt" Darina, but Darina is fine: "In you I'm going to dance again. You're not going to fail me are you?" Meg: "I'd die first!" And then we watch Meg and Ariane dance together in the film's final big splashy number, "Holiday for Strings." Ariane's former fiancé ("Whatever that child told her that was the end of me!") is seen in a box with a new girlfriend, Mr. Paneros is seen watching with Meg's showgirl aunt, Darina's eyes mist over as she watches, and the film ends. All has happened for the best. Everyone is happy.

There is quite a bit of archival material available about the production of *The Unfinished Dance*, including treatments, script iterations, memos, and censorship files. One of the most interesting responses to the film's story lies in the Production Code Administration files for the film (it was then called *Ballerina* too), in the form of a letter to MGM studio head L. B. Mayer in 1946.[52] The censors had a "serious question" about the "exact nature of the feeling of the little girl, Meg, toward Madamoiselle [sic] Bouchet. Certainly, there should not be the slightest whiff of suspicion that there is anything unnatural about her adoration of the ballerina." They ask for script revisions

Cyd Charisse and Margaret O'Brien in *The Unfinished Dance* (1947).
Collection of the author.

to make sure that the attitude of the child is no more than "hero-worship."
This is one of the only instances in my frequent examinations of PCA files
over the years that a child's sexuality has been so much as alluded to, and
it is one of the few times in which the possibility of lesbian sexuality is
admitted even by euphemism. But in fact *The Unfinished Dance* is a film in
which women play virtually the only significant roles, and female interaction, ambition, and emotion are the bases for all its narrative action. We will
return to this issue below.

Originally, the plot of *The Unfinished Dance* was to have been much closer
to that of the French film, including the major point that Cyd Charisse's
character (the names vary in some of the treatments) was to have been less
of an artist than Karin Booth's.[53] The prose with which ballet dancers and
ballet dancing are described in all of the available treatments is, to put it
mildly, purple. To wit, from Myles Connolly, in 1946:

> The orchestra plays, the curtain rises, the ballet begins. Karina
> [Darina], supported by the children's corps, makes the stage a won-
> drous place, animate with moving grace, radiant with color.
>
> Now, the children drift off, fade delicately into the shadows, and
> Karina is left sole mistress of the scene. And a superb mistress she
> is, making her body sing a song of exultant joy, a dithyrambic paean
> of life. . . .

> The children in the wings, the stage hands, all the roaming popu-
> lace of the backstage world are hushed as they peer from the dark at
> this miracle of moving light. . . . They are drawn slowly, inevitably, . . .
> pulled from the shadows of their conventionality and inertia by the
> other-worldly beauty being created before their eyes.[54]

In this treatment, when Ariane dances, in contrast, "she does not work the
miracle that Karina worked," and there is "none of that white magic" that
held everyone spellbound; "no one is carried away," except for Meg. The
problem with this treatment is that it presumes two dancing stars, one of
whom must be superb. Instead, the only trained dancer in the film, Charisse,
plays the part of the *second* dancer, thus seriously skewing the possibility of
remaining faithful to the French film's story.

To call the dancing in *The Unfinished Dance* uneven is therefore an
understatement. There is a lot of dancing, and except for the scene in which
Darina is dropped through the floor, virtually all of it is performed by Cyd
Charisse, backed up by corps of MGM dancers, any of whom (with the exception of the child dancers) bests the actor playing Darina in dance technique.
Charisse had been an MGM starlet for several years at that point, but her
dancing prowess far exceeded her acting abilities. Her first husband was a
well-known ballet master, Nico Charisse, and she had been a dancer with
the Ballet Russe de Monte Carlo before signing a contract with MGM (she
appears, uncredited, dancing the part of Soviet ballerina Galina Ulanova in
Mission to Moscow in 1943; see chapter 5).[55] So one of the problems *The Unfinished Dance* cannot overcome is that Ariane outdances Darina and therefore
cannot plausibly be the lesser talent. Nor is Margaret O'Brien—on her "hastily tutored toes," in Bosley Crowther's words, in "specially manufactured
ballets"[56]—at all convincing as a ballet dancer (despite the film's press-book
headline, "Margaret O'Brien masters ballet technique!"). Rather, it is hard
not to agree with the *New Yorker's* reviewer that Meg is "one of the worst
ballet aspirants I ever laid my eyes on."[57] In fact, *The Unfinished Dance,* billed
as a "magnificent, new kind of entertainment!" and a "thrilling, romantic
drama," was met with almost universal critical hostility, mostly by comparison to its French predecessor.

The fall through the trapdoor deserves a bit of attention on its own.
It is the most obviously melodramatic of the film's many melodramatic
moments, embodying both pathos and sensationalism, and it was featured
prominently in the film's advertising campaign as well. The performance of
Swan Lake during which the fall occurs takes place on a mirrored floor, and
while there is a prince—danced by an uncredited George Zoritch, a Ballet
Russe dancer himself, in a powdered wig and ponytail—his only duty is to
swing girls around rather than dance himself. The choreography, billed to

David Lichine (who was completely demoralized by the experience),[58] clearly has almost nothing to do with the *Swan Lake* pastiche that we watch and that we hear on the soundtrack. Karin Booth's dancing double jumps and leaps about performing predominantly cheerleader moves, and ultimately, as Meg pulls the lever to the trapdoor, we enter an entirely melodramatic universe in which nondiegetic sound and the image track and editing are all directed at creating suspense about the exact dispensation of disaster. As a square of mirrored flooring begins slowly to descend, Darina/Booth pauses in her dancing and then begins, to a completely different and ominous non-Tchaikovsky score, to circle the stage in an endless series of backward *chaîné* turns, her face to the ceiling. We cut back and forth, the shots shorter and shorter, between the mirrored square slowly descending, to her spinning ever and ever closer to the hole; and finally, to a crashing crescendo, she falls in ("She was dancing when it happened?" asks someone; "Yes, magnificently!" is the response). Here a performance of *Swan Lake* is turned into the equivalent of a girl tied to the railroad tracks, as extreme a rendering of an old-fashioned melodramatic moment as exists in any ballet film.

And yet, as perhaps realized by the PCA and its worries that the film was somehow "unnatural," or in however flawed and meretricious a fashion on dance terms or in relation to "realism," *The Unfinished Dance* clearly ends even more surprisingly than *Dance, Girl, Dance* or even *The Men in Her Life.* It is a woman's film in the sense that men occupy very little screen time.[59] Moreover, one of the few male characters, Ariane's suitor, is portrayed in his brief scenes as young, handsome, rich, charming, and extremely kind—and still he is easily discarded. But although Ariane's character is flat and her motivations underdeveloped—she is happy to be prima ballerina, she is happy to get married, she is happy to go back to being prima ballerina in an all-girl company—the result is a film that comes down on the side of a woman's career *over* home and family (if *The Unfinished Dance* is, as promised by its billing, a "romantic drama," the romance fails *except* between the women). More precisely, the all-girl world of the ballet is itself shown as a form of home, with mothers and children having the most profound interactions and somewhere in the background a paternal manager who pays the bills or a kindly "uncle" who washes your clothes and fixes your meals. Ballet is not only woman in *The Unfinished Dance;* it is a separate form of domesticity based both on spectacular display and close personal interaction and love between adult women and female children. And while I cannot claim to *like* the film much myself—it is simply unbearable for me to watch little tiny children dancing in toe shoes, and I have a hard time forgiving MGM for making *La Mort du cygne* impossible to see for so many years—it clearly had an effect on audiences somewhat akin to that of *The Red Shoes* the following year. So I will give someone else the final word on

Advertisement for *The Unfinished Dance* (1947).

Copyright 1947 Loew's.

The Unfinished Dance here, in a comment written for the Internet Movie Database (note, too, that *The Unfinished Dance* has now become somewhat of a lost film itself; it is as of this writing not available in any consumer video format):

> I am a grandma now, but as a five year old, I viewed this movie in a very small town theater. After I saw this movie with a five year old's eyes, I not only wanted to be a ballerina, but I wanted to be Margaret O'Brien. Not being able to have dance lessons, I danced on my own. My aunt made me a beautiful outfit, and I was in heaven. Now, move ahead 20 years. I have a daughter who wanted to dance, and of course I sent her for lessons. She is now a very successful and talented dance teacher. I would love for her to see this movie, but I don't know where, or how to get it. This movie has not only been an influence on one generation, but on two. I wish there were more movies of this caliber. Simple, but oh so good.[60]

IN HIS 1987 BOOK *Opera, Ideology, and Film* Jeremy Tambling writes extensively about Hollywood's "refusal to film operas but its willingness to plagiarise music and arias for stories of its own devising."[61] Tambling argues that in erasing the "conflictual drama" and oppositional elements common to even the most sentimental operas of the nineteenth century, Hollywood betrays a lack of interest in opera as drama in order to emphasize "grand opera" as a designation: opera becomes "spectacle, static, so unquestionable." Hollywood's approach to ballet in its 1930s and 1940s ballet films is similar in many ways to Tambling's description: ballet is a mood, "an accompaniment to romance," a way to signify art without actually having to *be* art. Especially in films that feature offstage icons, ballet's meaning can *only* be symbolic, a partial allusion to something meaningful, separate from the body's danced corporeal subjectivity and all the conflicts and contradictions that the dancing body invokes. In 1943 American dance critic Edwin Denby noted that dance expression and dance recording "are two separate functions in the cinema that rarely coincide."[62] Film, Denby claims, puts a dancer into "an intimate relation to the audience; she is therefore restricted to intimate effects and cannot use the full dynamic range of serious theater dancing. She is most successful when she looks not like a dancer at work, but like a non-dancer who incidentally does some winsome steps and when in expression she restricts herself to understatement."[63] Audiences are "embarrassed" to see a woman dancer work so hard; and while this effect is not restricted to film (sitting on the first row of a concert theater can produce the same effect), it is perhaps the primary reason, for Denby, that films of women ballet dancers seem "absurdly overemphatic."

Women working hard are no longer embarrassing to watch, and of course I believe it is likely that they never were as embarrassing to watch as Denby makes them out to be. Yet even with so little dancing in these films, or so much dancing performed by "hastily tutored" actors rather than carefully trained and dedicated dancers, the messages of the films were always at least ambiguous rather than being as reactionary as some of their narrative details would seem to imply. Ballet remains mysterious, foreign, and somewhat effete, even in *Dance, Girl, Dance*. It is identified by clothing, music, and mise-en-scène rather than dance or dance values (in *Days of Glory* even the tutus and theatrical mise-en-scène are only imaginary, gestural, mimed). Although training and its rigors are referred to from time to time or shown in bits, the connection of the dancer's training to her work, her art, is obscured. Indeed, ballet training is often represented as punishment inflicted by the powerful on the weak and therefore as something to be escaped whenever possible. But some of the most melodramatic films are also the most utopian, in feminist terms, with ballet becoming the route to success and fame, as well as personal fulfillment. To conclude more than this, we must first turn to the men who dance, to see how they fare in the lovely world of the ballet film.

3

The Man Was Mad–But a Genius!

Gender, Genre, and the Ballet Film through 1947, Part II

For an artist [love] is fatal. He must have his whole soul, his whole being, in his art–nothing else.

–The Mad Genius, 1931

The Great Petrov doesn't dance for fun.

–Shall We Dance, 1937

I'm going crazy! I'm insane!

–Gold Diggers in Paris, 1938

That guy went crazy the last time he danced, and loonies like him have a way of repeating themselves.

–Specter of the Rose, 1946

The number of classical Hollywood films with male ballet artists as protagonists can probably be counted on one hand: *The Mad Genius* (1931), with John Barrymore and Donald Cook, explicitly "based in some respects upon the life and work of Serge Diaghileff"; *Shall We Dance* (1937), a Fred Astaire–Ginger Rogers vehicle in which Astaire plays a tap-dancing American ballet dancer masquerading as a Russian; and *Specter of the Rose* (1946), written, produced, and directed by Ben Hecht, about an American dancer who is purportedly "a genius" but who is also psychotic. In addition, as discussed in the previous chapter, there are several male impresarios and teachers hovering around the edges of other films, most notably Ralph Bellamy's Steve Adams in *Dance, Girl, Dance* (1940) and Conrad Veidt's Rosing in *The Men in Her Life* (1941), as well as any number of uncredited dancers and dancing partners. Here I examine the ways that men have been positioned onscreen not simply as dancers performing ballet but as a different sort of filmed spectacle, as representations of a cultural and historical ambivalence about the aestheticized performing male body.

Women's status as spectacle in classical Hollywood cinema has been voluminously theorized since the 1970s, and recently some of the scholarly attention has shifted to spectacular men. But, as the editors of a 2004 anthology on masculinities in Hollywood and European cinema put it, the "systematic exploration of masculinities" developed as an "afterthought" of feminist film theory of the 1970s and 1980s.[1] It never constituted a field in the same way that feminist film analysis did because, among other things, the attention that *was* paid to masculinities occurred predominantly through gay and queer studies and was interested less in "representational 'norms'" of masculinity than in deviance therefrom, "thus sidestepping the investigation of heterosexual masculine structure."[2] In his 1983 essay "Masculinity as Spectacle," however, Steve Neale had already concluded that commercial films of virtually any genre had always depended on the display of male bodies.[3] While these bodies were no less fragmented or stylized or even scantily clad than those of women, there was "no trace of an acknowledgment or recognition of those bodies displayed solely for the gaze of the spectator" because the straight male would then have to confront his pleasure in erotically gazing at his onscreen ideal.[4] So, according to Neale, there is always a sound narrative reason for the characters in a film, and through them the film's audience, to look at a male body, and these looks "are marked not by desire, but rather by fear, or hatred, or aggression." If a male body is spectacularized, in other words, it is often beating something up or being beaten up itself. When a male star or actor *is* singled out for spectacular display that is not tied to violence—in a musical, for instance, or Rock Hudson's image in any Douglas Sirk melodrama—Neale concludes that the spectacularization is accompanied by, or coded in terms of, feminization, and the look of the spectator is therefore coded as feminine as well. One strategy for countering the discomfort produced by this process is to make sure that the spectacularized male is "doing something," in Richard Dyer's words, and that what he is doing has a compelling narrative function so that the erotic pleasure the gazing man feels at the sight of the male body does not come to the fore.[5]

Several anthologies on masculinities in film appeared in the early 1990s, all explicitly engaging or taking off from Neale's analysis.[6] They were also partly a result of concurrent developments in the American film industry, a resurgence of the male star as a marquee name in action cinema, neo-noir films, "postmodern westerns," and so on. The new anthologies focused on several similar themes: that masculinity in fact was never monolithic or represented as unequivocally normal in commercial cinema, that there are many types of masculinity being constructed by films (with genre as well as star image being major mitigating factors), and that masculinity is and always has been spectacular in ways that do not so easily map the gaze onto aggression, fear, or violence or, conversely, onto feminization. Steve Cohan, for example, in his 1993 essay "'Feminizing' the Song-and-Dance Man: Fred Astaire and the Spectacle of Masculinity in the Hollywood Musical," concludes that Astaire's colorful clothing and dance moves are substantially mediated by his professional prowess and abilities—Astaire is not feminized so much as he represents a different *mode* of self-presentation tied to well-known theatrical and show-business values.[7] Unlike John Wayne or Cary Grant, for example, Fred Astaire is a "highly theatricalized representation of maleness on screen which oscillates between, on the one hand, a fictional character grounded in the static and reductive binarism of traditional gender roles and, on the other, a musical persona whose energy choreographs a libidinal force that revises conventional masculinity and linear desire."[8]

For gay male spectators, the Hollywood musical and its several layers of performance—in the narrative, in the diegetic numbers and shows that populate musicals, in a star's onscreen and offscreen personas—were also usefully conceptualized as camp. Moe Meyer, in his study of camp politics and poetics, proposes that camp (or Camp) is both a queer discourse and a queer cultural critique, with parody, specifically, becoming "the process whereby the marginalized and disenfranchised advance their own interests by entering alternative signifying codes into discourse by attaching them to existing structures of signification."[9] Camp, as "specifically queer parody," is the only process "by which the queer is able to enter representation and to produce social visibility." Matthew Tinkcom's work on the MGM musical focuses on camp as the material but ambiguous signs of the film industry's closeted gay labor force, who work to "ensure the commodity's multivalence," its appeal to both queer and nonqueer consumers.[10] The difficulty of "identifying queer tastes at work means that the object has served to deflect attention from those who think in camp ways."

Steve Cohan articulates the camp dynamic further in his book on the MGM musical as a camp object, which includes a chapter on Gene Kelly titled "Dancing with Balls."[11] Cohan describes camp's "double function" as "a style and a strategy of passing," of queer men posing as straight by exploiting the slippage between the cultural categories of gender and of sexuality; he also discusses the omnipresent "manly/effeminate dualism" of Kelly's image.[12] Fearful always of being called a "sissy dancer," Kelly worked overtime to dissociate himself from the "balletic convention of the tights" and to emphasize dance's equivalence to athletics. By a circular process of reasoning, what Kelly danced was not ballet because he performed it in a sailor suit or in khakis and loafers or tennis shoes; and even if he was employing ballet technique and vocabulary, he could not be called a sissy because he was not wearing tights. Kelly's persona therefore negotiates the tension between *effeminacy* and *homosexuality* in an era known for its heightened anxiety about sexuality and gender, the 1940s and 1950s.[13] That Kelly's performances are always also camp performances derives from the "variable logic" and "gender hyperbole," Cohan writes, by which a dancing male must repeatedly insist on his manliness and virility, continually calling up and drawing attention to the specter of sissiness in order to disavow it.

But how did the male dancer come to be associated so strongly with effeminacy and sissiness in the first place? Do not baseball and football players wear tight pants, or basketball players display their bodies? Is the physical "something" that sports figures do so different from dancing? As was discussed in chapter 1, despite being acknowledged for his power and strength, Vaslav Nijinsky was considered "offensively effeminate" by critics who saw his performances in America in 1916 and 1917. Moreover, these assumptions about the "effeminate quality" of the male ballet dancer were already in place and were sometimes countered, in Nijinsky's case, by his "certain masculinity of strength and rhythm." Ramsay Burt, in his 1995 study of the male dancer in Western culture, points to several conditions, beginning in the nineteenth century, that fostered an attitude toward the dancing male that was at least tinged by homophobia.[14] First, the low status of the performing arts generally, and dance specifically (as a "non-verbal form"), contributed "to the exclusion of the male dancer from the realm of genius." Second, denunciations of the male dancer could also "draw on diatribes against the immorality of actors as a whole." But most significant in the end, Burt claims, is that "the male dancer displayed himself, and thus was in danger of infringing the conventions which circumscribed the way men could be looked at."

Yet there is no "simple linkage," Burt writes, "between homosexuality, homophobia and uneasiness at professional male dancers."[15] As we have seen, by the time of Fanny Elssler's appearances in America in the mid-nineteenth century ballet had come to be defined as an "idealized feminine world." Although there were still male dancers around who were "valued for their technical ability as dancers," many male roles were performed by women *en travestie,* thus reinforcing the links between voyeuristic looking (or leering) and the female rather than the male ballet body (the male dancer "must undoubtedly have got in the way of erotic appreciation of feminine display").[16] Moreover, and ironically, for many ballet critics it was not a male dancer's effeminacy that carried negative connotations but rather the "spectacle of the male dancer's strength and virtuosity" because "vigorous and manly displays of dancing" invoked working-class entertainment. In France in 1838 Théophile Gautier wrote that "nothing is more distasteful than a man who shows his red neck, his big muscular arms, his legs with the calves of a parish beadle, and all his strong massive frame shaken by leaps and pirouettes." In short, ballet's men were problematic both because they were purposefully displaying themselves in a feminized framework and because they, or their bodies, were too vigorous and manly for that framework. In either case the male dancer provoked anxiety, writes Burt, "not only in relation to class position but also in relation to the difference between homosocial and homosexual relations." If one enjoyed the spectacle of men dancing, one might also be interested in men.

When Serge Diaghilev presented Nijinsky to the West in 1909, the male dancer made a "comeback," in Burt's words. It is once again ironic that the resurgence of the male dancer was in this case "predominantly developed and promoted by homosexual men," but it was not at all ironic that the initial audience for the Ballets Russes, in contrast to the "almost exclusively male" audience for European and American ballet in the nineteenth century, consisted of "the elite of society, artists and those who, by supporting [Diaghilev's] enterprise, gained entry to that elite" (and most of his financial benefactors were women). It was "only with Diaghilev," Burt concludes, "that ballet became an area in which homosexual men became involved as artists and as audiences, and that a homosexual approach developed to the appreciation and interpretation of ballet."[17]

On these terms it is not hard to imagine why American audiences might be, at best or at least, confused by the male ballet dancer. Even if Nijinsky (or Mikhail Mordkin, or Adolph Bolm, or Michel Fokine, or any other Russian ballet dancer around) was hailed for his strength, vigor, and virtuosity, he was also always already participating in an art form whose elite and foreign status functioned both as excuses for any "eccentricities" and as the source of ballet's prestige, its value as cultural capital. Not all ballet men wore tights or were effeminate or were "sissies." Men ran most American ballet companies; George Balanchine looked and dressed more like Steve Adams in *Dance, Girl, Dance* than like Diaghilev or Nijinsky. Moreover, the performance context of ballet in America was never only elite; as discussed in chapter 1, its associations with burlesque house, music hall, and vaudeville (and eventually movie theater) were not so much regrettable lapses on the way to the opera house or concert stage but rather part of ballet's continuing, if fitful, presence in American mass culture. *Any* man dancing in these other "entertainment" contexts was also, therefore, potentially faced with what Olga Maynard referred to as the audience's fear of "the pervert on the stage."[18] Indeed, for almost twelve pages of her book Maynard harangues American audiences, as well as company directors, teachers, and choreographers, for assuming that male dancers are "sexually perverted," for believing that it is ballet itself that "induces emasculation and perversion," and for not accepting, and treating accordingly, male dancers as the "virile force" they really are. Maynard does not want to see a "bold, coarse truculence in the male dancer but to give him socially, artistically, and psychologically a position of significance in America parallel to the paramount male position of the man dancer in all other countries, civilized or non-civilized."

Maynard's polemic, to which we will return in chapter 5, derives from two claims: that there are no more "homosexuals" in ballet than there are in any other theater form (they are, she thinks, attracted to all the theater arts by makeup, costuming, and role playing), and that even if there are, it is not ballet's fault but the assumptions imposed on men by uneducated and prejudiced audiences and by unthinking ballet professionals. However, Maynard holds up Ted Shawn, Frederick Ashton, and Anton Dolin, who were all then closeted gay men, as paragons of the potential for theater dance and ballet to generate a virile, noble, and, in Maynard's mind, heterosexual masculinity. Shawn himself repeatedly argued that dance was not "pansy" or "sissy" (and that it was "best when woman was working in the home, taking care of the needs of her husband and children"),[19] thereby adapting his work and public life to remain "carefully within the bounds of propriety," in Ramsay Burt's assessment.[20] In fact, the aggressive, "tough" dancing performed by Shawn and the all-male troupe of dancers with which he toured the United States (as well as Canada, Cuba, and England) in the 1930s had inspired Gene Kelly. Maynard quotes Kelly, who was just receiving awards and kudos for his 1958 network television *Omnibus* program "Dancing: A Man's Game," as divulging that "seeing Shawn's Men Dancers as a high school student had been one of the great inspirations of his life."[21]

In short, we are now back at camp, so to speak, in one of the major senses that Cohan and Tinkcom speak of it: as the unacknowledged (by heteronormative ideology) labor of gay subjects. No less than the Hollywood musical and its appeal to ideals of heterosexual romance and marriage, classical ballet's best-known narratives are hyperbolic renderings of masculinity and femininity, producing images of what Richard Dyer calls the "perfect heterosexual couple"[22]—the prince and the princess, the nobleman and the maiden, the warrior and the temple dancer, and so on. Ballet's camp appeal is precisely the "spectacle of heterosexuality paraded as glittering illusion"; the very "abstraction of love in ballet renders it a kind of essence, not about women and men, nor about real people even, but the embodiment of an idea of human relationships that anyone can relate to." And if Gene Kelly needed to protest that dancing is a man's game and that it is just as athletic as basketball, baseball, or football (all equations he made in his *Omnibus* special), the fact remains that it is equally athletic and physically challenging for the female dancer, the ballerina, the very antithesis of all things manly and un-sissy.[23]

The ballerina's trained body and technical expertise support and also obviate the fragility of many of the roles she plays. But for certain men, too much interest in style and surface and decoration, in aestheticizing the body as *beautiful* and active and powerful rather than as merely active and powerful in the conquest of some goal, creates even more of the discomfort that Edwin Denby notes about films of women dancing "close-by." While for women the problem is that we are purportedly "embarrassed to see [them] work so hard,"[24] for men Denby's statement might be recast as a widely held discomfort with their not working hard *enough* or with their being too interested in the visual effects of their work and with concealing it behind a facade of beauty and art (one reason that the supposedly average American man of the 1940s and 1950s did not reveal his body but rather hid it in a boxy gray flannel suit).

Beyond camp, either as discourse or as a spectatorial/critical reading strategy, it seems that the male dancer in American cinema has to tread very carefully between the audience's presumed fear of the "ballet pervert" on the one hand and representational strategies that frequently align the spectacularized male body with revulsion, fear, and violence on the other. A further problem is that, irrespective of a film's stylistic excesses or lack thereof, the very *role* of the artist, *any* artist (painters, sculptors, composers), was already significantly loaded with perversion and pathology in American culture and its cinema. Nijinsky's insanity resonated so strongly and became a cliché of representation so quickly in part because he was fulfilling a sort of mandate in popular culture that the artist not only suffer but suffer spectacularly and pathologically. We have seen this in many of the women's ballet films discussed in the previous chapter, and we have considered how suffering and pathos inform the generic role of the ballerina in certain musical as well as nonmusical films. Not surprisingly, the few Hollywood films that overtly feature male ballet dancers as protagonists, with the exception of *Shall We Dance,* were labeled explicitly as melodramas and feature high degrees of action and sensationalism, as well as overwrought emotion.

Other films demonstrate a clear interest in visually feminizing or lampooning the male dancer to comedic ends, as well. *Gold Diggers in Paris* (1938), the final entry in Warner Bros.' *Gold Diggers* series, features a skinny loose-jointed and bug-eyed ballet master/dancer character named Padrinsky (Curt Bois) who supposedly leads one of the best ballet companies in the world, the "Academy Ballet of America."[25] Padrinsky speaks with an unidentifiable accent, wears baggy black tights and floppy silk shirts and scarves, and is such a weakling that he collapses if someone so much as slaps him on the back (he also trembles violently under stressful conditions and declares, "I'm going crazy! Padrinsky is nuts!" or "I'm going crazy! I'm insane!" before fainting). There are also several films from the mid-1940s onward in which men perform in tutus or in comic ballets of some kind where they are man-handled, in a word, by troupes of ballet girls. This feminization can be read pleasurably, as camp, and also as, or in conjunction with, the misogynistic as well as homophobic flip side of the dis-ease produced by the aestheticized male body—especially the *American* aestheticized male body. Beginning with *The Mad Genius,* then, regardless of their plotlines, American films can be said to employ three strategies, alone or in combination, for investigating and characterizing the male ballet artist narratively: a hyperbolic masculin-ization and accentuation of the character's heterosexuality, an association of his art with criminality or insanity, or parodying the whole idea of the manly ballet dancer through "sissy" histrionics, gender-bending, or cross-dressing. Whether their artists are truly or merely playing at being deranged, "loony," or gay, the strange fascination of the films I discuss below lies, again, in their ambivalence—their hope as well as their fear that there might indeed be an alternative style of masculinity, grounded not only in spectacle and specta-torship but in an appreciation of men in tights.

As should have become clear, the three full-length films I discuss first link up more or less chronologically with some of the women's ballet films of the previous chapter: *The Mad Genius* immediately precedes *Grand Hotel* in the early 1930s and, like *Grand Hotel,* makes use of ballet's iconic Russi-anness to define its characters and what they do (as well as where they do it, namely Europe). *Shall We Dance,* like *Gold Diggers in Paris,* falls into the cluster of films in the late 1930s and early 1940s that draw on ballet's increas-ing visibility on Broadway and in musical theater, and it engages some of the ongoing debates about how to make ballet American that I explored in chapter 1. *Specter of the Rose* is perhaps the most ambitious of the three films—a postwar attempt by a single writer-director-producer to make a film about art and artists that, when it is discussed at all today, usually is called a film noir (reviewers in 1946 aligned it with a "current trend in psychological mellers").[26] Based on director Ben Hecht's own short story, the film, like *Shall We Dance,* transposes its literary source's Russian dancer into an American masquerading as a Russian and its locations from Europe to urban America. More than probably any other American ballet film of the 1930s or 1940s, *Specter of the Rose*—made on a shoestring budget at Republic studios—was given a lot of serious attention in middle-brow venues, including those devoted to reviews and studies of American theater art. Most significant, I argue, is that it not only registers the burgeoning popularity of ballet in America but also, like the other mid-1940s lampoon films featuring men in tutus, struggles with the new "problem" of wartime and postwar masculinity (and, by implication, its "binary opposite"—femininity), using an iconogra-phy of art and/as violence.

Strangest Passion Man Ever Had for Another Man!

The Mad Genius need not have featured ballet at all, and that it did probably has much to do with the free publicity provided by the newsworthy death of Serge Diaghilev in 1929. According to John Davis, the primary impetus behind the Warner Bros. production was really the success of Universal's *Dracula* (1931).[27] Anxious to jump on the horror-film bandwagon, Warner Bros. produced *Svengali,* with John Barrymore in the title role, two months later. An adaptation of George du Maurier's 1894 novel *Trilby, Svengali,* like *Dracula,* featured a monstrous but strangely attractive man who exerted a malign and mysterious influence over various victims, and it, in turn, was successful enough at the box office to beget its own sequel with many of the same featured stars. The nominal literary source of *The Mad Genius* was a play by Martin Brown called *The Idol,* which was similar in subject matter to *Trilby* and *Svengali* but with a male character in place of the female Trilby. Davis argues that, despite having the "same theme and leading actors"—namely Barrymore, Marian Marsh, and Luis Alberni—*The Mad Genius* (directed by Michael Curtiz) became "something quite different." Davis places the blame for the relative failure of the film on its "unusual style and subject matter and the fact that it didn't fit comfortably into any genre."

The Mad Genius is certainly an odd film, odd especially if one tries to label it a horror film of the same type as *Dracula* or *Frankenstein* (another Universal box-office hit of 1931). *Dracula,* as mentioned earlier, happens to use the famous theme from Tchaikovsky's *Swan Lake* over its credits (apparently someone at Universal, in contrast to MGM in 1940 as discussed in chapter 2, knew that the ballet's music was in the public domain). But although Count Dracula is aristocratic, European, and somewhat effete, the film's appeal to its contemporary audiences, like that of *Frankenstein, The Mummy,* and other films of the well-known "horror cycle" of the early 1930s, seems to have been its ability to shock and frighten (undoubtedly in sexually inflected ways—Dracula exemplifies the attraction/repulsion dichotomy embodied in the attractive yet dangerous man) through supernatural or science-fiction means.

There is actually no monster at all, or even a real genius, in *The Mad Genius,* merely a very nasty and repellent man, Tsarakov (Barrymore), initially a (literal) puppeteer with a club foot who finds a young boy, Fedor, running loose and leaping fences "like a deer." Tsarakov turns Fedor into a great ballet dancer (the process by which this occurs is not shown) and then gets angry when the dancer falls in love and leaves him. Tsarakov has an assistant, Karimsky (played by Charles Butterworth, whose comic character is simply dropped into the film and who functions essentially nondiegetically—as one reviewer noted, Butterworth "is not fitted to such a story"), and a ballet master named Serge Bankieff (Luis Alberni). Serge is a drug addict, and Tsarakov controls Serge's access to drugs and thereby, until the end of the film, controls Serge as well. Donald Cook plays Fedor as a young man, "the greatest dancer of all time," who falls in love with his ballet-girl partner, Nana (Marian Marsh). Tsarakov fires Nana from what is variously identified as the "Ballet Impérial Russe" and "Les Ballets Russes," but Fedor will not renounce her. Instead, he quits, and they marry to live in Paris. Tsarakov, who still controls Fedor's contract, then makes sure that Fedor cannot dance in any of the opera houses of Europe.

Fedor attempts to find a new dance career but is unsuccessful as a cabaret "hootchy-kootchy" dancer. When he appears to Nana to be getting miserable away from the ballet ("Why do you play at being happy, Fedor?"), she goes to Tsarakov and agrees to leave Fedor, to become the mistress of a wealthy but sleazy count, if Tsarakov will allow Fedor to dance ballet again. Fedor rejoins Tsarakov's company and becomes a bit of a temperamental monster himself (the puppeteer has made the puppet dance; the mad genius has created a monster in his own image), but one night, on the premiere of a new ballet (a giant sculptural idol's head is the major element of the theater set), he sees Nana in the audience and they reunite. Serge, however, has gotten into Tsarakov's supply of "drug powders" and consumed them all; he goes insane and kills Tsarakov, who is revealed hanging, dead, from the idol's head as the curtain opens. Fedor and Nana live happily ever after.

As this plot synopsis suggests, despite being advertised as a "melodramatic gem in a gorgeous setting" there is not much action in *The Mad Genius* and no action that is horrific other than, arguably, Tsarakov supplying Serge with drugs (their transactions and Serge's injections are shown in silhouette only) and the final murder of Tsarakov (also shown in silhouette, until the curtains open to reveal his contorted body). The film's publicity campaign seems to have rested on two different sorts of attraction: its "weirdness" ("Barrymore portrays weird role in new Warner Bros. picture," or "Barrymore . . . in his most weirdly magical role") and its ballet credentials.[28] In the first case Barrymore is linked up with both Svengali and Frankenstein: "He creates the Frankenstein that destroys him!" or "He pours his genius into another man's veins—but his creation becomes an avenging god!" That these sorts of taglines have little to do with the film itself should be obvious, too. Fedor does not destroy Tsarakov nor avenge anything; Serge does. Tsarakov does not even seem to be "mad—but a genius!" as another tagline promises. As well, despite references to Diaghilev (or Diaghileff) of the "real Imperial Ballet" being the "basis" for the film and to the fact that the composer of the film's ballet music, Mosolov, and its choreographer, Adolph Bolm, had been Diaghilev's "associates," there is very little dancing in the film of any kind and very few scenes that derive their meaning from ballet or dance. In fact, despite publicity references to Mosolov and "four ballet scenes and a dress rehearsal," little of Bolm's work, and none of Mosolov's music, are included in *The Mad Genius*.

The scenes in *The Mad Genius* that truly earn the designation "weird" are early in the film, when we see the young Fedor jumping over those fences, in the rain, quite obviously with the aid of wires. Then we listen to Tsarakov's glowering and heavily accented speeches about Fedor's future: "What legs he has for dancing—look at him, like a deer! Nature fashioned him for that—his thighs like steel, yet plastic. That's the body I should have had—with my soul. A dancer's soul." Tsarakov invokes the Golem, Frankenstein, the Homunculus—"These are all dreams, brought to life by mortals"—to lead ultimately to the pronouncement of his own dream for Fedor: "I will make him the greatest dancer of all time!" But when we then fade to Berlin in "the present," to a ballet rehearsal featuring the now-adult Fedor, it is a constructivist ballet in which almost no one actually dances. We do not see Fedor do much of anything, much less leap like a deer; he and Nana, and the many other "dancers" populating the scene, pose statically or while waving their arms (Fedor's thighs are not impressive either). And although Tsarakov has presumably raised him, this Fedor speaks in a high midwestern accent. Serge screams and yells and says everything is no good (he calms down when Tsarakov gives him some drugs), and Tsarakov lurks around in a top hat pinching and stroking and whispering into the ears of ballet girls. The sets and decor are sumptuous (Fedor's and Nana's headgear resemble nothing so much as modern-day bicycle racing helmets, however), but from the beginning, Fedor is a nondancing dancing genius, Tsarakov's puppet, and ballet will become merely a "backdrop" against which very quotidian action will occur. Tsarakov seduces and discards dancing girls and concocts plots to get rid of Nana; Fedor and Nana leave the company and enjoy blissful married life in a cozy garret until Fedor's unhappiness gets the better of him; Nana goes off with the count; Fedor returns to the ballet. Serge is always looking for drugs, and Karimsky/Butterworth pops up from time to time to perform utterly superfluous comic patter. Not until the end of the film do we see Fedor (or his uncredited double) really *dancing,* in a sort of Aztec/Inca/Native American pastiche that features feathered headdresses, moccasins, loincloths, and so on—and the large idol's head on which Tsarakov's body will hang.

Because the real Diaghilev was already dead, *The Mad Genius* could employ his name in publicity (but not that of Nijinsky, whom Fedor is, of course, meant to resemble) without having to worry about libel suits. Warners could also advertise the film's links to the Russian Imperial ballet and even make free references to Ballets Russes repertoire. Some of the most arresting images in *The Mad Genius* are the two montages of gorgeous posters advertising Tsarakov's company, and their references to ballets, like *Le*

Pas d'acier and *Le Coq d'or,* from the Diaghilev company's actual repertoire. But if one went to *The Mad Genius* expecting to see the two ballets advertised in the film's publicity, by Bolm ("since Diaghileff's death . . . probably the world's greatest authority on the Russian Ballet," whose "work with the ballet sequences [makes] them of particular interest"), one would have to have been disappointed. Which brief bits are supposed to be the "Ballet Mechanic" [*sic*] and which ones "The Factory"? The "great 'Idol' ballet which climaxes the film" is easy to identify but occupies only a few seconds of screen time. The film's interest in Russian ballet, or Diaghilev or Nijinsky, is purely auratic, an equation of ballet vaguely with prestige but more specifically with moral and sexual decadence.

Tsarakov and Serge, not Fedor, are grotesque caricatures of popular conceptions of what motivates and supports artists and their work. Women are expressly things that the artist needs for "relaxation" and "inspiration" but nothing more. When the orotund count expresses a sexual interest in Nana, Tsarakov responds that, "as it happens, she is reserved for Fedor." But not for love: "For an artist, love is fatal. He must have his whole soul, his whole being, in his art—nothing else." All over the film's backstage mise-en-scène are women posturing and posing for pickup by men. Fedor's only crime, his great betrayal of Tsarakov, is that he falls in love with a woman and marries her. Fedor's return to Tsarakov's company after Nana agrees to decamp with the count as a sacrifice for Fedor's happiness makes Fedor's manners worse and his voice higher, but his brief and peevish outbursts do not warrant Tsarakov's response—"Isn't he magnificent? What temperament! What an artist! What a genius, huh?" Moreover, Fedor and Tsarakov spend little time onscreen together; the film expends enormous amounts of footage representing Tsarakov's erotic interests in a succession of women while doing almost nothing to show us that Fedor is a great dancer. Fedor himself is a model of heterosexual rectitude throughout. Tsarakov's "jealousy" of Fedor and Nana's romance, therefore, hardly measures up to the film's advertising or even to the camp values promised by it: "Strangest passion man ever had for another man!"

While other horror films of the early 1930s were successful at the box office, *The Mad Genius* was a critical and financial failure. The success of *Grand Hotel,* with its story line of the aging ballerina and her tragic life, the following year ensured that the ballerina would be the symbolic locus of the ballet film from then on (the unexpected death of Pavlova in 1931 helping to grant an extraordinary staying power to her legend). The imposition of the uniform interpretation of the Production Code in 1934 also served to put an end for a time, John Davis argues, to the cycle of horror films of which *The Mad Genius* is a part.[29] Dancing men did not disappear from commercial cinema; however, unlike poor Fedor they were much more likely to be successful at jazz and tap and "hootchy-kootchy"-style dancing than Imperial Russian ballet and, more important, to be tangential rather than central to a film's narrative.

The success of the dancing partnership of Fred Astaire and Ginger Rogers and their combination of ballroom and social dancing, tap, and Broadway-style "show dancing" arguably made the musical's dancing man into a less problematic figure than the male ballet danseur. Fred Astaire's slight figure and receding hairline meant that he would never be able to base stardom on physical pulchritude and the spectacle of his body as such (although in his first film, playing himself in *Dancing Lady* in 1933, he does appear in shorts and lederhosen). Rather, Astaire's links to spectacle and feminization were cloaked in sailor suits or a class-based rhetoric of the "man about town," the bachelor on the loose whose evening attire was frequently some version of a tuxedo or tails. Rogers's wisecracking all-American-girl image also helped "give him sex" (even as Astaire "gave her class," to paraphrase Katharine Hepburn's famous aphorism about the pair). In their eighth black-and-white film together Astaire's masculinity was secure enough—and the series desperate enough for novelty in subject matter—for him to play a ballet dancer. Again, while ballet dancing, its technique and vocabulary, were showing up more and more frequently in theaters of both the opera-house and Broadway variety, *Shall We Dance* seems to be the first film since *The Mad Genius* to employ the danseur as a protagonist, to engage his Imperial Russianness and his credentials as an elite performing artist to narrative ends.

You Want to Dwindle into a Shimmy Dancer

The plot of *Shall We Dance,* as of all Astaire-Rogers musicals, does not need much recounting. Fred Astaire's character is in love with Ginger Rogers's character (in this case, he has fallen in love with her photo and her dancing in a flip book), and he pursues her from Paris to New York to Europe and back again. She is annoyed by him, there is a misunderstanding about whether they are or are not married, he does something over-the-top to amuse and impress her, and by film's end they are performing together and embarked on a romance. There are, of course, songs, in this case composed by George and Ira Gershwin, and dances along the way. As has been true of several other ballet films to this point, ballet is used more or less as Jeremy Tambling's "accompaniment to romance" but also, and more significantly, as a representation of class values.[30] Jane Feuer has argued that American musicals routinely employ a "standard plot" that she calls the "opera vs. swing narrative."[31] Familiar to any fan of film musicals, these narratives involve an elite art, such as opera, that is put into conflict with a "popular" form, such as jazz or swing. Usually there is an older character who initially looks down on jazz or swing as inferior but who soon begins to tap his or her feet or snap his or her fingers in time to a "swinging" version of some operatic classic. Not all films that feature classical and popular music, or ballet and tap dancing, set them into conflict with one another, but those that do are clearly engaged, Feuer believes, in showing "what popular art can contribute to elite art, even while trying to affirm the kind of status and longevity elite art can lend to the musical film."[32]

In *Shall We Dance* Fred Astaire plays a Russian ballet dancer, Petrov—"the Great Petrov," as he is referred to by the owner of his ballet company, Jeffrey Baird (Edward Everett Horton). The film's opening shots, however, are of women dressed identically in tights and tutus, shot from the waist down, twirling in place for their ballet master (male, of course). We see Petrov first as a painted portrait of Astaire *en attitude,* eyes modestly downcast, being gazed at in some awe by a bellboy. We know that Petrov is truly worthy of admiration because after glancing briefly at the other portrait on display, of Baird (Horton), the bellboy takes out a pen and draws a moustache on Baird's face. Baird catches him in the act, while he is looking for Petrov ("Ou est Petrov?" Baird keeps demanding of the bellboy and eventually the ballet master; thus we learn that we are in Paris). Petrov is "in his room practicing his *grand* leap," but when Baird opens the door we hear taps and swing music. Petrov, dressed in belted tight pants and a floppy white shirt and soft ballet shoes, is in a tap-dancing frenzy. When Baird yells at him to stop, he discovers that Petrov has taps on his ballet shoes—"Sacrilege!"—and that he is dancing for fun: "The Great Petrov doesn't dance for fun!" The Great Petrov may not, responds Astaire, but "I do. Pete Peters, remember me?" Baird "forbids" Petrov to tap ("That's not art!"), but Petrov/Pete Peters wants to "combine the technique of the ballet with the warmth and passion of—this other mood." This "other mood" is not jazz, however; "jazz went out with the flapper," Astaire intones dismissively. Baird responds, "Fifteen years of the hardest work and you want to dwindle into a shimmy dancer."

But just what this "other mood" is *instead* of jazz is conveniently left hanging as Astaire begins thumbing through the flip book of photographs of Linda Keene (Rogers), a nightclub dancer. He has not met her yet, but he would "kind of like to marry her." That is his plan, and it sets into motion the rest of the film's plot and essentially does away with Astaire's relationship to ballet except as a disguise. It is a plot device by which he can confuse and irritate Linda Keene for a while, by making her think that he is Russian and effete. When handed his card, she scoffs, "Petrov? What's a Petrov?" *Her* manager replies, "Only the Russian ballet's greatest dancer." This, and her retort—"That's all I need to make things perfect, a simpering *toe* dancer!"— further align Petrov/Astaire, in her and the film audience's mind, with Nijinsky and his rumored effeminacy.[33]

Fred Astaire and Harriet Hoctor in a publicity still for *Shall We Dance* (1937).
Collection of the author.

Once Linda Keene learns that Petrov is really Peter P. Peters of Philadelphia, P.A., ballet disappears from the film until its final production number.
Feuer points out that the syntactic structure of *Shall We Dance* continually
reminds us, through its musical themes, that George Gershwin actually
accomplished with music what Petrov/Peters wants to do with ballet: namely,
Gershwin *did* combine concert music and popular song, did "bring a revital-
izing jazz influence to classical music."[34] *Shall We Dance,* however, initially
maintains a distance between ballet and the ballroom/tap dancing that

Astaire and Rogers perform. When Astaire dances in "Slap That Bass," the film's first real production number (in the impossibly luxurious and sparkling hold of a luxury liner, with an African American singer and musicians and the ship's engine itself providing the soundtrack for Astaire's movements), he is shown in a few ballet poses that function primarily as accidental tics—he throws them off, as though they are a bad habit, something of which he needs to break himself.

Petrov and Linda Keene dance together for the first time in "They All Laughed," which Rogers sings. She gets tricked into dancing with him, and he with her, and she still thinks he is a Russian ballet dancer. So he toys with her for a bit by prancing around doing ballet steps that she answers with incredulous facial expressions, in close-up, as well as tap steps before Astaire, of course, lets loose with his own explosive tapping and reveals his "true" identity. And an hour or more later in the film, when, in a nightclub on the roof of a skyscraper, the big ballet production number does occur, Astaire only briefly partners with American ballerina Harriet Hoctor (playing herself), his eyes downcast for most of the time, before Hoctor performs her own ballet solo. There is a corps of ballet girls in dark tops and white tutus who flutter around, too, as well as a group of chorus girls dressed, and masked, to look like Linda Keene. The plot's misunderstandings are resolved—they do not matter much, but involve Linda Keene's being "humiliated" by a photo of a dummy of herself, taken to be real, in Petrov's bed and rumors about Keene's being pregnant, none of which Petrov had any hand in—and Peter and Linda dance together, Astaire-Rogers style, and the film ends. Ballet has served its function, to align Astaire and Rogers with dance *art* as well as entertainment. Feuer's characterization of the myth of entertainment is at work here too: like many musicals pitting elite forms against popular, "entertainment is shown as having greater value than it actually does."

As conventional a musical as *Shall We Dance* is, and as highly stylized and farcical in its narrative action, it cannot be dismissed as a ballet film. Ballet's values are not merely overlaid onto a typical Astaire-Rogers film plot but help structure its meanings in ways that have everything to do with the changes that theatrical ballet, and therefore film ballet, was undergoing in the 1930s. Ballet's Russianness is now a masquerade, a comic gag; the real dancers are *Americans,* and they want to merge ballet's classicism and technique with popular American music and dance styles—with or without taps on their ballet shoes. The final number, with Astaire partnering Hoctor and in which, in Arlene Croce's words, "turned-in toe dancers rumble around in clumps," is choreographed to a lushly orchestrated version of "They All Laughed," merging Broadway's melodies with ballet's vocabulary.[35] Croce thinks that "not even in his satin *premier danseur* tunic can Astaire be taken for a ballet dancer," but she is even harder on Hoctor, who "can be taken for nothing human." Croce calls Hoctor a "contortionist," her style of danc-ing a "kind of primitive, pseudoaesthetic show dancing [that] was going out of fashion." In contrast, Croce claims, "classical" ballet was to be found, in Technicolor, in *The Goldwyn Follies* the same year, with Vera Zorina and Balanchine's American Ballet.

I brought up the problem for ballet history posed by dancers like Hoctor and critical assessments like Croce's in the introduction to this book. Here, though, Astaire's ballet body is the focus, and it was problematic not only for Croce but for his, or rather its, contemporary critics as well. Although *Variety*'s reviewer thought that *Shall We Dance* offered the "final proof" of Astaire's being the "head man as to dancing" because it contains some of his "best ballet work," the reviewer also notes that the Petrov-Peters "terpsicho-rean kidding" may have had an "ulterior motive"—namely to "immediately take the curse off those dainty ballet gestures so that no hard-boiled balcony can construe Astaire as having a rose in his teeth."[36] No matter how much "high art" *Shall We Dance* purports to contain, for Astaire his ballet dancing had to be combined with "ballet gagging,"[37] and a plot otherwise focused on pursuit of Ginger Rogers, in order to remove the rose from his teeth. Jenni-fer Fisher claims, in her discussion of *Shall We Dance* as "one of the earliest still-popular Hollywood musicals to prominently feature the high art–low art divide," that Astaire is "supposed to be a snob in this movie."[38] He is hardly that; Petrov/Peters wants to be a musical-comedy dancer much more than he wants (even after "fifteen years of the hardest work") to be a ballet dancer. Fisher also believes that, in the end, "it's not really ballet that gets identi-fied with the elitist label, because Petrov does not really inhabit that rarefied world. He is, we are told, a great ballet dancer, but he's off the pedestal in no time." Nevertheless, it is important to remember that the final production number in *Shall We Dance* depends for its effect on Astaire's being able to return to and to leave that pedestal at will (Fisher does not discuss Hoctor or any of the other ballet characters in the film). Jeffrey Baird is a snob, and one does not have to know much about camp to read him as a closeted gay character, his admiration for Petrov's art being no less an admiration for Petrov's body. Ballet is harmless to the health in *Shall We Dance*, however, something to which one can devote years of work and still end up rich, famous, and alive. You can pretend to be a Russian, but if you are male and you do so, people may think of you as a "heel-clicking hand-kisser," as Linda Keene does initially of Petrov. Once your Americanness is revealed, though, you might be able to get a girl like Ginger Rogers (if you do not instead want a rich boyfriend like Edward Everett Horton).

From *Shall We Dance* through the end of the 1940s, most male ballet characters in films were either the teachers and mentors of female protago-nists (*Dance, Girl, Dance, The Men in Her Life, The Unfinished Dance*) or engaged in even more overt and extreme "ballet gagging" than occurs in *Shall We Dance* (see *Gold Diggers in Paris*), a subject to which we will return at the end of this chapter. The growing popularity and ubiquity of ballet dancing in films and in theatrical venues as various companies toured the United States during the war partly explains Ben Hecht's decision to attempt another film featuring a male ballet protagonist, *Specter of the Rose,* in 1946. Nijinsky had also been in the news again in 1945, when rumors that he had been "slain by the Nazis" during the war proved untrue, and a few stories circulated about the possibility that the "mad genius of the ballet" was "regaining his reason" and might "dance for the world again—perhaps before a movie camera," as *American Weekly* put it.[39] A true oddity in American cinema, a labor of apparent love by Hecht (who not only adapted his short story for the screen but directed, produced, and financed the film largely with his own money), *Specter of the Rose* has been called everything from a "crude but courageous" minor masterpiece to a film about which novelist Saul Bellow said he would rather "eat ground glass than have to sit through a second time."[40] In current video guides, as well as in its contemporary reviews, the adjectives most frequently employed to describe Hecht's film are *bizarre* and *strange.* The morbidity of *Specter of the Rose* is impossible to miss, as are its melodramatic features—primarily an innocent young girl who is menaced by a sinister madman with a knife. The fact that the madman is also the film's hero is one source of the film's strangeness and deviance from expected models, with deviance itself—from Hollywood's conventional patterning of gender roles, bodies, dialogue, mise-en-scène, and so on—figuring as the film's most obvious formal device.

Let's Get This Straight

Hecht's short story "Specter of the Rose" is based loosely but obviously on the career, sexual notoriety, and descent into madness of Nijinsky. In the 1911 ballet *Le Spectre de la rose,* music by Carl Maria Von Weber and choreographed by Fokine, Nijinsky played the spirit of a rose that a young girl carries with her from her first dance and subsequently falls asleep dreaming about. Nijinsky danced in a famous costume made of pink silk rose petals (see the photo in chapter 1), and the ballet ended with his leaping out of the room, appearing to hover high in the air before disappearing through an open window as the girl awakes. In Hecht's story the Nijinsky figure is André Sanine, a "charming" Russian ballet dancer who was "at times a little disturbing," mainly because although André, in Hecht's words, "loved everybody and everything, he had nevertheless managed to avoid falling in love with one particular human being," that is, a woman.[41] When Sanine finally does marry, the "evil that was in him" comes to the fore as he strangles his wife and is subsequently locked in an asylum "for the criminally insane." On his release Sanine resumes his career and seems about to marry again; but instead of murdering his second wife, too, he throws himself out of a skyscraper window and, Hecht writes, falls "straight as an arrow, his arms lowered, his hands folded in front of him, and his feet [making] entrechats. His head was tilted gracefully to one side" (the story's final line is, "He was dancing as he fell").

The film's narrative is similar but much more involved and padded with subplots, and Sanine is no longer clearly a criminal. The police suspect that he murdered his first wife but do not have the evidence to prove it. Sanine himself tells the detective who is on the case, "Let's get this straight: I didn't kill her." Sanine has just been released from the asylum into the care of La Sylph (Judith Anderson), an aging ballerina and teacher, and is about to embark on a new tour despite La Sylph's misgivings about the soundness of his mind. Sanine takes as his partner a young ballerina, Haidi (played by American ballerina Viola Essen in the first of her two movie roles). Michael Chekhov plays a comic but "suspiciously rose-watered ballet impresario" (in the words of the New York Times's reviewer),[42] and it is he who utters the first line of the film: "Oh, the smell of art, the lovely smell of art; only you have preserved it in the world, La Sylph"—this in a dingy rehearsal studio full of sweating dancers. A journalist-cum-poet (who is also in love with Haidi), Lionel Gans (Lionel Stander), functions as an odd Greek chorus throughout the film, uttering some of the worst lines ever written, or some of the campiest ("I often cry at night, and the night becomes full of dancing words," or "To Haidi, who weaves a wreath of skylarks around her heart"). No such lines occur in the short story, nor, other than Sanine and Haidi (Nina in the short story), do these characters.

But by far the most interesting change from story to film is the fact that André Sanine is no longer a Russian but an American from the Midwest whose "real name is Paul Dixon." Sanine/Dixon is played by an American Olympic swimmer named Ivan Kirov, who had, according to the film's publicity materials, thought that "ballet work for men was the epitome of femininity" until he saw Prince Igor in 1939 and became convinced that "here was an art form that combined everything that he loved into one. Music, motion, body control, and beauty" (he started ballet lessons "the next day").[43] In her work on ethnicity in film, Sumiko Higashi points out that in many Hollywood movies "the threat of sexual difference . . . is displaced onto ethnic difference. Scapegoating is a common ploy used against ethnic groups."[44] This is true of Specter of the Rose (the film) but in a very complex sense: ethnic difference itself is displaced onto sexual difference. Although not explicitly mentioned, Nijinsky's well-known homosexuality is still present, connoted by ballet itself but reconfigured as "normal" criminal behavior. The suicide of the American Sanine is necessary, according to the film's narrative logic, not because he *is* a criminal (he may or may not be) but because he is a ballet dancer, because he "wants to be like Nijinsky was," a line from the story not uttered in the film (presumably because Nijinsky was still alive, there are no overt references to him in the film at all). Even Sanine's flagrant narrative *hetero*sexuality is belied by his spectacle status, his performing ballet for us nude from the waist up and dressed in tights, and, of course, by the fact that he seems to murder women, specifically his wives.

Moreover, despite the film's literally flowery title, most of the principals are ordinary modern working-class Americans, living in a dark and claustrophobic urban landscape (New York City, or a thinly disguised version of it). All of the mise-en-scène is seedy, and much of it is heavily shadowed. The plot, as might have been surmised by now, makes little sense; the characters are driven by weird obsessions and torments and are very noticeably alienated from their surroundings and from each other; sexuality is spectacularized and, in the process, made deviant and dangerous; and nothing seems certain about anybody's life but dread and despair. Virtually every character is caught in or by something from his or her past; everybody wants something they cannot have (La Sylph wants her youth and fame; the impresario wants a big hit and some respect; Haidi wants Sanine; Lionel wants Haidi; Sanine wants to be free of the memory of his first wife, Nina, and the music in his head that goes "bong!" or that "sounds like devils screeching"). In short, *Specter of the Rose* seems to be, in several senses, less the "art film" that Hecht and most of its contemporary reviewers designated it than a typical film noir. Indeed, *Specter of the Rose* is fascinating not only because it is a somewhat odd or bizarre classical Hollywood movie but because its protagonists resemble so many others in low-budget black-and-white films noirs of the 1940s. After seeing *Specter of the Rose,* in other words, it is easy to note that the protagonists of many American films noirs actually *all* resemble "artists" too, as Hollywood has characterized them over the years. Conversely, other film noir protagonists can be said to be afflicted with the problems facing all of the characters, especially the doomed Sanine, in *Specter of the Rose:* they are in many ways artists who are not able, or not allowed, to express themselves.

John Walker, for example, writes in his book *Art and Artists On Screen* that the goal of the Hollywood artist is essentially a romantic one, a "struggle . . . to overcome alienation or, if this is not possible, to find some other solution."[45] Because artists are alienated from society, they are conceived of as "beings who are *different* from ordinary people: they are . . . eccentrics, bohemians, lunatics, outsiders, rebels, iconoclasts. . . . They are still in touch with unconscious desires and forces—the erotic, the perverse, the obscene and the blasphemous—which 'straight' society has outlawed or repressed."

The expressionistically shadowed ballet studio in *Specter of the Rose* (1946), with Judith Anderson and Michael Chekhov.

Courtesy National Film Archive, London.

Although noir protagonists, on the other hand, are often ordinary people caught in the grip of extraordinary events, or driven by forces beyond their control, they can also be thought of as rebels, outsiders, iconoclasts, idealists, or romantics alienated from a society that does not understand them. According to Alain Silver and Elizabeth Ward's basic encyclopedic reference work on American film noir, noir protagonists encompass "two key character motifs": alienation and obsession.[46] As noir figures "struggle through their particular dark night of the soul, alienation is the common factor, the narrative constant" that links otherwise disparate features (and films) together. The second "key emotion in the noir universe," obsession, to "a certain extent . . . transcends such ordinary considerations as morality and causality." Alienation and obsession are the driving forces in *Specter of the Rose* ("story of violence mingled with love" is one of its press-book taglines) as well. The hero, if he is that, is a regular American guy who is going insane but does not know why.

Even though *Specter of the Rose* "plasters sticky tributes," as Arlene Croce put it, all over the "beauty of the ballet" while revealing "alarming gaps" in its author's knowledge,[47] from a ballet point of view its protagonists do not act enough like "real" artists, or certainly not real ballet artists. That is, there are more "alarming gaps" than evidence of what the art is, where it comes from, what it results in. More significant, most of the dancing we see is performed by a male rather than a female dancer. In addition to Sanine's "warm-up" dance, there is a single ballet set piece, a montage sequence (choreographed by Tamara Geva), and Sanine's final "madman's dance" in his high-rise apartment (which is less dancing than crouching menacingly and jumping on and off the furniture) before he leaps out the window. There is none of Weber's music or any recognizable choreography from the ballet *Le Spectre de la rose*. In their exploration of masculinities in Hollywood film, Steven Cohan and Ina Rae Hark write that "film theory has for the most part confidently [and, they believe, often erroneously] equated the masculinity of the male subject with activity, voyeurism, sadism, fetishism, and story, and the femininity of the female subject with passivity, exhibitionism, masochism, narcissism, and spectacle."[48] In *Specter of the Rose* it is the male body and the masculine subject who is fetishized, exhibitionist, narcissistic, passive, and spectacularized (Sanine calls La Sylph "Mommy"). Indeed, the noir "spider woman" in *Specter of the Rose* is Sanine himself, an *homme fatal* who lures women to his trap, whose power is located in his spectacular sexuality, and who ultimately must (therefore) die. Conversely, the noir male "detective" figure who tries to save the innocent from evil is not only Lionel, or the actual police detective, "Specs," who appears from time to time to ask questions, but the jaded and cynical Judith Anderson/La Sylph, who knows the whole story and who has seen everything.

Specter of the Rose signals, then, a sort of merging of romantic stereotypes of the artist as misunderstood, alienated, and obsessive outsider with modern notions of the individual, of modern "man," as misunderstood, alienated, and often obsessive. Hecht's film is a peculiar harbinger of how Hollywood will come to define modern gender identity generally, using much of the iconography previously applied to film treatments of rebel and iconoclastic and psychotic artists. Thus, Hecht's "tantalizing mixture," as *Theatre Arts* called it, of "rich human insight, screenwise technique and bald unadulterated hokum"[49] does not merely signal that Hecht cannot distinguish between what is good and what is bad taste (as Croce claims). The film "intrigues even as it repels" because the sort of sense it does *not* make brings to the forefront how awkward and complex conventional notions of gender and identity really are.

A B-studio product, *Specter of the Rose* was nevertheless unusually widely publicized and discussed, partly because it cost only a few hundred thousand dollars to make, partly because it was supposed to be about art and hence was a "film for the intelligentsia" rather than being the usual "crassly commercial" fare of Hollywood (as *Variety* put it).[50] Part of the weirdness of the

Ivan Kirov (Sanine) menacing Viola Essen (Haidi) before he kills himself in *Specter of the Rose.*

Courtesy National Film Archive, London.

film is due to its odd conjunction of low-budget and high-art aesthetics. It may indeed be that Hecht, as Jeffrey Brown Martin writes in his biography of him, "seems to have taken the ballet world [too] seriously, ignoring his own advice on the subject of ballet: 'The lesser the art, the more artistic the admirers.'"[51] In *Specter of the Rose,* Martin continues, "the people are besotted with their artistry. The ballet sequences . . . are only passably effective, adding to the confusion of how seriously the characters can be taken." Or perhaps Hecht was "venting his frustration at the emptiness and vindictiveness of the New York theatre world where he had had no major critical success since *The Twentieth Century* (1932)." So surely it is La Sylph, not the "ash-can" poet Lionel, who speaks most for Hecht: "We artists suffer so."

Ballet Gagging and Ballet Dragging

Although today it is hard not to laugh loudly and often throughout *Specter of the Rose,* most of that laughter clearly runs counter to the film's intentions— it is laughter at the film and its over-the-top or corny lines, its pretentiousness, its bizarre characters and situations rather than laughter with it, on its own terms. *Specter of the Rose* is not meant to be a film comedy, and its characterization of the male ballet artist in particular is not meant to be funny. There are some other films, however, of the mid-1940s in which the depiction of men dancing ballet *is* clearly meant to be hilarious. Most important, these men are often dressed, if not otherwise disguised, as girls. Although the proportion of screen time devoted to the ballet gagging (to repeat the term used in the *Variety* critic's response to *Shall We Dance*) and, sometimes, dragging is relatively small, the moments are virtually always emphasized by publicity—especially photographs—and noted by critics. Nothing much *happens* that matters in a cause-and-effect sense; all of the scenes could be cut from their films with no reduction in narrative comprehensibility. Indeed, it is the deployment of the ambiguously feminized male body as spectacle (ambiguously because all of the men are still clearly *men* and meant to be recognized as such) during and immediately after World War II that makes these moments, no less than the gender anxiety and ambivalence permeating *Specter of the Rose,* interesting and provocative as well as "funny."

The Laurel and Hardy comedy *The Dancing Masters* (1943) is one of the pair's last films, and despite its title it contains no musical numbers of any kind. "The boys" operate the "Arthur Hurry School of Dancing, Laurel and Hardy, Proprietors." They teach "every possible form of dancing: ballroom, tap, ballet, rhythmic, hula, . . . and jitter." Hardy teaches the advanced classes, made up of lethargic girls only, while dressed in a clown costume. Professor Laurel teaches the beginner's classes (also made up only of girls); he is dressed very much like Marie Taglioni, in a long tutu, a circlet of flowers for his hair, and extremely baggy tights (but no toe shoes). Suspended from obvious wires, he performs the "Dance of the Pelican" for his students, and it is not long after this sequence that all references to and plot significance of the dancing school drop away (except in relation to whether the rent on it can be paid), to be taken over by an insurance scam, a romance between young lovers, and the invention of a secret weapon.

Red Skelton also appears in a tutu, a pink one, in the Technicolor Esther Williams film *Bathing Beauty* (1944). Steven Cohan has written extensively about *Bathing Beauty*'s "camp dialectic" as depending on Skelton's "sissy persona," but he only mentions Skelton "in his pink tutu" a couple of times in passing, as though a man in a tutu is already so clearly and so conventionally campy that it is not worth further discussion.[52] Skelton plays a songwriter, Steve Elliott, who marries a college swimming instructor (Williams). Various complications and machinations by the film's villain (played by Basil Rathbone) mean that Skelton's Steve must win back Esther Williams's character all over again. To do so, he enrolls in the women's college at which his wife teaches. The film had been in preparation since at least 1940, under the title *Mister Co-Ed,* and the change to *Bathing Beauty* in 1944 "neatly condenses,"

Stan Laurel in *The Dancing Masters* (1943).
Courtesy National Film Archive, London.

Cohan believes, the "gender problematic set in motion" by the plot's requiring Steve/Skelton not only to enroll in a girl's college but to dress in girl drag.[53] Although, like *The Dancing Masters, Bathing Beauty* "makes no reference to wartime," the film "addresses cultural fallout from the sexual instability resulting from the war's deregulation of gender roles (hence the first title, *Mr. Coed* [*sic*]), but covers up this anxiety by asserting the primacy of male heterosexual desire for an unimpeachable feminine female (hence the second title, *Bathing Beauty*)."

What is interesting from a dance as well as film perspective about Skelton's pink tutu is that it was not present in early drafts of the script. Rather, at first our hero was to have been dressed in a chiffon tunic, which he refers to in one 1940 line as a "toga." Rather than tinkling ballet music, the class was to have been conducted to "two kettle-drums with different pitch, a triangle, and an East Indian temple gong."[54] Madame Zarka (Ann Codee), in other words, described in a 1943 script as "looking like a General Sherman tank," was not to have been teaching ballet but rather eurhythmics, a form of early twentieth-century improvisation-based movement and music study from Europe that influenced the work of many American modern-dance pioneers. The description of the chiffon tunic and the "frightening array of

Red Skelton in *Bathing Beauty* (1944).
Courtesy National Film Archive, London.

percussion" in the early drafts of the script would have made Steve Elliott risible not as a ballerina in drag but as a sort of swaying, genuflecting, and heavily draped version of Isadora Duncan, Ruth St. Denis, or Martha Graham. Sometime between August 1943 and October 1943 the scripts begin to refer to the scene opening with a "shot on premier danceuse [*sic*]" and a "lovely girl in regulation ballet dress" performing a "difficult ballet movement in solo," and Madame Zarka becomes a "temperamental Russian ballet mistress" teaching a "senior dancing class." And, therefore, Steve Elliott, too, will wear a "regulation ballet costume. Tights, tarlatan skirt, and ballet slippers tied in bows which stick out on each ankle. The girls go into a gale of giggles."

On the one hand, then, *Bathing Beauty* always wanted to feminize Steve Elliott through dance, but until very late in the game it was not to have been with ballet (indeed, the sign on the studio door in the completed film still reads "Madame Zarka / Eurhythmics"). On the other hand, putting Red Skelton in a pink tutu not only feminizes him in hilarious ways but registers the increasing visibility of ballet in American culture *as* something that feminizes men. Equally significant, not only does the severe Madame Zarka brutalize Skelton's body by making him stretch and pose unnaturally, but the other women in the class both laugh at him and dance him into the ground in much the same way that the wilis in the second act of *Giselle* dance men to their death. Skelton is a man in women's clothing, but he is not a good enough dancer to be a girl.

In *Something in the Wind*, a black-and-white Deanna Durbin vehicle with Donald O'Connor co-starring as her sidekick (John Dall is Durbin's love interest), a penultimate ballet featuring an unnamed male ballet danseur, as well as a host of women in toe shoes, is treated both seriously, as a work of dance art (it was choreographed by Eugene Loring) ostensibly being broadcast to the nation on television, and, finally, in comic fashion, with O'Connor replacing the danseur. Unlike that dancer (probably an uncredited Loring) who partnered and lifted the women with ease, O'Connor staggers under their weight, cannot keep them upright, and ends up smothered by piles of them and with a toe shoe in his mouth, like a riding bit. What is most odd about this is the lack of narrative context; we have not been told why there should be a ballet performance here nor why O'Connor should be dancing a comic version of it. Almost as soon as the ballet ends—was the comic version broadcast on television as well?—the film does too. While O'Connor's persona was already that of a juvenile with an elastic body who virtually always performed some comic dance in his films (*Something in the Wind* features other O'Connor numbers, too, one very similar to "Make 'em Laugh" in *Singin' in the Rain* [1952]), the inclusion of ballet again seems motivated by an implicit assumption that ballet feminizes most of the men who participate in it, yet it also is a spectacular, entertaining, and relatively popular high-art dance form. Since Deanna Durbin's star image was built on her operatic singing voice—and *Something in the Wind* features several opera set pieces by her and by well-known opera tenor Jan Peerce (playing a policeman)—ballet would seem to be superfluous, icing on an already heavily aestheticized cake.

The 1940s versions of ballet masculinity, then, include everything from the paternalistic but handsome Steve Adams in *Dance, Girl, Dance* to Red Skelton in a tutu in *Bathing Beauty* to the attractive homicidal maniac Sanine in *Specter of the Rose*. Again, the wartime and postwar films quite obviously participate in a phenomenon that has received extraordinary amounts of critical attention already, namely the "consequences for masculinity," as Kaja Silverman writes, of "a particular historical upheaval—that of World War II and the recovery period."[55] These films too "attest with unusual candor," in Silverman's words, "to the castrations through which the male subject is constituted." Moreover, "in order to shore up the ruins of masculinity, many of these films are obliged to confer upon a female character the narrative agency which is the usual attribute of a male character, thereby further undermining sexual difference." Certainly in most of the films described in this and the previous chapter—those from the 1930s and early 1940s as well—women function in far more complex ways than as muse or inspiration for the male artistic genius, or as abnormal deviations from domestic

Donald O'Connor and "ballet girls" in *Something in the Wind* (1947).
Copyright 1947 Universal Pictures.

ideology. As dancers and teachers, the women are artists in their own right. In part because of a cultural difficulty with imagining and therefore representing the male ballet dancer (ironically, a problem obviated by women's conventional association with spectacle and the body), a male dancer cannot, at this time, be other than a camp diva, a body whose erotic charge must be subsumed by violence, even comic violence. Thus, we have seen that women's agency is granted more primacy than that of many of these films' male characters. And while it is a conditional and fragile agency, it is ballet that makes it possible even as it also sometimes signifies morbidity and the difficulty of reconciling art and a "normal" life.

BY THE LATE 1940S, ballet as a mood, as a profession, and in no small sense as dancing had become quite a common feature of Hollywood films, nonmusical as well as musical. It was also becoming less and less Russian, although its Russianness was frequently acknowledged even if only to be questioned or disclaimed. And finally ballet was also being deployed in ways that further linked the form with femininity or a highly stylized or ambiguously performed masculinity. This latter issue can be discussed not only with reference to camp but also in relation to the scholarship on film melodrama with which I framed much of the discussion in the previous chapter. With the exception of the musical *comedies,* virtually all of the films discussed thus far bear traces of melodramatic concerns: pathos and overwrought emotion, certainly, as well as some degree of sensationalism. Linda Williams points out that neither pathos nor action alone but rather their dialectic defines film melodrama, the tension between power and powerlessness, agency and victimhood.[56] Ben Singer also writes of sensational melodrama's "oscillation between empowerment and imperilment," of the "intimate connection" between excitement and anxiety.[57]

The intimate connections between excitement and anxiety, empower-ment and imperilment, and, finally, the ballet film's tradition of morbidity *and* its capacity to imagine and represent what Angela McRobbie calls "a future state of being which promises reward, recognition, and happiness" come together most surprisingly, perhaps, in *The Red Shoes* in 1948.[58] A Brit-ish film with an international cast, *The Red Shoes* features performers who were, to a degree previously unmatched in commercial cinema, trained and competent, indeed in some cases already legendary, in the theatrical dance form that the film purports to represent. *The Red Shoes* is more about ballet dancing than any previous film had been, and its dancers and their danc-ing were a big source of the film's appeal to U.S. audiences and its effects on other commercial films as well. It even created a minor critical indus-try devoted to fighting new rounds in an invigorated dance-film debate, a debate that had profound consequences for the dance content of subsequent commercial films. But the glories of *The Red Shoes* are matched by a story that promulgates not only familiar and well-worn messages about women as victims or male ballet artists as perverts but about the functional incom-patibility of life and art. Yet it also served for many audience members, especially women and young girls in the United States, as a potent fantasy of achievement, a parable about remaining committed to goals other than those prescribed by domestic ideology. Indeed, so large does *The Red Shoes* loom in the ballet-film landscape, even now, that it seemed to demand, and has been granted, a chapter all its own.

4

If You Can Disregard the Plot

The Red Shoes in an American Context

ONE OF THE GREATEST ROAD-SHOW GROSSERS IN FILM HISTORY!
Up to January 1st, 1950 "The Red Shoes" was seen by 10,000,000 people
at $2.40!

64 Weeks in New York (and still running)
54 Weeks in Los Angeles (and still running)
53 Weeks in Chicago (and still running)
40 Weeks in Philadelphia
45 Weeks in Boston
21 Weeks in Washington
10 Weeks in Miami!

One of the most widely pre-sold motion pictures in publicity history!

Reproduced with this story is a cut of the by-now-famous "long legs" ad
used for "The Red Shoes" campaign. These legs are the best known in
the whole world of the motion picture today.

–U.S. press book for *The Red Shoes*

Hollywood films were representing the profession of ballet with considerable iconographic consistency by the late 1940s, marking it as a form of
highbrow art to which its practitioners were fanatically devoted and dedicated, their overriding ambition, whether male or female, to dance and keep
dancing. But, as we have seen, often Hollywood's ballet protagonists either
danced not at all (*Grand Hotel* [1932], *Days of Glory* [1944]), only a little (*The
Mad Genius* [1931], *Waterloo Bridge* [1940]), on "hastily tutored toes" (Maureen
O'Hara in *Dance, Girl, Dance* [1940], Margaret O'Brien in *The Unfinished Dance*
[1947]), or with the help of trained but uncredited dance doubles (*The Men in*

Her Life [1941], Karin Booth in *The Unfinished Dance*). Without dancing, it was difficult for audiences to understand ballet as a form of art worthy of quasi-religious devotion, extravagant dedication, and passionate attachment. *Specter of the Rose* (1946) did star a "real" theatrical ballerina, Viola Essen, *as* a ballerina, but even she was not allowed to dance much, and arguably no brief ballet montage sequence could compete with a plot otherwise concerned with a psychotic knife-wielding hero and the suspense of whether he will kill his second ballerina wife as he apparently had his first.

There was, however, no shortage of superb dancing, a lot of it ballet-based, to be found in American film musicals of the 1930s and 1940s. Lengthier dance interludes and dream ballets had become de rigueur in musicals with any kind of artistic pretensions at all following two theatrical events, the 1936 success of the Broadway musical *On Your Toes*, its "Slaughter on Tenth Avenue" ballet choreographed by George Balanchine, and the success of *Oklahoma!* in 1943, with its long "integrated" dream ballet, choreographed by Agnes de Mille. But not many of the longest dance interludes—five minutes or more—occurred in films that were financial successes. When *Yolanda and the Thief*, a Technicolor fantasy musical starring Fred Astaire and Lucille Bremer, showed a net loss at the box office of $1,644,000 in 1945, the failure was pinned on the film's most obviously unusual elements, in particular its fifteen-minute-long "surrealist" ballet, which was choreographed by Eugene Loring.[1] After another unconventional fantasy musical with a long ballet (directed, as had been *Yolanda and the Thief*, by Vincente Minnelli), *The Pirate*, starring Gene Kelly and Judy Garland, showed an even greater net loss—$2,290,000—after its release early in 1948, studio heads could reasonably claim that while the movie public still liked musical comedies, it was much less fond of surreal fantasy musical films with long fantasy ballets.[2]

But at the same time, theatrical ballet itself had become a more popular and familiar presence across the United States during and after the war years. Ballet or "toe" was now being offered by most if not all of the dancing schools of small-town America, their students driven to emulate not only the famous dancers they saw on tour but the dancing stars they saw on their local movie screens. Smaller regional companies were flourishing, albeit on a comparatively minuscule scale, in cities ranging from Atlanta to Salt Lake City to San Francisco and Los Angeles in addition to New York and Chicago. During the war itself the big classical ballet companies also had brilliant seasons, the Ballet Russe de Monte Carlo full of actual as well as nominally Russian prima ballerinas and danseurs performing capsule versions of the romantic warhorses, works by Balanchine, and Agnes de Mille's Americana ballet *Rodeo*, and Ballet Theatre boasting Alicia Markova and Anton Dolin (both Russianified Brits, as discussed below) in classic pas de deux, as well as newer "psychological" ballets by transplanted British choreographer

Anthony Tudor. Ballet Theatre also commissioned and performed works by American choreographers, de Mille and Loring included. But by 1947 dance critic Edwin Denby was writing that these big companies had "not kept the high standards they had reached" during the war, and Jack Anderson, referring to the 1947 Ballet Russe de Monte Carlo, spoke of "gloomy intimations of decline."[3] Ballet Theatre was actually disbanded, for lack of financial support, between May 1948 and March 1949.[4]

Into all of this stepped, figuratively if not literally, *The Red Shoes*. A Technicolor British film written and directed by Michael Powell and Emeric Pressburger and starring Moira Shearer, Anton Walbrook, and Marius Goring, *The Red Shoes* opened at New York's Bijou Cinema, a small five-hundred-seat Broadway "art house," on October 22, 1948.[5] Such art houses—unaffiliated, as were many of the films they exhibited, with any particular Hollywood studio—were themselves relatively new and were but one sign of Hollywood's gradually decreasing dominance as the purveyor of mass-mediated entertainment in the postwar era. On October 11, Lincoln Kirstein and George Balanchine's enterprising subscription-only Ballet Society metamorphosed officially into the New York City Ballet (as Ballet Society had metamorphosed from Balanchine's American Ballet and, in some sense, from Kirstein's American Ballet Caravan) and embarked on its first full season. And intimations of decline or no, from September 18 to October 10, 1948, the Ballet Russe de Monte Carlo enjoyed an outstandingly successful tenth-anniversary gala season at the Met, a season that, while providing nothing much in the way of novelty, reunited its famous artists with their best roles and in so doing rendered going to the ballet as glamorous an event as it had been in years.[6] Some of the artists who performed or whose works were performed during the gala season could be seen in *The Red Shoes* too. While it might be too much to say that *The Red Shoes* sparked an immediate rush for tickets to live ballet performances even in New York, Arlene Croce, for one, does claim that "it brought a new and young audience to the crucial first seasons of the New York City Ballet,"[7] a benefit one presumes must have applied to other companies as well.

The Red Shoes has become legendary, its name able to evoke *something* about ballet even in the minds of people who have never seen the film; conversely, it is already familiar to many people because it has remained available and in front of American audiences as a film and, now, in all sorts of video formats year after year. So it can be hard to understand fully the magnitude of the popularity of the film on its original release, the profound effects it had not only on a ballet consciousness in America but on other films as well. Its story is hardly novel and, indeed, seems to tread heavily on the already well-worn ground laid out by previous ballet films—only the names have been changed, as it were. An impresario, Lermontov (Walbrook), runs

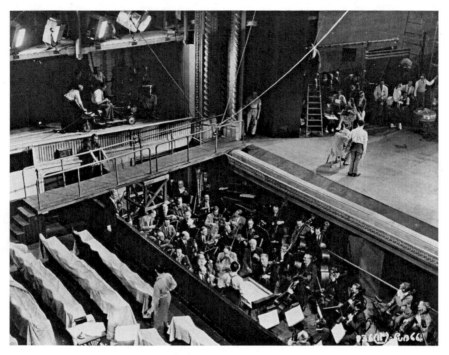

The Covent Garden stage set of *The Red Shoes.* The scene being filmed is Vicky's first audition for the Ballet Lermontov; Moira Shearer is visible on the right.

Courtesy National Film Archive, London.

the most famous ballet company in the world; he hires a young unknown English dancer, Victoria Page (Shearer), whom he grooms to take over the role of the leading ballerina, the Russian Boronskaya (Ludmilla Tcherina). Boronskaya has made the mistake of getting married. Lermontov hires a young English composer (also unknown) at the same time, Julian Craster (Goring), with whose music the Ballet Lermontov creates a new work, "The Ballet of the Red Shoes" (based on the Hans Christian Andersen fairy tale), in which Vicky becomes an overnight sensation. But Vicky and Julian fall in love, and when Lermontov discovers this, he fires Julian, and Vicky quits in protest. Vicky and Julian marry, but, bored and on holiday, Vicky agrees at Lermontov's urging to dance the "Ballet of the Red Shoes" once more, and Julian appears in her dressing room before the performance to demand that she return to him. Lermontov and Julian battle each other over the protests of the weeping Vicky, who, when Julian leaves, throws herself off of a balcony in front of a train and dies but not before asking Julian (who has rushed back, but too late, to make up with Vicky) to take off the red shoes. The performance goes on without her, a spotlight tracing her movements on the stage à la Pavlova's "final performance" after her death in 1931.

In addition to possessing a melodramatic story familiar from tragic ballets and also ballet history (perhaps most obviously the well-known saga of Diaghilev and Nijinsky), *The Red Shoes* did not feature stars whose names meant anything to the average American filmgoer. Even the names of Powell and Pressburger would have been unknown to audiences outside of major metropolitan areas. Nor did *The Red Shoes* receive universally glowing reviews following its U.S. release; indeed, as we will see, the film was panned more often than it was praised, especially in mass-market periodicals with national circulation. Given the box-office failure of so many previous ballet films, especially those released only a few months before *The Red Shoes*, the obvious question raised by its success is why the film was so potent, especially for American spectators. The British film industry had also experimented with ballet films in the 1930s and 1940s, none of them very successful either; yet *The Red Shoes* was also very popular in England. In short, what made ballet "work" in *The Red Shoes* as it had not before in either American or European films?

To address these issues, I first discuss the creation of *The Red Shoes* in Britain; it is one of the few ballet films whose archival and historical presence looms large, the loquaciousness of Michael Powell, Moira Shearer, and others involved in the film producing a detailed record of the processes by which ballet became imbricated as an always contradictory representation and ambiguously gendered embodiment of morbidity and ecstasy, life and death, achievement and failure, fulfillment and despair. Moreover, the production context of *The Red Shoes* functions as a sort of metanarrative about the relationship of ballet to the film industry and of the machinations and processes by which ballet's theatrical identity and the subjectivities of its practitioners were manipulated and objectified (not always successfully, and never without resistance) to fit the measure of a full-length commercial film. Some of this metanarrative, as well as various other news items, circulated anecdotally in American periodicals and newspapers well before the release of *The Red Shoes*, and these helped to create a climate of anticipation for it; quite a bit, though much of it incorrect or already out of date, was known to the reading public about *The Red Shoes* before it opened at the Bijou.

Then I discuss the film proper, not only through analysis of its film values or its melodramatic narrative but in relation to the dancers and dancing who occupy so much of its screen time. It is far from incidental that *The Red Shoes* does not feature actors pretending to be dancers but rather dancers who are acting, many for the first time, but who are playing dancers. And finally, I turn to the American reception of the film. *The Red Shoes*, distributed in the United States by Eagle-Lion, was released selectively in large cities before attracting wider audiences in road-show engagements, and initial reviews treated it not as an unusual film but as more of the standard backstage generic fare, with bad-mannered artists replacing the usual chorines, hoofers, and cigar-chomping showmen. This generic framework apparently had little parallel to its reception in Britain, and I am interested in how an intertextual prereading of *The Red Shoes* was made possible through an emphasis on its links to, as well as its differences from, the other ballet films we have already discussed. The class-based antipathy generated in Britain by *The Red Shoes* among certain ballet critics is quite startling as well, and examining this discourse in relation to the dichotomous U.S. reception also provides interesting and useful ways to consider commercial cinema's changing status in the mediascape, as well as that of classical ballet proper.

Art Is a Relaxation Directly Opposed to War

The 1930s and 1940s were a time of great ballet activity in Britain.[8] Several schools and companies were founded by native impresarios and choreographers, more than a few of them women, as a result of the interest in the form generated by Adeline Genée's residency at London's Empire Theatre in the teens (Genée remained an important figure in British dance training for decades), Diaghilev's regular Ballets Russes seasons, and, of course, Anna Pavlova's frequent visits (Pavlova's primary residence from 1921 was Ivy House, in the north of London). Marie Rambert's Ballet Club at the Mercury Theatre was founded in 1930, Ninette de Valois' Vic-Wells Ballet in 1931. The Vic-Wells became the Sadler's Wells Ballet in 1940 (and eventually the Royal Ballet in 1956). Both women ran schools as well, and their companies presented classics, some Diaghilev repertoire, and new works throughout the period. While some British dancers who had been working longer had already been given Russian names (Alicia Markova was born Alice Marks, and Anton Dolin began life as Patrick Healey-Kay, for example; and de Valois herself, who had been a soloist for Diaghilev in the 1920s, was born Edris Stannus in Ireland), during the 1930s Britain sought actively to establish ballet as *British* ballet, to assume the mantle of Diaghilev after his death in 1929. (Lincoln Kirstein brought Balanchine to America in 1933 for much the same reason.) Among the native talent that de Valois, in particular, wanted to nurture were two young dancers, both potential ballerinas: the dark-eyed Margot Fonteyn, whose real name was Peggy Hookham, and the red-haired Moira Shearer, born Moira Shearer King in Scotland.

As was the situation in the United States, some British ballet artists would end up working here and there in commercial films, partly because film work paid well and because the growth and increasing popularity of ballet made it attractive to producers looking for story material. Some historians call *Dark Red Roses* (1929) the first full-length British sound film, and

Margot Fonteyn, as herself, and Yvonne Marsh in *The Little Ballerina* (1947).
Courtesy National Film Archive, London.

it featured a wild incidental apache-style number danced by Anton Dolin, George Balanchine, and Lydia Lopokova, an authentically Russian Diaghilev ballerina. Ballet dancers, usually uncredited, can be seen performing in the numbers of various musicals after this time too. *Dance Pretty Lady* (1932; directed by Anthony Asquith) was the first British film adaptation of Compton Mackenzie's *Carnival*. Like the 1916 silent American version *The Ballet Girl, Dance Pretty Lady* had a happy ending, with all working out well for heroine Jenny Pearl. The barely glimpsed ballet scenes were choreographed by Frederick Ashton, who would soon become an important choreographer with the Sadler's Wells, and performed by dancers from Marie Rambert's company. Still another version of *Carnival*, this time following the book closely and therefore ending with ballet-girl Jenny Pearl's death, appeared in 1946; called *Carnival* this time, it was choreographed by a music-hall dance director, Freddie Carpenter, and featured his corps de ballet. In 1947 Margot Fonteyn appeared as herself in *The Little Ballerina,* in which a young girl who worships Fonteyn seeks to win a scholarship in order to train for the Sadler's Wells. The dancing was given prominence, but despite a beautiful rendering of Fokine's *Les Sylphides* with Fonteyn and partner Michael Somes, the acting (including Fonteyn's) was amateurish, and *The Little Ballerina* did not make much of a stir. Ironically, Fonteyn's increasing stardom in theatrical ballet is the main reason that she was picked to headline in a commercial film, and it was as a theater art that ballet mattered most in Britain, initially in the 1930s but even more spectacularly during World War II.

Although, as discussed, ballet also increased in popularity in the United States during the war, the arts as a whole meant something much more significant to a country that had been faced with and endured routine bombardment and threats of invasion for several years. As Meredith Daneman writes of the period in her 2004 biography of Margot Fonteyn, "War was terrifying, of course, but it could also, between air raids, be monumentally dull."[9] In an article titled "The Re-Birth of Ballet," published in the magazine *Film Reel,* the author reflects on the increased "following of this art" in recent years:

> This can be traced, like the increased interest in other forms of classic art, such as the opera and paintings, to a psychological reaction to the war years. Art is a relaxation directly opposed to war. And it is colourful, emotional yet restful relaxation a frustrated nation is seeking.
>
> Ballet is undoubtedly enjoying a re-birth both in this country and in America. Many new British and American ballet companies have been formed, and in Britain ballet companies on tour have received crowded houses which would have justified, had it been possible, extended dates. . . .
>
> But although ballet has been reborn as an entertainment it cannot be claimed to have gained the universal popularity of other forms of amusement, such as the cinema. . . .
>
> Shortly, however, I believe that ballet will reach its nearest approach to being a universal entertainment. Appropriately, this approach will come through the medium of the most universal entertainment—the cinema.[10]

The Red Shoes, the writer continues, would entertain "ordinary people" with "the beauty of the ballet," as well as the "beauty of [its] story, which incorporates backstage scenes revealing what ballet really means to those who make it their life." In addition, *The Red Shoes,* which had not yet been released at the time of this article, would be populated, acted as well as danced, by "some of the most famous ballet personalities of our time." With the situation described this way, one wonders not at the popularity of *The Red Shoes* at the box office in Britain but why the other films mentioned above did not also do well, since they, too, featured famous ballet personalities and "backstage scenes." The context for the popularity of a film about ballet in Britain, then, seemed certain in some senses but not others. Ballet was popular, but thus far British films with a ballet setting or story had not been—as Michael Powell and Emeric Pressburger well knew.

It Was Wonderful—A Fabulous Enterprise

The journey that ended with *The Red Shoes* was begun sometime around 1934, when British film magnate Alexander Korda announced the production of a film based on the life of Nijinsky, apparently to star Paul Muni.[11] Not surprisingly (given that Muni was not a ballet dancer), that project never materialized. In 1937 Korda again planned a ballet film, this time as a vehicle for his wife, Merle Oberon (Anton Dolin was also to appear, as well as to choreograph and arrange the dances), and he engaged a Hungarian scriptwriter recently arrived in Britain, Emeric Pressburger, to write it. Pressburger had not yet met Michael Powell, but the 1937 script was similar to that of *The Red Shoes* in at least two significant respects: the main character was a ballet dancer who has a new ballet created for her, and this ballet was itself to have been seen as the action of the film unfolded. Again not surprisingly, given both Oberon's lack of training as a dancer and the returns and critical opprobrium with which other British ballet films had heretofore been greeted by audiences and critics, this project never got off the ground either.[12] But in 1946 the idea of a ballet film was revived by Pressburger and Michael Powell, now partners in a production company called The Archers; Korda, however, was no longer interested (he and Oberon divorced in 1945). The Archers bought Pressburger's script back from Korda and offered it to J. Arthur Rank, for whom they were making *Black Narcissus* at the time.[13]

For the new ballet film the script was completely overhauled. In a 1973 interview Michael Powell described why, and how:

> There was naturally much more dialogue than story in the original. . . . And, of course, the ballet scenes originally consisted of a few shots of doubles dancing and somebody saying "Isn't she wonderful?" Then there were a few more shots of doubles dancing; it was that sort of thing. I remember that I was a bit shocked at the tremendously clever script, the way it was all worked out and was put together. Yet when you came to the ballet you saw her mentor watching and then, it said in the script: "She dances across the stage" or "Julian conducting and then she dances across the stage again." I could imagine close ups of Merle Oberon. . . . That conception, however, was as dead as mutton, but that side of it hadn't interested Emeric as much as the working out of the Diaghilev/Nijinsky story. That's all it is, of course, with Moira Shearer as Nijinsky. The original script had the same theme. I remember, quite clearly, reading it and saying to Emeric, "I think it's

a marvellous script, but I can only do it if a dancer plays the part."
This floored him a bit.[14]

Not only did Powell want a dancer in the leading role, but he wanted a
ballet to be the film's most interesting feature, although Pressburger would
later maintain that, even in the original script, he, too, "wanted to have a
film in which a work of art would not merely be discussed, but in which
it would *appear.* That was my aim."[15] Powell, however, repeatedly asserted
over the years that the idea of a long, complete ballet "really frightened"
Pressburger:

> He said, "You mean a long ballet—many minutes." I said, "Yes, about
> 20 minutes, I expect." "But you don't know anything about making a
> ballet." "Oh well, we'll soon find out. We've got all the talent in the
> world to draw on." I don't think he liked this at all, but he realised that
> if I didn't get my way, I wouldn't do it. Then he and Rank and . . . every-
> body found themselves with a ballet company, because, of course, we
> formed our own. . . . It was wonderful—a fabulous enterprise.[16]

The fabulous enterprise began with the hiring of dancer-choreographers
Robert Helpmann (who plays the Ballet Lermontov's Russian premier danseur Ivan Boleslawsky) and Leonide Massine (as Grischa Ljubov, the company's ballet master and character dancer). Helpmann, Australian by birth,
had been involved with British ballet since 1933; he also was well known as
an actor in straight plays. He had danced in the Vic-Wells and Sadler's Wells
companies and was a tremendously gifted theatrical figure, providing de
Valois with one of her greatest star attractions. Margot Fonteyn later said of
Helpmann, "There is no doubt that he was the absolute star of the company
in those days, the rest of us merely trailed along in the background. People
do not seem to realise nowadays just how much British ballet owes to Bobby
Helpmann. . . . He was a magnet that held things together in a remarkable
way."[17] As the "key member" of the Sadler's Wells, during the war Helpmann
was granted exemption from military service, and he demonstrated then
that he could choreograph as well, with such ballets as *Comus* and *Hamlet*
in 1942 and *Miracle in the Gorbals* in 1944. Although *The Red Shoes* would be
Helpmann's fourth movie as an actor, it was the first one in which he was to
dance, as well; in fact, Powell wrote that Helpmann was a glutton for work,
and Powell hired him to dance and act, stage, and choreograph.[18]

Massine, then in his early fifties and a ballet legend (he had begun his
career with Diaghilev's Ballets Russes as the anointed successor to Nijinsky),
had arrived in England in 1946 from America—where he spent the war years
with Ballet Theatre and touring with various Ballets Russes iterations—to
choreograph and dance in a stage version of Caryl Brahms's and S. J. Simon's

1937 comic mystery *A Bullet in the Ballet*. In America Massine had also choreographed and appeared briefly in some Hollywood shorts and a full-length feature, *Carnival in Costa Rica* (1947), a "Latin" pastiche starring Vera-Ellen in which Massine plays a "famous dancer" and performs in one number. When *A Bullet in the Ballet* closed before reaching London, Ninette de Valois stepped in and invited Massine to stage and dance in his own works for the Sadler's Wells. There he revived *La Boutique fantasque* and *Le Tricorne*, both originally choreographed for Diaghilev, and, while *The Red Shoes* was still in postproduction, *Mam'zelle Angot*, which had been choreographed in America for Ballet Theatre. Although many dance critics at this time were indicating that Massine's creative powers seemed to be waning or were out-of-date, as a performer he was still quite a wonder and, most important for Powell and Pressburger, he had significant "marquee value." Powell writes that he approached Massine about performing in *The Red Shoes* because it seemed that "Fate had brought us together just when I needed for the film all the genius of the world."[19] But Powell had, at first, some trouble filling the film's leading role.

Moira Shearer, born in 1926, had been dancing professionally in England since 1941, when she was an original member of Mona Inglesby's International Ballet (yet another English ballet company founded and run by a woman).[20] Shearer subsequently joined the Sadler's Wells, and by 1946, when the company reopened the newly restored Royal Opera House at Covent Garden with a triumphant revival of Tchaikovsky's *The Sleeping Beauty,* she was one of its principal dancers. In the first volume of his massive autobiography Powell writes in great detail of the lengths to which he had to go in order to acquire the services of Shearer (as the *New York Times* would put it in 1951, "Getting Miss Shearer into the movies has been as difficult as keeping most people out"),[21] but his account differs in many of its details from that of Shearer herself.[22] In 1979 Shearer described the situation for a book of dancers' recollections called *Striking a Balance:*

> *Red Shoes* was the last thing I wanted to do. I fought for a year to get away from that film, and I couldn't shake the director off. It was 1946, it was the first season at Covent Garden, and I was trying to cope with all the big, heavy parts. . . . Oddly enough, of all people it was Ninette de Valois who finally said, "For goodness' sake, do it. Get if off your chest and ours, because I can't stand this man endlessly 'round bothering us any longer. Why don't you just do it, and then it's done." And I said, "Yes, but then what? Can I come straight back into the company again and go on as if nothing had happened? Maybe you will then not want me back." She said, "Of course you come straight back." Which is what I did; I did all the work for six months, 4:30 in

the morning 'til 7:30 at night, Sundays too, and then I was back at Covent Garden again.[23]

Powell, on the other hand, describes rather a different turn of events, with de Valois being much more manipulative and with Shearer accepting the part, then changing her mind, then accepting it again, precisely because de Valois did *not* make it clear that Shearer could return to the company when the filming was over.[24] Powell also claims that he went so far as to travel to America to recruit a substitute that he never planned to use, to "catch" Shearer. Although Shearer never heard about this ruse (and therefore it could have had no bearing on her decision to take the part), there was an announcement in the magazine *Dance* in 1947, accompanied by a photograph, that an American dancer, Edwina Seaver, was going to "star in Michael Powell's forthcoming, British-produced film, 'Red Roses,' based on the Hans Christian Anderson [*sic*] fairy tale."[25] The title error is interesting, as is the fact that in June 1947 *The Red Shoes* was already in production, with Moira Shearer.

But if there ever was a way to make Ninette de Valois interested in *The Red Shoes*, it would have been to threaten to put a non-British dancer in the role of the world's most gifted ballerina. This would have been more of an affront to British ballet, and hence to her, than to Moira Shearer. Indeed, Powell writes that Robert Helpmann and others told him he should have asked Margot Fonteyn to take the role first, and that if he had, he would have had no trouble from de Valois.[26] Fonteyn's one experience with narrative filmmaking *(The Little Ballerina)* had revealed her, even to herself, to be a wooden actress no matter how divinely she danced. Moreover, de Valois apparently delighted in telling her most photogenic dancers, in an attempt to keep them strong against the blandishments of film agents, that, in the words of Fonteyn's biographer, "the transposition of ballet to celluloid was a vulgarity."[27] It nevertheless apparently irked Fonteyn "that the film industry should be in hot pursuit of another, prettier ballerina: her titian-haired colleague, Moira Shearer."

In an interview given around the time of the film's premiere Powell called Moira Shearer the "salient feature" of *The Red Shoes* ("If we had not found Moira Shearer we could not have made the film"), because without her the film's other salient feature, "The Ballet of the Red Shoes" (as it is billed in the opening credits), would not have been possible.[28] Powell and Pressburger needed Shearer—as well as fifty-plus other credited and uncredited ballet artists—to make *The Red Shoes* balletically "real" in a way that no other commercial film had been to that date. No dancing doubles, no one saying "Isn't she marvelous" as a star clumps around in blocky toe shoes or is intercut in close-up with long shots of a double dancing in her stead.

This mattered in the narrative, too, as we will see, but "The Ballet of the Red Shoes" itself had been planned and worked on continuously from the moment Emeric Pressburger agreed to the "fabulous enterprise," and it was worked out in abstract form well before production on the rest of the film was begun. The ballet, in short, was to be a cynosure; its setting would be a film in which the ballet's theme, that of Andersen's fairy tale (more or less), was duplicated. In his autobiography Powell even uses a paraphrase of the fictional Lermontov's description of the ballet to Julian Craster to describe the film's plot.[29] In other words, in Powell's mind it was primarily the idea of the "Red Shoes" ballet that motivated not only the film's unfolding but the process by which the ballet was put on the screen, that the film's scenes both presage the title ballet and are derived from it. Yet after the film was released and the critical assessments were in, Jack Cardiff, the film's cinematographer, wrote that everything in *The Red Shoes except* the ballet was made "to ordinary film standards."[30] Arguably Michael Powell and Emeric Pressburger had never been interested in making "ordinary" films, and Cardiff's remarks may have been defensive. For it was not the central ballet as such but the film's story, to which we will return in a moment, that proved to be its most controversial feature.

The Search for the Perfect Film

In his autobiography Powell writes that *The Red Shoes* was "another step, or was planned by me as another step, in my search for a perfect film, in other words for a 'composed' film."[31] Although the terms *perfect* and *composed* do not have the same meaning in other contexts, to Powell a perfect film was one in which cinema techniques, art direction, and performance all operated under "the authority of the music." The authority was given to the music by the fact that it was recorded first and the film shot and edited to playback, a technique also common to musicals but not so widely used in straight films. Powell's first attempt, he claims, at creating a composed film is a twelve-minute sequence in *Black Narcissus* in which "music, emotion and acting made a complete whole, of which music was the master."[32] Although music is important in many sequences in *The Red Shoes* and may have governed the way they were arranged and shot, Powell does not specifically describe them as composed sequences—other than, of course, the ballet sequences, particularly the central ballet, which is the aspect of the film that had most interested him from the beginning. The "Ballet of the Red Shoes" was to be something the likes of which no one had ever made or seen before.

The music for the "Red Shoes" ballet did not actually come first, however. Hein Heckroth had made a large color drawing for each camera shot and angle in the ballet, some 120 drawings in all. After Robert Helpmann approved the drawings (and hence the camera shots), they were assembled in correct sequence and Brian Easdale composed the music to fit the completed cartoon. The dancers performed to a playback of the finished score, recorded already by Sir Thomas Beecham and the Royal Philharmonic Orchestra.

Much of this information is from a March 1949 article in the trade journal *American Cinematographer*. Although the article spends more time describing 1,200-foot-candle 300 amp. water-cooled arcs and 225 amp. Mole-Richardson "Brutes," there is some discussion of the aesthetics of filmed dance and, in particular, of the artistic merit of "The Ballet of the Red Shoes."[33] The article maintains, for instance, that a new word, *choreophotography*, had to be coined to describe "the fusing of the two separate arts" (who might have used the term is not discussed; Cardiff himself came up with another term, *choreocinema*), and it also discusses the "intentions" of the ballet, that it includes "an impressionistic sequence in which the camera mirrors the ballerina's subconscious mind. As she dances, the characters in the ballet identify themselves with the personalities involved in her own life," and the ballet "is so very definitely a cinematic ballet that it could never actually be performed on a theatre stage"—as, indeed, is true of the finished product. But several paragraphs before, the same article describes, with no apparent sense of contradiction, a different intention entirely: that the ballet was intended to be filmed "without any cutaway shots, so that the motion picture spectator could imagine himself actually sitting in Monte Carlo Opera House watching it on the stage."

One need not expect knowledge of the finer points of ballet in *American Cinematographer*, a specialist trade journal (at one point it refers to the ability of dancers to jump high and calls it *balloon* rather than *ballon*), but this particular contradiction is interesting because it occurs over and over again, in other writing about the film—including many of the anecdotal mentions that began to appear in the United States while the film was in production. According to a June 1947 *New York Times* item that seems to be the first time the film was mentioned in the nontrade American press, for example, the ballet was to be "surrealist," but a month later the *Times* referred to Powell's directing the ballet "without any cuts to show that it is being performed in a theatre" and that there would even be a few seconds' "break in the picture . . . when the cameras draw back at the end of the ballet, giving the movie audience a chance to applaud if they are so minded."[34] Six months later, Heckroth was describing the ballet as being "subjective as well as objective," that the ballet would "combine the Andersen story of the girl who had to dance until she dropped with an impression of the thoughts passing through the girl's mind as she dances."[35]

In the completed ballet there are actually two backstage shots that interrupt the ballet and that return it from "surrealism" to "realism": Vicky's

Moira Shearer being filmed in the "Red Shoes" ballet. The shadows in the foreground are of production personnel.

Courtesy National Film Archive, London.

exit stage left after she hears a "wave" of applause, which turns visually into waves crashing against the stage, and her following reentry onto the stage from the wings. But there are no bits of intercut audience reaction, and the ballet as it exists makes no pretensions at all to being seen entirely from the front of the stage. But if the film was about people who work in classical, theatrical, ballet—a proscenium art—could the dance form, critics seemed to wonder, be manipulated successfully to fit another medium of expression and remain expressive *as ballet?* Is there a sense of choreography under the dancing, or do we merely remember Moira Shearer, in one writer's words, "spinning like a teetotum"?[36] One of the dance critics reviewing the film—and, as had increasingly happened with ballet films in the 1940s, most notably *Specter of the Rose,* ballet critics were asked to write their own reviews of films whose "specialist content" required "specialist knowledge"—wrote of Helpmann's "rambling choreography."[37] But the fact is that "The Ballet of the Red Shoes" has some 120 cuts, many of them discontinuity or "shock" cuts, so it could hardly have been *perceived* as anything other than "rambling." That is, it is the film that rambles, not its choreography; there are not many scenes in which choreography is the most important element—very little is performed by the large corps de ballet—and there are several places where there is dancing but not much choreography, the places where Moira Shearer essentially shoots across or wafts around the soundstage *en pointe.* Much of the ballet is, then, memorable in terms of film gimmicks—slow motion, process shots, any special screen effect. Nevertheless, there are also moments in which the dancing appears to exceptional advantage because it has been so beautifully performed and so calmly recorded.

Helpmann later called his own work in the "Red Shoes" ballet "undistinguished," which may be accurate in theatrical terms.[38] This does not mean that it is not a great experience, but it is a great *film* experience; more than the other dancing in *The Red Shoes,* it ends up driven as much by Moira Shearer's photogenicity as by ballet as an art form. Possibly because of the way the central ballet was planned, to order, to match a series of "artist's renderings," its energy is narrative rather than choreographic, especially in the early fair sequences, where the frame fills with highly stylized compositions and block after block of color and shape. The "action" rockets along almost in a panorama from stage right to stage left, a series of swiftly performed vignettes alternating with garishly decorated set pieces. Then, as Robert Helpmann, playing the girl's lover, is borne away into the distance by a crowd, leaving the girl alone in her cursed red shoes, the action reverses, from stage left to stage right, into and through the ballerina's "subconscious mind." The rolling along of the action is punctuated by little bursts of complicated cutting and Leonide Massine, as the maniacal shoemaker.

Whatever one thinks of "The Ballet of the Red Shoes" on film or on ballet terms, it was clearly meant to be *special*—it was the reason Powell wanted to make the film; it was the reason Powell needed Moira Shearer et al.; it was the most widely publicized feature, by far, of the film in both the British and the American popular, as well as trade, press. At least one writer suggested that the ballet should be removed from the film and shown on its own right, "to give spectators a chance to study it again and again."[39] But it would have been suited to being a removable artistic entity if it had *not* detoured into Vicky Page's subconscious or, more to the point, if her subconscious had been concerned less with larger plot details. For instance, the girl's dance with a newspaper, which turns into a man (Helpmann) and back again, relates to the windblown newspaper that Vicky steps on the night she has been told that she is to dance the lead in the new ballet. She sees in the article under her foot that the press in fact already knows about it, that her acquiescence was assumed, and perhaps she is momentarily chilled by the revelation of Lermontov's omnipotence. Julian's whistled minor melody in the same scene also turns out to be the actual music of the ballet's newspaper dance. Moreover, although the ballet duplicates the film's story, it also *presents* the idea that Vicky is falling in love with Julian and that Lermontov, who has already exhibited his scorn for married ballerinas and made various pronouncements about the incompatibility of life and art ("The dancer who relies upon the doubtful comforts of human love can never be a great dancer—never!"), is therefore becoming frightening in a way he has not been before. So although *The Red Shoes* is not a generic musical, the central ballet's fantasy elements *and* their relation to plot points function in ways that would already have been familiar to musical fans.

The aforementioned *Yolanda and the Thief,* for example, is about a con man (Fred Astaire) who is trying to fleece a gullible South American heiress, and he has tricked her into thinking he is her guardian angel. Songs and dances are inserted in typical musical-comedy style, but one number, the long dream ballet, is meant to show us the state of mind of Astaire's con man much as the "Red Shoes" ballet does of Vicky Page, even though the latter is supposedly taking place on a real stage in a real theater. Once it becomes a "state of mind" ballet, however, the "Red Shoes" ballet can be said to resemble any number of other love duets of musicals in which song or dance are used to move the story along, most usually to alter the relationships of the [heterosexual] couple from platonic or antagonistic to romantic. We are not really shown before the "Red Shoes" ballet that Vicky and Julian are in love—although their initially prickly relationship would also have been very familiar to fans of musical comedy—nor are we particularly aware of Lermontov as a figure who can destroy Vicky's life. But all of this is realized during the ballet. When the menacing figure of the Shoemaker changes into Lermontov, into Julian, and back again to the Shoemaker, we discover that these people control her life. When Julian leaves the orchestra pit to come conducting over the footlights, changing form on the way to become Vicky's dancing partner (in the shape of Helpmann's character Ivan), we determine that she is falling in love with him. This is not too different from, for instance, the Fred Astaire–Ginger Rogers "I Used to Be Colorblind" dance

Robert Helpmann and Moira Shearer in their "newspaper costumes" in the "Red Shoes" ballet.

Courtesy National Film Archive, London.

from *Carefree* (1938), where Rogers's character discovers that she is in love with Astaire's in a drug-induced dream. Especially now, so many decades later, the "subconscious" elements of the "Red Shoes" ballet are obvious but at the same time corny and campy. It has become hard for us to see it any longer as an innovative artistic whole, however much we may still respond to its "cosmoramic" (Jack Cardiff's word) effects, of the sort that prompted

Publicity still of Julian's and Lermontov's final battle over Vicky.
Collection of the author.

one English critic to write even in 1948 that "this, believe me, must be the nearest thing to a dope-addict's dream."[40]

In fact, much of the film's running time is spent showing us a whole world in which magic is commonplace and desirable but created with material things—wood, paint, fabric, sweat, muscular effort, and so on. The film seems to reveal the effort that goes into mounting a theatrical ballet, how things are done, the training and rehearsal and talent and skill it takes to get them done—in other words, it looks as if the film's producers were allowing the performers to do on the screen what they did in real life—but very little of this work, other than several steps we have seen in rehearsal, shows up in "The Ballet of the Red Shoes" itself. Because the emphasis of the central ballet turns away suddenly from dance to screen art, it replaces a seemingly realistic approach to ballet with a movie-conventional "lurid visual tone poem," the magic of the theater replaced by laboratory effects—some of them successful, some not.[41] The moment when the red shoes jump onto Vicky's feet is an effective device that instantly and comprehensibly transports us into both a cinematic and a ballet experience and that helps to make the red shoes the potent visual symbol they will remain throughout the rest of the film.

In the End She Dies

What are the red shoes meant to symbolize, however? Karen Backstein's 1994 piece on the film reminds us that the heroine of Andersen's parable "longs not to dance but to show off her beauty; her sin consists of a pride so strong that it leads her to disrespect God. But then, perhaps it isn't surprising that Lermontov [or, I would argue, Powell], who explicitly desires 'to create'—just like God—overlooks Andersen's moral."[42] Moreover, one of the most famous exchanges of dialogue in the film reveals more about the relationship of *The Red Shoes* to the stereotypes of other ballet films than to Andersen's moral. When Lermontov first meets Vicky and learns that she is supposed to be a ballet dancer, he asks her, "Why do you want to dance?" She responds, "Why do you want to live?" His answer to *her* question is, "Well I don't know exactly why, but I must," to which she replies, "That's my answer too." Not only is this virtually identical to, say, the initial exchanges between the Conrad Veidt and Loretta Young characters in *The Men in Her Life* ("The question is, how great is your desire, your ambition, to be a dancer?" / "Oh, I think I'd give anything in the world!") but Lermontov's desire to make Vicky into a "great dancer" (Powell might as well have added another line from *The Men in Her Life*, if he had to "kill her in the attempt") mimics the godlike desires of mad geniuses from too many other films to name.[43]

The red shoes, therefore, are primarily a symbol of destructive or compulsive behavior, because of the film's consistency in the way that it treats ballet not only as an art requiring tremendous physical discipline but as a "religion" that attracts a certain type of stereotyped personality. The film tries to use the props from the central ballet to duplicate aspects of the fairy tale in the surrounding narrative—Vicky pulling out her pink toe shoes to stroke fetishistically in the middle of the night, for example, a pair of red ones lurking there in the drawer—but the fairy tale seems manipulated by the protagonists to excuse rather than to cause their actions. *The Red Shoes* makes the *most* sense, then, not as an unusual film but as part of the long movie tradition I have described in these pages. It carries to the furthest extreme the themes of previous films like *Grand Hotel* and *Waterloo Bridge*, where the protagonists are like the characters they are supposed to dance, and Vicky's death becomes like the death of the Sylphide, of Giselle, of Odette: she is not killed by ambition, or pride, but by people she loves who betray her. The exceptionally sanguinary nature of Vicky's demise (she lies in bloody and torn tights on the railroad tracks) upset many critics, but the fact of her death is, we have seen, one of the least exceptional features of *The Red Shoes*. Vicky is doomed merely because she is a ballerina. Although the visually sumptuous films of Powell and Pressburger are often treated as

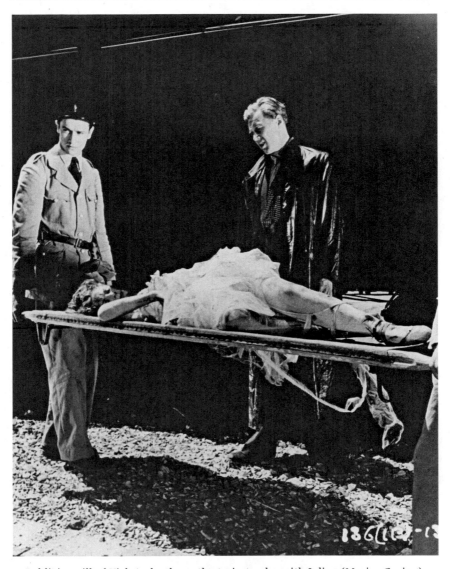

Publicity still of Vicky's death on the train tracks, with Julian (Marius Goring).
Courtesy National Film Archive, London.

anomalies in British cinema history—because, in Ian Christie's words, they were "created out of no obvious cinematic tradition"[44]—the *story* of *The Red Shoes* is but one entry in a long line of American and European films in which ballet is iconographically linked with excess and deviance, disaster and doom, as well as beauty and glamour. After Lermontov describes the ballet's plot to Julian (he is fondling the cast of a foot in a toe shoe as he does so), Julian asks "What happens in the end?" The audience familiar with these conventions could probably have done a pretty good job at coming up with Lermontov's answer: "Oh, in the end she dies."

Reading the Critics Out

Ian Christie claims that *The Red Shoes* produced "confused responses" among critics, and Julian Petley maintains that the films of Powell and Pressburger were greeted with "desperate dislike."[45] This has actually helped to contribute to the reputation of Powell-Pressburger films as auteurist and, most important, *atypical* masterworks that remained until very recently, as Christie writes, "the delight of mavericks and fellow-outsiders."[46] Christie does note that it is "important to dispel the notion that The Archers' films were subjected to uniformly hostile criticism, or that they were dismissed from serious attention. On the contrary," Christie continues, "a pattern emerged early in their career which balanced admiration with irritation in varying proportions."[47] Christie names a "wider critical dilemma" with which films like *The Red Shoes* and, in 1951, *The Tales of Hoffmann,* were also met: namely, "could they be judged merely as films, in view of their large dance and music content?"[48] But we know that rather than *The Red Shoes* creating this "critical dilemma," it was renewing the dance-film debate, carried out by dance, film, and theater scholars and artists, about how best to present dance through film.

It is important to remember, however, that to critics and audiences alike ballet, as dancing, still generally meant eye- and ear-filling spectacle, with lots of decor and costuming and characters. The notion of ballet as pure dancing to music was an exception to these rules at this point, and thus the ballets marked as "radical" tended to be those that were not so spectacular—for example, Frederick Ashton's austere *Symphonic Variations* in Britain immediately after the war or any of Balanchine's so-called abstract ballets. This accounts in part for some of the critical hostility with which the film was greeted, especially in England.

Just how vituperative were some of the attacks on *The Red Shoes?* Here is ballet critic Arnold Haskell's first review of the film in 1948, written, signally, for *Ballet Annual* of 1949, or after the film had begun to demonstrate its enormous box-office clout:

> Its story is idiotic; it always has been. The atmosphere of a Russian Ballet company on tour is entirely false. The acting is mediocre. . . . The fantastic ballet arouses one's admiration for its technical trickery but fits badly in what purports to be realism. To be absolutely fair, it must be said that, viewed out of its absurd context, as I first saw it, the ballet gains enormously even though Disney has done this whole

thing so very much better. The photography alone deserves unqualified praise. . . . As things are this glamourised twaddle can only do harm wherever it is seen by an unsophisticated public.[49]

Here is Haskell again, in 1951, as the film continued to run: "I can only think of [The Red Shoes] as the Red peril. Its false glamour is the very thing ballet must avoid if it is to survive as a serious art."[50] And yet again, the same year: "[The current] popularity [of ballet] is a little alarming, particularly when it is manifested by such tasteless efforts as The Red Shoes or the performances that have been given recently in the vast London sports arenas. One is forced to ask oneself, Is it all a boom like miniature golf?"[51] The hierarchy of tastes and taste cultures at work in Haskell's assessments of the perils of popularity is quite clear. Thus, it is tempting to dismiss his remarks as those of a snob whose own class-bound cultural capital was being usurped. Seen in the context of other, less commercially successful British and European ballet films, the hostility here seems part of a top-down anxiety about the nature of the mass audience and the mutability of taste culture itself. But Haskell's basic points are sometimes echoed by other British and American critics—namely the admiring of the central ballet's "technical trickery" while lambasting it for fitting badly in its purportedly realist context and, concomitantly, that the ballet, viewed out of its context, was interesting precisely as cinematic fantasy.

Of the fifteen film reviews from the British national press surveyed by A. H. Franks in his 1950 book Ballet for Film and Television (a book that makes great use of, and was itself made viable by, the popularity of The Red Shoes), he found only one that condemned the "Red Shoes" ballet itself.[52] Wrote Milton Shulman in the Evening Standard, "Now, Mr. Pressburger, if you do intend to introduce a new ballet presumably intended for the stage, is it then fair to have your ballerinas dancing in a set with the combined dimensions of the Grand Canyon and Salisbury Plain? And must it attempt to rival Walt Disney in everything but elephants with green polka dots?" Conversely, those who liked the ballet, among them C. A. Lejeune in the Observer, thought the same thing: "The highspot of the film is unquestionably the 'Red Shoes' ballet, specially devised for the film, and danced by Massine, Moira Shearer, and Robert Helpmann. To my mind the wedding of the movement and colour here is almost perfect, and to Hein Heckroth, who designed the production, I would gladly award the finest rose in my garden." Reg Whitely of the Daily Mirror referred to the "magnificently staged ballet scene" and hailed Moira Shearer as "a dancing discovery greater than Ginger Rogers"—a "queer comparison," as Franks notes.[53]

Of the American reviews, the only consensus reached among the many I surveyed was that, at two-and-a-quarter hours, the film was too long, and its dialogue and plot were worn and cliché-ridden (as indeed they were). *The Red Shoes* was just another "backstage story," in which, as *Variety* put it, "temperamental ballerinas replace the more conventional showgirls."[54] *The Nation* concurred: *The Red Shoes* "tells the story . . . of lives blighted by genius and a stubborn dedication to the muses. The heroine is compelled to dance, the hero to compose, and Anton Walbrook, as a combination Svengali-Diaghileff, to interfere in their love life. If you can disregard the plot, and it is the apparent intention of its creators that you should, the dancing should prove delightful."[55]

But, as in England, virtually everyone admired the central ballet, but not as a form of "cinedance" or "choreophotography" but simply as a big musical number. *Variety* continues: "a superb ballet of the Red Shoes . . . is staged with breath-taking beauty, out-classing anything that could be done on a stage. It is a colorful sequence, full of artistry, imagination and magnificence. The three principal dancers . . . are beyond criticism. . . . Then the melodrama resumes."[56] *Newsweek* reported that "for all its demonstrably good taste and better intentions, 'The Red Shoes' is a disappointing film, regarded either as special fare for the balletomane or strictly emotional entertainment for the average moviegoer. . . . Although [the screenplay] is more thoughtful than most, it is, basically, just another backstage story that reiterates the familiar conflict of love vs. career. It is also singularly uneventful for a film that runs almost two and a quarter hours."[57] The ballet itself, the critic continues, "is imaginative, colorful, and expertly danced. . . . But the resulting sequences float through a good half-dozen dreamlike and sometimes almost surrealistic settings which could not possibly have been fitted into the most elaborately equipped theater. It might have been more daring of the producers, and more to the point of the story at hand, if they had focused a single camera on a ballet troupe confined to the real stage for a single performance."

Time's reviewer called the film

> a lingering, calf-eyed look at backstage ballet's little world of overworked egos and underdone glands. Its theme is one of fiction's most moth-eaten: one must suffer for one's Art. . . . As in most movies that grapple with Art, the burden of the suffering falls on the audience, which is subjected to all the knitted brows, quivering nostrils, tossed locks—and tantrumacious bad manners—that cinemaddicts have learned to recognize as signs of artistic genius. *The Red Shoes* is such a spotty piece of movie craftsmanship that it is hard to believe that it is a major effort by Britain's crack moviemaking team, Michael Powell and Emeric Pressburger.[58]

But according to the *New Yorker*,

Nestling among the innumerable reels of "The Red Shoes" . . . is a fine ballet, vaguely based on a Hans Christian Andersen fairy tale. . . . The ballet is as interesting an item as you're likely to come across in a long time, . . . but pleasant as this interlude is, I can't say that the picture as a whole struck me as being very stimulating. The color gives most of the characters the complexion of the recently embalmed, and the dialogue runs to such doubtful extravagances as "The dancer who relies on the comforts of human love will never be a great dancer" and "Great expression of simplicity can only be achieved by great agony of body and spirit." These master thoughts may be valid, but a film that swarms with people given to talking that way is hard to endure for more than two hours, and this film lasts more than two hours.[59]

Some of the critical dissidence sparked by *The Red Shoes*—a dissidence that marks more recent scholarly assessments of the film as well—seems to derive from uncertainty about what the film was supposed to be. Although it sports much more opulent production values than had *Specter of the Rose*, it was clearly similar to other film melodramas based on some version of the Diaghilev-Nijinsky "mad genius" story. It was also quite like a musical, because there is a very long ballet close to the end of it (there are thirty minutes of film left once the ballet has ended). The long ballets in movies had all thus far been in musicals; even some of the films that also had ballet stories, for example *The Unfinished Dance,* had been advertised, albeit with some conditional language, as musicals. It was problematic not that *The Red Shoes* was hard to believe, or artificial, or even that it contained fantasy elements (musicals were and did all of these things, too) but that the conventional signals that allowed fantasy elements to occur in other films are missing in *The Red Shoes.* "The Ballet of the Red Shoes" is not a dream ballet; it is a theatrical performance, a dance version of the Hans Christian Andersen fairy tale in which a girl demands a pair of red shoes and, once she has them on, cannot stop dancing and eventually dances herself to death. There had been improbable stage spectaculars in other films (think Busby Berkeley musicals, which frequently set their wild and spatially impossible numbers in proscenium theaters) but not in other "straight" films, which is why the central ballet, lauded as a film ballet, ended up peculiarly divisive, too: it could never have happened on a stage, but some felt that they had been led to believe it could.

In short, *The Red Shoes* in the 1940s and 1950s was seen by many of its contemporary critics much as film scholars do today—but it is the valence of the film, the value of what earlier was disparaged, that has altered. What once was maligned about *The Red Shoes* and other Powell-Pressburger films are the same things that make them so admired by filmmakers like Brian De

Palma and Martin Scorsese today—their visual and auditory excess and garish color, their extravagance and pretentiousness and hothouse atmosphere,
their Europeanness. Arlene Croce maintains that *The Red Shoes* represented a
"cultural bonanza for Americans who were starved for the magic of London
and the Continent that had been cut off by the war."[60] Given the sorts of
reviews I have cited, in the end perhaps the biggest surprise about *The Red
Shoes* is that American audiences were so utterly fascinated by it.

After a bit of time had passed and as *The Red Shoes* showed "legs"—not
only in its advertising campaign but in terms of its longevity at the box
office—some reviewers did begin to attempt to account for the film's astonishing popularity. As *The Red Shoes* continued to rake in the money—by
1954 it had earned $5 million and joined *Variety*'s list of the "all-time top-
grossing pictures"—middlebrow organs of public opinion, like *Theatre Arts*
magazine, were also pondering the film's popularity in the context of Hollywood's well-known financial woes (with 1947 having been an exceptionally
bad box-office year):

> It is becoming increasingly evident that the British picture makers
> have in a few brief years reached a maturity not yet achieved by their
> much older but still adolescent American cousins. . . . The depression
> that has struck Hollywood is deeper than financial. It is psychologi-
> cal. . . . It is not more money that will make Hollywood a valuable con-
> tribution to the lives of picture goers. Hollywood must find maturity.
> This, in France, Italy and England already has happened. . . . New evi-
> dence comes to us from England in the current brilliant success *Red
> Shoes*. Here is combined intelligence, maturity, grace and beauty in
> the creation of a treasured experience that will remain with spectators
> long after the fabulous output of Hollywood has been forgotten.[61]

The *New Republic* called *The Red Shoes* "close to being perfect": it is "amusing,
beautiful, dazzling; it invades an area of enchantment with confident good
humor and maintains its style of elegance with casual sureness. . . . 'The Red
Shoes' is in Technicolor and the producers have made a real virtue of it. They
carry over into the dramatic scenes the cake-icing prettiness of the dance
episodes, and they make their locales—London, Paris, the Riviera—shine like
bright new color slides."[62]

I have spent some time myself trying to account for the film's popularity, to understand what seems to have made the film special for its general,
nonspecialist audiences. Maybe I can only recount really what makes it special for *me,* which has a lot to do with the very familiarity and conventional-
ity of its predictable plot. That *The Red Shoes* is morbid should be clear by
now; but so are many other films. I believe that the success of *The Red Shoes*
in an American context is tied paradoxically both to its "foreignness" (its

mood, its *mystery*) and to its familiarity (not only on the level of plot but in its bodies and their actions). This paradox is what I turn to now.

Images Are Everything

Michael Powell writes in his autobiography, "In my films, images are everything; words are used to distill emotion."[63] Perhaps this is why it turned out to be difficult to reconcile realism with fantasy in the script of *The Red Shoes*. The emotions distilled into words became extravagantly sentimental and cliched, and many critics, the ballet critics most obviously, derided the dialogue and the "ridiculous" story and ignored, or did not notice, that *The Red Shoes* was about ballet only as *Black Narcissus* had been about nuns. That is, both are about fanaticism or extreme devotion, themes well served by the subject matter but scarcely particular to them. The depiction of a manic world of dance was and remains a large part of the film's charm, however, and its scenes of backstage life demonstrably continue, to this day, to shape the way the film public thinks about ballet.[64] But we are, of course, really learning more about what the film's own Lermontovs—Powell and Pressburger, Heckroth, Cardiff, et al.—feel about it. Powell and Pressburger allowed the dancers to perform for the camera—and Powell claims to have given little in the way of direction to the dancers in their acting scenes—and then fashioned, from the recorded images, other images that supported the film team's creative design. There are several scenes, in fact, in which it is clear that the camera was simply trained on the dancers, the classroom scenes for example, so that Massine's character, Grischa, appears to dismiss class at the end of *barre,* a balletically illogical thing to do. Thus it is true that the film is not accurately a record of life in a ballet company—and Moira Shearer publicly pointed out, from 1949 on, that there is little, if anything, in the film that actually reflects the processes and procedures of life in a real ballet company[65]—but what Powell and Pressburger did require was that the art form be performed by the characters themselves. The movie's audience had to be able to see that what the characters did in the film—in class, in rehearsal—was the material source of what they would do in the dancing scenes.

But even the relationships of classroom to rehearsal to performance are treated in film-conventional ways. As is common arguably in all the movies discussed so far, no really burning questions, even aesthetic ones, are ever asked, and the Ballet Lermontov lives in a world so insular that it is comfortable, despite all the "tantrumacious bad manners" on display. The company choreographer never choreographs anything but masterpieces, the single premier danseur is perfect for every role, the decor and costume designs, by the kindly and ancient European Ratov (Albert Bassermann), are always superb. No hatred, little intrigue beyond that instigated by

Lermontov himself, no petty jealousy, just pleasant histrionics and temperament. You can see more sweat and grittiness and sense more physical discomfort in *The Red Shoes* than in any American movie about ballet to that time, certainly, but it is no wonder that the film might also attract people to the art, because it more than insinuates that the rewards for the hard work are fabulous—one can become world-famous overnight—and that the people among whom you will spend much of your waking and sleeping life resemble nothing so much as a happy family. Everyone, even Lermontov, is deep down inside rather kind; and when they are not, it is because they are anxious, or angry, or frustrated—all human emotions, all readily understandable, all temporary.

The Red Shoes begins to create its mood from the credits, a series of garish paintings (by Heckroth) that depict the voyage of the red shoes. The movie fades in to the roar of the crowd, one that has been queued for hours to get in to see the Ballet Lermontov; when the doors are unbarred, a flood of people pounds up the stairs to the upper balcony and, almost immediately, visual as well as aural elements build an atmosphere of foreboding. As the crowd rushes by in the claustrophobic stairwell, the camera picks out a playbill on the wall advertising the Ballet Lermontov, and as soon as we are able to tell what it is, it is violently but carelessly torn from the wall by the teeming hoard of closely packed bodies. Our first sight of the aristocratic Vicky (she even wears a tiny tiara in the shape of a crown), in a box with her aunt watching the "Heart of Fire" ballet through opera glasses, is musically almost terrifying. Even in scenes of rather straightforward exposition the mood is maintained by the way the scenes are framed and edited. When Vicky realizes, for instance, that she has been granted a position as a member of the Ballet Lermontov and will travel with the company to France, before the scene cuts from her joyous face we hear what seems to be a terrible scream that turns out in the next shot to be a train whistle. The physical intensity of many of the scenes in *The Red Shoes* is startling even now, as is their formal beauty, the way that the mise-en-scène is crafted to make mysterious the world in which these people are supposed to operate. One of the most famous and gorgeous sequences in the film is when Vicky is driven to and then climbs the steps to Lermontov's villa above the Bay of Monaco, where she learns that she will star in "The Ballet of the Red Shoes"—she figuratively and almost literally rises, as Powell writes, "from obscurity to stardom."[66] The film is also full of inscrutable glances and veiled expressions (often literally, by dark glasses), still waters running deep. But generally it is the way the film is shot and edited, the frequent use of tight close-ups, a particular handling of the tools of cinema technique, that creates the drama; mystery resides in the film's form rather than by anything inherent to the dramatic content of scenes about ballet dance and ballet dancers.

But I also do not want to underestimate the impact of the film's dependence on "real" ballet dancers, for this was certainly an important aspect of the film's publicity campaign. For years Hollywood had been putting non-dancers in dancer roles and then trumpeting their abilities as exceptional. "MARGARET O'BRIEN MASTERS BALLET DANCING TECHNIQUE" screams one *Unfinished Dance* press book headline, using poor David Lichine as the authority for O'Brien's being "one of the finest young dancers he has ever seen. In six months [sic] time she learned what most young ballet students must study years to accomplish."[67] Compared to O'Brien in *The Unfinished Dance,* or even to Cyd Charisse, Moira Shearer is a dancer who performs—and is given substantial screen time to perform—at a level far beyond that of any screen dancer to that point. We see her performing bits of *Swan Lake* (or *Lac des cygnes* as it is much more romantically named in the film), *Les Sylphides, La Boutique fantasque, Coppélia,* and, of course, "The Ballet of the Red Shoes," in rehearsal and in performance. However well known Shearer was in the relatively circumscribed milieu of wartime and postwar England, she was a dream object for American spectators: the beautiful and spectacularly talented young unknown. Moreover, Shearer lived up to the ballyhoo in a way that Margaret O'Brien never could.

I also have always adored the other strange and fascinating details of life in the ballet that the film contains. The film spurred me to study everyone else who appears in it too, and these details then became even more fascinating: Marie Rambert in the Mercury Theatre (you can see references to works by Antony Tudor and Frederick Ashton on the rain-soaked poster we are shown outside), where Vicky performs act 2 of *Lac des cygnes* on the tiny stage to a scratchy LP record.[68] Lermontov has given her permission to dance, and she catches sight of him, in a series of whip pans meant to mimic her spotting in a *piqué tour* sequence across the stage, watching her. When we see her frozen face in close-up, she is in full stage (not film) makeup, red dots at the corners of her eyes to make them stand out. There is a rehearsal call-board for the beautiful *Giselle* rehearsal at the Paris Opéra with its notices in Russian, English, and French—and when French is spoken in the film, it remains French; there is a modicum of immediate repetition in English. There is Massine dressed and marking steps for *Le Tricorne,* but, I later learned, with the exaggerated eyebrows from his *Gaîté parisienne.* Elsewhere he is seen in his famous "Chaplin" makeup for *Boutique fantasque* (which is credited to Massine in a program shown in the film), and when the orchestra is warming up for the premiere of the "Red Shoes" ballet, you can hear a lone musician practicing bits of *Boutique*'s music (the ballet was choreographed originally, like the other two, for Diaghilev). There is Robert Helpmann as Dr. Coppélius, a character role for which he was famous. It is remarkable how much *The Red Shoes* takes for granted, in other words, how

Moira Shearer posed on the Mercury Theatre stage set in *The Red Shoes*.
Courtesy National Film Archive, London.

much it assumes its audience knows. And if you do not "get" everything at once, surely you are going to (want to) figure it all out eventually.

I Can't Believe What That Man Did to Her!

The film's handling of gender roles is also interesting, on a number of sometimes paradoxical levels. Alexander Doty points out in his essay on the "aesthete-and-diva" sexual politics of *The Red Shoes,* onscreen and off, that the men "behind" *The Red Shoes* initially (and, in Powell's case, subsequently as well) demonstrated considerable contempt for the ballet women and men in their film on whom they would depend so much.[69] Producer Alexander Korda felt that the men associated with ballet "were a lot of poofs," and Jack Cardiff thought ballet was "sissies prancing about," although he claimed to have become a balletomane during the film's production.[70] The "aura of queerness" surrounding the film (Walbrook was gay, as was Helpmann) also included Powell and Pressburger themselves, Doty claims; Powell referred to his relationship with Pressburger as a "marriage without sex."[71] That the "men's club" of The Archers required the involvement of a talented woman, much less a young and inexperienced woman who was nevertheless neither cowed nor impressed by what geniuses they all were, seems to have irked Powell especially, in Doty's estimation (Shearer *was* impressed by the involvement and ballet credentials of Helpmann and, in particular, Massine). Given this creative situation, "it comes as no surprise to discover that a number of Archers productions include an onscreen male character who attempts to control or regulate the central female character(s) and the development of their heterosexual relationships."[72]

Despite this, which I find convincing as an argument, I would not be the first to call *The Red Shoes* a "feminist fable." On the one hand, Lermontov is a very romantic figure, much more romantic and appealing, as an actor and a character, than Marius Goring's Julian. Goring had no matinee-idol following in the United States as he had in England, and Vicky's romance with Julian was apparently quite easy for American audiences to ignore or to discount. When Julian starts issuing ultimatums, there is enough anecdotal evidence to support the assumption that some spectators simply fantasized that Vicky would tell him to get lost and keep on being a fabulous star herself. The rewards for being a star in *The Red Shoes*, both textually and extratextually (Shearer became a movie star too), were much more substantial and fulfilling than the rewards of being Julian's wife (this is true also of Boronskaya, whose marriage to an uncharacterized and unnamed elderly man brings her wealth but quickly returns her to the stage). The other men do not function too well as romantic figures either; Robert Helpmann looks perhaps the campiest, with his strange Astaire-shaped head and his bulbous chest, wearing a head scarf and a bathing suit in one scene, heavily made up and needing to pee in others. Massine's/Grischa's relationship with Boronskaya is one of the most affecting—they scream all the time but love one another dearly, and no display of temperament ever causes a lasting rift—but, well, he is old too, his teeth are brown, and he is very short. Shearer herself commands the screen and our attention and, for reasons not unrelated to the popularity of *The Red Shoes* itself, requires much less explaining away now than the other dancers whose work we watch, whose bodies we look at. Her body is sculpted but streamlined, her legs long, her dancing swift and precise; we can imagine her onstage today in a way that is not true of any of the other dancers in the film. Moreover, she subsequently not only went back to the ballet but made more films, worked in theater, wrote books and articles, and married and had four children—she did not have to die for her art, or for love.

The legend of *The Red Shoes*, however, remains strong: that it portrays a basic incompatibility between art and life. Powell claims that it is about dying for art, that art is worth dying for.[73] But the sense not of this logic but of the context by which we understand the film's gender politics has changed over the years. It is no longer easy, if it ever was, to see Vicky Page's suicide leap in front of the Riviera Express as death by Art. Instead, she seems pushed by those she loves who would rather possess her than support her. The film mainly illustrates the effect that ruthless personalities—the aesthetes, in Doty's characterization, as opposed to the "divas" like Vicky—have on the less powerful or the demure, and the trouble that powerful people can cause when their desires are thwarted. There is actually not much in the film that demonstrates that ballet and marriage are incompatible, but there is plenty to suggest that dancing for Boris Lermontov and marriage to Julian Craster are incompatible because both men are so egotistical and intolerant. Vicky Page does not now seem a fool, exactly, but her unhappiness is not caused by any real rift that exists between art and life (as Doty points out, Craster has no problems in this regard; nor did Moira Shearer herself); rather, she never risks being impolite or unladylike by telling either of these men that they are driving her crazy.

Even by those who have seen it, *The Red Shoes* is still often mentioned as a film about the conflict between art and life—but seldom by those who have seen it a lot. The inconsistencies become overwhelming on multiple, thoughtful viewings. The audience is given clue after clue, for example, that Lermontov is jealous of Julian not for keeping Vicky's mind off of her dancing but for keeping her mind off of him, Lermontov. Alex Doty strongly dismisses the "general cultural heterocentrism" that makes all of the many novelizations, synopses, reviews, and critical studies of *The Red Shoes* refer to Lermontov's jealousy of Craster rather than to the "gay impresario's vital investment in the diva as his erotically expressive stand-in."[74] Indeed, although Doty's reading is compelling and reasonable, it is not so easy to claim, as he does, that "[a]ll evidence onscreen and behind the scenes" is "to the contrary" of those who "insist upon heterosexualizing the Diaghilev-like Lermontov and his relationship with Page." After all, Vicky's dancing only becomes "impossible!" in Lermontov's eyes after he *discovers* her romance with Julian, not when the romance actually begins some weeks or months previously. Lermontov dismisses the prima ballerina whom Vicky replaces, Boronskaya (played by the "ample"—Powell's term—Tcherina), because, as he states, a dancer who relies on the comforts of human love and so on will "never be a great dancer—never!" And yet, as he says this, we are told by Massine/Grischa that Boronskaya is performing as she never has before—that she is dancing better *because* she is "in love" rather than in spite of it. And finally, there are a lot of publicity photographs showing Walbrook and Shearer in romantic clinches; I have never seen a single one, not even in press books, in which Shearer and Goring are in such poses.[75]

Moreover, Julian himself, as character after character states, is also so awesomely talented that firing him was probably as great a mistake on Lermontov's part as allowing Vicky to leave.[76] This is, perhaps, where the Diaghilevian elements of the film make the most sense, since Diaghilev

U.S. press-book detail, *The Red Shoes*, showing Lermontov and Vicky in a "romantic" pose.

Collection of the author.

seemed, at least, to be willfully capricious in his relationship with his artists. The firing of Nijinsky after he married was the source of the fictional Lermontov's action. And there is no slight inconsistency in Lermontov's willingness to *re*hire the married (hence "finished") Boronskaya in Vicky Page's place. And finally, the night that Lermontov actually finds out about the Vicky-Julian romance, he had booked a table for two at the best restaurant in Monte Carlo. Nevertheless, even in 1983, as revealed in Suzanne Gordon's book *Off Balance: The Real World of Ballet,* a student at the American Ballet Theatre school is reported as being "so moved and terrified by Moira Shearer's tragic end that she says she will never think of taking up with a man. 'I can't believe what that man did to her!' she exclaims. 'He made her choose between him and dance.'"[77]

Long Legs

One of the most startling things I learned about *The Red Shoes* from research in archives was the emphasis given to the "'long legs' symbol" in the film's U.S. public relations campaign.[78] Called the "most famous legs in the motion picture world today," the legs are not photographic but an artist's rendering of a pair of taut and crossed legs, in tights and *en pointe*, from the thighs down. They belong not to a real woman and seem to have almost nothing to do with the film's content or approach to ballet, yet they remain on the cover of the restored film's release on DVD. I cannot believe that the "long legs" symbol meant much to anyone besides the press agent who came up with it, but it does serve to set up another obvious effect of *The Red Shoes* and its popularity: its impact on the dance content of other films. (As mentioned, a film that has "long legs" in press-agent parlance is one that maintains its popularity over an extended period, which certainly fits *The Red Shoes*, too.) The "long legs" symbol could work as publicity for a number of subsequent musicals that all contain much more ballet than might otherwise have been the case pre–*Red Shoes;* indeed, such artists' renderings of impossible body parts, including legs in toe shoes, do show up in advertisements of other Hollywood ballet films.[79] The cachet given to Powell and Pressburger by the success of *The Red Shoes* enabled them to use some of the same production personnel, as well as performers (Shearer, Helpmann, Tcherina, for example), in their flamboyant Technicolor "composed film" *The Tales of Hoffmann* (1951), in which the dancers mouth the dubbed words of Offenbach's operetta as they dance the choreography of Frederick Ashton.

Gene Kelly would have had a career without *The Red Shoes,* but it did make long ballets viable commodities in Hollywood films again, too. When Kelly wanted to put a seventeen-minute-long ballet at the end of *An American in Paris* in 1950, he used *The Red Shoes* as evidence that classical ballet "could be done and had been done" successfully in popular films.[80] Michael Powell writes, "Gene Kelly told me that he ran *The Red Shoes* fifteen to twenty times for different executives at MGM before he got acceptance of his script . . . and then it was mainly because he had a foreign ballerina for the part—Leslie Caron. He was told that the success of *The Red Shoes* was due to the girl being foreign."[81] Saul Chaplin, who worked on *An American in Paris,* also remembers discussion of *The Red Shoes* and its "seventeen-minute ballet": *The Red Shoes* "had come out . . . and it was doing very well. That settled it. As long as they could do it, we *certainly* could do it, only do it better."[82] Once *An American in Paris* was released to wide critical acclaim and popular

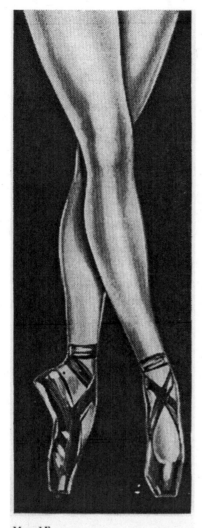

Mat IF

Most famous legs in the motion
picture world today are these,
symbolizing "THE RED SHOES,"
which opens . . . . . at the . . . . .
Theatre.

U.S. press-book detail, *The Red Shoes*;
the "long legs" ad.

Collection of the author.

success (it won the Academy Award for best picture in 1951, beating out *A
Streetcar Named Desire* and *The African Queen,* among others), no longer would
filmmakers have to hedge their bets in their dream ballets, as Minnelli had
in *Yolanda and the Thief,* by inserting a sprightly love song in the middle of
the dancing. So acceptable, in fact, did ballet become as a component of
movie musicals that even when an all-dance film such as Kelly's *Invitation*

to the Dance—made, primarily in England, for MGM in 1954 but not released until 1956—failed commercially, the failure was not blamed on too much ballet but on specifics such as the paucity of choreographic ideas and invention that marked Kelly's use of it, as well as on the poor quality of the special effects in the animated sequence.[83]

Moira Shearer did claim, vociferously and in public, to regret her participation in *The Red Shoes* from virtually the film's release on. Although it was her first film, made when she was twenty-one years old, it followed her throughout her life, freezing her forever at a point in her career when, as she put it, she was just about to make "a big jump forward" in both technical and artistic ability. She was preserved—in her own words "pickled"—too well too soon. While maintaining that "it is impossible for a participant to see it as the public sees it," she later wrote that it is the "colour, music and backstage story" that help to give *The Red Shoes* a "perennial allure,"[84] and indeed in the end the film is not so remarkable for anything in particular as much as for the balance it maintains among these effects. It was not just the long ballet, or the fact that the subject was ballet, or its stars, or its sinister mood, or its beautiful European scenery. *Tales of Hoffmann* had more ballet, more sinister a mood, and many beautiful effects, and the quality of its choreography and dancing was infinitely superior; but the film was cumulatively deadening, a little too garish and a little too vulgar for audiences and critics. The story of *The Red Shoes,* however conventional, remains moving, but I will always wonder what might have resulted had the filmmakers used the experience and knowledge possessed by their little ballet company, in addition to their performing abilities, to more coherent effect. Although the less ignorant one is about dance history the greater one's regard for the film because of the people who are in it and the era in ballet that it represents, there can also be a tendency to feel a certain amount of condescension toward it—partly because the technique is not virtuoso but mainly because it usually belongs to one's early years, so that it is something one is almost embarrassed to have been so affected by, with its "romantic view of art as diabolical," in Raymond Durgnat's words.[85]

THE QUESTION OF WHETHER art remains diabolical in the films that followed *The Red Shoes* will be addressed in the next chapter. Before moving on, however, I want to return briefly to melodrama, or rather melodrama's bodies. Much of the scholarship on stage and screen melodrama alludes in some way to the importance of the legibility and recognizability of the bodies that populate the melodramatic universe, where "the bodies of victims and villains must unambiguously signify their status," to quote Peter Brooks again.[86] An obvious question that now looms, after so many films, is who (or what) the villain *is* in a ballet film and how he or she (or it) is represented as such. Certainly we have met some quite apparent villains in a few films, regardless of how sympathetically we might be made to feel toward them from time to time—John Barrymore's Tsarakov with his club foot in *The Mad Genius*, Anton Walbrook's "attractive brute" and "cruel monster" Lermontov in *The Red Shoes*, marked visually as a vampire by his pasty skin and the white streak in his black hair.

But it is the ballerina who is given the most repetitive and consistent visual (and, often, aural, through the use of musical leitmotifs) treatment: tutus, toe shoes, tights, bird or flower iconography of various kinds. She is the character most frequently isolated from everyone else in the mise-en-scène, and only rarely are there others who are so easily identifiable by their bodies and clothing and, more and more frequently through the era we have been discussing, their bodies' actions as well. The ballet-dancing male is also more clearly or obviously visually different from other "ordinary" men who populate a film's visual field. In a film like *Dance, Girl, Dance*, it is no accident that the most powerful "normal" male onscreen, the impresario Steve Adams, is dressed like a mainstream businessman.

This brings up an interesting quandary. If the ballet film as a whole can be seen as a parable, to borrow Ben Singer's term once more, then it is impossible not to be fascinated by the way that ballet's body is perhaps itself the body of the villain, the sign of art's villainy, that which produces the ambivalence of pathos toward its victims but also the "agitation," in Singer's words, "that comes from observing extreme moral injustice, the feeling of distress, of being profoundly disturbed or outraged when we see vicious power victimizing the weak, usually involving some kind of bodily violence."[87] Is ballet's physical discipline—a physical discipline frequently represented, metonymically, as some sort of difficult and repetitive exercise, or through the "monsters" described above, but sometimes only mentioned in dialogue—the "bodily violence" that represses and injures its own bodies, bodies that must therefore be "rescued" by those who might promise normal life and domesticity? Is this not also indicated by the fruitlessness of some such attempted "rescues," with any deaths or incapacitating of the artists themselves (or of their loved ones) allegories of the works they perform? Even films that I have described as utopian to a degree—*Dance, Girl, Dance, The Men in Her Life, The Unfinished Dance*—are marked by moments of extreme pathos and violence.

Of course, the "highly expressive" mise-en-scène of film studies' "domestic" or "family" melodrama is well known.[88] There is often an "extreme compartmentalisation of the frame," in David Rodowick's words, "in which the decor of the home (via window and door frames, mirrors, partitions, grillework, etc.) is used to isolate the characters architecturally and emphasise the lack of human contact in their home environment."[89] The proscenium arch of the theater frequently functions this way in the ballet film as well, suggesting, perhaps, what is imagined to be the separateness and functional incompatibility of its way of life with "normality," even as the proscenium-as-frame is also employed as a malleable and permeable barrier. Performer and spectator frequently lock eyes in the ballet film across the footlights, indicating that extreme emotion can puncture the barrier. For those films in which a couple results from this textual mechanism it would be simplest to say that for "consummation" to take place both halves of the couple must move to the side occupied by the ballet's spectator, virtually always male: the proscenium must be crossed through and the theater life left behind. Yet there are films, among which I count *The Red Shoes* in its American context, in which the theater wins, in which the spectator who asks that the performer give up her avocation is cast aside in favor of a community of art and artists that sometimes, though not always, might also be a space where professional work and domesticity can potentially merge (the impresario and the ballerina might someday have a family of little dancers and impresarios of their own).

In addition, the utopian and communal dimensions that are usually thought to be more commonly ascribed to the film musical can sometimes trump the melodramatic, as it were, and greater realism of mise-en-scène or of dance ability does not necessarily correspond to greater reality in the plot's ability to reconcile art and life. *Dance, Girl, Dance, The Men in Her Life,* and *The Unfinished Dance,* for example, which are utterly risible in almost all ways relating to their depiction of the technique and training and practice of ballet itself, nevertheless function as potent counternarratives to *The Red Shoes.* What *The Red Shoes* can only acknowledge but not resolve except by death is blithely offered as a given in all of these films, *The Unfinished Dance* especially: that women have as much right to devote themselves to the pursuit of art as men do, and that becoming a fine dancer is a perfectly acceptable thing to give up rich and handsome suitors to work toward. My fondness for *The Red Shoes*—a fondness that, as I have mentioned, has nothing to do with Vicky's sanguinary demise or the choice that presumably led her to it—is also, then, itself ambivalent.

So was *The Red Shoes* more popular than all the other ballet films before it *because* of its morbidity or in spite of it? *The Red Shoes* comfortably confirmed or, rather, reconfirmed the opinions of those who wanted to believe the worst about art and artists and, particularly, the deviance and perversion of the ballet world (and, of course, it reified long-standing myths about the relationship of femininity and death in art). For such spectators, *The Red Shoes* was indeed, as Arlene Croce calls it, "a horror story . . . with dance supplying the main thrills."[90] But for others *The Red Shoes* made ballet real, tangible, professional, the extratextual relationship between its characters and the dance stars (or budding stars, in the case of Moira Shearer) who portrayed them a more potent message than all the film's renderings of well-worn conventions and platitudes. The morbidity and horror had been seen before; the ballet film with stars who were not only real theatrical dance stars but also potential movie stars, and who were demonstrably already reconciling art with life, was less familiar. Thanks to Hollywood-style bally-hoo, spectators could figure out that no one involved with *The Red Shoes* was likely to jump off a balcony in front of a train. They were having too much fun making art and becoming rich and famous.

Thus we arrive back at Arlene Croce's comment that *The Red Shoes* "capped the tradition of morbidity and raised the status of ballet in the movies at the same time. After that, things got healthier but duller."[91] It is a nice aphorism, but the situation, as we will see, is more complicated; health and, even more profoundly, disease, in fact, became governing metaphors in the postwar era on a number of cultural and political levels. While *The Red Shoes* and the increasing familiarity of ballet did substantially add to the number of dream ballets and women in toe shoes populating commercial films, there were fewer films with ballet protagonists made between 1948 and the end of the studio years in the 1960s than had appeared before, even if one excludes the silent features. The male ballet dancer as a significant character (one with lines, a name, some relationship to the action of the narrative) disappears almost entirely, not reappearing until the 1970s. At the same time, the Hollywood musical, partly under the influence of Broadway theater, worked to turn ballet into an American folk form, replacing the outward appurtenances of toe shoes, tutus, tiaras, and tights with gingham, jeans, sailor suits, khaki pants, and loafers. There are plenty of dancing men in *these* films, and they have been trained in ballet's techniques, but they do not look like the dancing men in *The Red Shoes*. In the next chapter I turn to the complex interactions of theatrical ballet, its dancers and their bodies, commercial cinema, and cold war politics in the 1950s. These interactions had lasting effects on what is frequently called the Americanization of ballet as an art form internationally from the 1950s through the 1970s, and help to account for how classical ballet could become the most familiar, success-ful, and lauded dance art while retaining, sometimes parodically, its aura of disease, decadence, and perversion—for its women as well as its men, their bodies as well as their hearts and souls—in the mediascape.

5

The Second Act
Will Be *Quite* Different

Cinema, Culture, and Ballet in the 1950s

I can't–I can't go on–my legs . . . I can't move–I'm paralyzed!

–Limelight, 1952

It isn't as if you have to be cooperative and reasonable like a normal human being. You're a ballerina–you're not supposed to be normal.

–Meet Me in Las Vegas, 1956

AMERICAN BALLET: Dance spectacle as performed by native dancers in New York City, through our provinces and the world entire in an international (melting-pot) manner, combining elements of the more suave and acrobatic Russian Imperial and Soviet Academies . . . pushed into a sharp, percussive, hard, clean accent, athletic and metrical which seems when exported to South America, Europe or the Orient, heartless, anti-theatrical (i.e. antipantomimic), under-clad, ill-decorated and relentlessly ingenious in its insistence on the academic classic dance as a propulsive or compulsive basis. . . .

 . . . We appear to the rest of the world exasperatingly capable of anything, good and bad. But there are not any paths of invention or range of performance that our home-grown dancers of energy find shut to them. This now happens to be untrue anywhere else in the world.

–Lincoln Kirstein, *What Ballet Is About: An American Glossary,* 1959

On October 9, 1949, the Sadler's Wells Ballet opened its first American season ever at the Metropolitan Opera House in New York City, with its own opulent full-length production of Tchaikovsky's *The Sleeping Beauty.* Ninette de Valois' British company was presented by impresario Sol Hurok, who had long been a supporter of ballet as popular entertainment but who had lately been having some bad luck with the companies he handled in the United States. According to one eyewitness chronicler of the event, dance historian Mary Clarke, the "Sadler's Wells in New York was more than a smash hit. It was the greatest ballet success ever known in that city, and rivalled the musical *South Pacific* in popularity and box-office takings (the Press, in fact, called the ballet *North Atlantic*)."[1] *Variety* placed the company's success on its front page in a banner headline: "Ballet Bowls over Broadway." It was reputedly the first time ballet had been headlined in this way since *Variety*'s founding in 1905.[2]

The Sadler's Wells Ballet was not already a well-known company in America, where audiences and some critics kept calling it the "Sadler Wells." The primary reason that tickets were selling out a full four months before the curtain would rise on the first scene of *The Sleeping Beauty*—indeed, the reason the tickets were put on sale four months in advance anyway ("for the first time in American theatrical history," according to Clarke)—was the presence of a single ballerina.[3] Not Margot Fonteyn, the company's official prima ballerina, but Moira Shearer, relegated that night to a third-act *divertissement*.[4] For many years since, Shearer's impact on the success of the Sadler's Wells in America has been dismissed either with a brief nod to the fact that "*The Red Shoes* had enjoyed great popularity in America" (Clarke's words)[5] or as something that the company's *real* success quickly obliterated and rendered moot. Because Margot Fonteyn herself did, in fact, dazzle audiences and critics that hot October Sunday night in 1949 in the starring role of Princess Aurora (while Shearer performed only in the "Blue Bird" pas de deux), whatever expectations Shearer's presence in the company might have generated quickly fell away or were abrogated by Fonteyn's triumphs.[6] The initial American season of the Sadler's Wells—which was followed by a second, and much more extensive, season and tour from 1950 to 1951 (when they visited thirty-two towns in the United States and Canada in the space of nineteen weeks)—was laid figuratively, then, at the feet of de Valois' protégée, Margot Fonteyn.[7] It was Fonteyn who appeared on the cover of *Time*, not Shearer;[8] it was Fonteyn who starred in the prime evening presentations of the company's other remarked-upon glories, its full-length classics (especially *Swan Lake* and, in the second tour, *Giselle*), as well as new ballets choreographed by the company's resident genius, Frederick Ashton.

This is not to take anything away from Fonteyn's abilities or her stature—which was indeed elevated tremendously by her reception in the United States. But more recently Fonteyn's biographer has again brought up what a lot of people were aware of at the time but apparently did not like to talk about—namely, *The Red Shoes*. The "difference which *The Red Shoes* made" to the growing fame of the Sadler's Wells, writes Meredith Daneman, "was, of course, all the difference in the world."[9] To Shearer's face, de Valois "laughed" at *The Red Shoes,* calling it "'ludicrous, so bad,' and [spreading] that around." Others, however, knew that de Valois had urged Shearer to do the film not as a "lark" or to get rid of Michael Powell who was "endlessly 'round bothering us" but as part of a strategic plan that began in late 1947 or early 1948, when discussions with Hurok to take the Sadler's Wells to America were initiated. As Clive Barnes explained to Shearer decades later about de Valois' interests in *The Red Shoes,* "My dear, she knew it would come out in '48, have an enormous showing all over America and be the perfect springboard for the company when you arrived in '49. She wanted you and Bobby [Helpmann] as forerunners—for Margot."[10]

Also in 1949, a special issue of the magazine *Holiday* was devoted to New York City, reporting specifically on how well the arts were faring therein and noting that New York was "on the way to becoming the artistic center of the world."[11] Museum and opera attendance was booming, but according to dance historian Lynn Garafola the major interest of the *Holiday* issue was "the great change since the First World War [in] public attitudes towards ballet." The magazine reported that "thanks to the New York City Ballet," which *Holiday* depicted in performance at the City Center for Music and Drama, ballet had "become firmly rooted in New York life." "Amazingly," Garafola states, "the company that had brought about this renaissance was only six months old."

While Balanchine's and Kirstein's New York City Ballet was indeed a significant addition to the cultural life not only of the city itself but of the nation as a whole (for reasons that will be discussed further below), clearly the company alone had not brought about the "renaissance" Garafola names. Garafola's 1999 anthology, *Dance for a City: Fifty Years of the New York City Ballet,* does not contain any mention of *The Red Shoes,* but it is hard to imagine that the New York City Ballet, no less than the Sadler's Wells, would have been quite as popular that first season without it. So I have begun this chapter with meditations on *The Red Shoes* in the context of "ballet bowling over Broadway" and New York becoming the "artistic center of the world" at the end of the 1940s because they serve to illustrate several important points under consideration here. First, they suggest that by the late 1940s, America, not Europe, had become the only place where a theatrical ballet company could become internationally successful, as Ninette de Valois knew. In contrast, Diaghilev in the teens had seen America as an artistic wasteland but maybe a cash cow; when it turned out the cash was not going to be forthcoming, he abandoned the enterprise altogether. Second, *in* America, ballet's increasing stature remained in fertile connection to its wide presence and fame as entertainment, particularly mass-mediated entertainment. There is always a distinction to be made about large urban centers like New York or Chicago, but still, just as *The Red Shoes* made "all the difference in the world" to the success of the Sadler's Wells, so did it, and a myriad other commercial films, to the growing audience for ballet across the United States. And in the 1950s television was increasingly featuring ballet in significant ways as well.

In fact, television's relationship to ballet in America is the source of one of my final introductory ruminations and brings up the chapter's arguably most bizarre subtopic. Jennifer Fisher's 2003 book *"Nutcracker" Nation* concerns the extraordinary popularity of the Russian ballet *The Nutcracker* in America, a popularity she locates with the first CBS television broadcasts, in 1957 and 1958, of the Balanchine version (danced of course by the New York City Ballet).[12] Fisher writes, in passing: "Even during the Cold War, when my mother was assuring her friends that my love for Russian ballet did not mean I was a Communist, most Americans appreciated *The Nutcracker*'s Russian heritage. Not its actual, detailed history. . . . But the general idea that the ballet is Russian has always appealed to Americans, providing as it does the assurance of 'the real thing.'"[13] A few weeks after I read this, I was going through an old scrapbook of my mother's and came across the program for the annual dance recital of the only dance studio in Vivian, Louisiana, in 1951. On its face the program quotes Russian dancer and choreographer Mikhail Mordkin: "Not that beautifully formed people dance, but those who dance become beautifully formed." Inside, the program lists several Russian ballet excerpts, noting that "*Les Sylphides* was first presented in St. Petersburg in 1908 [as] *Chopiniana* and assumed its present title when brought to Paris by Diaghilev."

Although the "Russianness" being invoked in both these instances is not Soviet Russianness but an Imperial, old-style, "White" Russianness, Fisher's remarks nevertheless struck me as a startling reminder that, as during World War I with all things German, Russianness *was* often equated with Sovietness during the 1950s and was demonized as a result. In Cecelia O'Leary's *To Die For: The Paradox of American Patriotism,* for example, O'Leary records the dilemmas faced by symphony orchestras during World War I, not only for playing German music—which then dominated the world of classical music—but also for having German conductors.[14] The Boston Symphony was not allowed to play in Baltimore in 1917 because of its German conductor, who was actually arrested by the Justice Department in 1918. As one politician exhorted a crowd during a protest meeting at the time, "What does art amount to when it is in competition with patriotism?"[15] During the 1950s, art's competition with patriotism would seem to have been even more protracted and contentious, as evidenced by the notorious HUAC investigations and the blacklisting of artists in Hollywood, television, radio, and the theater. But clearly not much seems to have been made of the Russianness of *ballet* during the cold war, not even in a tiny and very politically and culturally conservative town in north Louisiana.

Indeed, those who have studied the extensive and malign effects of red-baiting and McCarthyism on the film industry should be at least a bit startled to realize that the New York City Ballet was founded, with a Russian at its head, during the cold war to no great public outcry. More startling still perhaps is that 1957 Christmas *Nutcracker* television broadcast; Americans across the country not only watched Russian ballet, to Russian music, right in their own living rooms, but soon *The Nutcracker* would also become a strange, or strangely, American tradition, an annual holiday-season event supporting (still) any number of schools and regional companies across the country. But I have never come across any references in biographies or critical studies of Balanchine or of the New York City Ballet, for example, that discuss him or his company's success in the postwar era in light of or in contrast to what is so frequently referred to as "cold war paranoia." Hollywood films, on the other hand, have been exhaustively mined for their paranoid content, which was assumed by many scholars to have affected the entire country on virtually every level. What Michael Rogin refers to as the "political demonology" of this era often focused specifically on film and its industries: "Film, as HUAC investigators understood, was an intruder. It entered the unconscious of those who watched movies in darkened theaters throughout the land."[16] Geoffrey Smith famously wrote in the journal *Diplomatic History* in 1994, "Only now have historians begun to sense that [the cold war] became a rationale for nearly everything in American life and culture."[17] Is it merely that art, or at least ballet, was immune to politics, or ignored by it, or was the cold war warmer in some cases than others?

The short answer is no, that ballet is not immune to politics, and certainly not in the 1950s. In fact, ballet began to be very explicitly linked to national and international politics during this era. As Naima Prevots reveals in her 1998 book *Dance for Export: Cultural Diplomacy and the Cold War,* the cold war actually instantiated a whole new "official" attitude toward the arts in general and dance in particular, as from the mid-1950s on the U.S. government employed the performing arts, including modern dance and ballet, as a way to enhance America's image abroad.[18] Rather than relying only on popular entertainment such as Hollywood movies, which tended to present the nation as one of "gum-chewing, insensitive, materialistic barbarians" (to quote a New Jersey senator urging federal sponsorship of the arts), art would be employed to show that Americans were free, expressive, cultured, and inventive. Three ballet companies were eventually sent to the Soviet Union. Negotiations began in the 1950s about which companies would best represent America, with American Ballet Theatre eventually being the first to tour the U.S.S.R. in 1960, followed by the New York City Ballet and the Robert Joffrey Ballet of Chicago. The Ballet Russe de Monte Carlo was, however, rejected, on the grounds that its tired repertoire did not "give the world a vision of ballet that was contemporary, exciting, and made in the U.S.A." No, its repertoire was predominantly Russian.

Also, of course, there is an ever-increasing number of social historians, like Joanne Meyerowitz and Peter Filene, whose own research has suggested that the cold war was far from uniformly conservative or paranoid and who have identified sources of dissent within cold war culture itself.[19] Filene argues that the cold war was "fought primarily at an elite level. It pervaded and shaped the experience of ordinary Americans far less than historians would have us believe."[20] For Filene, then, "the story of Cold War culture is more ambiguous and complicated than Americans then or since have recognized." Again, one searches in vain for references to cold war politics in dance-history books (with Prevots' study a notable exception), even in sections that detail how the center of the ballet world did in fact complete its shift from Europe to New York City in the 1950s. Several film-studies scholars, among them Jane Feuer, Rick Altman, and Jerome Delamater, have indirectly acknowledged wartime and postwar politics in their discussions of the rise of the folk musical of the 1940s and 1950s.[21] But here, too, the issue is primarily framed in terms of the increasing integration of number and narrative in the musical as a genre, although Altman's lengthy study does address the development of the folk musical subgenre—with its darker overtones, its emphasis on family and/as community, its deployment of a mythic Midwest as the locus of American values—as a response to the nostalgia and ideological pressures of World War II and its aftermath. Moreover, as we well know by now, ballet's presence in movies is not just limited to musicals.

If this introduction seems somewhat disjointed, it is because the issues under consideration in this chapter shake out even less neatly than has been true up till now. There are a number of cross-currents at work, as in the 1950s themselves, and peculiar conjugations and paradoxes abound. I have been arguing that theatrical ballet acquired a new and broader but always ambivalent audience through ballet's increasing presence in commercial cinema from at least the 1930s on. But few histories of theatrical ballet, especially theatrical ballet of the postwar era, remark on this, as though the audiences for movies and theatrical ballet were separate, distinct. From the late 1950s, ballet was perceived by the U.S. government as a potential weapon in international culture wars that enhanced ballet's public recognition and stature at home. But at the same time, a significant degree of antitheatrical prejudice remained part of the public discourse about performing arts generally and ballet specifically. Even as ballet was "bowling over Broadway," or Walter Terry was writing in *Look* that "[b]allet isn't high-brow anymore" ("No longer box-office poison, ballet is fast becoming mass entertainment"), Sol Hurok and others were publicly bemoaning the fact that, in terms of American support for the arts, "the situation becomes steadily grimmer."[22] And, as mentioned in previous chapters, in 1959—one year before American Ballet Theatre was sent to the U.S.S.R. by the State Department—Olga Maynard was agonizing in print about the ballet audience and its fear of the "pervert on the stage."[23] It is relatively well known that President Dwight Eisenhower in the early 1950s began to purge "homosexuals" from federal payrolls,[24] but less well known is the fact that in the interests of cultural diplomacy he would send ballet companies and their numerous "perverts" abroad a few years later as federally sanctioned and sponsored cultural ambassadors.

The Hollywood musical also came to be identified in the late 1940s and 1950s by its long ballets; the commercial and, especially, critical success of big-budget Technicolor films like *On The Town* (1949), *An American in Paris* (1951), *Singin' in the Rain* (1952), *The Band Wagon* (1953), and a host of others—often MGM products—is inseparable from the increase in their deployment of ballet as dance. But the nonmusical ballet film, despite more flamboyant production values (more of them are in color too), seemed at first to remain almost as morbid, its artists often just as unhealthy or sexually perverse, as had been the case in the 1940s or before—except, paradoxically, for the Russians and, even more paradoxically, those Russians who were also Soviet. By the end of the 1950s, however, the conventions of the tradition of morbidity,[25] and of the cheerful boy-meets-girl structure and syntax of the musical itself, were no longer sufficient to sustain their narratives and had become something of a residue, or the object of often comic parody.

Improving the Entertainment Standards of the Community

Despite the list of big-budget successes above, Hollywood's own fortunes were in decline in the 1950s; the musicals named were so expensive to produce that they actually made relatively little profit. The decline had begun in the late 1940s—with 1946 being among Hollywood's most prosperous years ever, and 1947 (the year President Harry Truman officially declared a "cold war," of containment, against the Soviet Union) one of its worst. Several notable events conveniently mark the decrease in the big studios' hegemony over the acquisition of the American entertainment dollar.[26] First, Hollywood's compliance with the Office of War Information during World War II helped to grant it the status of an essential industry, exempting it from wartime restrictions and rationing; price controls on materials and labor also helped Hollywood earn large profits through the end of the war. But by the late 1940s, inflation raised the prices of virtually everything—from the lumber with which sets were constructed to film stock itself (which increased enormously in price in just a few years), as well as the giant labor force that the studios held under contract—even as theatrical attendance began what would turn out to be a permanent and inexorable decline. Second, the Justice Department resumed its antitrust activities, with what is commonly known as the "Paramount decrees," a consent agreement entered into by the major studios that controlled the means of film production, distribution, and exhibition. The agreement forced the biggest studios to divest themselves of one of the three over the period between 1948 and 1952; those that owned them chose to sell their theaters. Third, HUAC's investigations into "communist activity" in Hollywood in 1947 and again in 1951 (and 1953, 1955, 1956, and 1958) led to the blacklisting of many of its most talented, and successful, writers, directors, and actors.

In addition, the Production Code, Hollywood's self-censorship mechanism that had substantially determined the narrative trajectories of Hollywood films since the early 1930s, was first challenged officially and then permanently undermined in the 1950s. The 1952 "*Miracle* decision," as it is usually called, finally granted movies the First Amendment protection they had been denied back in 1915. This development sounded the eventual death-knell of the Hollywood film as always already "family fare" that upheld the sanctity of heterosexual marriage and the integrity of the government and religious institutions, refused the depiction of graphic violence or the exercise of human sexuality (or its results—the word *pregnant* had not been uttered in a Hollywood film for at least two decades), and outlawed "sex relations between the white and black races." The prohibition of "miscegenation" had had particularly malign effects on the racial politics of American cinema; since by far the majority of Hollywood narratives feature one or more major romance plots, it relegated to minor or specialty roles virtually all actors of color appearing in studio films. Musicals themselves began to seem puerile and naive, no longer convincing as coded representations of male-female relations, where the physical contact of the romantic "couple dance" took the place of more overt expressions of adult sexuality.

The Miracle, the attempted censorship of which had provoked the lawsuit that resulted in the "*Miracle* decision," was a short 1948 Italian neorealist film by Roberto Rossellini released in the United States in 1950. And another hard fact for Hollywood to bear was the growing competition it faced from small independent producers and foreign films, exhibited often in art houses (into one of which *The Red Shoes* had first been booked). These films, which seemed so refreshingly honest about matters of sexuality, politics, and religion, also affected the content of American films. So, of course, did the little box with the bulging glass screen and the rabbit ears in the now increasingly suburban living room. Widescreen and stereo sound thus became the industry norm by the end of the 1950s, too, except for cheap "exploitation" films and "teenpix" aimed at an adolescent youth market. Yet another of the paradoxes of the 1950s in film terms, then, is that Hollywood ratcheted up the level of sex and violence and epic spectacle to compete with television and more "adult" European fare, even as it made more and more "safe" films to avoid roiling conservative waters. Many exhibitors, striving to heed official demands "to improve the entertainment standards of the community," were finding that previously reliable "family fare" was producing "sorry returns."[27] Again, it is usually seen as ironic that the most glorious Technicolor musicals with the biggest and most spectacular numbers were made in an era that also heralded the genre's demise in the 1960s. MGM's big CinemaScope and Technicolor musical in 1957 was *Silk Stockings*, starring Fred Astaire, who was then fifty-eight years old; MGM also made that year, in black-and-white and on a relative shoestring, *Jailhouse Rock*, with Elvis Presley. The latter film produced, not surprisingly from our vantage point at least, much the bigger financial return.

Despite demographic changes and Hollywood's own shifting fortunes, or perhaps because of them, the most obvious difference between pre–and post–*Red Shoes* "movie ballet" is the variety and sheer ubiquity of ballet across a wide range of films (musical comedies, "ballet mellers," espionage films, biopics, drawing-room comedies and farces, even several "all-dance" films, among which I include Powell and Pressburger's 1951 *Tales of Hoffmann*), most with far higher production values than had been the case in the 1930s or 1940s. Ballet dancing is everywhere, whether integrated into the narrative or not; and with few exceptions, the dancing is performed by trained theatrical dancers. More significant, these dancers are far more *recognizable* to us today as ballet dancers because of the increasing attenuation of the ballet line, the increasing fitness of the ballet body, the increasing emphasis on virtuoso technique, and, across the decade, an increase in abstraction, of dance for dance's sake. But if the offstage icon fades away—few if any films are about ballet dancers who are not also shown dancing, although the dancing may still be performed by a double—even the trained dancers who take on film roles in ballet films frequently play characters whose horizons are still limited by their dedication to the art and, more troublingly, by their gender. At the same time, and again paradoxically, ballet's wider presence and larger identity in the mediascape means that the narratives of ballet films, especially their conventional constructions of the ballet artist, become even more obviously just one part of an intertextual nexus of the meanings that ballet possesses at this time. By the end of the decade it is clear that the message of a film as expressed in dialogue and plot comes to matter less than the message of a film's ballet bodies and their abilities—not only their ability to dance but to become rich and famous movie stars as a result of their dancing prowess. As in the case of *The Red Shoes*, these films, despite their frequent tragic outcomes, function equally as fantasies of achievement and as cautionary tales about the incompatibility of art and life. If there was a capping of the tradition of morbidity, in other words, it occurred not with *The Red Shoes* but in the films of the decade that followed it.

If You Can Disregard the Plot (Again)

In fact, the line from a *Red Shoes* review that I used as the title of the previous chapter can be used as a sort of mantra for the ballet film in the 1950s. A brief summary of the narratives of a few of the era's films gives an idea of just how familiar the plots would have been: a young dancer is training in New York but falls in love with a sailor whom she will marry and follow to a life of happy domesticity in a midwestern town; a Scottish soldier falls in love with a beautiful young Russian ballet dancer in postwar Austria, but she kills herself; a beautiful young ballerina who believes her legs are paralyzed recovers and becomes a world-famous dancer but loses an older man she loves; a beautiful young dancer gives new inspiration to a male impresario who falls in love with her, but on the same day she dies, and his dreams and creativity are crushed; a ballerina falls in love with an American soldier, but when she believes he is dead she becomes a prostitute, only to discover he is still alive after all (yes, *Waterloo Bridge* was remade in the 1950s). The number of beautiful young ballerinas increases exponentially, and as these descriptions indicate, they are incredibly desirable and romantic figures. Read narratively, it would be quite difficult to support Croce's assertion that things are "healthier," but contra Croce, it is the familiarity of the unhealthiness that itself becomes dull.[28] Not surprisingly, the pervasive aura of Pavlova and dying swans, disease and perversity, comes by the end of the decade to be a source of humor in films that otherwise treat ballet quite seriously. Since everyone knows that a ballerina is "not supposed to be normal," she can deploy her identity in ways calculated to achieve her own ends.

We have seen comic self-reflexivity in the ballet film before: in *Shall We Dance* (1937), where the ballet dancer's presumed Russianness is deployed strategically by Fred Astaire as the American Pete Peters, who is pretending to be the Great Petrov. Or in *Dance, Girl, Dance* (1940), where the assumption that ballerinas must be birds or flowers (rather than figures of "today") is derided. Or in *The Philadelphia Story* (also 1940), where child actress Virginia Weidler dons toe shoes and speaks French as an act designed to exhibit a horrifying, if comic, level of snooty Main-Line pretentiousness. And of course Stan Laurel performing the "Dance of the Pelican" in a long white tutu or Red Skelton in a short pink one both lampoon assumptions about the correct gender of the ballet practitioner (leaving aside the gender *and* species issues of the animated tutued and toe-dancing animals in Disney's 1940 *Fantasia*). Films of the 1950s are similar in their comic treatments, but they more frequently turn received wisdom on its head. The sketch in *The Philadelphia Story* is an act, a disguise, but the assumptions that give it its comic edge remain in place. In a film of the 1950s, on the other hand, the assumptions themselves are often shown to be wrong. And ultimately, it is dancing that functions most significantly in this regard, its glories trumping any nonsense in the narrative about ballet's malign effects on life, health, sanity. Men are not absent, but they are rarely given narrative identities as ballet dancers. Rather, they are either dancers à la Gene Kelly or Fred Astaire, performing ballet-based choreography but strenuously avoiding any association in the plot between what they are doing and the "sissy" art of ballet; or they are ballet dancers, often uncredited, who perform for us on the screen but who are nameless and characterless—male versions of the film showgirl, in other words. Or, finally, they are once again nondancing impresario/geniuses, for whom dancing women function increasingly as muses.[29]

To trace these developments across time, I will focus most on films made from 1952 to 1956 in which ballet dancers—always women—are main characters: *Limelight* and *Hans Christian Andersen* (both 1952), *The Story of Three Loves* (specifically its first section, "The Jealous Lover") and *The Band Wagon* (both 1953), *Dance Little Lady* (1955), and, more briefly, *Gaby* and *Meet Me in Las Vegas* (both 1956). It should be noted at the outset that in not one of these films is the ballet protagonist Russian. There are, however, several films in which "Russianballet" is the only ballet there is, and I am going to start with these, my goal being to contextualize the issue of the "American-ization" of ballet in film, as well as theater, and to be able to understand why ballet could seem the ideal vehicle for promulgating American values abroad and also remain the source of significant amounts of hostility and "fear" among some segments of the American audience.

This Is the *Real* Ballet Russe

Russian ballet makes several noteworthy cameo appearances in American films during and following World War II. In 1943, in *Mission to Moscow*, it made perfect political sense to glorify the Soviet ballet of our wartime allies; thus, Eleanor Parker, playing the daughter of ambassador Joseph Davies (Walter Huston), can gaze through her binoculars at Galina Ulanova (played by an unbilled Cyd Charisse in her second film) and exclaim, "I like this even better than the Ballet Russe in New York," to which her Soviet host responds, "This is the *real* ballet Russe." The dancing, with Charisse (then going by the name of Lily Norwood) partnered by an uncredited Michael Panaieff (a real Russian dancer, who began performing in the United States in the 1940s and choreographed the dancing here and in several other films), is brief, shot primarily in extreme long shot and in a closer overhead shot (the film is in black and white). If there is a queasy edge here, it comes from the simultaneous beginning, during the ballet itself, of the Moscow purges, and ballet is neither seen nor referred to again.[30]

In *Never Let Me Go* (1953), on the other hand, a black-and-white MGM film that features overt references to and inserted documentary footage of Stalin, reporter Philip Sutherland (Clark Gable) falls in love with a Russian ballerina, Marya (Gene Tierney), who is, naturally, "a swan"—"the number four swan, to be exact"—and apparently dances nothing but *Swan Lakes*. Because ballet is not mentioned in early drafts of the script (the Marya character is simply a "Russian bride"), I assume that ballet was added precisely because of its, or *Swan Lake*'s, amorphous association with romance, especially doomed romance.[31] Tierney is not a bad actress but she is an abysmal dancer, despite all assertions in the film's press book that had Tierney "not chosen a film career she might have been an outstanding ballerina," claims made "on record" by the film's choreographer (he also dances and acts briefly), Anton Dolin.[32] Marya's lines, and Tierney's accent, render much of the dialogue hilarious ("Can you feel my heart pushing?" she asks Philip/Gable their first night alone. "It's like little animal. Has much movement!"). When Philip and Marya marry, Philip is unable to get his bride out of Russia legally, so he makes plans to go in himself and spirit her away across the Black Sea. But, just like the happy ending mandated for *Swan Lake* by Soviet authorities, ballet itself is treated lightly and quite positively in *Never Let Me Go*. Marya has no intention of giving up the ballet after their marriage: "I would not stop dancing!" And she is going to teach their children to dance: "Dancing gives them pretty bodies. You want our children to have pretty bodies, yes?" And during the months that Philip spends devising the plan that will get Marya into his hands—during a performance of *Swan Lake*—Marya rises to become prima ballerina in the company, a position she has always planned to achieve. No anguish or despair waiting for her new husband to rescue her, she just keeps on achieving her career goals.

Moreover, the performance of the first-act pas de deux from *Swan Lake* that we do see in *Never Let Me Go* is performed (in long shot, of course, but also in long takes) by renowned but uncredited Sadler's Wells ballerina Violetta Elvin, partnered by Dolin. And then, as planned, Marya collapses onstage and Philip, pretending to be a doctor, takes over, simultaneously invoking and rendering spurious the association of the ballerina-as-swan with disease and death. There is an ambitious and evil Russian ballerina who lurks about Marya, played by Belita (a single-name actress who made several other mostly low-budget films in the 1940s and 1950s playing ballet dancers, ice-skaters, and swimmers—sometimes all three in the same film), who almost scotches their plans—until Philip points out that she will be prima ballerina herself once Marya is gone.

Possibly the most famous "good Russians" of the era occur in the aforementioned MGM widescreen Technicolor musical *Silk Stockings,* in 1957, based on a Cole Porter stage musical of 1953 that was itself based on a 1939 (nonmusical) Ernst Lubitsch film, *Ninotchka,* advertised as the first film in which "Garbo laughs!" In *Silk Stockings* (as in *Ninotchka*), nostalgia for Russia as a land of "blinis and sour cream" is opposed to the U.S.S.R.'s steel factories and workers; a land of "hospitality," good food, and dancing, to gulags and Siberia. Belita once again plays a Russian ballet dancer (there is no ballet in *Ninotchka*) in a brief scene where she is shown pirouetting and then leaping into the lap of and strenuously kissing a comical "commissar of the arts" who has promised "to make [her] prima ballerina." Despite its obvious generic claim to being a fluffy "champagne" musical comedy, the queasy edge is stronger in *Silk Stockings* than perhaps any other of the films of the era, in part because it is a glossy musical featuring comic songs about Siberia, in part because its sexual politics are so reactionary. Cyd Charisse plays a dour Soviet commissar who becomes a simpering "woman" by giving herself up to the pleasures of Western consumer culture and to an American movie producer, Steve, played by Fred Astaire.

But, in terms of the Americanization of ballet that occurs across the decade, the most interesting interaction of the Russian and the American in the 1950s occurs in two Technicolor musical biopics, *Million Dollar Mermaid* (1952), about Australian swimmer Annette Kellerman and starring Esther Williams, and *Tonight We Sing* (1953), based on the life of impresario Sol Hurok, played by David Wayne. Both films feature interpretations of Anna Pavlova and, therefore, competing versions of her best-known solo, *The Dying Swan.* In the first film Pavlova is played by Maria Tallchief and in the second by Tamara Toumanova.

However odd the casting may seem, having the Russian Pavlova played by the Native American, Oklahoma-born Tallchief was solid and conventional star politics. Maria Tallchief was then among the most famous ballerinas in America, the biggest star of the New York City Ballet and married to George Balanchine. Her "ideal ballerina's legs—long, shapely, strong but not muscular," had even appeared on the cover of the 1952 *Holiday* magazine mentioned earlier, a real-life version of the "long legs" *Red Shoes* advertising campaign. Conversely, employing Tallchief to impersonate the most famous Russian ballerina of all time also made Russian ballet's Russianness nothing to worry about, easy for an American dancer to assume, to perform, to discard, to assimilate. Indeed, Americans are better, the casting implies, at dancing ballet than the Russians are or ever were. Tallchief/Pavlova here also serves as inspiration to Williams/Kellerman, assuring her that just as they

Maria Tallchief as Anna Pavlova in *Million Dollar Mermaid* (1952).
Courtesy National Film Archive, London.

now say there is only one Pavlova, someday they will say, "There is only one
Annette Kellerman" (and, by implication, "only one Esther Williams" and
"only one Maria Tallchief").[33]

There was no apparent political fallout for the Russian Toumanova,
who had starred in one of the most pro-Soviet of all wartime films, *Days of
Glory* (1944) (see chapter 2), nor would there be for her impersonation of
Pavlova in *Tonight We Sing*. Toumanova performs several ballet numbers,

Tamara Toumanova as Anna Pavlova in *Tonight We Sing* (1953).
Courtesy National Film Archive, London.

the longest of which, an excerpt from the pas de deux from *Don Quixote*, was one of Toumanova's best-known showstoppers rather than Pavlova's. And in general, it is not Toumanova's flamboyant, flashy, rather brittle dancing that matters but her accent and face and, again, Toumanova's fame itself. Both *Million Dollar Mermaid* and *Tonight We Sing* are marked by their pleasure in ballet as a form of star-based spectacle, with stardom—here acquired in theatrical ballet first—serving, rather than "Russianness," as the marker of authenticity. *Tonight We Sing* opens with Toumanova dancing before we even know that she is going to be playing Pavlova.

A final, somewhat anomalous Russian ballerina occurs in a British film distributed in the United States by United Artists, *The Man Who Loved Redheads* (1955), starring Moira Shearer. This adaptation of a Terence Rattigan play called *Who Is Sylvia?* concerns an upper-class boy who meets a redheaded girl and falls in love with her and then spends the rest of his life pursuing women who look like her. Shearer plays both the girl and the three later iterations of her, and by far the longest segment of the film is devoted to the third version of the redheaded girl in the person of Olga, a "temperamental but tender," in the words of the *New York Times*'s reviewer, Russian ballerina (there is no ballerina in the play) who performs, with

John Hart, a beautifully staged version of the third-act pas de deux from *The Sleeping Beauty* (arranged and with some new group choreography by Alan Carter).[34] All reviewers agreed that the ballet performance, as "clean and sharp as it is" (according to *Time*), has nothing to do with the rest of the film.[35] But the character of Olga is significant not only as yet another attractive and appealing Russian but also for the lines she utters—one of which I borrowed to serve as this chapter's title—when she finds out her middle-aged lover is married, not a spy but merely a boring civil servant, and is going to leave her to go back to his family, lines that simultaneously acknowledge and scorn ballet's tradition of morbidity: "After all, it is only the first act of *Giselle*. The prince, disguised as the peasant. But you need not fear anything. . . . I shall not go mad, and die, and come back as a ghost. The second act will be *quite* different."

What should one make of all these good Russians in 1950s films, especially in films that predate the death of Stalin in 1953 or the declining political power of HUAC and Joseph McCarthy after his condemnation in the Senate in 1954? Clearly the "Russian" of Russian ballet does come to stand in this era for a "good" Russia, a romanticized "lost" Russia of art and music, but these films, in combination with the others I explore below, begin to suggest ways in which ballet's meanings were being negotiated much more overtly in relation to nationality in the 1950s. With ballet "firmly rooted" in the life not only of New York but in small towns across the country, and with federal sponsorship of the arts, beginning with Eisenhower's Emergency Fund for International Affairs in 1954, developing as a means to counter Soviet notions of the United States as, again, a society of "gum-chewing, insensitive, materialistic barbarians," it certainly would be difficult to conclude that ballet was simply so innocuous, so fanciful or decorative, as not to matter in any overtly political sense at this period in American culture. Moreover, it is well known that avant-garde painters and painting, such as Jackson Pollock and abstract expressionism, were controversial at home but employed abroad to "promote America's creative freedom" in direct opposition to Soviet-style social realism.[36] On the one hand, classical ballet's aesthetic credentials seem much less problematic than those of abstract expressionism, but on the other hand, they certainly clash with various ingrained and emerging cold war attitudes about sexuality.

In the early 1950s, panic over the "corrosive influence" of homosexuality initiated purges of gay men and lesbians from the federal payroll, and in 1953 Eisenhower issued an executive order barring gay men and lesbians from all federal jobs. Thus, when hearings were held requesting continuance of the Emergency Fund for the arts in 1955 and 1956, it is perhaps not surprising that there was substantial resistance to paying even relatively meager sums to support the performing arts.[37] Given all that has been discussed in the previous chapters, I believe that any hostility might well have been a sign that this or that congressman simply had seen some ballet films in the 1930s and 1940s and thus associated the art form, especially in relation to its men, with perversion and disease, as well as a certain fluffy prettiness. While Prevots believes that any opposition to supporting the arts with federal dollars came simply from ignorance rather than distaste or hostility, Olga Maynard did devote quite a number of pages in 1959 to arguing that male ballet dancers are not all homosexual (although "There have always been, and there remain, a number of homosexuals in ballet and the theatre in general," ballet cannot be held responsible for the fact).[38]

So ballet was both full of homosexuals and so fine and so finely representative of America's achievements in the arts that it could be sent abroad to represent "us" as exemplary of our good taste, our creative freedoms, our talent and ability, and so on. And in the late 1950s the United States hosted several soviet dance troupes, beginning with the Moiseyev dancers in 1958 and followed soon by the Bolshoi. Interestingly, one of the first things that *any* state entity, capitalist, socialist, or communist, does to proclaim its international status is to found a classical ballet company—China, Cuba, many Latin American countries, and of course in some sense the United States, too, all have done this. But given the attitudes demonstrated in the congressional hearings Prevots recounts, or in Maynard's book, it cannot be said that ballet just does not matter politically in the 1950s. In fact, the success of Eisenhower's program, and of artists as cultural ambassadors, helped pass a 1958 bill establishing a National Cultural Center, which led to the shaping and development of the National Endowment for the Arts six years later.[39] The unironic ambivalence or contradictions in American culture and politics at this time are ultimately what are most fascinating: ballet was growing in popularity locally at the same time that the pervasiveness of cold war paranoia required Jennifer Fisher's mother to assure her friends that love for Russian ballet did not automatically make one a communist. Hollywood as an industry was bowing to HUAC on all sorts of levels at the same time that it was making films in which Russian ballet was the most appealing it arguably had ever been (or has been since), as well as employing ballet as a dance form to raise its own prestige levels.

Much of the ballet in 1950s films was *not* identified as Russian, however, and this is one of the most significant things about them. The only politics they invoke relate to sexuality and gender. As mentioned, male ballet dancers virtually disappear as protagonists from films of the era (although the camp turn continues; in *Knock on Wood* [1954], for example, an espionage comedy, Danny Kaye plays a ventriloquist who accidentally drops into an opera-ballet performance, where he hilariously partners Balanchine ballerina Diana Adams in a harem number). Sans the outward appurtenances of the danseur (tights especially), the male "dancer with balls," to employ once more Stanley Donen's famous characterization of Gene Kelly's persona, instead populates the folk musical subgenre and its many ballet set pieces (to which we will return).[40] Ballerinas, on the other hand, are everywhere—French, British, American, Danish. Most of the films I discuss below, with the exception of Charles Chaplin's *Limelight* and Vincente Minnelli's *The Band Wagon,* are obscure now, but they were all widely reviewed and did reasonably well at the box office on their original releases. Ironically, *Limelight* was Chaplin's last American film because of his refusal to submit to HUAC questioning and the revocation of his reentry permit to the United States after a worldwide *Limelight* promotion tour. The American Legion called for a boycott of *Limelight* as well, denouncing Chaplin, who had never become a U.S. citizen, as a communist "fellow traveler." The narratives of the films are, as mentioned, conventional, already familiar (the "second act" is not different on the level of story, in other words); but this allows for greater degrees of self-reflexivity, of satire, of cultural carelessness—of assuming that "the normative" is so hegemonic that no evidence need be supplied of its validity.

Moreover, the increase in the dance quotient in films of the era—the disappearance of the offstage icon—cannot simply be seen as "adding spectacle" in the usual senses that feminist film theory would imply. That is, the dancing does not render the women into passive, inactive, and fetishized objects of the heterosexual male gaze. Nor are the films mere imitations of *The Red Shoes,* although there are a few jaded aesthetes and geniuses looking for inspiration and finding it in the faces and bodies and dancing of young ballerinas. It is the fact that Hollywood continued to rely on outworn, clichéd, and highly stylized renderings of the dancer's life and existence, as against the extraordinary emphasis, in promotion and publicity materials, on the dancer-as-star and the complexity of ballet as a form of dance art, that makes the films so interesting and "different."

The Dancing's Excellent But the Comedy's Poor

Chaplin's *Limelight,* "the story of a ballerina and a clown" as an opening title card states, is set in London in 1914, invoking the era of Compton Mackenzie's *Carnival.* The camera tracks from the street to end up finally on a young woman, with heart-shaped Pavlova-like face and dark hair, lying with closed eyes in a bed. As the camera continues its perambulations around the room, we see that a suicide is in progress—bottle in her hand, oven wide open, towel crammed under the front door. Chaplin, playing an over-the-hill alcoholic music-hall clown named Calvero, rescues the young woman, Thereza (Terry, played by Claire Bloom)—who refers to herself as "helpless," "destitute," "ill"—and takes her under his wing. Given the adjectives Terry applies to herself, and her inability to speak without breaking down in tears, it is not at all a surprise to find that she is "a member of the Empire Ballet," or was until her legs became paralyzed suddenly.

Calvero decides that Terry's paralysis is mental rather than physical, diagnosing it as "psychoanesthesia," and she begins soon to dance again. Terry's story is mirrored in the new ballet for which she wins the lead role, the story of Harlequin and Columbine, which begins with Columbine's death in bed and ends with her return as a spirit, to dance with and inspire her mourning lover. There is even a troupe of other wili-like spirits, à la *Giselle*, who accompany Columbine's appearances, and in fact the story of the film concerns Calvero's redemption as well as Terry's. On opening night of the new ballet, Terry's paralysis returns—"I can't go on—my legs ... I can't move!" Calvero slaps her and orders her onstage, and she becomes an overnight success. (Calvero asks her the next morning, "How's it feel to wake up famous?") Calvero also has a new chance onstage that night, but judgment about the show, which Calvero overhears, is that the "dancing's excellent but the comedy's poor." Crushed by his own failure at professional rejuvenation, Calvero removes himself from Terry's life and resumes the alcoholism that had killed his career. Although she is shown in a montage sequence dancing in the capitals of Europe, Terry remains attached to Calvero and very dependent on him. He dies in the wings, watching her dance after his own "return performance"—a gala benefit in which Chaplin and Buster Keaton perform an extended comedy act—and presumably Terry will remain famous and is free now to marry the young composer who has been following her around for years.

Limelight was written, directed, and scored by Chaplin, and according to end credits the choreography of the ballet was by Andre Eglevsky, Melissa Hayden, and Charles Chaplin too (with the corps de ballet led by Carmelita Maracci). Eglevsky dances the role of Harlequin, is never named as a character, and has no presence other than as dance spectacle. Hayden, then a principal dancer with the New York City Ballet, doubles for Claire Bloom. She is therefore shown only from the rear or in long shot on the stage where the lack of facial and physical resemblance—of body shape, stance, gesture, and so on—is less noticeable. The choreography is repeated several times; the same steps are performed during the audition, the ballet itself on opening night, in the montage sequence, and in the final shots as Calvero dies offstage. Hayden's technique bears little resemblance to music-hall ballet or, more significant, earlier film ballet, not even Vera Zorina's; it is, by comparison, athletic, sharp, pulled-up, the muscles taut, with control and precision visible in every movement, and with little emotion conveyed through either gesture, facial expression, or larger physical movements. Ironically, its recognizability as ballet to audiences now comes from Balanchine's aggrandizing in American ballet of "a sharp, percussive, hard, clean accent, athletic and metrical," in Lincoln Kirstein's words.[41] Andre Eglevsky, on the other hand, is a "softer" dancer of what was becoming an old-fashioned ballet-russe style; his positions are less angular and less clearly defined in space, his turnout is not as extreme, his toes are not always pointed, and so on—nor, again, does he have a name, or a voice, or any other narrative identity in the film. As with Maria Tallchief's appearance as Pavlova in *Million Dollar Mermaid* the same year, the dancers seem to have been selected as exemplary through their theatrical credentials, and clearly American women dancers were becoming well known. The ranks of American male ballet dancers, however, were less populated. Even Eglevsky, a renowned Russian-born French dancer, is featured only to dance; he is just a spectacular body in tights. And most of his "tricks"—jumps, beats, multiple turns—are performed, with ease, by Hayden as well.

Ballet's performance in *Limelight,* then, makes the dancing, spectacular Terry the utter opposite of the narrative's helpless, passive, pessimistic Terry. And whether intentional or not, the narrative's derivative plot resembles nothing so much as a sequence of moments from *Giselle,* with Terry first inspiring Calvero with her innocence and youth as Giselle does Albrecht, then Calvero's death, like that of Giselle, in turn inspiring Terry, protecting her, with Terry now in the role of Albrecht—melancholy, but redeemed and inspired by love. Moreover, the type of ballet performed by Melissa Hayden, its athleticism and lack of legible emotionality—as against Terry's/Bloom's frequently extravagant or hysterical acting style—makes the ballet "stick out" from the period narrative surrounding it. Although *Limelight* certainly can be called melodramatic, the sheer technical brilliance of its dancing works against the morbidity of the narrative and its protagonists.

A similar disparity exists in *Hans Christian Andersen,* a heavily fantasized musical biopic produced by Samuel Goldwyn about the Danish fairy-tale writer whose name had been featured so prominently in *The Red Shoes.* One of Goldwyn's biggest box-office successes, the Technicolor *Hans Christian Andersen* features a number of lengthy ballet sequences, including a "Little Mermaid" ballet that takes place in the titular character's mind, all starring French ballerina Zizi Jeanmaire (billed simply as Jeanmaire). Christensen is played by Danny Kaye, who is a cobbler infatuated with Doro, the Danish ballerina Jeanmaire plays. Doro is kind to him, but she is married to her rampaging ballet master Niels (Farley Granger), and at the end of the film she sweetly and sympathetically sends Andersen on his way. Doro is a romantic figure but an unattainable one; thus, there is little suspense in the plot that is not manufactured by melodramatic split-second timing alone. That is, Andersen comes upon an argument between Doro and Niels and leaves believing that Doro is miserable. But we see that the couple's spat is just a temperamental display; Doro and Niels make up, and passionately, immediately thereafter. This dialectic of argument and reconciliation continues throughout the film, and everyone recognizes it except Andersen; he writes "The Little Mermaid" as a message to Doro that he can rescue her from what he imagines to be her plight. But it is not a plight; it is a film convention: the artist as temperamental. As Andersen's young friend, the boy Peter (Joey Walsh), puts it clearly if anachronistically, "What funny people they are over there [in the theater]. First they laugh and kiss, then they scream and beat each other. Kinda crazy." Despite starring Danny Kaye, *Hans Christian Andersen* is a melancholy film with few if any jokes, little comedy, and the only romance that of a cranky married couple.

According to several accounts, *Hans Christian Andersen* was planned to star Moira Shearer, dancing to choreography by Balanchine; I imagine that the plot's incoherence would only have been magnified by their participation. Shearer withdrew from the project because she was pregnant, and Jeanmaire as replacement meant Jeanmaire's mentor and husband, Roland Petit, would be engaged as choreographer. Petit dances, too, as "The Prince" in the "Little Mermaid" ballet. Danish dancer Erik Bruhn plays "The Hussar" in the other big ballet production number, the "Ice Skating Ballet." The former is an expressionistic *Red Shoes*–style extravaganza, with great slashes of painted bright or garish colors everywhere. The latter, which occurs earliest in the film, is narratively placed as a dress rehearsal in a theater. After watching Jeanmaire and Bruhn and an uncredited corps de ballet dance in the lengthy fast-paced and explosively performed production number, there is a pause for applause; one imagines that the audience watching the film in the 1950s might have obliged, given the spectacular speed and difficulty of the dancing. But instead Niels bursts into a tirade: "All right, all right, we'll do it all over again. Ladies, the pirouettes were impossible. Gentlemen, the lifts have to be higher. The ballerina's performance I won't begin to discuss—that would take until tomorrow morning. Take your places, we'll do the entire thing again." At this point Jeanmaire/Doro flounces off, and their temperamental display begins, the one that Andersen mistakenly takes as a sign that Niels is abusing Doro, who must therefore be saved from him. Again the ballet's men, including Erik Bruhn or Roland Petit, are not given narrative identities as characters.

In her well-known essay "The Self-Reflexive Musical and the Myth of Entertainment," Jane Feuer employs several classic MGM musicals of the 1940s and 1950s to analyze how they worked to establish entertainment "as having greater value than it actually does," a value that always exceeds art as art.[42] One of the components of the myth of entertainment is "the myth of spontaneity," that the best performances are the result of effortlessness

Cyd Charisse, Fred Astaire, and Jack Buchanan in a publicity still showing rehearsals for the doomed "art" production in *The Band Wagon* (1953).

Collection of the author.

rather than calculation or even apparent rehearsal. Feuer discusses the myth of spontaneity with particular reference to *The Band Wagon*, released the year following *Hans Christian Andersen*. I mentioned *The Band Wagon* and its countering of art and popular culture a bit in the introduction to this volume. Art is represented by ballerina Gabby (Cyd Charisse) and her ballet-master boyfriend (James Mitchell), as well as Jeffrey Cordova (Jack Buchanan) and his penchant for outré theatrical versions of the classics. Popular culture is embodied in hoofer Tony Hunter (Fred Astaire) and his musical-comedy pals Lester (Oscar Levant) and Lily (Nanette Fabray). Feuer claims that Cordova's early pretentious and "arty" productions in *The Band Wagon* are unsuccessful because in them labor eclipses performance; we are never shown a completed number from the first Cordova show, only the toil and contrivance that goes into them. *The Band Wagon*, Feuer writes, "suggests that Cordova fails because he has been unable to render invisible the technology of production in order to achieve the effect of effortlessness by which all entertainment succeeds in winning its audience." Conversely, the later numbers in *The Band Wagon*, when Tony Hunter and friends take over and Gabby ditches her ballet boyfriend and learns to hoof as well, are very successful, and the diegetic show in which they are performed (but which we do not see in rehearsal) becomes a big hit (and Gabby and Tony are destined to marry).

In *Hans Christian Andersen,* however, we watch a performance that, on film terms, is clearly meant to be successful; the amount of screen time devoted to it and the pause for applause at its end are signs of its intended significance as entertaining spectacle. Moreover, it is a rehearsal in the narrative but a complete and polished musical number in the film. Niels's derisive response, then, makes no sense in regard to what we have seen—*especially* the ballerina's performance that he criticizes so severely, or Bruhn's lifts, which could scarcely be "higher." Thus, what Feuer claims about contrivance, art, and demystification in *The Band Wagon* needs some adjustment to apply to *Hans Christian Andersen.* Feuer writes, "Although Cordova's *Oedipus* is said to be successful with audiences in the film, the extent to which it is demystified for us undercuts its status as a successful show." In *Hans Christian Andersen,* on the other hand, we might rework Feuer's formulation as follows: "Although Niels says that the 'Ice Skating Ballet' is unsuccessful because it is badly performed, the extent to which it is mystified for us by being performed perfectly undercuts its status as an unsuccessful show."[43] Because of how the film has presented ballet to us formally, as entertainment as well as "high" art, Niels's outburst is jarring and rings false. Jeanmaire's sunny temperament throughout the film also foregrounds the performative basis of artistic temperament; as in *The Red Shoes,* everyone who seems angry is not, and everyone who seems an evil genius is just a sensitive guy putting on an act.

The Band Wagon, as Feuer notes, does a much better job of managing the myth of entertainment, and it is a canonical golden-era Freed-unit musical that has been the subject of extensive critical attention already. That *The Band Wagon* nevertheless seems so conventional now is undoubtedly because it renders yet another variation of the well-worn "opera vs. swing" plot structure that we have already discussed, because it *does* work hard to make entertainment, in dance terms, superior to an "art" form like ballet. Charisse dances one short "straight" ballet on a diegetic theatrical stage early in *The Band Wagon,* and is dutifully lauded as "fantastic," "beautiful," and "magnificent" by spectator Astaire (and this ballet has a pause for applause at its end, too). And *The Band Wagon* also makes note in its plot of the increasing significance of ballet in the mediascape; Cordova claims that it is Tony who is outmoded, whereas ballet is "modern" and "today." But ballet "straight," according to the myth of entertainment, is not as valuable as ballet mixed with hoofing, or ballet performed in ordinary clothes, in ordinary settings, without toe shoes and tutus (or men in tights). In both *Hans Christian Andersen* and *The Band Wagon,* ballet's bodies are valuable because they can do so *many* extraordinary things and, in the case of both Jeanmaire and Charisse, their legs are so long and lovely, so easily fetishizable, no less than the body-less legs in the *Red Shoes* "long legs" campaign or on the cover of the 1952 *Holiday*. These things can also be said of the male dancers in both films, and the films' own ambivalence about ballet-dancing men means that they are shown but not discussed, seen but rarely heard, feminized both by their tights and the performance frames in which they are isolated from the narrative. James Mitchell's character, who orders Gabby around and who has apparently controlled her career until she meets up with Tony and Jeffrey Cordova, is signally never shown dancing in *The Band Wagon*; he is instead made a flamboyantly macho boor and disposed of relatively quickly.

I Tell You Paula Cannot Live Unless She Dances

Although virtually the entire 1950s in some sense forms its own cluster of ballet films, 1952 and 1953 are particularly packed with vehicles whose main characters are ballet artists. Like *Limelight*, several are morbid or melancholy in terms of the plot but, like *Hans Christian Andersen* and, albeit to a lesser extent, *The Band Wagon* or *Never Let Me Go*, contradictorily transcendent on the level of the performance of ballet as dancing. This is even more the case with 1953's three-part *The Story of Three Loves*, or rather its first "story," "The Jealous Lover." (I have saved this film for last, but it was actually released about five months before *The Band Wagon*.) It does star Moira Shearer, in what turned out to be her only American film (made soon after giving birth to her first child), as a ballerina named Paula, with James Mason as a vaguely defined ballet genius named Charles Coudray. The choreography is by Frederick Ashton, who was then still with the Sadler's Wells and considered to be something close, if not superior, to a British George Balanchine. *The Story of Three Loves* and its three-part structure—the stories are all told in flashback and are loosely connected by virtue of their "belonging" to characters who happen to be traveling on the same ocean liner—was part of a trend of multi-part feature-length films that, one imagines, were conscious or unconscious responses to the programming and configuration of network television broadcasting. Little academic notice has been paid to the film, except by a few Vincente Minnelli scholars; Minnelli directed its middle story, Gottfried Reinhardt its other two, including "The Jealous Lover." But "The Jealous Lover" is noteworthy both for its dancing and because it is perhaps the clearest representation of the inability of conventional plots at this time to reconcile their own attitudes about the incompatibility of art and life. After about the first thirty-five minutes of *The Story of Three Loves*, only burlesque or parody of the stereotypes and clichés of the ballet film will be possible.

The story of "The Jealous Lover" was written by John Collier, and his complete handwritten treatment, on yellow legal sheets, survives.[44]

Throughout the treatment, the protagonists, Paula and Coudray, are referred to as "Moira" and "Mason," so clearly they were cast before there was a story to put them in. The plot Collier comes up with is that Coudray is seeking inspiration and finds it in the person and (ballet) dancing of Paula, who, unbeknownst to Coudray, has been forbidden to dance because of her weak heart. If she dances, it will kill her, but she does it for Coudray anyway, and then she dies, leaving him alone to face the future in despair. Collier's story thus participates in Western culture's long tradition of using art "to dream the deaths of beautiful women," to quote Elisabeth Bronfen's formulation again,[45] and his ideas about what ballet is and where it comes from mimic many other films about artists in which "inspiration" is at once the most precious and the most elusive of the artist's commodities. Moreover, the story also reiterates what Susan Felleman calls "an ancient and mythic scenario of genius and muse, of master and subject, by focusing (as is usual) on the normative, white, heterosexual couple of older man and younger woman."[46] Collier assumes that Coudray (or Mason) is the artist, while Paula (or Moira) is the muse. But regardless of Collier's intentions, the film cannot sustain this dichotomy, for Coudray remains impotent throughout, while Paula and her dancing begin, and end, as powerful signifying forces by whom and by which the film as a text, no less than Coudray, Mason, or Collier, is held helplessly in thrall.

Here is Collier's rendering of what it is that "Mason" does: "To me, ballets are a very personal job. From the very first vague idea, every step, every grouping—it all has to come out of *me*. Designers, composers, choreographers, dancers—they're the stuff I work with, do you understand? All that stuff about eating people alive, temperament, tantrums—what people don't realize is—it's my WORK." In the film itself this is collapsed into a shorter exchange, as Coudray explains that he is not an actual composer or painter himself: "But I think more boldly than a real musician or a real painter. . . . Composers, choreographers, painters—they know how, I know *what*." It is hard not to notice that while none of this describes the act of creation in relation to ballet—not even Diaghilev claimed to be an artist—it does do well as a characterization of the processes involved in making Hollywood films, in which the "me" is the film itself that depends on the "stuff" of the labor of other artists. Collier has no way to describe what it is that ballet dancers do—he seems to know nothing about ballet but adores it—except in utterly expressionistic and vague terms, as in this rendering of Paula improvising for Coudray in his studio: "That's it—float, float! / (And other more technical terms). / After a moment or so he ceases to 'conduct' her. He watches, his eyes growing more and more alive and excited. He crosses to easel; watches Moira as she approaches the first climactic pose, takes a brush and draws a few rapid lines."

The "genius" (James Mason) and his "muse" (Moira Shearer) in a posed publicity still for the "Jealous Lover" section of *The Story of Three Loves* (1953).

Courtesy National Film Archive, London.

In the film, the notion is also promulgated that the dancer cannot know or understand the significance of what she herself is doing. Coudray calls Paula "my dear little whatever you are" and asks her the rhetorical question, "Do you happen to know what you're doing?" while waving his hands and pointing vaguely to her body after she has stopped dancing. What excites him is that she is "going to be of some small help to [him], perhaps, possibly," and he demands that she go with him to his studio to be of that "help." He sneers when she hesitates (because she knows, after all, as do we, that she has been forbidden to dance because of her bad heart), assuming that she is afraid that he has some prurient interest in her: "I don't know who you are, but let me tell you, you flatter yourself." When she still hesitates, he sneers harder, condemning her for giving up dance "for what's presumably some sort of—bliss." "If there's one thing I hate it's a jealous lover," he growls.

But Paula does decide to go with Coudray to his studio, and after she dances for him—to an arrangement of parts of Rachmaninoff's "Rhapsody on a Theme of Paganini"—it turns out that his interest is not strictly in her dancing after all. After her final "dying swan" pose and the end of the music, Coudray rushes to her, and there is a long romantic kiss in response to her gasped question, "Have I helped you at all?" Then there is another long kiss as he tells her that she's a dancer, she's dancing itself, she's music, she's a poem, she's a joy. He rapturously plans their life together as, he believes, she is changing her clothes, but of course she has escaped out a side door and run back home, where she dies after telling her aunt how she danced and how wonderful it was. But if the story of "The Jealous Lover" is a quite conventional version of what people who know little about ballet think that it consists of and who "makes" it, ultimately what Coudray is, does, and says bears little relation to what we see Paula do, or, just as significant, to what the film's publicity says it is that Moira Shearer, as Paula, is doing either. Regardless of the framing story, Shearer's dance performance, of choreography by Frederick Ashton, clearly matters most.

The first actual glimpse we get of Shearer, however, is also conventional: her legs, dancing at what turns out to be an audition for Coudray. She performs Ashton's difficult choreography, to some of the fast bits of the same Rachmaninoff music, ending with a sequence of turns. Coudray is barely attentive at first, but just as his waving hand and stare indicate that he is beginning to become involved, she collapses. Coudray sniffs and mutters and loses interest as Shearer/Paula is carried off prostrate and protesting, "It's *not* my ankle, it's *not* my ankle!" to her aunt (Agnes Moorehead), with whom she lives. We hear someone calling a name—the next dancer to audition—and it turns out to be the dancer who will star in the Coudray ballet, the shipboard discussion of which initiated Coudray's flashback (an earnest young man wants to know why such a masterpiece was only performed once). The next scene takes place in the aunt's opulent London apartment; the doctor and the aunt are discussing Paula's condition. The aunt herself used to be a ballerina—and a "great one," the doctor says—and she recounts how since Paula was a little girl Paula has "lived for her dancing. There is nothing else for her. It's the meaning of life to her." She pauses, and then expostulates, "I

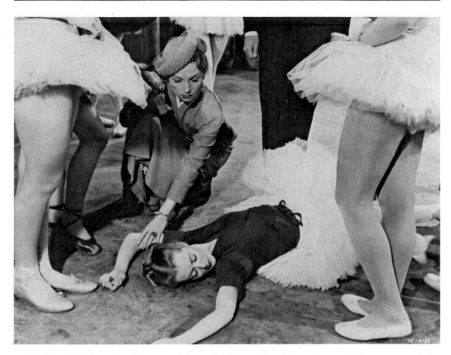

Publicity still of Moira Shearer with Agnes Moorehead from the audition scene of the "Jealous Lover" segment, *The Story of Three Loves.*

Courtesy National Film Archive, London.

tell you, I tell you Paula cannot *live* unless she dances!" To which the doctor replies, "And I tell you plainly she cannot live if she does."

When Paula enters the room, beautifully dressed and looking healthy as a horse, she guesses the diagnosis but exhibits little emotion about it. The aunt says to her, "We'll learn to like other things." Paula replies, in the last line of the scene, "We'll try." Rachmaninoff's music returns as a bridge to the next scene, a diegetic theatrical performance of Coudray's new ballet, the ballet for which Paula earlier auditioned. There are numerous flagpoles and waving pennants onstage, but the ballet is abstract, lots of people dancing in flowing orange and yellow costumes. Paula is watching from a box, tears in her eyes. During the curtain calls Coudray is pulled onstage by the leading dancers, where he makes a couple of awkward bows. A dissolve finds Paula still in her box in the now-deserted theater, and after an editing ellipsis she is shown walking onto the empty stage. Her crazed facial expression in close-up—lips parted, eyes darting from side to side—and the reflected echoing music on the soundtrack indicate that she is listening to the music in her head, and as the camera places her body, in long shot, in the center of the frame, she begins to dance. The music becomes closely miked, and for almost two and a half minutes, with no cuts, we watch Shearer dance. She wears a blue evening gown, with one long white glove on her left arm. The point of view is from the front, straight on. Then the camera cuts to the flies, where Coudray/Mason is watching. He starts yelling at her to "hold it" and so on, and when she stops dancing—which "spoils it" for Coudray—he heads down to the stage, and they begin their exchange about how she should come to his studio to be of "some small help" to him. He asks her in the taxi on the way, "What *can* you love more than dancing like that?"

Once they arrive at Coudray's studio—which, as the *New Yorker*'s reviewer noted, "is roughly the size of the Bolshoi Theatre . . . and equipped with just about everything an artiste could desire except an oxygen pump"[47]—Coudray expects Paula to "do" what she was doing in the theater. He points vaguely at the ground and stands there expectantly, waiting for her—still dressed in her evening clothes and high heels—to inspire him. Eventually he shows her to a room with costumes, "things for her hair," and some perfectly fitting toe shoes and tights, and waits again for her to emerge and serve as his muse. He also provides music—again Rachmaninoff's "Rhapsody," on a record. Shearer does emerge, in a white costume with a long skirt, and begins with the same choreography we saw in her performance alone on the theater stage. But this time she continues dancing for some six and a half minutes, with no breaks, in very long takes punctuated by a few close-ups. Eventually, as the famous adagio section of the music comes to an end, she is folded up on the floor and Coudray, who has been absent visually from most of what we have been watching for so long, gazes at her adoringly and at last figures out that she is breathing strangely and rushes to her side, where they will kiss and he will tell her she's a joy and that he wants her with him always. The audience is in on the knowledge that Paula has a weak heart; but at no point, until the music ends, does any part of the dancing suggest that Paula/Shearer is in other than perfectly honed physical and technical shape. It is a virtuoso performance of difficult and lovely choreography; as itself, it is already the result not only of "inspiration" in the feeble senses that the script has defined it but of obvious and careful collaboration between choreographer, dancer, and film technicians. Neither Collier's story nor the script are about ballet, yet ballet is clearly the cynosure of "The Jealous Lover" as a piece of filmmaking.

Moreover, the prestige value of Frederick Ashton's participation in *The Story of Three Loves* cannot be discounted; the Sadler's Wells had just completed its second, and enormously successful and well publicized, U.S. tour in 1950–1951, with Ashton's name featured prominently as one of the creative forces behind the company's success. And Shearer herself, as a developing star image, had been disproving the messages of morbid ballet films for some time by 1953. *The Red Shoes* had explained that women could not

She is not dead after all; Moira Shearer in Paula's dance costume in *The Story of Three Loves*. Publicity photos like this, of film-narratively tragic ballerinas being glamorous Hollywood stars and doing normal and healthy things, were part of ballet's increasing allure in the 1950s.

Courtesy National Film Archive, London.

be great ballet dancers or world famous unless they gave up "the doubtful comforts of human love" and subjected themselves to the whims and desires of tyrannical aesthetes. But Shearer had not died on the train tracks; she had instead become a cheerful and cheerfully rich world-famous ballet dancer, a budding film star, *and* a wife and mother. The story of "The Jealous Lover" maintains that ballet is something created by a single genius who is inspired, rather like a movie producer, by the labors of other artists and who somehow creates ballets even though he does not know "how" anything is done. But the dancing in "The Jealous Lover" is choreographed and performed by people trained and adept in the art form in question; whatever mystical elements occur in the process of artistic creation, we are not witnessing the result of the manipulation of sketches and wooden models and wires and swatches of fabric by a brooding connoisseur alone in his urban loft. The defining characteristic of the genius here actually is his impotence, his very inability to work and to create. And more and more of the audience, and more and more critics, were noticing the discrepancies in the plot's version of ballet as against the subtext provided by Shearer's and Ashton's participation in the preparation of the film's own ballet art.

The reviews of "The Jealous Lover" acknowledged both the glossiness of the film's production values and its generic sentimentality, as well as the tired implausibility of its premise. *Commonweal* called the "vignette" absorbing and beautiful but cautioned that you "may grow impatient with this girl whose love of dancing is so great she cannot stop even after being warned by her doctor that she must."[48] *Newsweek*'s reviewer called the ending of the story "well and early telegraphed," but until it occurs, "Miss Shearer is radiant."[49] Parker Tyler in *Theatre Arts* admired the film's entertainment value, and Shearer's solo, for which "some of the credit, naturally, must go to its distinguished choreographer, Frederick Ashton."[50] The *New Yorker*'s review was especially caustic; Mason is "required to make out that he is a new-day Diaghilev, inventing a ballet while Miss Shearer skips about his studio" to his "ecstatic coaxings," and the reviewer hopes that Mason's love scene with Shearer "was as embarrassing for him as it was for me."[51] This "high-toned nonsense" ends when Shearer's "poor heart at last quits for keeps, and after taking a header down a stairway she trundles off to the beyond."

Broad, Hokey Ballet Meller; Dubious Seller

As mentioned, the exact designation "ballet meller" was first applied in 1954, in a *Variety* review, to the British film *Dance Little Lady*. In fact, the melodramatic structure of *Dance Little Lady* was named as an element in its predicted commercial failure outside of the United Kingdom (where quotas against the importation of features from Hollywood helped "local" fare to achieve more success than it might have otherwise).[52] It was the very rigidity of its screen conventions that damned it to derision, especially its insistence that the ballerina's life be a tragic one. *Dance Little Lady* concerns a dancer who is regarded as a meal ticket by the manager she marries. So villainous is what all reviews refer to as her "worthless husband" that when the ballerina is severely injured in an automobile accident—never to dance again, she will be told by her doctors—on her way home from the celebrations attending to her debut at Covent Garden, he deserts her and their child to run off with another dancer. The jilted wife gradually falls in love with the sympathetic doctor who supervises her recovery, and she begins to train her daughter to dance too. What *Variety* called the "major melodramatic twist" occurs when the husband, now a talent scout, returns from Hollywood and decides to take his daughter away from her mother and to put her to work on the screen. The worthless husband is redeemed by a house fire; he implausibly rescues his daughter from a flaming roof that firefighters cannot even reach, before dying in the flames himself and leaving wife and doctor to marry, and wife, doctor, and daughter to live happily ever after. The melodramatic elements of *Dance Little Lady* are obvious, the villain clearly marked as such by his extraordinarily brutish behavior and his wielding of power over the weak and victimized heroine and her child.

If the ballet meller no longer works at this point in the 1950s, however, it cannot be because melodrama itself ceased to function in meaningful ways or to address cultural concerns in an ameliorative fashion. The film melodrama of the 1950s, in fact, has generated more critical literature than arguably any other era in sound-film history, especially what film studies calls the "domestic" or "family melodrama" (an academic subgenre into which *Dance Little Lady* would obviously fall). Indeed, melodrama had achieved what David Rodowick calls "considerable formal and stylistic diversity" in the 1950s, being incorporated even into "well-defined genres like the western and gangster film" that then became "heavily determined by their melodramatic content."[53] The 1950s melodramatic imagination inserted men as fathers into the "global network of authority," represented by the nuclear family, with women "mirrored in this network by their relationship to men as wives, mothers, daughters, etc." What Rodowick ends up asserting, though, is that melodrama was unable during this time fully to reconcile the family, as the domestic version of a "social system defined by patriarchal authority," with the "restlessness of desire within the individual characters," especially its women. "Split between madness and authority," Rodowick concludes, the 1950s film melodrama was unable to evolve as "either a fully affirmative or fully subversive form" but instead offered only a "partial solution" to the problem of individual action and agency in a patriarchal and paternalistic framework. *Dance Little Lady*—despite its cardboard characters, stereotypical plot (wrote one British reviewer, "one can wager one's entire fortune that if the heroine of a film is a ballet dancer she is bound, before many minutes have passed, to meet with a crippling accident"),[54] and outrageous coincidences—does raise the possibility that the father and the husband are at once the villain and also constitutive of family happiness and a child's sunny temperament and talent. Ballet, conversely, is no longer *only* associated with tragedy but also is the new family's source of joy and success.

Try Again, Gaby

After *The Story of Three Loves* and *Dance Little Lady,* ballet protagonists cannot be defined by morbidity except as an element of camp, or of a self-conscious performance of morbidity and, or as, outrageous displays of temperament. The history of the ballet elements of the third remake in 1956 of *Waterloo Bridge,* called *Gaby,* bear this out. *Gaby* stars Leslie Caron, a trained ballet dancer, *as* a ballet dancer, French this time. John Kerr plays Greg, her "Yank paratrooper" boyfriend. Updated to World War II right before D-Day, *Gaby* was advertised by MGM as a "vibrant wartime romance, filmed in Cinema-Scope and color."[55] Its title tagline is "The love story of *Gaby.*" *Gaby* is a true remake of the 1940 film, not a new adaptation of Robert Sherwood's play; and Production Code Administration and MGM script files show that the remake had been in the works for some years, since the early 1950s at least.[56] One of the most noticeable, and startling, differences between the 1940 *Waterloo Bridge* and *Gaby* is that, rather than the heroine being more or less forced into prostitution by circumstance—poverty, illness, the desire to help out the friend, Kitty, who has cared for and protected her—the plot in *Gaby* turns on the fact that Gaby sends Greg away on what should have been their wedding night. As in the earlier film, they cannot marry because of various wartime regulations that they have misunderstood, and Gaby wants to wait until they are married the next day before sleeping with Greg. Instead, of course, Greg is recalled to the front, and the marriage does not occur. When Gaby learns from Greg's aunt that he has been killed in the D-Day invasion, she torments herself for, in essence, not having had sex with him before he died: "I was cruel to him. I was so cruel. That last night, I sent him away. I made him leave. . . . Oh, I should have let him stay!"[57] Gaby's "contrite woman's heart," as some of the film's posters proclaim, "sends her into the arms of other men—seeking to give them all that she had denied her own sweetheart! Then Greg returns . . ."

On the one hand, the publicity for *Gaby* and its emphasis on love and romance matches that of the earlier film, and surely, given the clear emphasis on what the PCA called *Gaby*'s "unacceptable justification of illicit sex," Gaby's fate should have been no less severe—death—than that of Myra in 1940. On the other hand, the PCA's influence was waning by the late 1950s, and the disjunctions in *Gaby*'s generic identity suggest that MGM hoped the film would appeal to those seeking sensational subject matter masked as "drama," as well as those who were satisfied by high production values, musical numbers, and a tragic romance.[57] In chapter 2 I quoted Mary Ann Doane in reference to Myra's fate in *Waterloo Bridge*. Doane writes that Myra "must die" because "prostitution is absolutely irrecuperable. Myra's fiancé, Roy, can cross class lines in order to become engaged to her, but once she slips into prostitution, she is lost, her death inevitable."[58] But although Gaby is even more clearly possessed of an "excessive sexuality," she does not die. Moreover, she and Greg walk off together into the future, all forgiven, all understood. Gaby is actually still a ballet dancer, gainfully employed, throughout the film; but we never hear strains of *Swan Lake*, and Gaby's participation in ballet is treated as part of her romantic allure—Greg falls in love with her during a ballet performance (it is the "first time I've ever seen a ballet," he says), as in the earlier film—but otherwise not emphasized except as the locus of the orphan Gaby's chosen and supportive "family."

In fact, the process by which *Waterloo Bridge* became *Gaby* is a record of the gradual erasure of ballet's metaphoric significance to the narrative and its characterizations. Early script treatments from 1953 and 1954 alternately made Gaby the star of the ballet that Greg (called Jim in some versions) attends, and the disapproving and tyrannical "Madame" of the earlier film is here too, but male. And Gaby is again fired for missing a performance, forcing her to be "desperately humble—groveling before [the ballet master/impresario]" to appease his "swollen ego," so that in concentrating on the "strict discipline" that classical dancing "demands, there will be no time for remembering the past." And *Swan Lake* is present too, as one of the ballets Gaby performs before she dies in an air raid. The flashback structure is also maintained—Gaby's story is the memory of her lover as he watches a ballet with his aunt. In other words, *Gaby* was originally a refilming of *Waterloo Bridge* with different nationalities and names. By 1955, the flashback structure and many of the ballet scenes and their "swollen egos" are gone, but Gaby has sent Greg away, and he has married someone else. There is another version in which Gaby is hit by a car and dies in "Jim's" arms. But in the ultimate version—the film itself—Gaby lives. And ballet, despite Caron's star image being associated with ballet and dancing, becomes simply Gaby's job, not a predictor of her fate. When Gaby is explaining tearfully to Greg's aunt why she cannot marry Greg, the reason she gives is that she "just can't leave the ballet." Her aunt responds, "Try again, Gaby," as though to say that no one can get away with palming off the incompatibility of life and art anymore. (One of the most hilariously self-reflexive scenes in *Gaby* is when Greg, by phone, tells his aunt that he is going to marry Gaby: "I just met her over here. She's a dancer. Hello? Aunt Helen? Are we disconnected? That's right, a French dancer. Hello?")

Press-book advertisement for the remake of *Waterloo Bridge* (1940), now entitled *Gaby* (1956), as a love story rather than a tragic romance.

The Art before the Coarse

David Caute writes that ballet in the West in the 1950s and 1960s "increasingly avoided stories, dramas, heroes, heroines, villains, dénouements, dying swans. Dance was developed as an *en-soi*, a thing apart. . . . The external referent, the story, . . . had been deliberately cauterized. Abstraction prevailed."[59] As all of the films discussed in this chapter suggest, this is much less true of ballet in commercial cinema. Where an individual ballet "number" might eschew a narrative framework, the function of ballet in any film is always part of a story and, often, at least through the early 1950s, a melodramatic story at that. It is not, then, that things had become "healthier but duller" immediately after *The Red Shoes*, but by the mid-1950s the generic unhealthiness of the ballet artist had itself become dull, the subject of parody, because of the increasing amounts of competing information about ballet available in the popular press, in theatrical performance and publicity about it, and in local training venues and opportunities. There was more dancing in films, much of it based on ballet technique, but it was marked differently than the elite theatrical art of swans and princes and pointe shoes—namely the sort of ballet that Gene Kelly usually performs, or that is found in folk musicals ranging from *On the Town* to *Oklahoma!* According to Jane Feuer, ballet in America had in fact changed "in such a way as to make itself accessible to Hollywood," by eliminating overt references to the aristocrats and court language of traditional ballet:

> Choreographers such as Eugene Loring *(Billy the Kid)*, Agnes de Mille *(Rodeo)* and Jerome Robbins *(Fancy Free)* made what the dance critic Edwin Denby calls "local colour" ballets out of American folk material—cowboys and sailors. Even more significantly these choreographers frequently dispensed with the unnatural classical lines of ballet to introduce a more natural and spontaneous dance style based on American folk stance and gesture. . . . If classical ballet seeks to conceal all effort, and modern dance seeks to reveal all effort, then musicals seem to want to naturalize all effort.[60]

Making ballet accessible to Hollywood was not necessarily on the minds of those who were working to Americanize classical ballet. Rather, as discussed in chapter 1, ballet had been part of American popular culture, as well as elite art, from at least the 1920s on, its nimbleness of style, derived paradoxically from the flexibility and adaptability of the technical vocabulary of the classic *danse d'école*, continually blurring whatever boundaries demarcated the "low" from the "high." George Balanchine's abstract ballets, especially for the New York City Ballet in the 1940s and 1950s, also were incorporating "American folk stance and gesture," whatever this might mean, even as they increasingly amplified the "unnatural classical lines of ballet." But the point is well taken that the American film musical of the 1940s and 1950s did often either disguise the classical basis of the dance technique and training of many of its best-known performers or, conversely, if a dancer's popular image was already linked to ballet (Cyd Charisse, Leslie Caron), their performances were increasingly jazzed up or "naturalized" as musical-comedy "show-dancing."

An enormous amount of scholarship has been devoted already to the "golden age" of the American film musical in the 1940s and 1950s as the apotheosis of studio art-making. Films like *On the Town, An American in Paris, Singin' in the Rain,* and *The Band Wagon,* and their big ballets (so-named in reviews, whether they are performed in toe shoes or not), all have been the subject of extensive critical analysis in a number of frameworks—for the way in which they exemplify trends toward the increased stylistic integration of number, narrative, mise-en-scène, and performance; as gay male camp; as signs of the authorship of Hollywood genre as a social-industrial construct and of individuals such as Gene Kelly, Stanley Donen, and Vincente Minnelli.

Jerome Delamater's *Dance in the Hollywood Musical* spends a lot of time, as does the work of Feuer and Rick Altman, on the meanings of the dance content of musicals of the era in relation to changes in the genre's requirements over time and in response to other influences such as the Broadway musical, popular music, or television (Delamater even calls the integrated musical the "*dance* musical").[61] I will not discuss the dance content of such musicals in any depth because many others have already done so, but it does make sense to address the issue of ballet's relationship to the aesthetic status, in academic scholarship particularly, of the "integrated musical."

Delamater lays what he sees as the rising importance of dance as an "essential cinematic code" or "controlling factor" in the Hollywood musical of the 1940s and 1950s on the concomitant participation in the genre of "trained dancers and genuine choreographers."[62] And by "trained" and "genuine" he means "ballet" or "ballet-based." Ballet, in fact, "[lent] a more serious approach to dance" in film "and would provide better dancers than had previously been available," and Delamater sees "a move from popular, vernacular dance to ballet" as a "trend that has been manifested throughout the history of the musical." But given the primacy of integration as what Delamater calls the "platonic ideal" of the Hollywood musical—by which the entire film emerges as a "unified cinematic experience" rather than a loose sequence of more or less spectacular numbers driven by the skills of idiosyncratic performers—it is difficult to understand how ballet, especially recognizable or iconographically classical ballet as has been discussed in these pages, functions as an element that *can* be integrated, especially into the folk musical subgenre as opposed to a backstage musical such as *The Band Wagon* or even *Singin' in the Rain*. Ballet technique certainly is, as stated, more and more visible as the underlying basis of the movement and gestures of film dancers from the 1940s through the 1950s; this is not only true of "nominal" ballet dancers like Charisse (previous to her film career a member of one of the American Ballet Russe companies) or Caron (brought to Hollywood from Roland Petit's Ballets des Champs-Elysées) but of musical comedy dancers like Vera-Ellen or Mitzi Gaynor or Carol Haney or Marge and Gower Champion (Marge Champion's father was Ernest Belcher, a well-known dance teacher in Los Angeles). But ballet as an element of narrative is very difficult to integrate, unless the technique is disguised as vernacular through costuming, setting, and so on.

Toe shoes alone have always presented "integration" problems to movies, even to movies about ballet, because they are so intractable; it is hard to get them on, or off, quickly or easily. Indeed, the goal of the theatrical ballet dancer is to get them on to *stay* on, not only with ribbons and elastic but sometimes with glue in the heels and toes. So in every scene in *The Red Shoes*, for example, in which toe shoes must be removed, an edit covers up a preparation that has taken place off-camera. In the "Red Shoes" ballet itself, when the Priest removes the shoes from the Girl's feet, the knots in the ribbons have been untied and the heels of the shoes folded under, so that they can be slid off like bedroom slippers. And at the end of the film, when Vicky is lying bleeding on the railroad tracks, the ribbons are tied in bows at the front of the ankle and, again, the heels folded under so that Julian can remove them. Toe shoes, one might say, are the *material* reason why so many film ballets in non-ballet-based stories are dream ballets. While tap shoes can *look* ordinary, toe shoes never occur as a feature of ordinary dress.

Integration of number and narrative does not apply to Gene Kelly's all-dance *Invitation to the Dance,* which began production in 1952 but was not released until 1956; it has no spoken dialogue or "explanation" for the dancing, nor any overarching "unifying" narrative. It is a collection of three long dance numbers, two of them explicitly ballets, that feature some of the best-known American and European ballet dancers of the time (Igor Youskevitch, Tamara Toumanova, Claire Sombert, Diana Adams, Carol Haney, Tommy Rall, and the ubiquitous Belita). But it was Kelly's "commercial" routines, especially his "oh-so-cute little dance with some animals and cartoon figures," that indicated, to *Time*'s reviewer, that "Hollywood just cannot bring itself to put the art before the coarse."[63] Yet the two ballet sequences in *Invitation to the Dance*—or, rather, Kelly's "artistic pretensions," as Arthur Knight wrote in *Dance Magazine,* in combination with Kelly's choreography, which "rarely rises above the obvious"—were actually reviewed as being the weakest things in the film.[64] Gene Kelly's desire to be taken seriously as a choreographer and as a dancer required that he work in the idiom of classical ballet, that he become a younger and American version of Balanchine, unfettered by the constraints even of the skeletal narrative that surrounded Balanchine's ballets for *The Goldwyn Follies* (1938). So while ballet was becoming the technical basis for much of the dancing in Hollywood musicals but being disguised, or "naturalized," as vernacular or folk dancing, ballet—with tutus and toe shoes—remained Hollywood's ideal of dance art.

At the same time, in the 1950s there were many films that thought ballet significant and entertaining enough to plunk it down in the middle of the film, baldly unintegrated, except in a very specific narrative sense, as a stand-alone "number." It makes a little narrative sense that the Russian ballerina Olga in *The Man Who Loved Redheads* should perform some ballet; but it is as a performance by Moira Shearer and John Hart that the number derives its entertainment as well as aesthetic value. There is no attempt to integrate the ballet into the film otherwise, nor is there any apparent interest in integrating anything in the film into a "unified cinematic experience." Delamater calls musicals that do not exhibit an interest in integration on his terms "thirties musicals," regardless of when they were made, as though they

EXCITING WOMEN enact life's Drama, it's Loves, it's Laughter, it's Beauty!

MGM presents in color by TECHNICOLOR Invitation to the dance

starring GENE KELLY
TAMARA TOUMANOVA · IGOR YOUSKEVITCH
direction and choreography GENE KELLY · produced by ARTHUR FREED
a Metro-Goldwyn-Mayer picture

Part of the failed advertising campaign for Gene Kelly's all-dance *Invitation to the Dance* (1956), which substantially downplays the film's ballet in favor of "exciting women" and sex appeal. The leopard-skinned Belita pictured so prominently occupies very little screen time in the film, and Kelly is illustrated only as a smiling face. (It is also worth noting that copywriters even in 1956 were not always clear about the difference between possessives and contractions.)

Collection of the author.

are throwbacks to an earlier, more primitive era.[65] But Hollywood certainly invested enormous amounts of money even in the 1950s on "thirties musicals," including a couple "about" classical ballet dancers.

You Say Art to Them, and They Say, Art Who?

In 1956 *Meet Me in Las Vegas* starred Cyd Charisse as a possibly American, possibly French ballerina named Maria Corvier. She is described as the first ballerina ever to appear in a Las Vegas casino, and the sign advertising her gig at the Sands labels her "premiere ballerina" of the "Ballet de France." She travels with an older companion, also a former ballerina (played by Lili Darvas). And she has a suave but paternalistic manager, Pierre (Paul Henried), who has signed her up at the casino to make money while he stays back in New York fooling around with ballet girls who dance *Swan Lake.* Maria is frigid, repressed, and, or because, she spends all her time either onstage, rehearsing, or resting. When she gets excited, she takes "cold showers." The only man in her life is Pierre, who is using her as a cash cow.

Enter Chuck (Dan Dailey), an unlucky rancher/gambler who grabs Maria's hand as he places a bet and discovers that she brings him luck. He convinces her to go out with him that night to gamble, and they win money all over town. When he takes her to the country to meet his mother, oil erupts from a dead well, and formerly recalcitrant chickens suddenly lay loads of eggs and things of that sort. But of course, this being a musical, Chuck and Maria fall in love. Once they are in love, they are (as anyone could have told them) no longer "lucky." So they part, but eventually they come back together. Their final plan is to spend six months on the ranch, six months touring with the ballet. The closing shot of the film is of Chuck/Dailey kissing Maria/Charisse, who is wearing a tutu and toe shoes; as the kiss goes on, her legs tighten into phallic arrows as she rises *en pointe.*

Meet Me in Las Vegas was publicized as an "M-G-M Goldmine of Entertainment" (much like a television variety show, but longer and in widescreen and color) because it features a "flock of guest stars," many in cameos—Lena Horne, Frankie Laine, Frank Sinatra, Sammy Davis Jr. (in voice-over only), Pier Angeli, Debbie Reynolds, Eddie Fisher, Vic Damone, and on and on.[66] It was shot partly on location in Las Vegas, a "big, bland tribute" in the *New Yorker*'s words, "to the wonders of Nevada's gambling center."[67] Charisse dances in two extended and beautifully photographed ballet sequences choreographed by Eugene Loring—an abstract rehearsal number with everyone in tights and leotards only and a version of *Sleeping Beauty* in modern dress, where Charisse is knocked out by a volleyball (rather than being pricked with a needle by an evil sorceress) before being woken by a boy in white ducks and a golf shirt. At first glance, *Meet Me in Las Vegas* would seem to be yet another promulgation of Feuer's myth of entertainment, as well as her "opera vs. swing" plot. The final big ballet is the comic "Frankie and Johnny" (narrated by Sammy Davis Jr.), jazzed up and choreographed by Hermes Pan, with Charisse and all the other women dancers wearing high heels and fishnet stockings. But the film never makes ballet into something that is not entertaining and valuable on its own. Maria/Charisse becomes successful in Las Vegas as a ballerina, and she already knows how to dance in a jazzier style; it is not something she has to learn to do to make herself accessible or palatable to audiences. Instead, all of the comedy comes from playing with the stereotype of the ballerina as countless other films, American films in particular, have portrayed her, and the most pointed satire is directed at the audiences whose money Maria and Pierre will be taking: "You say art to them, and they say, Art who?" Pierre says. He also tells her to do whatever she wants to do because she does not have to be "cooperative and reasonable like a normal human being"; she is a ballerina, she is "not *supposed* to be normal."

But Maria *is* normal, in a sense that the film approves of: wanting to marry for love but also wanting to work. Pierre's paternalistic treatment of Maria is self-serving ("a ballerina shouldn't think," he tells her, and he calls her his "big baby"), and his assessment of ballet dancers turns out to be misguided (he tells Chuck that ballerinas are "nervous creatures" and that he has not met a "ballerina yet who didn't *live* on applause"). However wacky the notion might be in practical terms that Maria and Chuck will spend six months on the ranch and "six months wherever the ballet is," Chuck ends up loving ballet and treating it respectfully, as something that is crucial to Maria's happiness rather than a de facto barrier to it.

There are no numbers in *Meet Me in Las Vegas*, then, in which dance, *especially* the ballet, functions as what Delamater calls "exterior manifestations of a character's interior feelings."[68] Ballet is not the vehicle for psychological expressivity, whether in dreams or romantic duets. It is, however, undeniably gendered as feminine. Again, no male ballet dancers are given names or characters; they are present on the screen in large numbers, but only the ballerina has a narrative identity—an imbalance that is hardly progressive in terms of gender politics on some levels (even a haughty ballerina like Maria Corvier ends up answering to "Bunny") but on others interesting for how the male dancers are truly "only" objects of the gaze, while the female dancer, the ballerina, functions much more as a transfigurative object: the man who watches is changed, not merely reassured, by what he sees. After Chuck watches Maria dance for the first time, she says, "I thought you didn't care about ballet." He responds, "That's what I thought too. But I was wrong."

FOR ALL INTENTS AND PURPOSES, there are no fictional, narrative American ballet films, as I have been describing them, from the end of the 1950s

Cyd Charisse in a posed MGM publicity shot from around the time of *Meet Me in Las Vegas* (1956).

Collection of the author.

through the decade of the 1960s. There are ballet characters around the edges—the spoofed and sped-up "Russian" ballet company in *Bye Bye Birdie* in 1963, Toumanova as a Soviet ballerina-spy in Hitchcock's *Torn Curtain* in 1966, Catherine Deneuve as a dance teacher in *Les Demoiselles de Rochefort* in 1968, for example—and at least one full-length commercial all-dance film, *Black Tights,* in 1962, starring Cyd Charisse, Moira Shearer, Jeanmaire, Roland

Petit, and Petit's new Ballet de Paris. And beginning in the mid-1950s concert documentaries with titles like *Ballet de France* (1955) or *Stars of the Russian Ballet* (1956) were being released in art houses, with the number increasing during the 1960s as well.

The defections from the Soviet Union of Rudolf Nureyev in 1961, Natalia Makarova in 1970, and Mikhail Baryshnikov in 1974—and their subsequent appearances in gossip columns and tabloids across the United States—not only made ballet international news again but helped produce the well-known "dance boom" of the 1970s. Although, thanks to television, commercial films arguably could no longer be called the primary promulgators of popular culture by this time, Baryshnikov's appearance in *The Turning Point* (1977) helped make that film one of the most financially successful ballet films of the century. By *The Turning Point,* despite Balanchine's well-known aphorism that ballet was "woman," the attention was beginning to focus more obviously, even in the narratives of ballet films, on ballet's star men. Overall, the biggest change in ballet films both of the 1970s and 1980s and since, in the new cluster of films that appeared around the turn of the twenty-first century, lies in their retooling or reassigning of racial, gender, and sexual identity politics in stories that are otherwise extremely conventional—duller, *pace* Croce, if not always healthier. These films, their contexts, and their bodies are the topic of the final chapter of this book.

6

Turning Points

Ballet and Its Bodies in the "Post-Studio" Era

Ballet is an adolescent passion. . . . It gave me only turned-out feet and anemia.

—Leslie Caron, 1963

If you're going to make a big commercial movie about Nijinsky, you better stick to terms that can be understood by even the dimmest member of the audience, someone who still thinks of ballet as a lot of odd people wearing tights and tutus and clomping around on their toes.

—Review of *Nijinsky*, 1980

This is a *film*—this is *forever*.

—*Dancers*, 1987

Hip-hop can't take you the places that ballet can.

—*Honey*, 2003

In 1965 and again in 1968, *Time* magazine devoted cover stories to ballet.[1] In the first case, the focus was on Rudolf Nureyev, who had defected in 1961 and had rapidly become one of the biggest male ballet stars the world had seen. His partnership with Britain's reigning but "aging" *prima ballerina assoluta*, Margot Fonteyn, made them "the hottest little team in show biz," the article reports, he a "glittering young prince in the first bloom of creative life," she the "alabaster beauty of elegant refinement," a "dying swan in the last flutter of a shining career." As superstars, Fonteyn and Nureyev attracted "scores of people to the ballet who would not know a pirouette from a pratfall," and they thus "symbolize, in fact, a major resurgence in the dance, long culture's most neglected child." The figures that *Time* cites to demonstrate dance's increasing presence are the growth from 75 dance companies across the United States in the mid-1950s to 225 "amateur, semiprofessional, and professional" companies a decade later. Although *Time* quotes Balanchine's oft-repeated edict that "ballet is woman," the focus of the piece is on the men, the "resurgence of the male virtuoso" who belies the image of the male dancer as "pansy," replacing it with, say, that of Jacques d'Amboise, who could "pass as a halfback for the New York Giants rather than what he is, a principal dancer for the New York City Ballet."

In the 1968 feature story the attention is again on male dancers and choreographers, particularly those who, like Robert Joffrey or Gerald Arpino or Paul Taylor, were "far out, flashy, mod, mind-bending. Not even the new cinema," the article continues, "has done as much as dance has to free itself from the rules, clichés and conventions of the past." Balanchine and the New York City Ballet, and American Ballet Theatre, still maintained certain romantic classics in their repertoire—*The Nutcracker* was a Christmas staple of Balanchine's company, and American Ballet Theatre frequently mounted a full-length *Swan Lake*. But one company director, Brian Macdonald, is quoted as claiming, "The days of *Swan Lake* and *Giselle* are gone forever." Europe, *Time* adds, might still be operating "pretty much in the shadow of Petipa and Fokine," but in the United States ballet had become an "eclectic hybrid: it borrows what it needs from classical ballet, modern dance, jazz, rock 'n' roll and pop art—and it goes on from there." Moreover, while the popularity of ballet had become such that the country was developing "more female dancers than it can productively use," there were still not enough men to go around—this even though the "percentage of homosexuals" in ballet was "diminishing," from "about 90%" to a "ratio [of] about 60 to 40."

That this "new" ballet was creating and depending on "new" kinds of ballet bodies is clear from the 1968 *Time* story as well. Not only did the "line of hopefuls" now stretch around the block when the School of American Ballet held auditions, but those who were accepted were "properly proud and even a little haughty." In the words of Nanette Glushak, then a seventeen-year-old SAB student, "We saw a movie of Pavlova the other day, and I can tell you that she was pretty bad. I don't think she'd get accepted here today. She just wasn't good enough." And in another sign of dance's purported social acceptance in the three years since the publication of the 1965 cover story—in addition to the "proliferating schools" in big cities ("They're like bookies—there's one in every basement," reported one Manhattan teacher)—the number of professional and semiprofessional companies in the United States had risen by 1968 to "at least 450." Financial support for the arts remained a "nagging problem," but since 1963, both the Ford Foundation and the National Endowment for the Arts had contributed close to ten million dollars to support dance companies, by far the majority of which were ballet companies.[2]

By the time Mikhail Baryshnikov defected in 1974, *Time,* along with most other popular weekly and monthly magazines, was featuring regular columns about dance. But "Only a clairvoyant," *Time* wrote in 1975, "could have predicted that Ballet Dancers Rudolf Nureyev and Mikhail Baryshnikov would be this season's top box office draws in Manhattan."[3] Baryshnikov, "The Leningrad Kirov Ballet's latest runaway genius," was driving audiences "to frenzy." Once again, the current "dance explosion" is pointed to, and once again its driving forces are star male dancers, choreographers, and company directors, especially Balanchine. Nureyev, the focus of this column, "is so famous that he cannot remember the last time he met someone who had not heard of him."

The attention paid to the men in this era does not mean that there were no more star ballerinas, but there was no one on the order of a Pavlova or a Fonteyn (besides Fonteyn herself, now too a "dying swan" in the professional sense). Natalia Makarova's defection, also from the Kirov, in 1970 attracted nowhere near the attention that those of the male dancers did, although she was given star billing at American Ballet Theatre or any other company with which she danced. (When she partnered Baryshnikov for his American debut, however, the raves were for him. Clive Barnes, in a tone that resembles many other reviews, called Baryshnikov "the hottest thing on two legs," "sculpturally pure," a "Donatello in movement," and so on.)[4] In some sense, the most famous ballerina in the world became a generic *body,* the "Balanchine ballerina," who, or which, would from the 1960s and 1970s on come to stand in metonymically for the American woman ballet dancer generally. This "new generation of ballerinas" consisted, in Lynn Garafola's words, of "teens with the slim-hipped sexiness of a Pamela Tiffin or Twiggy. More than ever, the accent was on youth."[5] The American ballerina was no longer a woman but a fantastically proficient girl, thin, with big eyes in a tiny head—"pinheads," some critics called them, dancing machines, claimed others. And there were, again, "too many of them," in comparison to the men.

But while ballet was more popular and more famous than ever, there were virtually no narrative ballet films after the 1950s until *The Turning Point* in 1977. Instead, there were documentaries and performance films like *The Royal Ballet* (1960), *Belles and Ballet* (1960, featuring the work of Maurice Béjart), *Black Tights* (1962, the all-dance film), *An Evening with the Royal Ballet* (1965), *Romeo and Juliet* (1966, with Nureyev and Fonteyn), *Bolshoi Ballet 67* (1966), *The Tales of Beatrix Potter* (1971, choreographed by Frederick Ashton and performed by the Royal Ballet), and *The Children of Theatre Street* (1977, about the Kirov's ballet school). Nureyev starred in his own feature-length theatrical documentary, *I Am a Dancer,* in 1972, and the PBS television series *Dance in America* began its intermittent but decades-long run, as part of the umbrella series *Great Performances,* in 1976. Moreover, many of the Hollywood films discussed in these pages could be seen—albeit cut, with commercials, or panned-and-scanned—on television, too, randomly representing the art form to audiences who perhaps linked the films' characterizations of ballet and dancers both with the documentary images and the stories circulating about the "new" ballet featuring superstar men and gloriously beautiful, thin, and agile young women.

Despite the good number of films from the 1970s through the past few years to which the moniker "ballet film," even "ballet meller," could be applied—from *The Turning Point* to *The Company* (2003)—I am covering them in the same chapter because I believe that most, if not all, of the films of these decades tend to work variations on, but do not substantially reconfigure, the generic narratives and iconographies already discussed at such length. By the 1970s the film industry was of course freed from many of the strictures of representation that marked the classical "studio" film; but although the sexuality of the ballet body could become an overt rather than deflected topic of narrative discussion and representation, sex as sex remains for the most part heterosexual and romantic.[6] With few exceptions, ballet in narrative cinema continues through the first years in the twenty-first century to function much as it did in classical Hollywood's heyday, when the film musical placed popular entertainment forms (however ballet-based their dance techniques may have become) against ballet as formal and stiff but also pleasantly romantic and beautiful, or as a sign of "status and longevity."[7] Hip-hop and other forms of "street dancing" have now replaced tap or jazz as the "swing" in the "opera vs. swing" narrative, and partly as a result, the racial and ethnic identity of the narratively defined ballet body has become much less emphatically white over the past several decades, a nonwhite body frequently serving as the semantic marker of the vitality and value that the elite art of ballet must acquire "from the street" in order to remain, or become, interesting to new audiences and new generations. Concomitantly, the institutionalization of ballet not as one of many competing but equally valuable dance alternatives but as Wendy Buonaventura's "colossus bestriding the world of dance" has challenged the simultaneously elite and subcultural identity of ballet and its artists in the classical Hollywood film.[8] Ballet not only has an aura of prestige but of *power* in many of the films I discuss in this chapter. In addition, commercial cinema now pays some (but not much) attention to the body as the site and sight of "real" disease—anorexia and bulimia for women (*Center Stage*, 2000), AIDS for men (*Alive and Kicking*, 1996, but British)—and a new clinical realism occasionally (though, as we will see, hardly always) replaces the indeterminate suicidal psychoses and/or fatal but nondisfiguring varieties of unspecified illness of the earlier ballet film. There is also a noticeable change in the formal structure of the ballet film that operates in complex interaction with the phenomenally heightened technical proficiency of even the humblest "gypsy" or chorus dancer since the 1970s and 1980s, who now must not only be possessed of a "ballet body" but be astonishingly virtuosic in a wide variety of dance styles (there are still a lot of "hastily tutored" movie actors starring as dancers too, however). As professional dancers in all show-business forms have become more acrobatic, prodigious, and highly trained, film form now tends to minimize the integrity and ability of the dancing body. Rather than showing dancing and the dancer through mobile camerawork and in longer unbroken takes, editing—especially extremely short takes and discontinuous or shock cuts—has come, regardless of the skill or theatrical credentials of the dancers (or nondancers) whose work is filmed and included as an element of spectacle in any narrative ballet film from *The Turning Point* on, to stand in for the energy and activity that dancing itself represented to audiences of the 1930s, 1940s, and 1950s.

These variations aside, many if not all of the more popular ballet films of this period return to, indeed depend on, the most stubborn ideas and assumptions about the gender and sexuality of the ballet body and its inability to be "normal," working and reworking the ballet meller's conventions into pastiches of energy and achievement, beauty and disease, glory and despair, life and death, or else working variations on the "myth of entertainment," that art is better when it is popular. I will discuss some representative films from the 1970s and 1980s—among them *Slow Dancing in the Big City* (1978), *Nijinsky* (1980), *Fame* (1980), *Six Weeks* (1982), *Flashdance* (1983), and *Dancers* (1987)—virtually all of which are related to or attempt to exploit the success of *The Turning Point,* a film I therefore explore at some length. If I leave films out, or do not devote huge amounts of attention to them, it is again because the ground has become so well-trodden here that detailed exposition would be as redundant as the films themselves. At the turn of the twenty-first century, a new cycle of films appeared, beginning with *Billy Elliot* and *Center Stage* (both 2000), followed by *Save the Last Dance* (2001), *Honey* (2003), and *The Company;* and at the time of this writing there is no sign that the cycle has yet run its course (see, for example, *Step Up* [2006]).[9] These films—or more precisely the longevity of the concerns of the ballet film as a mode—matter because they signify the continued relevance of the ballet film and the need for ways, still, to circulate and mediate, literally and figuratively, our feelings about an ambivalent yet powerful attraction to the mute but expressive spectacular performing body.

Dancers Have Such Ugly Feet

By *The Turning Point* in 1977, the sensational popularity of the nominally heterosexual Nureyev and Baryshnikov and, concomitantly, the extremely feminine but also, because of her youth, androgynous "Balanchine ballerina" certainly affected the gender politics of ballet, and therefore ballet films generally. *The Turning Point* was produced and directed by Herbert Ross, who was married to one of the best-known American ballerinas of the 1940s and 1950s, Nora Kaye. Ironically, Kaye's original name was Koreff; she was born of Russian parents, in Brooklyn, but the climate for dance was such by mid-century that she changed it to sound more American. The take on ballet that *The Turning Point* offers is free from much anguish about whether ballet is or is not a worthwhile profession to take up in the "present day"; it assumes that America, specifically New York City, is home to the best ballet in the world; and nobody dies as a result of desiring to be, becoming, or being in love with or related to a ballet artist. The film grossed an "amazing" amount ($17 million), profiting from and contributing to the "dance boom" just as it was "reaching a peak of excitement," as Nancy Reynolds and Malcolm McCormick put it—a "peak" that was "fueled" by the defection and spectacular American presence of Baryshnikov, who is, not coincidentally, one of the film's stars.[10] He plays a Russian dancer named Yuri who has become principal dancer with the "American Ballet Company," a thinly disguised version of American Ballet Theatre.

While not many of the reviews of *The Turning Point* mention *The Red Shoes*, several subsequent studies of dance and film relate the two by virtue of what is presumed to be their anomalous status—they are both films with ballet stories featuring ballet dancers (instead of movie stars playing dancers) that caused a rush to ballet schools and led to a more pronounced presence of ballet in the mediascape generally. We have seen that there were many commercial films that had ballet stories other than *The Red Shoes*; in fact, one of the most notable impacts of *The Red Shoes* was on the dance content of other ballet films. But oddly enough to us, perhaps, ballet in *The Turning Point* was seen by several journalistic film reviewers—those who wrote about the film before its wide release, in the *New York Times* and *Variety*, for example—as supplementary rather than necessary to the film's overall effectiveness. *Variety* claimed that the "ballet atmosphere," while contributing "dramatic color," was "really incidental to the universality of the human emotions involved" in the film's story and that the "background setting could have been the business world, the campus, anything."[11] The *New York Times* wrote that *The Turning Point* was "a backstage film about the ballet rather than a ballet film. . . . The method is that of show-biz not art."[12] The question is how, and by what means, *The Turning Point* managed to be both a "peak" in the 1970s "dance boom"—and, moreover, as we will see, its popularity did help launch a cycle of other ballet films—and a film "about people and not dance," a story of "complex human life with feeling and compassion" to which dance was "incidental."[13]

The tagline on posters for *The Turning Point* read, "The generations change. But the choices remain the same." The two top-billed stars are well-known Hollywood actresses, Shirley MacLaine and Anne Bancroft. Baryshnikov is third-billed. MacLaine plays a former dancer, Deedee, married to another former dancer (played by Tom Skerritt), who lives in Oklahoma; the couple run a suburban ballet school and have three children. The eldest daughter, Emilia, played by "real" ballet dancer Leslie Browne, aims to be a professional dancer, probably, if she can figure out what she wants; the second teenaged daughter, of whom we see relatively little, is "normal," not interested in dance but instead devoted to all things domestic (cooking and cleaning); the youngest child, an adolescent son, also might want to be a ballet dancer, although he is a sports nut and is given other excessively heterosexual characteristics as well.

The story concerns what happens when the American Ballet Company visits Oklahoma City, and Deedee reunites with Emma (Bancroft), who was once her best friend and chief rival in the company. Emma got the big part that she and Deedee were competing for twenty years ago; Deedee instead—on Emma's advice, we learn—got married to her ballet-dancer husband and had a baby (partly to prove he "wasn't queer," we also learn), and Emma remained with the company and became a big star. But Emma is now, like Deedee, middle-aged and therefore increasingly out of fashion as a dancer and an artist. Childless and unmarried, she helps Emilia, her godchild, to get into the company and move with it to New York City over the summer; Deedee and son go along. When Deedee takes up with an old flame she runs into on the New York streets for a one-night stand, Emilia, who has that same day learned—in the sort of coincidence of timing so familiar from other ballet mellers—that Yuri has betrayed her with another budding ballerina in the company, rejects Deedee and punishes her by moving in with Emma and behaving as though Emma is the more valuable parent figure.

Several reviewers called *The Turning Point* a melodrama and a woman's picture, linking it to other "soap operas" and tear-jerkers of the past in the well-known generic senses of the term. Emma envies Deedee because Deedee is a wife and mother, and Deedee envies Emma because Emma is a star. As the *New York Times* noted, the film's dilemma is "old hopes rekindled," and, "as all of us know, an old hope never dies in fiction of this sort, no matter how many tears are pumped on it."[14] Deedee, much the bigger focus of the story, blames Emma for convincing her not to have an abortion all those years ago, so that she never got to know whether she would have scored herself in the part that made Emma the star (but then she would not have had Emilia either). The narrative climax of the film is a scene involving Deedee and Emma alone, an exchange of blame after Emilia's debut in a big ballet gala, that culminates in an out-and-out hair-pulling catfight on the windswept and (unrealistically) deserted plaza in front of Lincoln Center. Deedee screams that Emma is a bitch who is trying to steal her daughter and her affections because she is a bitter old woman who has no children of her own; Emma shouts that Deedee was always second-rate and got married because she was no good and she knew it. The physical part of the fight becomes comical in the end, the women succumbing to giggles as they pummel each other. They instantly resolve their differences—Deedee *was* a rival to Emma, Emma admits, which is all Deedee wanted to hear—and together turn their focus to the new young ballerina, Emilia, whose life and career choices are recapitulating their own and on whose dancing and then freeze-framed image the film fades out.

I well remember the *Turning Point* phenomenon as a college-aged dance student, and the film's appeal had nothing, for me and my friends, to do with the nominal star actresses and any of their old-fashioned dilemmas. For us, the film functioned most as a fantasy not about the "turning points" affecting the older women but the glamorous fairy-tale life of the ingenue, Leslie Browne/Emilia, and her philandering boyfriend, Baryshnikov/Yuri. Today I certainly watch the film as much for the all-too-brief glimpses of other famous historical personages, such as British ballerina Antoinette Sibley, playing a dancer who has various amounts of husband material standing by to make sure that she will *not* "end up like Emma," or legendary Russian ballerina Alexandra Danilova, playing an aging Russian dancer reduced to coaching and in whose apartment Deedee and Emilia live during the summer, or the big gala montage sequence featuring everyone from Suzanne Farrell and Peter Martins to Fernando Bujones to Richard Cragun and Marcia Haydée performing bits of their most famous roles. But arguably the appeal for the "new generation" itself was the manifestly unrealistic fantasy, a fantasy that we did know was a fantasy, that one could still be "discovered" in Oklahoma City and, with a little luck, become an overnight sensation in New York. And in the process become one of Mikhail Baryshnikov's sexual and romantic conquests.

Baryshnikov's dancing occupies far more screen time than that of Leslie Browne; but he is not the uncharacterized spectacular male of earlier ballet films, although he might appear so to viewers coming to the film now without much knowledge of Baryshnikov's fame in the 1970s. Yuri has lines, he is sometimes funny, his actions create plot perturbations, and he is a fabulous dancer, but we are told virtually nothing about his background or what motivates him as an artist (he has a big Nijinsky poster in his beautiful apartment, for those who knew who Nijinsky was). What the film depends on and makes use of is what Baryshnikov already meant in the 1970s, from the news items, gossip columns about his numerous girlfriends, and, for ballet fans, articles circulating about him in *Dance Magazine.* Yuri "was" the real-life Baryshnikov, the hypermasculinized token spectacle of action and virility and danger who was also, in the end, safe and sweet (his nickname was "Misha"), tender, helpful (just like the heroes of the roles we watched him dance). Indeed, the fantasy of *The Turning Point* also differs from that generated by and about ballet in *The Red Shoes*, in ways that I profoundly believe but cannot prove. That is, if young dancers at the time had a fantasy investment in *The Turning Point*, it was as much about sexuality as achievement, or the achievement *of* adult sexuality in a pre-AIDS age where one could be on the pill and shock one's mother (as Emilia does Deedee) but not otherwise get into any kind of serious trouble for sleeping around (Deedee calls Yuri a "horny little Russian," but Danilova's character approves of the sexual liaison as "good for Emilia").

Moreover, everyone was aware—and it was widely publicized in much that was written about the film in dance venues—that Leslie Browne was already *not* a ballet star, nor was she likely to become one. *The Turning Point* was reportedly written for Baryshnikov and Gelsey Kirkland (whose subsequent notorious exposés of ballet are addressed further below). We could identify with the backstage world of the ballet, especially the classes—there is a beautiful close-up shot of hands taking the worn wooden barre to begin that daily ritual—and rehearsals, but we also already knew that nobody, or, more precisely, nobody female, became a ballet star overnight anymore in the dance world of the United States and its big companies. It was virtually impossible even to get into the School of American Ballet just to study, so many fabulously accomplished and rail-thin Balanchine ballerina bodies would one have to compete against to do so. In fact, no one except the defecting Russians had become overnight sensations in the ballet world in years.

Just as the young Moira Shearer became more famous than Margot Fonteyn and came in for a fair amount of sniping because of her "technical limitations" at the time of *The Red Shoes*, so did Leslie Browne get criticized after the film's release for not being of "real" ballerina quality or ability. Browne was a soloist with American Ballet Theatre, the daughter herself of married American ballet dancers (and the goddaughter of Nora Kaye and Herbert Ross). Her big moment in *The Turning Point* is dancing a 1970 Alvin Ailey solo, presented as being revolutionary and daring because it is "abstract" and thus far out of the purview of the technical and emotional capabilities of Emma, for whom it was originally intended. But by 1977 Ailey's solo (in *The Turning Point*, shown as choreographed by a gay white male), while beautiful, was not startling or unusual; as Arlene Croce wrote of the film, "Isn't it a bit late for the abstract revolution in ballet to be taking place?"[15] Emilia's ascent to stardom is supposedly based on merit, and Browne's body is very much in the mold of the Balanchine ballerina—thin to the point of emaciation, long

Leslie Browne in the audition scene of *The Turning Point* (1977).
Copyright 1977 Twentieth Century–Fox.

legs, small head, big eyes—and clothed often in tattered but revealing pastel leotards and tights and gauzy skirts; her body frequently glistens with sweat but she is never out of breath. We watch her mother bandage her bloody toes in gory close-up, and Emma at one point remarks that "dancers have such ugly feet." But nothing about ballet, other than being or becoming "old," is presented as really ugly (or smelly, or exhausting, or unfair, or even difficult). Once Emilia has been seen onstage by New York eyes, her future is assured; she will dance with Yuri again, and the company's repertoire, including a revival of *The Sleeping Beauty,* is going to be built around her stardom. Emilia and Yuri will make the company rich or at least fiscally sound, and presumably neither will be afflicted by the sorts of problems faced, or, it is more than implied, created by Emma and Deedee.

And no less than *The Red Shoes, The Turning Point*'s "point" about the impossibility of reconciling life and art in the case of the older stars of the story is belied by the historical truths on which the film was at least partly based. Browne's parents were married and both dancing with [American] Ballet Theatre when she was born, and although they did not become big ballet stars, they were able both to have professional ballet careers and to have a "normal" family life that included children. Nora Kaye was already a star with Ballet Theatre when Browne's parents joined; there was no rivalry between Kaye and Isabel Mirrow, Browne's mother, for example.[16] At the same time, however, while Moira Shearer made several other well-known

Anne Bancroft as the aging Emma contemplating her future in *The Turning Point*.
Copyright 1977 Twentieth Century–Fox.

films and remained a ballerina in the Sadler's Wells Ballet (her forward progress blocked there, like that of many ballerinas from the 1940s through the 1970s, only by Fonteyn's hegemony in the company) and also married and had a family, Browne's "overnight" fame never translated into true stardom, although she appeared in two other films, both also directed by Herbert Ross. Her final film, *Dancers* (1987), in fact serves as a bitter commentary on any "fantasy of achievement" that *The Turning Point* and its "backstage musical" story (success in the show guarantees success in love) might represent.

And yet even to speak of "normal" family life as something that a profession in the arts might preclude or ruin is to realize how conventional a melodrama *The Turning Point* is, despite what *Newsweek* called its "sophisticated '70s awareness."[17] Certainly it employs a quite hoary ballet-meller trope, the mother who will realize her thwarted professional ambitions through her daughter, varying it by adding a competing surrogate mother who attempts to steal the child's affection and esteem in order to fill her own empty nondomestic life. The ideals in which the film trades are the nuclear family headed by a heterosexual male, the wife always already a mother; she might work outside the home, but even then some female entity in the family must run the household, as the so-called "normal child," the middle daughter, does in *The Turning Point*. The film's tagline is thus a melancholy commentary on the continuing force of the Manichean universe of the ballet meller—the generations change, but the choices, in white American middle-class culture, remain the same, between "normal" life and, for women, essentially anything else. The most obvious change that *The Turning Point does* work on the ballet meller, if not on the musical genre as well, is related not to the fate of protagonists Deedee and Emma but to the ultimate failure of the fairy tale of overnight success. We might have loved the escapist fantasy of Emilia's rise to stardom, but we did know that it was not "true," that no one, certainly not Leslie Browne, was going to be plucked from the corps to dance with Mikhail Baryshnikov in the pas de deux from *Don Quixote* at Lincoln Center.[18]

"Rockies" in Toe Shoes

Broken hearts and jealousy aside, at least *The Turning Point* exhibits few signs of the sorts of morbidity that mark *The Red Shoes. The Turning Point* still makes comments about ballet men needing to prove they are not gay (why?), and some of its toes are still bloody, but its overarching message, beyond its adherence to basic "family values," is that it is no fun to grow old. Despite how crucial I believe ballet and ballet stars were to the film's success among the dance-crazed, it is nevertheless easy to understand why *Variety* would think that ballet is "really incidental" or that the film's background setting could have been "anything." Several other of the films that followed hard on the "amazing" success of *The Turning Point* are even more conventionally melodramatic.

Slow Dancing in the Big City features Paul Sorvino as what the *New York Times* called a "plain, ordinary big lug" named Lou who falls in love with a ballerina, Sarah (Anne Ditchburn), an "exotic hothouse flower of a dancer" who moves into Lou's brownstone.[19] A "'Rocky' in toe shoes," *Slow Dancing in the Big City* makes both Lou and Sarah into dreamers seeking their big break. Sarah was born rich and beautiful (Ditchburn was a Canadian ballerina), whereas Lou is working class; his desire for Sarah adds a superficial touch of class struggle to the film, but what supersedes all other plot divagations is that Sarah has an unnamed crippling disease that will put an end to her dance career immediately after she performs triumphantly in the premiere of a new "modern" ballet (the costumes are ragged loincloths, and the men dance in bare feet; the women wear toe shoes). Sarah literally loses the ability to walk as soon as the ballet is over, but Lou is waiting in the wings to carry her out to receive her ovation, and then, presumably, away to a happy nondancing life together. Although there are subplots involving Lou's efforts to save an eight-year-old Puerto Rican drug addict (the child dies), Lou's infatuation with Sarah drives the plot. And the infatuation itself comes about in familiar ways: he sees her dance, and he is smitten. "You're a poet," Sarah tells Lou over dinner; "You're beautiful," he replies.

Reviews of *Slow Dancing in the Big City* were, in general, bad, and it was not a box-office success. My friends and I went to see it because it had dancing in it, but we thought it hysterically funny and mimicked Ditchburn's bizarrely tight-lipped style of locution and the sentimental but "tough" dialogue on our way out of the theater. Even more risible to us was *Six Weeks* (1982), in which Mary Tyler Moore plays the mother of a preternaturally "gifted" California child ballerina who is dying of leukemia (Anne Ditchburn plays the role of an assistant choreographer who is named Ann Ditchburn). Dudley Moore appears as a local politician attracted to the mother, and the two take the girl to New York City, where she assumes the lead in a performance of *The Nutcracker* and then, within hours, dies. Here, the disease is given a name, at least, but to be ill enough to die from leukemia, we all thought, probably precluded performing any lead role in a full-length *Nutcracker* in the hours immediately preceding one's demise.

In contrast, in the early 1980s *Fame* and *Flashdance* were incredibly appealing, although the function of ballet in each is somewhat dissimilar. The ballet-dancing character in *Fame* was but one member of a large group of diversely talented students at New York City's High School for the Performing Arts. Antonia Franceschi played the foul-mouthed and bitter WASP ballet student Hilary Van Doren, who for ambiguous reasons—because she "digs his black ass" (she says this first in French), for thrills, or to rebel against her oblivious and cold parents (especially a stepmother)—enters into a sexual relationship with Leroy (Gene Anthony Ray), a bad-boy African American street dancer at the school, by whom she becomes pregnant. The scene in which Leroy and Hilary notice each other differs significantly in its racial but not gender politics from similar scenes in earlier films. Hilary, dressed in pale pink, is dancing ballet alone in a studio, where Leroy watches mesmerized from the sidelines; she finishes dancing and winks at him, he smiles, and they hook up. But after an extended monologue later in the film, in close-up, in which Hilary tearfully lays out the effects of having a baby on her ballet career (she turns out to be in the waiting room of an upper-class abortion clinic, and the scene ends with a shot of Hilary's blank face after the receptionist nurse asks whether she is going to pay with "Master Charge or American Express"), Hilary and her Balanchine body disappear completely from *Fame*'s narrative (she can be seen as one of the crowd of dancers who perform in the final musical number).

Ironically, in *Fame* Hilary is nobody's muse; she intends to be a star, and her dream is to be "doing all the classical roles before I'm twenty-one." But it is her own technical proficiency and perfect (skeletally thin and muscular) body and beauty, as well as her father's money and her toughness, that are going to get her where she wants to go; she is not really singled out as conspicuously or *unusually* gifted otherwise. In this sense *Fame*'s ballerina functions as a metacommentary on the trope of the sacrificial mother (Hilary does not want to live out her ambitions through *her* child), but the film otherwise has no place for her to go.

Flashdance, on the other hand, depicts ballet itself as a goal only, the dream achievement of its working-class, racially mixed, welder/exotic dancer heroine Alex (Jennifer Beals). In a sense, the Hilary of *Fame* is the sort of dancer Alex yearns to be, but Alex is not able to break down the class and race barriers that would allow her simply to study at a snotty ballet company school and thereby achieve her vague ballet desires. However gritty and realistic the welding and strip-club scenes feel, ballet and its practitioners are treated, in the fashion of melodrama, as somewhat villainous; the point of the film seems to be to show that Alex, from the wrong side of the tracks, can breach the fortress of elite art through pluckiness, spunk, and break dancing. But Alex is already a self-supporting adult with a huge urban-industrial apartment and her own dance floor; her yearning is not the problem. It is the film's ignorance about ballet that makes it so ludicrous and so easily the "fantasy of achievement" that Angela McRobbie labels both this film and *Fame*.[20]

More obviously than any classical Hollywood musical, *Flashdance* utilizes the "opera vs. swing" narrative to suggest that ballet is a moribund, effete, and stiff form that has been waiting for a break-dancer to bring it to life and make it relevant. At the same time, Alex's audition for the ballet school—performed to a recording of Irene Cara singing "What a Feeling" (Cara had sung and played a character in *Fame* as well)—functions like the big finale to a classical musical, a triumph in itself that brings the performer success in show business (here, art), as well as romance. Alex's rich boyfriend and former boss, Nick (Michael Nouri), is waiting for her after her (successful) audition (he has brought along her dog, some roses, and his Porsche), and the film ends on a freeze-frame of the couple in a smiling embrace. *Flashdance*'s big attraction was thus not its ballet; there is no ballet dancing in the film, just nasty [white] girls who stretch and pose in leotards and toe shoes and pink tights while they stare at and whisper about Alex as she walks through the halls of the ballet academy and dares, however briefly before fleeing the scene, to stand in line to apply for admittance. Rather, it was break dancing that helped propel the film into the status of a mass-media sensation. Jennifer Beals was not a dancer herself, however, and although the producers initially sought to keep her dancing doubles' names a secret (there were, apparently, three dancers doing Alex's work in the final audition number—Marine Jahan doing the dancing, Sharon Shapiro the slow-motion dives through the air, and Crazy Legs, a male break-dancer, the various break dancing spins and so on), the scandal of the deception caused more of a stir than the fact of the doubles themselves.[21]

Publicity still from *Flashdance* (1983) of Jennifer Beals as Alex, represented as out of place in the midst of ballet's white upper-class bodies.

Copyright 1983 Paramount Pictures.

As is obvious from the sheer number of bodies appearing together as the same character (Jahan does the dancing in the strip-club numbers too), all of the dancing in *Flashdance* is heavily edited, with short shots and slow motion intercut into a frenzy of movement only rarely dependent on or derived from the integrity of the dancer's body. The panel of judges who audition Alex in the penultimate scene go from dour and disgusting (one blows his nose repeatedly, one puffs on a large cigar) to astonished and happy; pop music, editing, slow motion, and floor spins, along with jazz shoes and leg warmers (and torn sweatshirts worn as fashion accessories), will make Alex and her several bodies into the saviors of ballet and its effete invisibility. In turn, by conquering ballet and the elite culture with which ballet is associated (the school Alex is auditioning for is housed in a museum), Alex has "taken her passion" and "made it happen," one of the film's most famous taglines. She too will become a Rocky in toe shoes.

Competing with the Sylph

Ballet in *Flashdance* is demonized at the same time that its (female) bodies and status are represented as desirable; and a similar dichotomy, the pathology of ballet as feminine and misogynistic, became the focus of more attention in the 1980s. In the 1940s and 1950s, mass-market magazines had frequently detailed how grueling dancing in the movies was and how hard stars from Ginger Rogers to Vera-Ellen to Leslie Caron or Cyd Charisse had to work during filming to "keep their weight up"; conversely, advice columns sometimes pointed to dancing itself, often using the same stars as sources or examples, as a good and fun way to keep the weight off.[22] But in the 1960s, Leslie Caron was quoted in a number of articles speaking to ballet's damaging effects on her body—"turned out feet and anemia"—and the life of a ballet dancer, in contrast to that of an actor, as being "dull, uninteresting, stupid and dirty."[23] Although ballet had often been associated with pain and suffering, its particular relationship to the female body became more of a focus with ballet's increasing hegemony in the dance world. The publication of a spate of books with titles like *Competing with the Sylph: Dancers and the Pursuit of the Ideal Body Form* (1979), *Off Balance: The Real World of Ballet* (1983), and, perhaps most famously, *Dancing on My Grave* (1983)—ballerina Gelsey Kirkland's best-selling autobiographical account of her attempts to satisfy the impossible demands of Balanchine that she be abnormally thin, feminine, and superhumanly athletic and virtuosic—was part of a wider concern with women's bodies and the eating disorders, such as anorexia and bulimia, that were affecting more, or more publicly affecting, Western girls and young women.[24] Balanchine did not invent the ideology of thinness for women dancers (although Joseph Mazo wrote that when you "think about dancers—long-legged, slender girls who move as quickly as delight—you are thinking about [Balanchine]. He invented them").[25] Rather, for Balanchine America was already the "land of lovely bodies."[26]

Bernard Taper, one of Balanchine's biographers, claims that Balanchine's classicism was itself "a contemporary classicism—designed to be seen by twentieth-century eyes and make its effects on twentieth-century nerves. The classic vocabulary of steps is employed in a different way from [Marius] Petipa: extensions are higher, movements may be faster and more staccato, combinations are more complicated and intense."[27] Dance anthropologist Judith Lynne Hanna reiterates this, calling contemporary ballet "at once antitechnology in its physical recoiling from the enslaving machine and protechnology in its emulation of the machine's precision, economy, and speed. . . . [E]levation and extension [are] higher, speed greater, body sleeker and as angular as the skyscraper, and movements sharper."[28] When asked, Balanchine was inclined to explain his preference for bodies "like toothpicks" (his words) in visual terms: it was possible to "see more" of the dance if less of the body was there. And Lincoln Kirstein, who worked so hard to have ballet accepted as the American dance art, also saw the highest good in surrendering of the self to dance: "What can be clearly seen in any well-executed [ballet] performance," he wrote in 1978, "is a group of beautiful young people in the prime of health, trained for a rigorous profession, working in transparent harmony according to metrical laws superior to their individual wills or accidental preferences."[29] That ballet would not exist without these "beautiful young people," and that these young people had needs and desires of their own, became, to Kirstein as well as Balanchine, an increasingly irritating problem.

Although men are as prone as women to develop dance injuries, men are more likely to be coddled through them; there are simply fewer men to go around. Yet when a degree of protest began in the 1970s and 1980s to be made about the New York City Ballet's low wages, long hours, short seasons, lack of health insurance or retirement benefits, especially for the corps de ballet, Kirstein simply turned his own argument on its head: "A straw man [sic] was conceived and labeled 'the Balanchine dancer,' generally speaking a lanky girl with a pinhead, a zombie, computerized past 'soul.' Since alternatives to classic ballet usually invoke 'self-expression' as salvation, and since the 'self' of most aspirants is dubious as to both maturity and information, . . . opposition to [Balanchine's] direction was only logical."[30] Thus, opposition to the bizarre conditions under which women ballet dancers worked rendered one immature and ill-educated; what Kirstein ignores is the extent to which being immature and ill-educated can be a potential result of a life spent in American ballet. Toni Bentley's 1982 *Winter Season: A Dancer's Journal* details both her reverence and regard for Balanchine as a mentor, a genius, and a father-figure and her ambivalence about how the "family" of the New York City Ballet reacted to its "children's" attempts merely to assert themselves, through strikes and other collective actions to gain living wages and health and disability insurance, as the adults that they in fact were.[31]

Yet there is something awry in the prevalence of the notion, across many areas of culture even today, that ballerinas *only*, not modern or postmodern or musical-comedy dancers, not models or actresses or athletes or college students (etc.), are anorexic neurotic pinheads. It is certainly an issue about which many of Balanchine's dancers are heatedly responsive; many assert that they did *not* feel themselves to be mere instruments, children, or mindless automatons. But some certainly did, Gelsey Kirkland being the most sensational example. It is more often at the corps de ballet level that dancers are likely to perceive themselves to be interchangeable, and it is here that anorexia, apparently, is more endemic (and it is not incidental that the labor unrest at the New York City Ballet occurred near the end of Balanchine's life—he died in 1983—at a time when many dancers at the company had never even met him). One subtext of this book has been the role that commercial film has played in the internalization of images about ballet and its bodies, and this applies not only to the conventions and iconography of narrative films and their ballet characters but, on a broader level, to photographic media that record time and space, to what dancing bodies are supposed to be and look like. Remi Clignet has noted that both film and video allow the comparison of past and present or of individual performers with themselves or with others. Film therefore "exacerbates competition because it enables actors and dancers to compare their successive performances and to internalize with greater ease the requirements of their own standards."[32] If Balanchine began by desiring the bodies of women that he saw in American movies, the women (and men) that he helped "create" as dancers were, knowingly or not, defining and refining their bodies and technical capabilities in relation to those earlier images and representations.

There is little, however, in the narratives of the ballet films of the period to indicate any particular problem with the contours of the female body. The body can be diseased, as in *Slow Dancing in the Big City* or *Six Weeks,* but, again, the ballet body had routinely been associated with disease and pathology in American popular culture for decades. The four interchangeable bodies that dance in *Flashdance* actually function more as component parts to a dancing machine than any Balanchine ballerina ever did. However, the *Flashdance* bodies are fit, muscular, and neither fat nor abnormally thin; they are racially and ethnically diverse, and one of them is male passing as female. Not until the end of the century did ballet films begin to consider the topics of ballet and body image in concrete terms; it is tempting to think of the dearth of ballet films focused on women *or* men in the 1990s as having something to do with a crisis of representation, an inability to conceive any longer of the ballet body as pathological in some amorphous sense when it really *was* becoming associated with life-threatening illness.

Ironically, the popularity of the 1980s ballet film as woman's film—or, more colloquially, "chick flick"—was based, at least partly, on the sexual attraction of the films' men, who functioned less as the sort of patriarchal mentor figures discussed above than as ways into sexual experience and, or as, independence and rebellion. None of the post–*Turning Point* films already discussed cared much about the men *except* as heterosexual bodies, even when they had names, lines to speak, or dances to perform. But there were at least two films that took the dancing man as their explicit subject, although neither of them, despite being expensive and handsomely mounted—with much bigger budgets than the 1980s chick flicks—succeeded at the box office. In fact, both films indicate the continued difficulty of representing the aestheticized male body as something other than pathological; moreover, they are both products of the *Turning Point* team of Herbert Ross and Nora Kaye.

Genius. Madman. Animal. God.

In contrast to *The Turning Point, Nijinsky* (1980) and *Dancers* (1987) are quite fevered melodramatic reworkings of two of the best-known story-myths of ballet's history in America. The above tagline to *Nijinsky* is suggestive enough, and the working title of *Dancers* was *Giselle*. It was inevitable, in the new age of film frankness, that someone was going to take on Nijinsky as a subject to explore overtly as opposed to the coded versions of *The Mad Genius* (1931), *Specter of the Rose* (1946), and their ilk. The success of *The Turning Point, Fame,* and *Flashdance* also ensured bigger budgets and therefore production values for new ballet films. *Nijinsky*—with George de la Peña as Nijinsky, Alan Bates as Diaghilev, and Leslie Browne as Romola de Pulsky, the corps dancer who married Nijinsky—was eagerly awaited by dance aficionados given its *Turning Point* lineage. One problem for the new project, however, was that the subject himself was a dancer legendary for being the best the world had ever seen; since no films exist of his dancing as there do of, say, Pavlova, his reputation had been mystified arguably beyond the ability of any film to represent him. One either had to find a dancer who might live up to Nijinsky's reputation as a dancing god (perhaps Nureyev or Baryshnikov, who had both frequently been compared to Nijinsky) or else not show him dancing at all. Ross chose to use another soloist from American Ballet Theatre, a fine enough dancer but not as virtuosic technically as audiences raised on Nureyev and Baryshnikov had grown used to.

Another problem posed for any filmmaker is the relative lack of narrative excitement of Nijinsky's later years; diagnosed with schizophrenia in the late teens, he spent the rest of his life as basically a family man, taken care of by his devoted, indeed hagiographic, wife and daughters and moving into and out of asylums and hospitals in Europe until his death in 1950. Therefore, the film covers basically a few months, the exciting period from 1912 to 1913, when the Ballets Russes de Monte Carlo mounted Nijinsky's scandalous and scandalizing *L'Après-midi d'un faun, Le Sacre du printemps,* and *Jeux.* But Nijinsky's own ballets were manifestly unlike the romantic or even classical but "abstract" works that dot *The Turning Point.* The novel techniques required to perform them, at the time part of the scandal the works aroused, are not as flashy as ballet's other pyrotechnics of difficult beats, multiple turns, jumps, speedy and intricate footwork—which American audiences of the 1980s had been educated to think of, especially in relation to male dancers, as signifiers of ballet quality.

Nijinsky's ballets as mounted in Ross's movie (no film records exist of any of the original choreography) resemble camp interpretations of modern dance—flat frontality and angularity, flexed feet and hands, clenched spasms of frenetic movement alternating with beautiful but static tableaux. And of course, there are no tutus anywhere or, except for the two women of *Jeux,* toe shoes either. Not even *Specter of the Rose* in 1946 had dared to dress its male lead in a costume sewn with pink rose petals (as discussed in chapter 3, the 1911 ballet *Le Spectre de la rose* is about a young girl who dreams of the spirit of a rose); *Nijinsky* does, although the costume is significantly modified and toned down in its fluffiness from original photographic renderings of it.[33] Nijinsky's famous high and hovering "leap through the window" at the end of *Le Spectre de la rose* is predictably created through the filmic trick of slow motion, which turns out to make a leap much less impressive as a sign of prowess than simply watching it in real time.

Like *Specter of the Rose,* though, the perturbations of *Nijinsky*'s plot arise from the simultaneous subject/object status of the male lead, who is the victim, along with Romola, of an appealing but monstrous Diaghilev. If Diaghilev resembles Lermontov in *The Red Shoes,* it is because Lermontov was also supposed to resemble the historical Diaghilev; both characters are marked as vampire villains by the white streaks in their black hair. Most reviews pointed out that Diaghilev, through Alan Bates (and like other villains of the genres of melodrama or horror), commands much more attention onscreen than any other actor or dancer, including the titular subject. And as had been the case with many, many other films, the skills and abilities required of fine dancers, or even stage actors, do not automatically make them fine film performers (Leslie Browne dances not at all, except in one scene intended to demonstrate how *bad* a dancer Romola herself was). Diaghilev is a more interesting figure than anyone else in the film, which is perhaps why a *New York Times* review of *Nijinsky* is entitled "Pointeless."[34] Although Herbert Ross was "the great popularizer of ballet," the clichés of *Nijinsky,* and the lack of astonishing dancing in it, leave the film with a lot of what the reviewer politely terms "holes." Nijinsky marries Romola, and Diaghilev rejects him; Nijinsky loses his reason and is shown, at the end of the film, in a straitjacket, staring into space à la Norman Bates in Hitchcock's *Psycho.*

The film seems on the one hand to suggest that Diaghilev drove Nijinsky insane through the force of his, Diaghilev's, domination and will, that without Diaghilev Nijinsky was nothing. Moreover, Nijinsky's need for Diaghilev's guidance caused Nijinsky to subsume his own heterosexuality—he rips Romola's clothes from her in an ecstasy of lust—or to disguise it as homosexuality in order to retain Diaghilev's support and guidance. In this sense, *Nijinsky* resembles the 1977 Ken Russell film *Valentino,* in which Rudolf Nureyev played the silent movie star also as a somewhat timid character, bullied by a conniving, lesbianish wife and hounded by rumors about his uncertain virility, and as a fiery, temperamental *artiste.* Nijinsky appears in *Valentino* as well, played by British ballet danseur Anthony Dowell; one of the best-known scenes in the film is the ballroom dance that Valentino and Nijinsky perform together.

On the other hand, *Nijinsky* reproduces all of the stereotypes of ballet's male "perverts," and audiences familiar with these stereotypes would easily have been able to perceive Nijinsky's insanity as itself a sign of his and ballet's perversion. Nijinsky is also, like Sanine in *Specter of the Rose,* the relatively passive object of everyone's gaze; Nijinsky's genius and temperament—his status as a god—all were part of his dancing, not of his ordinary personality. Temperamental outbursts became more common as a result of the depredations of his illness, but Nijinsky himself was, from most accounts, taciturn, not interested in much beyond dancing, quite boring to be around. So to have a male lead be intriguing by virtue of the aestheticization of his body, to make "him" alluring primarily, if not solely, as a beautiful mute object, shows how clearly the spectacular male dancing body still functions as a problem for mainstream commercial cinema even in the 1970s and 1980s. Gay ballet men are not perverts; but neither are they heterosexual, which American mass culture represents materially as the locus of the normative through "ordinary" male dress and purposeful, unflamboyant gestures and movements.[35] John Travolta's three-piece-suited disco-dancing body, to compare another famous example, poses much less of a predicament on these terms for *Saturday Night Fever* (1977) than it does to *Staying Alive* (1983), in which Travolta's "strutting" working-class Tony Manero becomes a Broadway stage dancer with an oiled body, a loincloth and a headscarf, and pointed toes.

But again, the female dancer's body and its contours also were starting to be considered pathologically, or as signs of a pathology that was at once a real disease, anorexia (sometimes conflated with bulimia), and a representation of the perceived misogyny of ballet itself. AIDS began to take its toll on the ranks of male dancers and choreographers after the 1980s, but few if any films acknowledge this in relation to dance and dancers; the only film I know of that deals with a male dancer with AIDS is *Alive and Kicking* (1996), which drew on the scandal of Nureyev's death from AIDS in 1993, and it was a British production that had limited American release.[36]

Pure Youth, Light, Energy, Joy

The box-office failure of the expensively mounted *Nijinsky* was perhaps a factor in returning Ross's final ballet film to clearer chick-flick territory, and at least one reviewer called *Dancers* (1987) a "sequel" to *The Turning Point;* it stars Mikhail Baryshnikov and features, in a much smaller role, Leslie Browne. But *Dancers* was an even bigger critical failure than *Nijinsky*—a true bomb, universally lambasted and disappearing from theaters very quickly after a splashy opening and tremendous amounts of gooey publicity.[37] This may be a good sign; I find it to be one of the most unbearably pretentious ballet films ever, a sort of cinematic revenge fantasy, because, quite simply, it tries to make *Giselle* into a star vehicle for a *man*—and not in any interesting gender-bending or even apparently intentional camp way (although *Dancers* may indeed provoke a camp response, or gasps of disbelief, today). It is disheartening to be disappointed by any film that focuses so much on a male ballet star's body, especially when the body belongs to "Misha" at his prime (the credits put Baryshnikov's, and Baryshnikov's name only of all the stars, above the title; and the poster consists primarily of a huge close-up of Baryshnikov's blue-eyed face). The trouble is the film's *attitude* toward its subject, the simultaneous glorifying of the misogynistic male and his body as the sign that this *Giselle* is somehow a "new," more relevant work, because it is now the product of hyperbolically heterosexual male genius not only at the level of direction, choreography, staging, and production but of *dancing*.[38]

The plot of *Dancers* is meant to double that of *Giselle*, but it cannot really do this and be about a male ballet superstar who arrives in Italy to make a film of the ballet for, by, and about him. Moreover, the reason that Anton ("Tony"), Baryshnikov's character, gives for why he cares about the project is that he knows that film, unlike ballet itself apparently, is *"forever."* So his future reputation, his status as a genius, is at stake. But Tony is in a creative funk, jaded, unhappy, and uninspired, which bothers him. Tony has become, in his own words, a man with "no feelings." But this is not by choice: "It feels terrible not to have feelings," he complains; "You think it's easy?" Tony is not much interested in the ballerina role of *Giselle*, the manifest glory of the ballet as a work of art. The ballerina who is dancing the lead in the film-within-the-film, Francesca (Alessandra Ferri), is just one of his old girlfriends, someone with whom he still occasionally sleeps when other of his regulars are not available. She may be a great dancer (and good in bed), but she does not make *him* feel anything. Thus, once Tony sleeps with a woman, that woman—regardless of any other characteristic she might have, including beauty, talent, or a sense of humor—automatically becomes part of the world about which he cannot bring himself to care, but with which he continues to divert or distract himself.

In other words, the story of Giselle, as *Dancers* recasts it (literally and figuratively), is really that of a duke, Albrecht, also now a "man with no feelings" but with nothing otherwise really to complain about. It is not that any character in a romantic ballet is well delineated or that he or she cannot be interpreted and reinterpreted on any number of levels. The figures of aristocrat and peasant girl are stock, cardboard on the level of psychological motivation and so on (this is true of all melodramas). But Albrecht does not usually spend much time onstage in the ballet or do much dancing. In act 1 he is the vehicle of Giselle's end of innocence, a nobleman who likes to slum as a peasant with his buddy and who desires the very young, unspoiled, and beautiful Giselle, maybe as a conquest, maybe because he falls in love with her. He is, however, already betrothed, and he does not give any signs as the ballet is written of really wanting or planning to give up the princess who wears his engagement ring. Indeed, one of the elements that has made Giselle into the prime test of the ballerina's art is how well she is able to invest Giselle's flat virginal innocence in act 1 with something more resonant—personality, for lack of a better word, or spunk, anything to make her betrayal by Albrecht matter as more than an upsetting of a placid, sweet dimness. Whether Giselle's heart condition, a flaw that makes her physically as well as psychically delicate, or instead suicide using Albrecht's sword is the cause of her death at the end of act 1, the success of the famous "mad scene"—her heart and reason shattered by the revelation of Albrecht's perfidy, Giselle relives the stages of their romance in broken, halting steps as Albrecht looks on in horror—depends on the contrast of its pyrotechnics with the delicacy and grace of the character's preceding incarnation.

In act 2, the "white" act, in which Giselle is a wili, one of a tribe of virginal girls betrayed and dead before their wedding day and who therefore roam the woods at night dancing any man they find to death before sunrise, Albrecht usually has even less to do. He wanders around in sorrow and throws himself on Giselle's grave, and later he supports Giselle in several pas de deux (he performs a couple of variations within these, too). Giselle's role is to protect him as he begins to tire, dancing more energetically herself and hiding Albrecht from the other wilis who want him to die. As dawn breaks, Albrecht is saved, Giselle returns to her grave, and the ballet ends. Albrecht usually is left alone onstage, but sometimes his father and friends and future bride rush onstage to rescue him.[39]

In Dancers, however, Baryshnikov/Tony makes Albrecht into someone looking for "meaning." One of Tony's old friends says to him, "You seem empty." Yes, he is; he is dancing, Tony says of himself, "without a spark." He finds the spark, "pure youth, light, energy, joy," in the person of an adoring and virginal young American corps dancer, Lisa, played by Julie Kent. Tony decides to hang out with her a little and asks her to "please try to think of [him] as just a guy," even though he has a pretty huge reputation as a lady-killer, as well as a ballet star (Lisa does not seem to have heard anything about his womanizing). Kent's role is to be young and sweet while she adores Tony; she has a high-pitched childlike voice and a Balanchine body, but we do not really see her dance. (In a mawkish "making of" article in Vogue, "Misha" himself says of Kent, "Look at her. . . . I first saw her two years ago, when she was fifteen, and I thought then, Here is the beauty of a woman in

Publicity photo of Baryshnikov "warm[ing] up with some barre work" in *Dancers* (1987).

Copyright 1987 Cannon Films.

the body of a child").[40] Lisa's innocence is also signaled by a normal family back home (parents, that is, and brothers and sisters) that she misses, and while she acquires an Italian admirer her own age with whom she rides around on a Vespa in a long tutu and toe shoes, she is still the answer to Tony's dilemma. In Lisa he *sees* what Albrecht saw in Giselle. But Lisa misunderstands her function for Tony and runs away crying when she eventually realizes that he has several girlfriends already. *He* is sure that she has decided to commit suicide, and the film intercuts his search for her outside the theater with the "mad scene" taking place within it (melodrama's interest in coincidence and last-minute rescues are at the fore here). But Lisa is not suicidal, she was just upset; moreover, she forgives Tony because he is a "great artist," and she decides she was happy to be his muse for even just a little while. "You made me cry," she tells him, but she means through his *dancing,* and this in turn means that Tony is no longer "empty." He has been revivified by the adoration of a virgin.

Even more grating is Leslie Browne's role in *Dancers.* She plays one of Tony's former brief conquests, an almost-ballerina named Nadine who has a young child by another philandering male dancer and who hates men for all they have done to her, for avoiding their adult responsibilities. When Lisa early says of Tony that she has never seen him before, except onstage, Nadine snaps back, "You're gonna wish you stayed in the audience." Nadine dances the role of Queen of the Wilis, but she is clearly never going to play Giselle herself; she is already, in her late twenties, too old. Worse, when Tony is not getting what he wants from his wili queen, he goads Nadine, onstage and in public, into using her despair, of which he himself is a major motivating cause, to be a better evil man-hating bitch in "his" ballet. But all ends happily. Once the filming is over, Nadine and the father of her child reunite, the star of *Giselle* (the ballerina star, that is) has been recruited to dance leads with another big company, and Lisa is going to go back home, having experienced a tiny bit of sorrow but undamaged and virginal still. The film ends with Albrecht/Baryshnikov dancing, alone and in slow motion, the better for us to adore his new fullness and maturity as an artist.

I have been more than a little snide about *Dancers*, but I would be snide about any ballet film that insinuates that having a main character who is a pathologically narcissistic philandering heterosexual male somehow is "progressive" on the level of gender politics and representation because, as such, he is "normal" or "ordinary."[41] No "perverts" or sissies here, just a "regular guy" who happens to be a ballet dancer who has been looking for love in all the wrong places (in fact, Tony is one of the biggest monsters of any ballet film described so far). And I will admit that my distaste for the film, despite its beautiful dancing, is probably also linked to other of its malign effects on my and my generation's own youthful fantasies, those I described in relation to *The Turning Point,* for example. If *The Turning Point* engages, as I argued (echoing Angela McRobbie), as much for its interest in the achieving of adult but nondomestic sexuality as for any fantasies of professional conquest, then *Dancers* redirects that fantasy and signifies its impossibility in ways that I also find very disturbing. It turns out, *Dancers* suggests, that Emilia in *The Turning Point* was already past her prime as she danced into her freeze-frame at the end of the film, because she could no longer truly function as a virginal muse—as "youth, light, energy, joy." Her future, rather, was as Nadine—with a child and an immature husband and, more important, doomed because of the promise that she no longer holds, the mystery that she no longer is.

In some sense this is true of a huge percentage of Hollywood heroines (and not just those of ballet mellers or musicals), who must always be just on the brink of greatness rather than actually competing with men in any professional field. Certainly some older ballet mellers were happy to punish the woman who actually *achieves* fame and success by robbing her of "normal" family life and "love." The true cipher in *Dancers* is therefore Alessandra Ferri, Giselle herself; we watch her dance, with and without Tony, and she has to be good enough, *great* enough, for Tony to allow her to star in his "forever" film. Tony does not, after all, kick Francesca/Ferri out and put Lisa/Kent in her stead. But other than the fact that she is tough, has a viable career of her own, and has sex with but does not love Tony, there is nothing that *Dancers* can tell us about this "real" Giselle, the mature, sexual, accomplished, *experienced* woman and dancer who portrays her (or about any male dancer who is not flagrantly and spectacularly heterosexual). Despite the film's final inclusive title—and its dedication to Nora Kaye, who died early in 1987—Ferri herself knew what *Dancers* was really about, and it was not Giselle: "It's about Misha, of course. It's the Baryshnikov story."[42]

I Don't Want a Childhood. I Want to Be a Ballet Dancer!

On certain obvious levels, it is not hard to understand why the big-budget ballet movie all but disappeared from movie screens during the 1990s. In addition to the disappointing performance of films like *Nijinsky* and *Dancers* at the box office, the era was rapidly becoming one in which "high concept" action films loaded with computer-generated special effects alternated with smaller, low-budget independent films, all of them competing for what was seen to be a dwindling audience that was more and more miserly with its out-of-home entertainment spending. Theatrical dance schools and companies might have been flourishing or struggling, depending on location and other variables, but ballet's status as a "colossus" remained secure. No other theatrical dance form could any longer come close to superseding it in terms of attendance figures, training and school enrollments, and financial support and sponsorship.[43] *The Nutcracker* remained an annual theatrical Christmas event across the country, with television supplying Baryshnikov's American Ballet Theatre version, filmed for PBS in 1977 and shown many times since, with Gelsey Kirkland. Cable and satellite television technologies and their burgeoning numbers of channels—and a concomitant need for programming to load onto those channels—led to the appearance of several networks devoted to the performing arts from the late 1980s on as well. If some of those channels have since disappeared, the programming that they supported can still show up intermittently on the ever-growing digitized broadcast spectrum. Ballet companies also found ancillary markets among the new delivery forms; the New York City Ballet, for example, became affiliated with a series of exercise videos designed to help "anyone" achieve the strength, grace, and toned body of a Balanchine ballet dancer, male or female.

Ballet was thus available as popular culture and as art in the 1990s, but it reappeared in several commercial films from 2000 to 2003, marking both a familiarity with it as the most easily identified and hegemonic theatrical dance art and an ongoing ease with employing it as deviant or morbid, at worst, or still in profound thrall to the "myth of entertainment," at best. Given the ubiquity of ballet in the late twentieth-century mediascape, it was perhaps inevitable that these new films would be such weird conflations of the older ballet film's iconography and generic conventions, of the ballet body's notoriety in relation to newer forms of illness and perversity, of various sensational tell-all biographies and autobiographies, or of the ballet dancer—of *some* ballet dancers—as crossover or media stars who act rather than dance, who sell watches in *New Yorker* ads, who can be found teaching in the local university dance department. In films ranging from *Billy Elliot* and *Center Stage* to *Save the Last Dance* and *The Company*, the basic mode of the ballet film continues to be either the melodrama (with "numbers") or the "backstage" musical. This does not mean that these films are not otherwise diverse or interesting or of high quality on any number of other levels. But in terms of the uses to which they put ballet—classical ballet, especially, as indicated by the grind of the daily class, the tyranny of the ballet master or mistress, the rigidity of the art's requirements for success within its elite ranks—the films serve as a sometimes depressing, sometimes joyfully incoherent recapitulation of everything that has come before.

Center Stage, for example, follows a group of young adults admitted to the "American Ballet Academy" in New York. Only "three boys and three girls" will be allowed to advance to "the company" after the workshop performance at the end of the year. One of the girls, Jody (Amanda Schull, a member of the corps de ballet of the San Francisco Ballet in "real life"), has the "wrong body type" because she does not have perfect turnout; her feet in first and second position do not line up perfectly along a straight line. Maureen (Susan May Pratt), the "best dancer," has a pushy stage mother who has driven her to anorexia. Another eats normally and so is "too fat" to dance and is kicked out. The character of Eva Rodriguez (Zoë Saldana) is the dark-skinned Latina rebel, not properly respectful to the teachers or the school's dress code or regulations about gum-chewing in class. But she is the most authentically talented, we know, because she is the only one who cries during a performance of bits of *Swan Lake* and *Romeo and Juliet* put on by the stars of the company. The boys range from gay and African American (he injures himself before the big performance) to excessively heterosexual, with the "normal guy" dancer, Charlie (Sascha Radetsky), mooning after Jody throughout the film. She, in turn, has been preyed upon by the big dancing star of the company, Cooper (American Ballet Theatre principal Ethan Stiefel), who picks her to be in his ballet but who after sleeping with her once ignores her (after the night she spends in his apartment, she thinks they are "together"). When Jody realizes she has been used, though, she easily switches her affections to the "right" boy, Charlie. And the anorexic girl confronts her mother and gives up ballet to be with her medical-student boyfriend—thus allowing the discipline case, the rebellious Eva, who did not get a starring role in the final performance, to dance in her stead and wow everyone and get accepted into the company.

Jody wows everyone too in Cooper's new "pop ballet"—it has a motorcycle in it, the guys wear jeans and leather jackets, she wears red toe shoes, and it is performed to rock music—and is going to become a prima ballerina with his new pop company, where she will not need perfect turnout. Pushy stage moms and arrogant company directors are the villains, but they turn out to have human sides after all.

Center Stage was recognized as the genial recycling of old material that it of course was ("no cliché left untwirled," as Entertainment Weekly put it).[44] There is the obligatory, but now anachronistic, "jazz class" that Jody sneaks off to, against the rules—where, to her surprise, she finds Cooper, the company's big star, dancing too, clearly a regular. "Why can't all dancing be this fun?" she asks him. Instead of a rigid set of formal exercises, monochromatic "uniforms," doleful classical piano music, and teachers who rail against her for not having the "ideal body type," this class has regular cool people, male and female, talking and laughing and sweating in all sorts of colorful and fashionable clothing, and a teacher whose only correction or direction is to scream, "Dance the shit out of it!" The film has bloody toes, jokes about who among the men (or boys, as they are referred to throughout) is gay or straight ("Fresh meat!" no matter what), references to the competitive ones as bitches or pricks, the company as having a "stick up its ass" because it frowns on profanity or jazz, and on and on. Some of the dancers are played by dancers who cannot act very well (Julie Kent appears again, as the company's skeletal prima ballerina), some by actors who are shown either dancing in close-up or being portrayed by doubles, in long shots. As was common even in The Turning Point or Dancers, but in contrast to many of the most famous dance numbers of the classical Hollywood musical, the dance performances are the most heavily edited scenes in the film. Even when the dancer is truly performing as a dancer, the film performs harder, working to make the film's form, rather than its subject matter, the source of the most energy and excitement.

Billy Elliot is a smaller independent British film (it premiered in the United States at the Austin Film Festival later that same year) that became a "sleeper hit"; it had an estimated budget of $5 million and grossed, in less than a year, close to $22 million.[45] Its background is the 1984 Miners' Strike in the United Kingdom, the eponymous hero a motherless eleven-year-old boy (Jamie Bell) who likes to dance and who is lured into a local community-center ballet class (he is supposed to be taking boxing lessons) by a cantankerous but good-hearted middle-aged, chain-smoking ballet mistress (Julie Walters). When Billy's father and older brother, who are participating in the strike, find out what he is doing, they are infuriated. Ballet is "not for lads, Billy. Lads do football, or boxing, or wrestling—not fuckin' ballet." But Billy does not want to be a lad: "I don't want a childhood. I want to be a ballet dancer!" His teacher arranges for Billy to audition for the Royal Ballet School,

Still the most dependable laugh in any ballet film, the uncomfortable male in proximity to girls in tutus. Publicity still of Jamie Bell as Billy in *Billy Elliot* (2000).

Copyright 2000 Universal Studios.

and after the predictable ranting and violence of his father and brother against the idea, they have a change of heart and support Billy through his audition at White Lodge, where his body is examined, humiliatingly and in scenes that are chilling for their likely realism, as though he is a race horse. Billy's audition, his and his teacher's own pop choreography, appears to have fallen flat, but once he gives a speech about the "fire in [his] body," the "electricity" he feels when he is dancing, his success is assured, although that of the Miners' Strike is not. The film flashes forward to the day that father and brother make it to Covent Garden for the performance of Billy, now an adult, in what turns out to be Matthew Bourne's revisionary *Swan Lake,* in which the swans are men. But we see only one single leap into freeze frame of the adult Billy's dancing double in his feathered breeches before the film ends.

The feel-good appeal of *Billy Elliot* is not to be sneered at, and it uses dance (albeit once again heavily edited, as though for a music video) in ways that hark back to the European art cinema's merging of subjective and objective planes of reality, as well as the generic conventions of Hollywood film. Billy's exuberant tap dancing through the shabby streets of his town is sonically dreamlike (his taps sound as loud as those of Gene Kelly or Fred Astaire, although he is not wearing tap shoes), and, while he does not make a very convincing ballet dancer, ballet is not the subject of the film. Besides the politics of class, it is ballet's link with homosexuality, with being a "poof," that drives the narrative's conflicts. As Gary Lewis, who plays Billy's father, helpfully explains in the "making of" featurette that showed on cable television stations and is reproduced on the film's DVD, the reason Billy's father is so outraged at the idea of Billy being a ballet dancer is that "he thinks that the ballet, getting involved in ballet dancing, something so clearly effeminate, will lead to his son becoming a homosexual, and this just does not happen in mining communities." It *does*, of course, happen in mining communities; and Billy has a friend who *is* a "poof" but a good guy. The film leaves open the question of Billy's sexual orientation, however, and just what might be causing the tears we see in his father's eyes right before Billy's entrance as a swan. In terms of the "opera vs. swing" narrative, Billy might just as easily have wanted to be an opera singer as a dancer; but *Billy Elliot's* sexual politics require that ballet, and the threat to heteronormativity that it represents to, and as, the male body, be the "opera" here.

She Was Dying While I Was Dancing!

Another big box-office success, *Save the Last Dance* (2001), also employs some of the creakiest of ballet-meller clichés but not any that relate to the male dancer and his body. Ballet is girl's work again, the dream of achievement that intersects with disaster and death. It is in some senses a significantly more melodramatic updating of *Flashdance*, with the girl, Sara (Julia Stiles), forced to move in with her working-class divorced father on "Chicago's gritty South Side," as the film's publicity puts it, after her not-working-class mother is killed on the way to Sara's audition for Juilliard. Now a white girl in a "bad" black neighborhood, Sara becomes the friend of African American Chenille (Kerry Washington) and Chenille's brother, Derek (Sean Patrick Thomas). Sara and Derek share a love for club dancing and become a couple. When Derek finds out about Sara's dream "to become a world-class ballerina," he takes her to a Joffrey performance. But having seen the "goofy/happy" expression on Sara's face while she was watching the emaciated Joffrey ballerina and her partner onstage, Derek urges Sara to take up her dream again, that she "can do it"; she was "born to do it." But Sara resists, because she believes that her "stupid audition" and "stupid dream" killed her mother ("She was dying while I was dancing!" she exclaims tearfully).

With Derek's encouragement, however, Sara starts taking ballet classes so that she can get into shape for another Juilliard audition. And Derek helps inject "dirty hip-hop dance" into her choreography. Sara screws up the beginning of her audition just like Alex does in *Flashdance*, but, once she gets going, her dancing, and the hip-hop music, cause the judges to bop along in ecstasy. The formerly snippy and rude ballet-master judge is so wowed by her dancing that he breaks the rules: "Miss Johnson, I can't say this on the record yet, but welcome to Juilliard!" A final clinch with Derek, and the film ends, Sara on the brink of her dream, and still with Derek. The clear links to *Flashdance* in the film's structure are not meant to minimize the significance of *Save the Last Dance* and its interracial romance, which is, but for a few comments that are narratively rationalized as jealousy, treated lightly. The appeal of the film was built on the controversy generated by an interracial romance that was not treated as controversial.

But oh, Sara's, or rather Stiles's, dancing. At least Sara's body is not exceedingly thin, in contrast to the Joffrey ballerina whom she watches with Derek. Otherwise, Stiles might as well be Margaret O'Brien in *The Unfinished Dance*. Moreover, there is a "making of" featurette for *Save the Last Dance* as well, and not only does Stiles refer to the character of Sara as a "nerd" (because she likes ballet), but the ballet choreographer for the film, Randy Duncan, was compelled somehow to gush over Stiles's ability to "pick up" ballet so easily, "in just a month" and so on. Stiles tells us that the hip-hop dancing came much more easily to her than the ballet, because she did not take ballet as a kid but she does like to "go to clubs." And Thomas refers to what Stiles does as "formal classical ballet," whereas his character, Derek, just does what he "feels" ("It's not formal or classical, it's just like raw hip-hop"). No one is speaking the truth here—not the choreographer about Stiles's abilities (she is, if possible, a worse "ballet aspirant" than Margaret O'Brien), and not even Thomas about the "raw hip-hop." The featurette itself shows the work that went into the *choreography*, by Fatima, of the hip-hop dancing as well, and the halting attempts of both stars to learn its patterns and moves. Fatima speaks of the difficulty of "jelling the two styles," but the choreography hardly matters in the end. As is true of most, if not all, of the dancing—of any kind—in films of this period, the editing creates more energy than the dancers' bodies are allowed to.

And while there are a couple of "real" ballet dancers seen for a few seconds in the course of *Save the Last Dance*, I believe that the use of ballet in the film overall speaks most to ballet's current relegation to nothing particularly reviled, nothing particularly esteemed, something familiarly accepted, if not understood, as high art, the realm of the snooty or the "nerd."[46] What is perhaps most interesting about the recent films is the way that the race of the ballet dancer is no longer treated as any sort of barrier. In *Flashdance*, part of the drama, or melodrama, was that the heroine was scorned by ballet ostensibly because of her working-class and racial status; her triumph was to make ballet accept her and her skills, by implication recognizing its own deficiencies in the process. In *Honey* (2003), in contrast, Jessica Alba plays an African American girl who saves inner-city children from the streets by holding hip-hop dancing classes. Her dream is to be a choreographer, but she does not want to do ballet—not because she is not allowed to, however, or is rejected by it; rather, she has been doing it for years, and it just is no longer as interesting an art form to her as hip-hop. It falls to her mother (Lonette McKee), sighing, to invoke ballet's metonymic function as an all-purpose but outmoded fantasy of achievement: "Hip-hop can't take you the places ballet can—all that *real* dance training." But *Honey* shows the opposite; that hip-hop is "real," not boring and outdated ballet, and can take you anyplace you want to go.[47]

What Before Was Life Is Now Art

Robert Altman's film *The Company* (2003), the final film I will discuss at any length, is a narrative feature that was produced by and stars a Hollywood celebrity, Neve Campbell, and has a screenplay written by Barbara Turner. But its publicity promises that the film shows us "real ballet dancers . . . doing what they normally do," and Altman called the film "both a fiction and a profile of a real ballet company," Chicago's Joffrey Ballet (the same company whose dancers appeared so briefly in *Save the Last Dance*).[48] Campbell stars as Ry, a career Joffrey dancer, and we watch her move through her everyday dancer's life—class and rehearsal—as well as work as a cocktail waitress (ballet does not pay enough), play pool, acquire a cute cook boyfriend, perform in several ballets, injure her arm (mildly) in the film's final number. Along the way we meet, but do not get to know, several other dancers, Ry's own stage mother, and the narcissistic director of the company (played by Malcolm McDowell), who is a standard-issue impresario interested in money, prestige, and authority but who avoids making decisions like the plague and flees all difficult confrontations. Joan Acocella refers to Altman's method, perfected throughout his thirty-year career as a director, as "parachuting," whereby "you drop down into a subculture, gather up a lot of piquant detail, mix actual members of that world with actors, weave together a few dozen narrative threads involving these people, and get out before your curiosity is exhausted."[49]

The Company is a useful film on which to end because its publicity campaign, and its extratextual relationship to Altman's previous film oeuvre, engages, more or less overtly, many of the topics that have been addressed in this book: questions about ballet as dancer and as dancing, as performance and as way of life, as "reality" and as "fantasy," as popular culture and as art. On the one hand, theatrical ballet as an art form, which by now should be well understood, communicates primarily through the performativity of bodies and appurtenances that are at once normative and transgressive in relation to gender (the roles performed onstage and in the classroom versus the androgyny of the female ballet body or the hypermasculinity of the gay or heterosexual male ballet body). In ballet films like *The Company,* on the other hand, the bodies of dancers, choreographers, and movie stars also speak, and the issues of subjectivity in relation to the "mute" bodies of dance, of language as communication, of gesture and acting and the formal and formally expressive "languages" of film and, now, video (*The Company* was shot on high-definition video) become, in many ways, the "content" of Altman's and Barbara Turner's film. According to Bill Nichols, narrative fiction can "answer more fully [than documentary] to the question of what it feels like to occupy a given body,"[50] yet *The Company* employs documentary techniques not only to show us performance as a theatrical, professional public event but also to give us access to the social and material contexts of those performances as based in feeling, intensity, labor, training, and the effort of bodies. Earlier ballet mellers seemed to make art into life, to make art the governing feature *of* life (art was sometimes fatal in these cases); but, as we have also seen, films themselves perform realism as well as the reality *of* performance, such that, in Acocella's words about *The Company* specifically, "what before was life is now art, or trying to be."

Just what *performance* is has received quite a bit of attention recently, as has performance as one sort of subject matter that films can "have."[51] For some scholars, most famously Peggy Phelan, performance is an oppositional and de facto political practice by virtue of the ontological "liveness" that makes performance distinct from all the saving/recording/documenting/circulating forms of mass-mediated representation.[52] Indeed, Phelan locates performance only in the "maniacally charged present"—and hence in disappearance. But, as Philip Auslander notes in response to Phelan's claims, there has been a progressive diminution of distinctions between the live and the "mediatized," even in the work Phelan examines.[53] And, "If live performance cannot be shown to be economically independent of, immune from contamination by, and ontologically different from mediatized forms," Auslander concludes, "in what sense can liveness function as a site of cultural and ideological resistance"?

In recent scholarship on film performance, any association of performance with liveness, as "that which disappears," has all but disappeared itself, or is ignored. The three editors of a 2004 anthology on contemporary film performance, *More Than a Method: Trends and Traditions in Contemporary Film Performance,* position themselves not against liveness but against what they see as the prevalent "supposition" that "film audiences encounter performances that have been modified by the work of directors, editors, cinematographers, makeup artists, music composers, and others."[54] Further, the anthology's three editors believe "that understanding ways in which texts mediate performances is crucial in studies of text-spectator relationships as well as cultural studies of star images." Yet in another 2005 anthology called *Theater and Film,* editor Robert Knopf again writes that, "At base, we can probably all agree that theater is live and exists in the moment, whereas film consists of a performance or story preserved, indeed most would say *constructed,* on celluloid."[55]

If one brings the term *performativity* into the mix, the discussion becomes even more complicated; the presentation or embodiment of the self in any social environment, not only within the explicitly marked frames of the theater or other public or commercial exhibition formats, is also clearly *performance,* and there is an ongoing interest in how social performance, as it were (for example, of gender and sexuality, class, race and ethnicity, age, ability/disability, and so on), intersects with and marks (and is marked by) the identity politics of theatrical or fictional public performance modes and their strategies of embodiment.[56] Thomas Waugh's work on performance in documentary film suggests that "[d]ocumentary performers 'act' in much the same way as their dramatic counterparts except that they are cast for their social representativity as well as for their cinematic qualities, and their roles are composites of their own social roles and the dramatic requirements of the film."[57] One way to talk about ballet performance in a film, then, or the way that a film performs ballet, would be to bracket out performance in the social sense and focus on a theatrical, "professional" mode, a "proscenium" mode as such; this is how genres like the musical, and the ballet film as I have defined it, treat dancing, even when it takes place on the street or in a rehearsal hall rather than on a theater stage. But the performance of the actors in a narrative film, or the performance by the film of the acting in a film's story, or even the behavior and actions of documentary subjects (Waugh's "documentary performers"), then must become that "other kind" of performance, the ordinary everyday "social" variety, even though it is also clearly still "proscenium" performance if one thinks of a narrative film as a sort of theatrical framing device. And here, too, we could still discuss all film performance with reference to its *construction* through choices, mechanisms, and devices including acting, narrative and narration, shot scale and camerawork, lighting, editing, and sound manipulation.

In *The Company,* then, as in many other films already discussed, we have both "documentary performers" and "actors," but they are not always whom you think they are. We do not know, in fact, who most of the people are whom we are watching in *The Company* because they are not identified, not spoken about, not placed in a context *other than* that of what is supposed to be "reality" but is often also theatrical performance: much if not all of the dancing we observe is designed to be seen on a proscenium stage.[58] *The Company*'s script, although containing some scenes that were constructed and written, is according to its screenwriter "essentially just a year with those dancers."[59] Altman's remarks about "those dancers" are instructive: "I cannot take 30 ballet dancers and make them actors. That's why I'm not giving anybody any lines."[60] With no lines (the dancers do speak, but mostly casual improvised dialogue), how can the narrative framework produce Bill Nichols's "question of what it feels like to occupy a given body"? Who speaks in *The Company,* and do we understand what they and their bodies are saying?

Despite *The Company*'s "high reality quotient," in Acocella's words (and in Altman's; he claimed in the DVD's "making of" featurette that for him *The Company* represented a "new style of filmmaking" that would "forever change" him), she also notes that its "wavering tone" is something that is common to all Altman films, then admits that it is a "lazy movie all around" and that Altman's engagement with the subject "isn't very deep." Few ballet films, we have seen, have had anything but a wavering tone, nor has their engagement with ballet been very deep either. There are not one but three injuries in the "plot" of *The Company;* McDowell's character is supposed to be first-generation Italian American but he sounds just like Malcolm McDowell; the ballets the film reproduces are mostly "trite and dated," as Robert Gottlieb puts it, so "second-rate" that he thanks Altman for reminding us all (especially New Yorkers) just how "slick and empty" the Joffrey's repertory is.[61] The Altman film most closely related to *The Company* in working method and effect would probably be *Nashville* (1975), in which professional singers who are amateur actors playing characters interact with professional actors who are playing characters who are professional singers. As Robert Self puts it, "An irony in Altman's narratives is the energy devoted to creating a verisimilitude in acting that ultimately must be read not as naturalistic but as expressionistic."[62] However much Altman, Barbara Turner, and even Neve Campbell swore to the "reality quotient" of *The Company,* it, too, because it *is* a ballet film, turns out to be a highly unrealistic performance of reality.

As this book has shown, ballet has a long history of being used quite melodramatically and conventionally by Hollywood films, often characterized narratively as a disease, as a religion, as an avocation, but more rarely as trained dancing that depends on the dancer's subjectivity as well as his or her body and that is a form of personally rewarding labor.[63] Ballet also has a history, and that history can be found, I have argued, in "tin cans" as well as in the interaction of the bodies and brains of different generations who pass on what otherwise *does* substantially "disappear" on being performed. But quite a bit of strange mystifying stuff is still written that attempts to deny the significance of mass-media ballet (much as Altman, Barbara Turner, and Neve Campbell deny or ignore the preexisting tradition of the Hollywood ballet film into which *The Company* so clearly fits). For example, Toni Bentley (a former dancer with the New York City Ballet, and the author of the aforementioned *Winter Season*) wrote in 2005 in the *New York Review of Books:*

A beautiful ballet doesn't speak of or refer to loss directly as can poetry, painting, or music; it is an act of loss itself, laid bare, and all the more moving for it. For the same reason it is perhaps the bravest of the arts, the one whose practitioners—dancers—risk all for mere transitory moments of beauty. . . . Unlike those arts that exist in a form outside the artist himself—painting, sculpture, poetry, prose, music—dance only exists . . . in that dancer, in that moment. And [the choreographer's] work, too, only existed in that body, in that ballet, on that stage.[64]

Bentley further claims, "At best [the dancer's] work exists as a memory—and we all know how reliable that is. A dancer will never even see himself, or herself, dance." Not even on film or video? For Bentley, video (she ignores film entirely) might be "technically useful," but it produces a "distorted, backward, two-dimensional, miniature rendition of a dance that inevitably erases complexity from any performance. It records, at best, steps, but never depth. Even other live performance—singing and acting—can now be accurately preserved on digital disks." Here, Bentley couches the matter in terms of *accuracy* of preservation as well as the "live moment." What *is* Altman doing in *The Company*, then—preserving ballet performance badly (even though in its original format *The Company* was not of course "miniature" but quite the opposite) but preserving the "other live performance," *acting*, well? (Singers and actors would likely also be astonished to learn that "digital disks" represent them accurately.) But Acocella claims that the "greatest stroke of realism" in *The Company* "is its dance sequences," precisely because the camera's closeness to the dancers reveals, more clearly than she has "ever seen it before on screen," the work of, the dignity of, the dancers themselves. "Above all," she writes, "we see movement, physical effort: every bend of the waist, with the costume fabric wrinkling; every lift of the leg, with the muscles quivering."[65]

Despite this, and the references to documentary authenticity in the film's publicity, there is relatively little documentation of the performance of dance and dancers in *The Company* that is not cut into and away from, often to what might be called "narrative concerns" (in this case the stars), in the manner typical of any old Hollywood musical or ballet meller (although there is less of the frenetic cutting that marks other recent films). In Robert Self's discussion of *Nashville*, he speaks of the way that professional singer Ronee Blakley's acting "has the ring of the amateur, which, coupled with the random camera setups and live sound recording, enhances the documentary quality of the film."[66] In *The Company* the problem is somewhat different, because it is the *star* who has the unmistakable "ring of the amateur," not as an actor but as a dancer.

Proclaimed a fabulous dancer—though not a ballet star, which Acocella also takes to be a sign of the increased realism of *The Company*—both within the film and in the publicity material produced about it, Neve Campbell, despite having trained in ballet for several years and possessing what looks like a "ballet body," is glaringly an amateur. Indeed, the amount of publicity and promotional material devoted to assuring us that Campbell was "really" a good dancer, qualified to be a "real" Joffrey dancer "without question" (in Altman's words), and with testimonials dutifully produced from Joffrey personnel that valiantly describe Campbell as a "beautiful and dedicated artist" who "worked hard" and was "disciplined" and "very focused"—all this speaks to the film's desire to perform the ballet authentically, or perhaps to Neve Campbell's desire to be a ballet dancer, since she produced the film so that she could star in it.[67] Equally significant, by making Campbell's skill the proof of the film's authenticity, by locating the film's realism most vociferously in its star's abilities, the film becomes part of another long-lived tradition in Hollywood cinema discussed in these pages. The sign of any film's value as the authentic performance of an elite performing art is whether a star has the credentials to perform that art, and we have seen the numbers of testimonials generated by "experts" that, were the stars of the films (whether *The Men in Her Life, The Unfinished Dance, Never Let Me Go,* or *Save the Last Dance*) not movie stars, they could easily be professional ballerinas—they are that talented.

Ballet itself has, again, two obvious registers of performance: dancing, which is predominantly silent but which has all kinds of meanings on its own relating to gender, class, sexuality, narrative; and speaking *about* ballet, as well as speaking that comes from the ballet body when it is not dancing. This is not, of course, the case in *The Company,* or any other ballet film, because it has actors in it, and a plot, however skeletal, in which performance is also of narrative events—having conversations, going to parties, crying because you have been dumped by your boyfriend, working as a cocktail waitress. In Thomas Waugh's study of documentary acting, he names two modes: *representational,* or when subjects "perform 'not looking at the camera,' when they represent their lives or roles, the image looks natural, as if the camera were invisible, as if the subject were unaware of being filmed"; and *presentational,* in which the subject "openly acknowledges and exploits [film's] performance components," a convention Waugh says that documentary inherited from its sibling, photography.[68] But it could just as easily have been inherited from performance modes like ballet or other theatrical entertainments, in which the audience's attention is solicited directly. In *The Company,* sometimes the ballet is being performed realistically; sometimes the dancers employ a presentational style, sometimes a representational style. Sometimes actors are acting; sometimes dancers are acting with that "ring of the amateur." But this is true of the ballet when it is being performed by actors; there, in fact, the ringing is even louder.

So are the boundaries between the registers of performance, in *any* of the films discussed in this book, too clearly marked or not marked clearly enough? Might this ambiguity account for the perplexity with which so many ballet films were greeted by critics and audiences? *The Company* certainly shows that minimizing melodrama in the narrative, or getting rid of the dying swans and madmen, does not produce authenticity or realism automatically. And this, as I hope I have shown, has always been the case with ballet's interaction with commercial cinema.

IN CONCLUDING THIS CHAPTER, I also conclude the book itself. Because I began with an anecdotal discussion of how I first became interested in ballet and film, I would like to end with some defiantly inconclusive and also anecdotal remarks pertaining to how my relationship to the subject matter changed as the project developed. When I was a ballet student, my understanding of the ballet film was stuck at the level of realism in many ways, in that I was mainly affected by whether a given movie was "right" or "wrong" in how it represented the world of the ballet that I was so sure I knew well. Although I was a lot younger, of course, I was not that far from Arnold Haskell or Arlene Croce in my point of view, because I, too, thought that Hollywood's ballet stories were generally puerile and ridiculous and excessively melodramatic and morbid. Certain lines, like the "sometimes toe shoes" remark from *The Band Wagon* that I quoted in the introduction, drove me crazy, as did the sight of any number of nondancers attempting actually to *perform* ballet in these films. However manifestly bad the dancing was, the plot usually required that someone eulogize it ("This child has poetry in her feet!"), and that offended me, too. If I had begun this book then, my mission would have been to show the world that what commercial cinema had been proffering as ballet, in musicals or nonmusicals or even feature-length documentaries, was either not ballet at all or else (and this was usually when the dancing was "old") was an inferior version of it. I was not really interested in the films as films, just as records of the progress of ballet and its bodies over time to the perfection of "now," the glory "ballet boom" years of Baryshnikov, Makarova, Kirkland, and above all Balanchine. Even when I became more astute about issues of historiography, visual culture, and dance's interaction with mass-mediated forms of representation, I was still, many years ago, more likely to side with Arlene Croce about what a bad dancer Harriet Hoctor was or to insist that a film like *The Unfinished Dance* was so awful as to be worthy of no attention other than derision. Even *The Red Shoes* was only good when Moira Shearer was dancing; only she was recognizably skilled and of the correct body type.

As I hope has become clear, however, my consciousness has been heightened, and I work much harder now not to apply what John Chapman refers to as "the methods of evolutionary history" to the dancing and dancers of the mass-mediated past. But I also am at pains to remember that the basis of my dance-history education was often itself precisely evolutionary, and Chapman details many of the ways that scholars wrote about ballet "as if [the past] were a direct pipeline to the present, as if ideas once born stand intact, impervious to the ravages of time, eventually making their way to the present."[69] Chapman quotes Agnes de Mille's claims in her 1963 *Book of the Dance* that the "style and deportment" of princes and nobles of the fourteenth century have been passed down "exactly" through "our ballet exercises straight from one generation to the next."[70] He also refers to how Lincoln Kirstein's standard history of ballet links the "positions of the arms and feet in Greek theatrical dancing" as "remarkably similar to classic Franco-Italo-Austro-Anglican ballet," and Chapman quotes Alexander Bland's remarks in another well-known history that "[a]ll the seeds of modern ballet from fairy tale to erotic duets and abstract ritual were planted in [ancient] Egypt."[71] And such claims were made without what I thought of as *real* proof, the proof that I had once believed to be ineluctable, photographic records. In fact, given the evolutionary history I had so well internalized, I once did not think it would be very difficult at all to argue, indeed to prove, that a particular film ballerina was bad, because if her leg was not completely taut and straight and muscularly defined in extension, if the toe was not perfectly pointed and the foot's arch bulging and obvious, if the arms were not held just so, if the body itself was not sculpted, lean, and, yes, pin-headed, and if she could not do more than a triple pirouette, then I was confident that the evidence itself would make my case.

I am, then, an ambivalent product of an erstwhile unambivalent past. I now recognize the complexity of commercial films as modes of address, as generic constructs, as representations of gender, sexuality, competence, cultural attitudes, and so on. And I believe now that even films I would once have considered *wrong* about ballet, like *The Unfinished Dance,* were actually *right* about it in very interesting ways—that a woman's dance career might be as valuable, even more valuable, to her than a rich boyfriend or husband, that domesticity was not the natural or desirable goal of all women, that women's partnerships and professional identities could be as fulfilling and joyful as any heterosexual romantic relationship. But I still cringe when I watch untrained dancers wobble around in toe shoes, or when a manifestly second-rate performer is lauded as a genius. Conversely, I now understand that the Balanchine ballerina's body is only one kind of dance instrument, and that dance talent does not inhere in leanness or muscle definition or length of leg. So when an actress like Neve Campbell in *The Company* can identify herself as a full-fledged ballerina because her body makes her look like one, that, too, is wrong, misleading. Despite all publicity to the contrary, Neve Campbell is not a "real" dancer (and I still would be happy to shout, to anyone who would listen, that Julia Stiles's character in *Save the Last Dance* would *never* get into Juilliard).

I also acknowledge that ballet once represented a quasi-feminist fantasy of achievement for me, a form of physical mastery that was personally gratifying and that flew in the face of everything I was expected to do or to want. I took ballet's inherent value for granted, though, because I saw it everywhere around me, in all of my teachers, my classmates, the stars we idolized, the fact that there *were* ballet stars. But this also meant taking for granted that my body was not the right size and shape ever to be that of a professional ballet dancer, and that there was nothing to be done about it, not even "getting" anorexia. It was my fault, not ballet's, and the standards were, again, immutable and always had been; the deviations from these standards presented by the evidence of and from the past merely underscored the superiority of the present. About all of this I am, of course, also ambivalent now, for I know that American ballet's "perfect" bodies and their extraordinary technical virtuosity have been achieved at a price not only to some who have devoted their lives to achieving them (or perhaps had their lives devoted for them by stage mothers and so on) but to ballet's ability to be an even remotely accessible fantasy of achievement for everyone. In the 1920s, 1930s, and 1940s, ballet was a seller's market from the point of view of the professional aspirant; if you loved ballet and were at least minimally technically competent and musical, there was a good chance that the Ballet Russe de Monte Carlo would hire you (if you were male and wanted to dance, you could get by with even fewer qualifications). By the 1960s and certainly the 1970s, the buyer's market prevailed; there were more than enough female ballet hopefuls to go around, and professional companies could choose from a broad range of equally superbly trained and proficient dancers with particular body types. It is the stuff of dressing-room legend among would-be dancers today that the first cut in any audition is made on the basis of body type alone—you never get the chance to show them how well you can dance, or what is almost as important on the level of feeling, how much you *want* to dance.

Wanting to dance, needing to dance, dying to dance have been weird and paradoxical constants of all of the narrative films I have discussed here, and it is one of the deepest and most resonant truths that, in the end, aches and pains notwithstanding, ballet feels fabulous to do. As Richard Dyer puts it in reference to the first ballet classes he took when he was in his mid-thirties: "[I]t was wonderful. For me it was a revelation that I could feel elegant and graceful in my body, that movement need not just be good for me because it made me fit and strong, but because it made me feel good about my body."[72] Ballet for Dyer, as for me, is "a dream of living in harmony with one's body"; it provides a sense of somatic accomplishment, it is something ineffably beautiful musically as well as visually, and even the most rudimentary components of its vocabulary and technique—*barre* work, for example—do figuratively and somewhat literally embody the fact that one is part of a very long tradition. Ballet may not have come down to us unchanged since the fourteenth century, but ironically one of the most appealing effects of the filmed past of ballet is the heightened sense of a link to its traditions, its myths, even its sometimes ridiculous assumptions. It is not just doing daily class or performing the ballet classics that connects one to the tradition of ballet but of figuring out Moira Shearer's opening steps in the "Red Shoes" ballet and performing them oneself (and at least imagining that one can do them almost as well). The physicality of film can produce a sense that, in being another's body and performing another's steps, one has begun to *understand* those others and their histories and their bodies, and this too is all part of the ongoing appeal of ballet's commercially filmed past and its continually circulating availability. A true awareness of the accomplishments of the performers of the past whose history has been "pickled" by film, to quote Shearer again, means being humble in the realization that one's own achievements will one day seem inferior to the accomplishments of someone else's present. And if some of the most resonant films as fantasies of achievement are awful as records of ballet in performance, some of the most beautiful dancing takes place in films whose stories and characterizations are risible, trivial, or insulting.

Other spectators from other fields may, of course, react in similar ways to other bodily expressions of the past—the films of Olympic-figure-skater-turned-movie-star Sonja Henie, for example. Although, compared to ballet, there has been no sustained tradition of "figure-skating films," one might certainly assume that today's budding or professional figure skaters would look back on the midcentury body and technical ability of a Sonja Henie and feel superior in all ways, but in fact this seems not to be the case. Internet message boards suggest a much more complex response, with one poster about Henie's skating in *Sun Valley Serenade* (1941) calling it "breathtaking" and another writing that "Sonja's skating routines seem tame compared to what's expected of today's skating competitors but she's graceful as ever on ice," and yet another waxing lyrical about how Henie "glides effortlessly into the viewer's heart, while balancing on a thin edge of silver, suspended over frozen water."[73] A recent film like Disney's *Ice Princess* (2005), in which a high school physics nerd gives up a scholarship to Harvard to achieve her dream of succeeding as a figure skater (she starts training a few months before she enters some sort of regional finals competition), is not only structured very much like a ballet film narratively but asks us to believe that the inexpert fumblings of its nonskating star (Michelle Trachtenberg) and the long-shot pyrotechnics of her skating double make her dreams, and the price she is paying to achieve them, seem reasonable. But still, *Ice Princess,* too, provoked heated responses from fans who adore and are inspired by its strange post-feminist message (we are asked to accept that a young girl choosing figure skating, wearing lots of makeup, and "looking hot" is rebelling against the more traditional and confining Harvard-educated physicist role that her mother and society expect her to fulfill) and those who are appalled by it, and those who admire its skating and those who think it was nowhere near good enough to enable the protagonist to become the star she wants to be. "As a figure skater myself the movie seemed unrealistic. Ask any skater that has seen it they will probably say the same thing," writes one Internet poster; but another, also a self-professed figure skater ("the greatest sport of all time"), claims, "I totally agree with almost everything that happened in this movie."[74] On the other hand, men who figure skate, like ballet dancers, are still largely the stuff of film comedy, and conversely, women who desire to compete in a traditionally male-dominated sport, like boxing, must deal with something akin to the semantic tropes of ostracization and opposition that mark the plight of the male ballet dancer even in recent films. Beyond this, the comparison arguably does not hold, for sports films lack the strong tradition of morbidity of the ballet film, although they are in most cases also fantasies of achievement. The road to success may be hard, and long, and bloody, and men may even prance about spectacularly, nearly naked and sweating in slow motion, but achievement in sports, as an individual or on a team, is already a socially sanctioned route to glory, respect, wealth, and any other fame- and achievement-related superlative.

Despite ballet's relative ubiquity in the mediascape, then, it would be difficult, even now, to say confidently that ballet has achieved an unambiguous status as a widely approved dance art, however solid its status in relation to other forms of theater dance. As a film presence, ballet does function sometimes relatively normatively as a profession, as a type of paid labor, as a "body" of knowledge and tradition, and as an art form, but it is always also a constant arbiter of mass-cultural ambivalence about art, especially art that depends on an aestheticized performing body. There are many more ballerina bodies around now than there used to be (like Neve Campbell's), but this also can mean that bodies that are not the right size and shape will be excluded, regardless of their abilities, from professional consideration (and some of the most visually perfect and accomplished "Balanchine bodies" may be hiding secret diseases). And while male ballet bodies have become more common too, the idea of a man dancing ballet (or figure skating, for that matter) is still employed as a dependable source for a homophobic cheap laugh.

Regardless of one's own relationship to the art form, or whether one's young daughter or son goes to weekly ballet classes, or one's college-aged child decides to major in dance at the university level, ballet is still likely to be encountered first as a part of the vast pastiche of media images with which many if not most homes are bombarded on a daily basis. As is well known, these ancillary markets increasingly are more significant to a contemporary theatrical film's bottom line than ticket sales at the local multiplex. Perhaps more to the point, even the most obscure or initially unsuccessful of the films discussed here are, generally speaking, still around, no longer locked in tin cans but more or less perpetually available, electronically and digitally mediated, as "new." To this day some of the most popular home-market channels remain those that show uncut and sometimes restored prints of films, with the video, DVD, and Internet markets also delivering all kinds of movies to new audiences in their living rooms or, increasingly, home theaters.[75] And once they are delivered to their new audiences, these films become the topic of new forms of discourse, evaluation, and judgment. Ballet and its bodies in narrative cinema are now, as they have been for so many decades, parables and images of personal status and achievement, and of subcultural identity; of high art, and of cheap entertainment; of change and progress, and of stasis and stereotype; signs of *our* status and achievement in the world, and also of decadence and strangeness. No less than its practitioners as Lincoln Kirstein described them in 1959, ballet still, in its mass-mediated forms and by its mass-mediated artists, is made to be "exasperatingly capable of anything, good and bad."[76]

NOTES

INTRODUCTION

1. See Naima Prevots, *Dancing in the Sun: Hollywood Choreographers, 1915–1937* (Ann Arbor, Mich.: UMI, 1987). An Academy Award was given for dance direction in 1935, 1936, and 1937; thereafter, for reasons that remain mysterious, the award was discontinued.

2. "Ballet's Fundamentalist" [cover story], *Time*, Jan. 25, 1954, 66–74: "I'd seen the movies. So many beautiful girls. Healthy girls—good food, probably. A country that had all those beautiful girls would be a good place for ballet" (71). The "Ginger Rogers" quotation is from Bernard Taper, *Balanchine* (New York: Times Books, 1984), 151.

3. Jane Feuer, "The Self-Reflexive Musical and the Myth of Entertainment," in *Film Genre Reader*, ed. Barry Keith Grant (Austin: University of Texas Press, 1986), 442.

4. Jane Feuer, *The Hollywood Musical*, 2nd ed. (Bloomington: Indiana University Press, 1993), 55.

5. Jerome Delamater, *Dance in the Hollywood Musical* (Ann Arbor, Mich.: UMI, 1981); Rick Altman, *The American Film Musical* (Bloomington: Indiana University Press, 1987).

6. John Chapman, "The Aesthetic Interpretation of Dance History," *Dance Chronicle* 3 (1979–80): 254–274.

7. Joan Acocella, "No Bloody Toes Shoes," *New York Review of Books*, Feb. 26, 2004, 7. See also Joni M. Cherbo and Margaret J. Wyszomirski, eds., *The Public Life of the Arts in America* (New Brunswick, N.J.: Rutgers University Press, 2000), esp. chap. 1, "Mapping the Public Life of the Arts in America."

8. Arnold L. Haskell, *How to Enjoy Ballet* (New York: Morrow, 1951), 111.

9. Rudolf Arnheim, *Film as Art* (Berkeley: University of California Press, 1957), esp. the sections from 1933.

10. All information in this paragraph from Anatole Chujoy, ed., *Fokine: Memoirs of a Ballet Master*, trans. Vitale Fokine (Boston: Little, Brown, 1961), 261–263.

11. Within the framework of the large debate, the literature takes many forms. There were columns with titles like "Cinema Chatter" and "Jollywood Jottings" in dance magazines of the 1920s and 1930s, and occasionally these addressed issues of adaptation as well—what dancer or choreography appeared best in film,

with Hollywood film being the mode in question. A few early articles are more nuanced: see, e.g., Betty Carue, "The Motion Picture's Influence on the Dance," *American Dancer,* Jan. 1929, 26, 29, which relates rising standards of audience appreciation of theatrical dance to dance in the movies. When theatrical choreographers (like Fokine) arrived in Hollywood, they frequently were also asked about the relationship of dance and film: see, e.g., Ivan Narodny's profile of Albertina Rasch, "Dancies Preferred: Albertina Rasch on Film Ballet Technique," *Dance,* April 1930, 27, 64.

Much of the dance-film literature comes from Britain, although it is often about American films. Ballerina Alexandra Danilova wrote "Classical Ballet in the Cinema" for *Sight and Sound* 4 (autumn 1935): 107–108, in which she takes as a given film's ability to preserve choreography and performance. Arnold Haskell, however, perhaps because film's popularization of ballet threatened its status (and therefore his own, as a ballet critic), wrote almost always negatively about film's effect on ballet; he was "sickened" by the possibility of ballet's becoming fodder for a mass audience: see, e.g., "Voyage into Space," *Ballet Panorama* (London: Batsford, 1938), 109–112, as well as *How to Enjoy Ballet,* 111–112. See also H. L. Perkoff, "The Screen and the Ballet," *Sight and Sound* 7 (autumn 1938): 122–123; David Vaughan, "Dance in the Cinema," *Sequence* 6 (winter 1948/1949): 6–13; A. H. Franks, *Ballet for Film and Television* (London: Pitman, 1950), and "Ballet in the Cinema and on Television," in *Approach to the Ballet* (London: Pitman, 1952), 285–298; director Anthony Asquith's "Ballet and the Film," in *Footnotes to the Ballet,* ed. Caryl Brahms (London: Black, 1951), 231–252; Peter Brinson, "Ballet in Two Dimensions: The Cinema," in *Ballet: A Decade of Endeavor,* ed. A. H. Franks (London: Burke, 1955), 169–184, followed by Franks's own essay on ballet and television.

Interesting American entries into the debate include Edwin Denby, "A Film of Pavlova" (Aug. 1, 1943) and "Dance in the Films" (Aug. 8, 1943), both for the *Herald Tribune,* repr. in *Edwin Denby: Dance Writings,* ed. Robert Cornfield and William MacKay (New York: Knopf, 1986); John Martin, "Introduction to a Catalogue of Dance Films," *Dance Index* (1945): 60–61; Walter Terry, "Motion Pictures and Dance," *Dance* 20 (Oct. 1946): 22, 36–38; Arthur Knight, "Dancing in Films," *Dance Index* (1947): 180–199 (and his earlier piece, "Toward the Dance Film," written as Arthur Rosenheimer Jr., in *Theatre Arts* 26 [Jan. 1942]: 57–63); George Balanchine, "Ballet in Motion Pictures," in *Dance Encyclopedia,* ed. Anatole Chujoy (New York: A. S. Barnes, 1949), 313–314; and Mary Jane Hungerford, "Motion Pictures and Dance," also in Chujoy's *Dance Encyclopedia,* 314–318 (but dropped from later editions; Balanchine's entry remained). In 1951 Hungerford complicated matters by referring to Hollywood films "centered around dancing themes" (e.g., *The Red Shoes*) as "all-dance films"; see her "25 Years of Sound Films," in *25 Years of American Dance,* ed. Doris Hering (New York: Dance Magazine, 1951), 139–151. See also Arthur Todd, "From Chaplin to Kelly: The Dance on Film," *Theatre Arts* 35 (Aug. 1951): 50–51, 88–91. Allegra Fuller Snyder attempted to define categorically the possibilities for the interaction of film and dance in "3 Kinds of Dance Film: A Welcome Clarification," *Dance Magazine,* Sept. 1965, 34–39: there is "choreocinema," a term she borrows from John Martin (the film "dances" but need not record dancers; abstract films like Fernand Léger's *Ballet mécanique* [1924] fall into this category, as do many animated films), "notation" ("the more methodical and mechanical it can be, the better"), and, most problematically, "documentary," in which category she places the musicals of Fred Astaire. Gardner Compton, in "Film Dance and Things to Come," *Dance Magazine,* Jan. 1968, 34–36, refers directly to Snyder's three categories but as the "record" film ("used to preserve [a performance] for posterity"), the documentary or "teaching film," and finally choreo-cinema. Choreo-cinema and/as "cine-dance" was the focus of an entire issue of *Dance Perspectives* (summer 1967), edited by Arthur Knight, in which noncommercial filmmakers such as Snyder, Maya Deren, Shirley Clarke, and Stan Brakhage discuss their own films. *Dance Magazine* had an intermittently appearing column called "Dancefilms" beginning in the 1960s, too. Arlene Croce's "Dance in Film," in *Afterimages* (New York: Random House, 1977), 427–445, deals with dance as just "one kind of human activity the camera can capture as well as any other." More recently, see Stephanie Jordan and Dave Allen, eds., *Parallel Lines: Media Representations of Dance* (London: John Libbey, 1993); Sherril Dodds, *Dance on Screen: Genres and Media from Hollywood to Experimental Art* (Basingstoke, U.K.: Palgrave, 2001); the final chapter, "Dance in the Movies (1900–2000)," in Nancy Reynolds and Malcolm McCormick, *No Fixed Points: Dance in the Twentieth Century* (New Haven, Conn.: Yale University Press, 2003); and Judy Mitoma and Elizabeth Zimmer, eds., *Envisioning Dance on Film and Video* (New York: Routledge, 2002), which comes with a DVD of dance-film examples. But see also Toni Bentley, "The Master [George Balanchine]," *New York Review of Books,* March 10, 2005, 12–14, whose antimedia stance is discussed further in chapter 6. For whatever reasons, the dance-film debate is missing from several places where one might expect to find it; e.g., *Film and the Arts in Symbiosis: A Resource Guide,* ed. Gary R. Edgerton (New York: Greenwood Press, 1988), makes no mention of dance, nor does Brigitte Peucker's *Incorporating Images: Film and the Rival Arts* (Princeton, N.J.: Princeton University Press, 1995).

12. All quotations here from Martin, "Introduction to a Catalogue of Dance Films," 60.

13. Haskell, *How to Enjoy Ballet,* 113–114.

14. Haskell, *Ballet Panorama,* 111–112.

15. Sally Banes, *Dancing Women: Female Bodies on Stage* (New York: Routledge, 1998), 8.

16. Arthur Knight, introduction to "cine-dance" issue of *Dance Perspectives* (summer 1967): 6–11.

17. There are several resources available that catalogue filmed dance performances of all kinds, and they usually include commercial feature films and shorts. See, e.g., David L. Parker, ed., *Guide to Dance in Film* (Detroit: Gale Research, 1978); John E. Mueller, ed., *Dance Film Directory: An Annotated and Evaluative Guide to Films on Ballet and Modern Dance* (Princeton, N.J.: Princeton Book Company, 1979); Dierdre Towers, ed., *The Dance Film and Video Guide* (Princeton, N.J.: Dance Horizons, 1991); Louise Spain, ed., *Dance on Camera: A Guide to Dance Films and Videos* (Lanham, Md.: Scarecrow Press, 1998).

18. See George Balanchine, *Balanchine's Complete Stories of the Great Ballets,* ed. Francis Mason (New York: Doubleday, 1954).

19. There are many basic book-length histories of ballet. See, e.g., the extensive work by Ivor Guest on ballet from its beginnings through the early twentieth century (*The Ballet of the Enlightenment* [Princeton, N.J.: Princeton Book Company, 1997], *Ballet under Napoleon* [New York: Dance Horizons, 2002], *Gautier on Dance* [London: Dance Books, 1986], *The Romantic Ballet in England* [London: Phoenix House, 1954], *The Romantic Ballet in Paris* [Princeton, N.J.: Princeton Book Company, 1982], *The Dancer's Heritage: A Short History of Ballet* [London: Dancing Times, 1974], to list just

a few); see also his biographies of Fanny Elssler, Fanny Cerrito, Arthur Saint-Léon, Adeline Genée, and many others. Other useful general works include Susan Au, *Ballet and Modern Dance* (New York: Thames and Hudson, 1988); and Reynolds and McCormick, *No Fixed Points*. Works on American ballet, and works related more to specific companies or individuals, are listed in the notes to chapter 1.

20. Richard Dyer, "Entertainment and Utopia," in *Genre: The Musical*, ed. Rick Altman (London: Routledge, 1981), 175–189.

21. For a review of the formation and constitution of the canon of film feminism see Judith Mayne's introduction to her *Framed: Lesbians, Feminists, and Media Culture* (Minneapolis: University of Minnesota Press, 2000), xi–xxiii; and Patrice Petro, *Aftershocks of the New: Feminism and Film History* (New Brunswick, N.J.: Rutgers University Press, 2002), especially chaps. 2 and 9. For the foundational text on the "male gaze" and cinema see Laura Mulvey, "Visual Pleasure and Narrative Cinema" (1975), in *Issues in Feminist Film Criticism*, ed. Patricia Erens (Bloomington: Indiana University Press, 1990), 28–39. See also Mulvey's *Visual and Other Pleasures* (Bloomington: Indiana University Press, 1989).

22. Angela McRobbie, "*Fame, Flashdance*, and Fantasies of Achievement," in *Fabrications: Costume and the Female Body*, ed. Jane Gaines and Charlotte Herzog (New York: Routledge, 1990), 39–58. See also Angela McRobbie, "Dance Narratives and Fantasies of Achievement," in *Meaning in Motion: New Cultural Studies of Dance*, ed. Jane C. Desmond (Durham, N.C.: Duke University Press, 1997), 207–231.

23. All quotations here from Ann Cooper Albright, *Choreographing Difference: The Body and Identity in Contemporary Dance* (Hanover, N.H.: Wesleyan University Press, 1997), 3. See also Christy Adair, *Women and Dance: Sylphs and Sirens* (New York: New York University Press, 1992); Sally Banes, *Writing Dancing in the Age of Post-modernism* (Hanover, N.H.: Wesleyan University Press, 1994); Ann Daly, *Done into Dance: Isadora Duncan in America* (Bloomington: Indiana University Press, 1995); Banes, *Dancing Women*; Lynn Garafola, ed., *Rethinking the Sylph: New Perspectives on the Romantic Ballet* (Hanover, N.H.: Wesleyan University Press, 1997); Keryn Lavinia Carter, "Constructing the Balletic Body: The 'Look,' the Sylph and the Performance of Gendered Identity," in *Reframing the Body*, ed. Nick Watson and Sarah Cunning-ham-Burley (London: Palgrave, 2001), 112–127; Julia L. Foulkes, *Modern Bodies: Dance and American Modernism from Martha Graham to Alvin Ailey* (Chapel Hill: University of North Carolina Press, 2002); Helen Thomas, *The Body, Dance and Cultural Theory* (London: Palgrave, 2003); Wendy Buonaventura, *Something in the Way She Moves: Dancing Women from Salome to Madonna* (Cambridge, Mass.: Da Capo Press, 2003). See also many of the essays in Susan Leigh Foster, ed., *Choreographing History* (Bloomington: Indiana University Press, 1995); Ellen W. Goellner and Jacqueline Shea Murphy, eds., *Bodies of the Text: Dance as Theory, Literature as Dance* (New Brunswick, N.J.: Rutgers University Press, 1995); Susan Leigh Foster, ed., *Corporealities: Dancing, Knowledge, Culture, and Power* (New York: Routledge, 1996); Desmond, *Meaning in Motion*; Sondra Horton Fraleigh and Penelope Hanstein, eds., *Researching Dance: Evolving Modes of Inquiry* (Pittsburgh, Pa.: University of Pittsburgh Press, 1999); Lisa Doolittle and Anne Flynn, eds., *Dancing Bodies, Living Histories: New Writings about Dance and Culture* (Calgary, Canada: Banff Centre Press, 2000); Jane C. Desmond, ed., *Dancing Desires: Choreographing Sexualities on and off the Stage* (Madison: University of Wisconsin Press, 2001). As will be discussed, ballet is sometimes demonized in feminist considerations of dance, and while there is much in these

analyses with which I agree, I also want to explore a broader range of representations of ballet than theatrical performances, classroom technique, or the "fairy tales" on which ballets are based; see also note 48.

24. Quoted in Balanchine, *Balanchine's Complete Stories of the Great Ballets*, 387.

25. The 2005 documentary *Ballets Russes* (Dana Goldfine/Dan Geller), about the various post-Diaghilev incarnations of "Ballet Russe" companies, features Wilkinson discussing her five years with the Ballet Russe de Monte Carlo; although her dancing colleagues were very supportive, she was eventually forced to quit the company because of racism by southern audiences, including an invasion of one performance by the Ku Klux Klan. See also Jack Anderson, *The One and Only: The Ballet Russe de Monte Carlo* (New York: Dance Horizons, 1981), 222–225.

26. Daly, *Done into Dance*, 162.

27. Albright, *Choreographing Difference*, xviii, 3.

28. Banes, "Power and the Dancing Body," in *Writing Dancing*, 44.

29. For an overview of "body studies" see Thomas, *The Body, Dance and Cultural Theory*, esp. 214:

> One of the major criticisms of recent body studies is that there has been an over-attention to theory at the expense of empirical analysis. That is, body studies on the whole fail to offer concrete evidence to substantiate or develop the theoretical stances adopted. Another is that body studies tend to use the body as a focus for studying something else (for example, consumer culture, gender, race and ethnicity, risk, health and illness, technologies of the body), with the result that the body simply disappears as it is brought into discourse. Yet another criticism is that the dominant image of the body that emerges from body studies is static and immobile, a frozen entity locked in space and time. Moreover, while body studies researchers sought to overcome the dualisms in western thought, they have also been criticised for shoring them up.

30. Steven Cohan, "'Feminizing' the Song-and-Dance Man: Fred Astaire and the Spectacle of Masculinity in the Hollywood Musical," in *Screening the Male: Exploring Masculinities in Hollywood Cinema*, ed. Steven Cohan and Ina Rae Hark (New York: Routledge, 1993), 46–69; Brett Farmer, *Spectacular Passions: Cinema, Fantasy, Gay Male Spectatorship* (Durham, N.C.: Duke University Press, 2000); Matthew Tinkcom, *Working like a Homosexual: Camp, Capital, Cinema* (Durham, N.C.: Duke University Press, 2002); Steven Cohan, *Incongruous Entertainment: Camp, Cultural Value, and the MGM Musical* (Durham, N.C.: Duke University Press, 2005).

31. Alexander Doty, "The Queer Aesthete, the Diva, and *The Red Shoes*," in *Flaming Classics: Queering the Film Canon* (New York: Routledge, 2000), 105–130.

32. Richard Dyer, "Classical Ballet: A Bit of Uplift," in *Only Entertainment* (New York: Routledge, 1992), 43; Olga Maynard, *The American Ballet* (Philadelphia: Macrae Smith, 1959), 321.

33. Croce, "Dance in Film," 441; Dyer, "Entertainment and Utopia"; McRobbie, "*Fame, Flashdance*, and Fantasies of Achievement."

34. See, among many examples, Christine Gledhill, ed., *Home Is Where the Heart Is: Studies in Melodrama and the Woman's Film* (London: BFI, 1987); Mary Ann Doane, *The Desire to Desire: The Woman's Film of the 1940s* (Bloomington: Indiana University Press, 1987); Marcia Landy, ed., *Imitations of Life: A Reader on Film and Television Melodrama* (Detroit, Mich.: Wayne State University Press, 1991).

35. Rick Altman, *Film/Genre* (London: BFI, 1999); Steve Neale, *Genre and Hollywood* (London: Routledge, 2000); Ben Singer, *Melodrama and Modernity: Early Sensational Cinema and Its Contexts* (New York: Columbia University Press, 2001).

36. Steve Neale, "Melo Talk: On the Meaning and Use of the Term 'Melodrama' in the American Trade Press," *Velvet Light Trap* 32 (fall 1993): 66–89.

37. Otis Stuart, "*Dancers:* The Movie," *Ballet Review* 15 (fall 1987): 70.

38. Peter Brooks, *The Melodramatic Imagination: Balzac, Henry James, Melodrama, and the Mode of Excess* (New Haven, Conn.: Yale University Press, 1976).

39. Peter Brooks, "Melodrama, Body, Revolution"; and Tom Gunning, "The Horror of Opacity: The Melodrama of Sensation in the Plays of André de Lorde," both in *Melodrama: Stage, Picture, Screen,* ed. Jacky Bratton, Jim Cook, and Christine Gledhill (London: BFI, 1994). See also Brooks's *Body Work: Objects of Desire in Modern Narrative* (Cambridge, Mass.: Harvard University Press, 1993).

40. Catherine Clément, *Opera, or, the Undoing of Women,* trans. Betsy Wing (Minneapolis: University of Minnesota Press, 1988).

41. Carolyn Abbate, "Opera; or, the Envoicing of Women," in *Musicology and Difference: Gender and Sexuality in Music Scholarship,* ed. Ruth A. Solie (Berkeley: University of California Press, 1993), 235.

42. Banes, *Dancing Women,* 10.

43. According to Cherbo and Wyszomirski, art and entertainment in the United States "interact and are interdependent in important ways and areas that pertain to all and face similar policy issues" (*The Public Life of the Arts in America,* viii); moreover, together they are America's second-largest export product and have been for some time.

44. Arlene Croce, *The Fred Astaire and Ginger Rogers Book* (New York: Galahad Books, 1972), 119; Croce, "Dance in Film," 433.

45. Moore's remark is in Ginnine Cocuzza, "An American Premiere Danseuse [Harriet Hoctor]," *Dance Scope* 14 (fall 1980): 50. Haskell called Hoctor "light as a feather, with a dignity that triumphs over surroundings and audience," in *Balletomania* (London: Gollancz, 1934), 278. Hoctor was trained by Louis Chalif and Ivan Tarasof in New York.

46. Review of *Shall We Dance,* dir. Mark Sandrich, *Variety,* May 12, 1937.

47. G. B. Strauss, "The Aesthetics of Dominance," *Journal of Aesthetics and Art Criticism* 37 (fall 1978): 73–79. In relation to the "deathly slim" female ballet body see also Carter, "Constructing the Balletic Body": "In our contemporary moment [the dominance of the ballet body] has reached a crescendo in tandem with a push toward slimness within the general female population—a push for which balletic fashion may be in fact responsible in some degree" (124). On the other hand, Susan Bordo's *Unbearable Weight: Feminism, Western Culture, and the Body* (Berkeley: University of California Press, 1993), which contains several chapters on twentieth-century anorexia and its cultural contexts, does not refer to ballet and its dancers' bodies at all.

48. Buonaventura, *Something in the Way She Moves,* 233, 259. As mentioned, several feminist writers also deplore ballet's effects on women, although often the analysis is based on the narratives of romantic ballets such as *Giselle* or *Swan Lake* or, as in Buonaventura's case, on the stories of commercial films like *The Red Shoes.* See also the chapter titled "Titillating Tutus: Women in Ballet," in Adair, *Women*

and *Dance* (82–118); and Rachel Vigier, *Gestures of Genius: Women, Dance, and the Body* (Ontario: Mercury Press, 1994), whose chapter on ballet is titled "Ballet Masters: Colonizing the Body" (53–62). An assessment of the female ballet body as transgressive and as "object of the patriarchal gaze" is in Carter, "Constructing the Balletic Body." See also Felicia McCarren, *Dance Pathologies: Performance, Poetics, Medicine* (Stanford, Calif.: Stanford University Press, 1998). Further review of the "ballet as bad" literature and its arguments, and how ballet has been placed against modern and postmodern dance, can be found in Thomas, *The Body, Dance and Cultural Theory,* 164. In contrast see Jennifer Fisher, *"Nutcracker" Nation: How an Old World Ballet Became a Christmas Tradition in the New World* (New Haven, Conn.: Yale University Press, 2003). For Fisher, "wanting to be a 'princess' in the ballet world was not the unliberated fantasy of a deluded, oppressed woman—it was a job description. I had not grown into a woman who waited for my prince"; rather, Fisher saw "in images of Pavlova, and ballet in general, ways of being that made life seem full of possibilities" (126).

49. James Naremore, *More Than Night: Film Noir in Its Contexts* (Berkeley: University of California Press, 1998), 255.

50. Banes, *Dancing Women,* 61.

CHAPTER 1   A CHANNEL FOR PROGRESS

1. Anatole Chujoy, in *The Dance Encyclopedia,* ed. Anatole Chujoy (New York: A. S. Barnes, 1949), 232–234. Virtually all of the information cited in the next few paragraphs can be duplicated by any number of histories of ballet. I have chosen Chujoy's encyclopedia because it was one of the first works I consulted and learned from, along with George Amberg, *Ballet in America: The Emergence of an American Art* (New York: Duell, Sloan, and Pearce, 1949); Olga Maynard, *The American Ballet* (Philadelphia: Macrae Smith, 1959); and Selma Jeanne Cohen, ed., *Dictionary of Modern Ballet* (New York: Tudor, 1959). In addition, the publication of these books was itself a signifier of the growing presence of dance in the United States, especially ballet, following World War II.

2. Chujoy, *Dance Encyclopedia,* 235.

3. Ibid., 102–103.

4. All quotations in this paragraph from ibid., 237, 189–190.

5. See, e.g., Amberg, *Ballet in America;* Maynard, *The American Ballet.* See also note 1 of this chapter.

6. Information here comes from the first two sections of Paul Magriel, ed., *Chronicles of the American Dance: From the Shakers to Martha Graham* (1948; repr. New York: Da Capo, 1978); Lillian Moore, *Echoes of American Ballet* (New York: Dance Horizons, 1976); Maynard, *The American Ballet,* 15–26.

7. In Robert C. Allen, *Horrible Prettiness: Burlesque and American Culture* (Chapel Hill: University of North Carolina Press, 1991), 88–89. See also Maynard, *The American Ballet,* 16–18.

8. Maynard, *The American Ballet,* 17.

9. Ibid., 18–19.

10. Ibid., 19.

11. Information and quotations here from ibid., 19–22.

12. Information and quotations here from George Freedley, "The Black Crook and the White Fawn," in Magriel, *Chronicles of the American Dance*, 65–79.

13. Maynard, *The American Ballet*, 25.

14. Quotations here from Amberg, *Ballet in America*, 9.

15. Here and next sentence from Maynard, *The American Ballet*, 26.

16. For a history of pejorative views of actors and theater performers see Jonas Barish, *The Antitheatrical Prejudice* (Berkeley: University of California Press, 1981), esp. chaps. 10–14.

17. Plot summary from American Mutoscope and Biograph Catalogue (1898), www.imdb.com/title/tt0229464/plotsummary (accessed July 16, 2007).

18. Maynard, *The American Ballet*, 26.

19. Information here from Maynard, *The American Ballet*, 24–29; Amberg, *Ballet in America*, 10–17. Again, virtually any history of ballet in America will contain this information, discussed in very similar terms.

20. Arguably the definitive study of Pavlova, which reproduces many documents pertaining to her image in popular culture in facsimile, is Keith Money, *Anna Pavlova: Her Life and Art* (New York: Knopf, 1982). "Russia's Poetess" is quoted on 401–402.

21. Chujoy, *Dance Encyclopedia*, 357.

22. All from Money, *Anna Pavlova*, but information available from many other sources.

23. Article reproduced in facsimile in Money, *Anna Pavlova*, 402–403.

24. Quoted in Elizabeth Kendall, *Where She Danced* (New York: Knopf, 1979), 180.

25. Quotations here from Money, *Anna Pavlova*, 408–409.

26. Descriptions of Pavlova's surviving film sequences can be found in ibid., 337–338, 411–413.

27. Agnes de Mille, *Dance to the Piper* (Boston: Little, Brown, 1951), 41 (in a chapter devoted to de Mille's adoration of Pavlova).

28. Victor Dandré's biography *Anna Pavlova* (London: Cassell, 1932) is, in Keith Money's words, "at times deliberately misleading" (*Anna Pavlova*, 415), but it was the source of many of the most resonant Pavlova legends, including the ones mentioned here. It was, of course, rushed into print immediately after Pavlova's death.

29. Keith Money describes how the premiere of Pavlova's *Dumb Girl of Portici*, rather than the opening of the Diaghilev-Nijinsky season at the Metropolitan Opera House in April 1916, "managed to scoop the theatre page headlines in New York" (Pavlova was not even in town; she was in Salt Lake City at the time). See Money, *Anna Pavlova*, 229.

30. See Henry F. May, *The End of American Innocence: A Study of the First Years of Our Own Time, 1912–1917* (Chicago: Quadrangle Books, 1964), 243–244. See also Peter Wollen, "Fashion/Orientalism/the Body," *New Formations* 1 (spring 1987): 5–33; "impeccable modernity" is from Kendall, *Where She Danced*, 118.

31. The standard work on the contemporary critical reception and impact of the Ballets Russes in the United States is Nesta Macdonald, ed., *Diaghilev Observed by Critics in England and the United States, 1911–1929* (New York: Dance Horizons, 1975). See also Lynn Garafola, *Diaghilev's Ballets Russes* (New York: Oxford University Press, 1989); and several of the essays in Lynn Garafola and Nancy Van Norman Baer, eds., *The Ballets Russes and Its World* (New Haven, Conn.: Yale University Press, 1999). On Gertrude Hoffman see Kendall, *Where She Danced*, 75–76, 83–85.

32. Reviews and the reception of Nijinsky in the United States, and all quotations here, in Macdonald, *Diaghilev Observed,* 172–181, 183–213.

33. The most detailed biography of Nijinsky is Richard Buckle, *Nijinsky* (New York: Penguin, 1975).

34. Macdonald, *Diaghilev Observed,* 174.

35. Kendall, *Where She Danced,* 85.

36. In her article "Ballet Satire in the Early Broadway Revue," *Dance Scope* 13 (winter/spring 1979): 44–50, Barbara Naomi Cohen discusses the satirical references to ballet in commercial musicals of the 1910s and 1920s and concludes that the many "affectionate satires of the celebrities of the Russian Ballet" were not only statements about American entertainment values but also records of the "increasing assimilation of European ballet tastes" (50). The status of ballet as "high" art remains secure in these musicals, which may be why, as Cohen notes, "Nijinsky's presumed effeminacy," while remarked upon in reviews of his ballet performances, "was seldom a topic for satire" (46). Buster Keaton parodies ballet and performs as a ballet dancer in a film-within-a-film in *Free and Easy* (1930).

37. On Broadway, Balanchine choreographed ballets for *On Your Toes* (1936, which included the famous ballet "Slaughter on Tenth Avenue"), *Babes in Arms* (1937), *I Married an Angel* (1938), *The Boys from Syracuse* (1938), and *Louisiana Purchase* (1940), among several others. In Hollywood, he was the dance director (choreography was not referred to as such in film credits until the mid-1940s) for ballet numbers in *The Goldwyn Follies* (1938), *On Your Toes* (1939), *I Was an Adventuress* (1940, which featured a short special-effects-laden "Swan Lake"), and *Star-Spangled Rhythm* (1942), all with his then-wife Vera Zorina.

38. See relevant entries in Chujoy, *Dance Encyclopedia* (including the second edition, edited by Chujoy and P. W. Manchester [New York: Simon and Schuster, 1967]). See also Amberg, *Ballet in America;* or Maynard, *The American Ballet.*

39. Doris Hering, "Don't Forget the Backbend, Harriet!" *Dance Magazine,* Dec. 1965, 112–117.

40. The term *pinhead* was apparently first applied to the Balanchine ballerina by critic R. P. Blackmur in 1956. See also chapter 6.

41. Lincoln Kirstein, *Blast at Ballet: A Corrective for the American Audience* (New York: Marstin Press, 1938), 45.

42. Information and quotations here from Deborah Jowitt, *Time and the Dancing Image* (New York: Morrow, 1988), 69–102.

43. See Kendall, *Where She Danced;* Jowitt, *Time and the Dancing Image,* chaps. 2–4; Ann Daly, *Done into Dance: Isadora Duncan in America* (Bloomington: Indiana University Press, 1995).

44. Daly, *Done into Dance,* 9–10.

45. Ibid., 16.

46. Isadora Duncan, *The Art of the Dance,* ed. Sheldon Cheney (New York: Theatre Arts, 1969), 49.

47. All here from Daly, *Done into Dance.*

48. Ibid., 207–208.

49. Ted Shawn, *The American Ballet* (New York: Henry Holt, 1926).

50. See Kendall, *Where She Danced*, chaps. 6 and 7; Jowitt, *Time and the Dancing Image*, sec. 3, for discussion of Denishawn in the United States.

51. In Walter Terry, *Ted Shawn: Father of American Dance* (New York: Dial Press, 1976), 67.

52. All quotations in this paragraph from Shawn, *The American Ballet*, 37, 39, 26.

53. All quotations in this paragraph from ibid., 7–8, 20–22, 39–40.

54. Ernestine Stodelle, *Deep Song: The Dance Story of Martha Graham* (New York: Schirmer, 1984), 53.

55. Julia L. Foulkes, *Modern Bodies: Dance and American Modernism from Martha Graham to Alvin Ailey* (Chapel Hill: University of North Carolina Press, 2002), 152.

56. Ibid., 154.

57. Ibid., 3.

58. When asked by Kirstein to come to New York to found a ballet company, Balanchine famously responded, "But first a school" (see Jennifer Dunning, *"But First a School": The First Fifty Years of the School of American Ballet* [New York: Viking, 1985]).

59. Kendall, *Where She Danced*, 136.

60. See the 2005 documentary *Ballets Russes* (Dana Goldfine/Dan Geller), for an accessible history of the post-Diaghilev Ballets Russes in the United States. Books include Jack Anderson, *The One and Only: The Ballet Russe de Monte Carlo* (New York: Dance Horizons, 1981); and Kathrine Sorley Walker, *De Basil's Ballets Russes* (London: Hutchinson, 1982).

61. Again, see the Goldfine/Geller film *Ballets Russes*; as well as Anderson, *The One and Only*; and Walker, *De Basil's Ballets Russes*.

62. The information in this paragraph can be found in Chujoy, *Dance Encyclopedia*, as well as in any number of other works on American dance history.

63. Kirstein, *Blast at Ballet*, 41–45.

64. For information on American Ballet Theatre and its history see Charles Payne, *American Ballet Theatre* (New York: Knopf, 1979).

65. For more on Hurok's colorful relationship to ballet in the United States see his *S. Hurok Presents . . . The World of Ballet* (London: Robert Hale, 1955).

66. Mark Franko, *The Work of Dance: Labor, Movement, and Identity in the 1930s* (Middletown, Conn.: Wesleyan University Press, 2002), 107.

67. See Kirstein, *Blast at Ballet*, Part Two, "The Great Conspiracy."

68. Ibid., 86.

69. Ibid., 45.

70. Bernard Taper, *Balanchine* (New York: Times Books, 1984), 151.

71. For a discussion of Kirstein's and Martin's views see Franko, *The Work of Dance*, 113–123.

72. Foulkes, *Modern Bodies*, 176.

73. Quoted in ibid., 159. Modern dance did succeed in institutionalizing itself somewhat but only in relation to a few specific individuals (like Martha Graham or, later, Merce Cunningham), and as Sally Banes argues in her book *Terpsichore in Sneakers: Post-Modern Dance* (Middletown, Conn.: Wesleyan University Press, 1987),

the problem for "historical modern dance" was that it had made "certain promises with respect to the use of the body and the social and artistic function of dance that had not been fulfilled. Rather than freeing the body and making dance accessible even to the smallest children, rather than bringing about social and spiritual change, the institution of modern dance had developed into an esoteric art form for the intelligentsia, more remote from the masses than ballet" (xv–xvi). By the 1960s, modern dance had "ossified into various stylized vocabularies" (xvi), and its professional and pedagogical organizations were no less hierarchical and autocratically run than any ballet school or company. Ironically, the wide variety of diverse and iconoclastic avant-garde and postmodern dance of the 1960s and 1970s—which sought to dispense with the expressionism, specialized technical virtuosity, and heavy narrative basis of modern dance (and, of course, ballet)—would also acquire "the status of a new academy," in Banes's words, and some of its dance-makers (Twyla Tharp most obviously) eventually returned to work in ballet and commercial theater (19). Of course, neither modern nor postmodern dance ever became as popular at the box office as classical ballet, and as Tharp's case indicates, classical ballet continues to draw into itself many of the formal innovations and movement qualities, if rarely the actual performing bodies, of even the most avant-garde dance styles.

74. Quoted in Foulkes, *Modern Bodies,* 157–158.

75. Ibid., 158.

76. Quotations here and in the next sentence are from Mark N. Grant, *The Rise and Fall of the Broadway Musical* (Boston: Northeastern University Press, 2004), 259.

77. Ann Barzel, "European Dance Teachers in the United States," *Dance Index* 3 (April–June 1944): 93. Barzel's lengthy essay also includes illustrations from a 1917 "mail order lesson in ballet" (89). See also Walter Terry, *On Pointe! The Story of Dancing and Dancers on Toe* (New York: Dodd, Mead, 1962). The American blocked toe shoe also enabled weird hybrid forms such as "toe tapping," or tap dancing in toe shoes; see also the specialty acrobatic toe dancing of Edna Sedgwick in the Alice Faye musical *You're a Sweetheart* (1937).

78. Franko, *The Work of Dance,* 123.

79. Virtually any biography or autobiography of a dancer who worked in the United States in the middle years of the last century contains some section on life in Hollywood, since so many ended up being lured there by the comparatively huge amounts of money offered for what seemed to be little enough effort. Often the daily grind of moviemaking is presented as crassly unpleasant, not only because of "endless interruptions and interminable waiting around," in dancer Sono Osato's words, but because of Hollywood's preference for glamour and spectacle and physical pulchritude, especially, over the dancers' own technique and talent in what they believed was the superior form of art. See, e.g., A. E. Twysden, *Alexandra Danilova* (London: C. W. Beaumont, 1945), 126–128; Sono Osato, *Distant Dances* (New York: Knopf, 1980), 251–257; Vera Zorina, *Zorina* (New York: Farrar, Straus, Giroux, 1986), 150–151, 167–200; Maria Tallchief, with Larry Kaplan, *Maria Tallchief: America's Prima Ballerina* (Gainesville: University Press of Florida, 2005), 163–167.

80. David Van Leer, "What Lola Got: Cultural Carelessness on Broadway," in *The Other Fifties: Interrogating Midcentury American Icons,* ed. Joel Foreman (Urbana: University of Illinois Press, 1997), 171–196.

CHAPTER 2   THE LOT OF A BALLERINA IS INDEED TOUGH

1. Here and below are from Steve Neale, "Melo Talk: On the Meaning and Use of the Term 'Melodrama' in the American Trade Press," *Velvet Light Trap* 32 (fall 1993): 66–67.

2. All information here is from the press book for *Dance, Girl, Dance*, Cinema-Television Library, University of Southern California (USC), Los Angeles.

3. Review of *Dance, Girl, Dance*, dir. Dorothy Arzner, *Variety*, Aug. 28, 1940.

4. Neale, "Melo Talk," 75.

5. Ben Singer, *Melodrama and Modernity: Early Sensational Cinema and Its Contexts* (New York: Columbia University Press, 2001), 37; Steve Neale, *Genre and Hollywood* (London: Routledge, 2000), 202.

6. Rick Altman, *The American Film Musical* (Bloomington: Indiana University Press, 1987).

7. Richard Dyer, "Entertainment and Utopia," in *Genre: The Musical*, ed. Rick Altman (London: Routledge/BFI, 1981), 175–189. The "tradition of morbidity" is from Arlene Croce, "Dance in Film," in *Afterimages* (New York: Random House, 1977), 441.

8. Singer, *Melodrama and Modernity*, 14.

9. Review of *The Ballet Girl*, dir. George Irving, *Variety*, Jan. 28, 1916.

10. All quotations here are from *Variety*, March 2, 1917.

11. Plot summary is from the American Film Institute Catalog, Silent Films, www.afi.com/members/catalog/AbbrView.aspx?s=1&Movie=13980&bhcp=1 (accessed July 31, 2007).

12. Plot summary is from the American Film Institute Catalog, Silent Films, www.afi.com/members/catalog/AbbrView.aspx?s=1&Movie=10768&bhcp=1 (accessed July 31, 2007).

13. Plot summary is from the American Film Institute Catalog, Silent Films, www.afi.com/members/catalog/AbbrView.aspx?s=1&Movie=12385&bhcp=1 (accessed July 31, 2007).

14. American Film Institute Catalog, Silent Films, www.afi.com/members/catalog/AbbrView.aspx?s=1&Movie=13461&bhcp=1 (accessed July 31, 2007).

15. Peter Brooks, *The Melodramatic Imagination: Balzac, Henry James, Melodrama, and the Mode of Excess* (New Haven, Conn.: Yale University Press, 1976); Singer, *Melodrama and Modernity*, 7.

16. Singer, *Melodrama and Modernity*, 7.

17. All quotations here are from Brooks, *The Melodramatic Imagination*, 199, 204–205.

18. Peter Brooks, "Melodrama, Body, Revolution," in *Melodrama: Stage, Picture, Screen*, ed. Jacky Bratton, Jim Cook, and Christine Gledhill (London: BFI, 1994), 18.

19. Singer, *Melodrama and Modernity*, 7.

20. All quotations here are from ibid., 44–49, 224.

21. Ibid., 137.

22. Ibid., 53–54 (my italics).

23. Ibid., 49.

24. Information on the film's background and production can be found in Thomas Schatz, *The Genius of the System: Hollywood Filmmaking in the Studio Era* (New York:

Pantheon, 1988), 108–120. For information on *Grand Hotel*'s many iterations across time see Lydia J. King, "*Menschen im Hotel/Grand Hotel:* Seventy Years of a Popular Culture Classic," *Journal of American and Comparative Cultures* 23 (summer 2000): 17–23.

25. Vicki Baum, *It Was All Quite Different* (New York: Funk and Wagnalls, 1964), 286.

26. See Keith Money, *Pavlova: Her Life and Art* (New York: Knopf, 1982); and discussion of Pavlova in chapter 1 of this book.

27. All quotations from Vicki Baum, *Grand Hotel,* trans. Basil Creighton (London: Garden City Press, 1930), 27–28, 49, 109.

28. Money, *Pavlova,* 393. The original source is Victor Dandré's biography *Anna Pavlova* (London: Cassell, 1932), 360.

29. Baum, *Grand Hotel,* 23.

30. MGM remade *Grand Hotel* in 1945 as *Weekend at the Waldorf,* and there the character of Grusinskaya has been replaced by a movie actress, Irene Malvern, played by Ginger Rogers (Irene Dunne and Katharine Hepburn were also considered for the role). According to 1943 scripts and notes from the MGM Collection at the Cinema-Television Library at USC, the remake was initially to have been a musical but with little remaining from the original story (one script iteration begins in the present at the Waldorf and introduces the *Grand Hotel* characters in comic/ romantic flashback). The musical idea was dropped entirely by 1944, and the film became an "exciting, romantic comedy-drama" whose appeal was strongly linked to the glamour and lavishness of the Waldorf-Astoria itself, reproduced at MGM in nearly perfect detail. Clearly it would have been difficult to make a musical-*comedy* version of *Grand Hotel,* because so many of the parallel stories end quite tragically; *Weekend at the Waldorf,* in contrast, concludes with everyone romantically and cheerfully paired up, and it is tempting to speculate that MGM just did not see a way to employ a Russian ballerina as a happy and fulfilled romantic lead in 1945. There is one comic reference to the earlier film ("Why that's straight out of the picture *Grand Hotel!*" exclaims Rogers to Walter Pidgeon, who has pretended to be a jewel thief for a bit; and he replies, "That's right—I'm the baron, you're the ballerina, and we're off to see the wizard") and one number in a nightclub that features some girls in tutus and toe shoes. The credits, however, claim only that the film was "suggested by a play by Vicki Baum."

31. Jeremy Tambling, *Opera, Ideology, and Film* (New York: St. Martin's, 1987), 44.

32. Rasch was a Viennese dancer who became a choreographer with her own troupe of dancers in Hollywood; see Frank W. D. Ries, "Albertina Rasch: The Hollywood Career," *Dance Chronicle* 6 (1983): 281–362.

33. Elisabeth Bronfen, *Over Her Dead Body: Death, Femininity, and the Aesthetic* (New York: Routledge, 1992), xi. Bronfen's book has chapters on paintings, novels (including *Carmen*), poetry, and even Alfred Hitchcock's film *Vertigo* (1958) but no mentions of opera or ballet.

34. The best discussion of women and morality in pre-Code Hollywood remains Lea Jacobs, *The Wages of Sin: Censorship and the Fallen Woman Film, 1928–1942* (Madison: University of Wisconsin Press, 1991).

35. Dodie Smith to Sidney Franklin, memorandum, Nov. 25, 1939; all information here is from the four folders on *Waterloo Bridge* in the MGM Collection, Cinema-Television Library, USC.

36. Mary Ann Doane, *The Desire to Desire: The Woman's Film of the 1940s* (Bloomington: Indiana University Press, 1987), 119. Johnston's words are from "Femininity and the Masquerade: *Anne of the Indies*," in *Jacques Tourneur* (London: BFI, 1975), 40.

37. In press-book promotional material Adams's big ballet is referred to as "the lavish 'Morning Star' ballet sequence," but that name belongs, in fact, to the smaller incidental piece that Judy makes up; Madame Basilova secretly watches Judy (or rather O'Hara's double, from behind) dancing and then calls Adams to make the audition appointment. Press book for *Dance, Girl, Dance*, Cinema-Television Library, USC.

38. Lincoln Kirstein, *Blast at Ballet: A Corrective for the American Audience* (New York: Marstin Press, 1938). For further discussion of Kirstein's argument see chapter 1.

39. Michael Renov, *Hollywood's Wartime Woman: Representation and Ideology* (Ann Arbor, Mich.: UMI, 1988), 38.

40. Lady Eleanor Smith, *Ballerina* (New York: Bobbs-Merrill, 1932).

41. Production Code Administration (hereafter PCA) files, Margaret Herrick Library, Academy of Motion Picture Arts and Sciences, Los Angeles. Columbia Studios has no archives of any kind.

42. Review of *The Men in Her Life*, dir. Gregory Ratoff, *Time*, Nov. 17, 1941, 93.

43. Bosley Crowther, review of *The Men in Her Life*, dir. Gregory Ratoff, *New York Times*, Dec. 12, 1941.

44. Review of *The Men in Her Life*, dir. Gregory Ratoff, *Motion Picture Herald*, Oct. 25, 1941.

45. Review of *The Men in Her Life*, dir. Gregory Ratoff, *Hollywood Reporter*, Oct. 29, 1941.

46. Review of *The Men in Her Life*, dir. Gregory Ratoff, *Daily Variety*, Oct. 29, 1941.

47. Review of *The Men in Her Life*, dir. Gregory Ratoff, *Motion Picture Daily*, Oct. 22, 1941.

48. One of the most famous sequences in Disney's animated classic *Fantasia* (released as a roadshow attraction in 1940, in wide release in 1942) is that featuring tutu-attired and ballet-dancing hippos, elephants, crocodiles, and ostriches.

49. See, e.g., *New York Times*, June 17, 1944.

50. "Film Fest Unearths Buried Dance Treasure," *Dance Magazine*, July 2000.

51. Quotations here and in the next paragraph come from seventeen reviews excerpted in *Motion Picture Review Digest*, Dec. 26, 1938, 7.

52. Joseph Breen to L. B. Mayer, Aug. 15, 1946, PCA files, Margaret Herrick Library, Academy of Motion Picture Arts and Sciences, Los Angeles.

53. MGM Collection, *The Unfinished Dance*, Cinema-Television Library, USC.

54. "Ballerina" (treatment), April 16, 1946, by Myles Connolly, MGM Collection, *The Unfinished Dance*, Margaret Herrick Library, Academy of Motion Picture Arts and Sciences, Los Angeles.

55. The best information on Cyd Charisse's performing career is found in Jean Claude Missiaen, *Cyd Charisse: Du ballet classique à la comédie musicale* (Paris: Henri Veyrier, 1979).

56. Bosley Crowther, review of *The Unfinished Dance*, dir. Henry Koster, *New York Times*, Oct. 31, 1947.

57. John McCarten, "Give Us a Waltz, Professor," review of *The Unfinished Dance*, dir. Henry Koster, *New Yorker*, Nov. 8, 1947, 114.

58. See Nico Charisse [Cyd Charisse's first husband, and a well-known Hollywood dancer, teacher, and dance director], *Ballet for Today* (Culver City, Calif.: Murray and Gee, 1951), 140–143.

59. I have written elsewhere about what I call "women's musicals," musicals that depend not only on a woman star's marquee value and name recognition but also on her performing talent, especially as a dancer. See Adrienne L. McLean, *Being Rita Hayworth: Labor, Identity, and Hollywood Stardom* (New Brunswick, N.J.: Rutgers University Press, 2004), chap. 3.

60. "A movie that changed my life," posted Jan. 20, 2000, Internet Movie Database, http://imdb.com/title/tt0039938/usercomments (accessed June 27, 2007).

61. All quotations here are from Tambling, *Opera, Ideology, and Film*, 44, 47.

62. Edwin Denby, "A Film of Pavlova," *Edwin Denby: Dance Writings*, ed. Robert Cornfield and William MacKay (New York: Knopf, 1986), 135.

63. Quotations in rest of this paragraph are from ibid., 136.

CHAPTER 3   THE MAN WAS MAD–BUT A GENIUS!

1. Phil Powrie, Ann Davies, and Bruce Babington, eds., *The Trouble with Men: Masculinities in European and Hollywood Cinema* (London: Wallflower Press, 2004), 1.

2. Ibid., 2.

3. Steve Neale, "Masculinity as Spectacle: Reflections on Men and Mainstream Cinema" [1983], repr. in *Screening the Male: Exploring Masculinities in Hollywood Cinema*, ed. Steven Cohan and Ina Rae Hark (New York: Routledge, 1993), 9–20.

4. Quotations here and in the next sentence are from ibid., 18.

5. Richard Dyer, "Don't Look Now: The Instabilities of the Male Pin-Up," in *Only Entertainment* (New York: Routledge, 1992), 110.

6. Among the first was Steven Cohan and Ina Rae Hark, eds., *Screening the Male: Exploring Masculinities in Hollywood Cinema* (New York: Routledge, 1993). For an overview of this material see the introduction to Powrie, Davies, and Babington, *The Trouble with Men*, 1–15.

7. Steven Cohan, "'Feminizing' the Song-and-Dance Man: Fred Astaire and the Spectacle of Masculinity in the Hollywood Musical," in *Screening the Male: Exploring Masculinities in Hollywood Cinema*, ed. Steven Cohan and Ina Rae Hark (New York: Routledge, 1993), 46–69.

8. Ibid., 63–64.

9. Quotations here and in the next sentence are from Moe Meyer, "Reclaiming the Discourse of Camp," in *The Politics and Poetics of Camp*, ed. Moe Meyer (New York: Routledge, 1994), 11.

10. All here from Matthew Tinkcom, *Working like a Homosexual: Camp, Capital, Cinema* (Durham, N.C.: Duke University Press, 2002), 46.

11. Steven Cohan, "Dancing with Balls: Sissies, Sailors, and the Camp Masculinity of Gene Kelly," in *Incongruous Entertainment: Camp, Cultural Value, and the MGM Musical* (Durham, N.C.: Duke University Press, 2005), 149–199.

12. Cohan, *Incongruous Entertainment*, 9.

13. All here is from Cohan, "Dancing with Balls."

14. Ramsay Burt, *The Male Dancer: Bodies, Spectacle, Sexualities* (New York: Routledge, 1995), 22.

15. Ibid., 24.

16. Quotations here and below are from ibid., 27–28.

17. Quotations are all from ibid., 76, 78.

18. All quotations from Olga Maynard, *The American Ballet* (Philadelphia: Macrae Smith, 1959), 312–323.

19. Quoted in Burt, *The Male Dancer,* 108.

20. Ibid., 110.

21. Ibid., 42.

22. All quotations from Richard Dyer, "Classical Ballet: A Bit of Uplift," in *Only Entertainment,* 43.

23. See David Anthony Gerstner, "Dancer from the Dance: Gene Kelly, Television, and the Beauty of Movement," *Velvet Light Trap* 49 (spring 2002): 48–66.

24. Edwin Denby, "Dance in the Films," in *Edwin Denby: Dance Writings,* ed. Robert Cornfield and William MacKay (New York: Knopf, 1986), 136.

25. The entire plot of *Gold Diggers in Paris,* which features typical Busby Berkeley numbers that are only tangentially connected to their narrative placement as stage performances, hinges on the mistaking of the chorines in a nightclub called the "Club Ballé" for dancers in the "Academy Ballet," run by Padrinsky. To avoid bankruptcy, the nightclub's owner, played by Rudy Vallee, pretends that his girls are in fact "toe dancers," and he hires a down-and-out ballet master to teach them; then they try to win a dance competition in the "Paris Exposition." They do, but with "show dancing" (or rather a Berkeley film number), not ballet. Other than the few scenes with Padrinsky, and some shots of girls in toe shoes, ballet has little significance to the film's narrative or its musical numbers.

26. See, e.g., *Variety,* May 22, 1946.

27. All here from John Davis, "When Will They Ever Learn? A Tale of Mad Geniuses, Scientists, Artists, and a Director (also Mad)," *Velvet Light Trap* 15 (fall 1975): 11–17.

28. All quotations are from the press book for *The Mad Genius,* British Film Institute, London, microfiche.

29. Davis, "When Will They Ever Learn?"

30. Jeremy Tambling, *Opera, Ideology, and Film* (New York: St. Martin's, 1987), 44. See also chapter 2 in this book.

31. Jane Feuer, "The Theme of Popular vs. Elite Art in the Hollywood Musical," *Journal of Popular Culture* 12 (winter 1978): 491–499. See also Feuer, *The Hollywood Musical,* 2nd ed. (Bloomington: Indiana University Press, 1993), 54–65.

32. Feuer, *The Hollywood Musical,* 62. See also the plot of *Gold Diggers in Paris.*

33. As do the lines referring to insanity and "going crazy" by the male dancer character Padrinsky in *Gold Diggers in Paris.*

34. Feuer, *The Hollywood Musical,* 61.

35. All here from Arlene Croce, *The Fred Astaire and Ginger Rogers Book* (New York: Galahad Books, 1972), 122–123.

36. Review of *Shall We Dance,* dir. Mark Sandrich, *Variety,* May 12, 1937.

37. Review of *Shall We Dance,* dir. Mark Sandrich, *Motion Picture Herald,* May 8, 1937.

38. All here from Jennifer Fisher, *"Nutcracker" Nation: How an Old World Ballet Became a Christmas Tradition in the New World* (New Haven, Conn.: Yale University Press, 2003), 62–63.

39. Ursula Trow, "Nijinsky: Out of His Twilight," *American Weekly,* Oct. 28, 1945, 9.

40. Quoted in Doug Fetherling, *The Five Lives of Ben Hecht* (Canada: Lester and Orpen, 1977), 153.

41. All quotations from Ben Hecht, *The Collected Stories of Ben Hecht* (New York: Crown, 1945), 378–387.

42. Review of *Specter of the Rose,* dir. Ben Hecht, *New York Times,* Sept. 2, 1946.

43. Press book for *Specter of the Rose,* Cinema-Television Library, University of Southern California (USC), Los Angeles.

44. Sumiko Higashi, "Ethnicity, Class, and Gender in Film: DeMille's *The Cheat,*" in *Unspeakable Images: Ethnicity and the American Cinema,* ed. Lester Friedman (Urbana: University of Illinois Press, 1991), 130.

45. All here from John A. Walker, *Art and Artists On Screen* (Manchester, U.K.: Manchester University Press, 1993), 16.

46. Quotations from Alain Silver and Elizabeth Ward, eds., *Film Noir: An Encyclopedic Reference to the American Style* (Woodstock, N.Y.: Overlook Press, 1979), 4–5.

47. Arlene Croce, "Dance in Film," in *Afterimages* (New York: Random House, 1977), 441.

48. Cohan and Hark, introduction to *Screening the Male,* 2.

49. Quotations here are from "The Films in Review," *Theatre Arts,* May 1946, 277.

50. Review of *Specter of the Rose,* dir. Ben Hecht, *Variety,* May 22, 1946. *Specter of the Rose* was reviewed in all of the major news weeklies, as well as in *Saturday Review* and *Theatre Arts; Life* magazine featured the film and its "shattering climax" (the "madman's dance") in a special spread (June 10, 1946, 84–88).

51. All here is from Jeffrey Brown Martin, *Ben Hecht: Hollywood Screenwriter* (Ann Arbor, Mich.: UMI, 1985), 169.

52. Cohan, *Incongruous Entertainment,* 66, 69.

53. Quotations here and below are from ibid., 69.

54. All quotations are from the script collection for *Bathing Beauty,* Margaret Herrick Library, Academy of Motion Picture Arts and Sciences, Los Angeles.

55. Quotations here are from Kaja Silverman, *Male Subjectivity at the Margins* (New York: Routledge, 1992), 52.

56. Linda Williams, *"Playing the Race Card": Melodramas of Black and White from Uncle Tom to O. J. Simpson* (Princeton, N.J.: Princeton University Press, 2001).

57. Ben Singer, *Melodrama and Modernity: Early Sensational Cinema and Its Contexts* (New York: Columbia University Press, 2001), 295.

58. Angela McRobbie, "Dance Narratives and Fantasies of Achievement," in *Meaning in Motion: New Cultural Studies of Dance,* ed. Jane C. Desmond (Durham, N.C.: Duke University Press, 1997), 220.

CHAPTER 4   IF YOU CAN DISREGARD THE PLOT

1. Hugh Fordin, *The World of Entertainment* (New York: Doubleday, 1975), 172.

2. Ibid., 212.

3. Edwin Denby, "A Briefing in American Ballet," in *Edwin Denby: Dance Writings*, ed. Robert Cornfield and William MacKay (New York: Knopf, 1986), 526; Jack Anderson, *The One and Only: The Ballet Russe de Monte Carlo* (New York: Dance Horizons, 1981), 139.

4. For details of Ballet Theatre's financial situation see Charles Payne, *American Ballet Theatre* (New York: Knopf, 1977), 156–163.

5. For more about *The Red Shoes* and its marketing as a "roadshow attraction" and as a British import see Sarah Street, *Transatlantic Crossings: British Feature Films in the United States* (New York: Continuum, 2002), 109–114.

6. Anderson, *The One and Only*, 139.

7. Arlene Croce, "Dance in Film," in *Afterimages* (New York: Random House, 1977), 439.

8. There are many books about the history of ballet in Britain; among the ones I consulted are Peter Noble, ed., *British Ballet* (London: Skelton Robinson, 1950); Mary Clarke, *The Sadler's Wells Ballet* (London: Adam and Charles Black, 1955); and Alexander Bland, *The Royal Ballet: The First Fifty Years* (New York: Doubleday, 1981).

9. Meredith Daneman, *Margot Fonteyn: A Life* (New York: Viking, 2004), 143.

10. All quotations from Orville Raimond, "The Re-Birth of Ballet," *Film Reel*, 8–9. The magazine has no volume or issue numbers and is undated. Moira Shearer is featured on the cover, and I assume it was printed in 1947 or 1948 (the film had apparently not yet been released when the article was written).

11. Mark Connelly, *The Red Shoes* (London: Tauris, 2005), 4.

12. See Karol Kulik, *Alexander Korda: The Man Who Could Work Miracles* (London: W. H. Allen, 1975), 317; Michael Powell, *A Life in Movies: An Autobiography* (New York: Knopf, 1987), 611. See also Mary Clarke, "Saturday's Children," in *Ballet Annual*, vol. 9, ed. Arnold Haskell (London: Adam and Charles Black, 1954), 106. Clark writes that the original project "fell through on the declaration of war in 1939," but Powell attributes the falling-through to "romantic escapades" involving Merle Oberon and David Niven that were "enough to make Alex hesitate about investing half a million in *The Red Shoes*."

13. *Black Narcissus* was released in 1947. After the success of *The Red Shoes* Powell and Pressburger would rejoin Korda's London Films; it was there that they made their ballet version of Offenbach's operetta *The Tales of Hoffmann* in 1951.

14. Kevin Gough-Yates, *Michael Powell*, quotation from an interview published in Brussels, Belgium, in 1973 by the Royal Film Archive of Belgium and the National Film Archive of Great Britain, 18.

15. Quoted in Monk Gibbon, *The Red Shoes Ballet* (London: Saturn Press, 1948), 51.

16. Gough-Yates, *Michael Powell*, 18.

17. Keith Money, *The Art of Margot Fonteyn* (London: Reynal, 1965), n.p.

18. Powell, *A Life in Movies*, 643.

19. Ibid., 642.

20. Books about Moira Shearer include Pigeon Crowle's early *Moira Shearer: Portrait of a Dancer* (London: Faber and Faber, 1949); and Hugh Fisher's *Moira Shearer* (London: Adam and Charles Black, 1958). Barbara Newman interviewed Shearer for *Striking a Balance: Dancers Talk about Dancing* (Boston: Houghton Mifflin, 1982). Shearer

also provided me with an enormous amount of information herself over the years about working on this and other films.

21. "Again It Is Shearer," *New York Times Magazine*, April 1, 1951, 22.

22. For Powell's account see Powell, *A Life in Movies*, 618–620, 625–626, 633–634.

23. Newman, *Striking a Balance*, 96.

24. Powell, *A Life in Movies*, 625–626.

25. *Dance* 21, June 1947, 8. Seaver, later known as Edwina Fontaine, was a dancer who was with the Ballet Russe de Monte Carlo from 1944 to 1949, apparently brought there by Balanchine; she had studied at the School of American Ballet (Jack Anderson, personal communication).

26. Powell, *A Life in Movies*, 620, 626.

27. Here and below are from Meredith Daneman, *Margot Fonteyn*, 201–202.

28. Michael Powell, quoted in an interview with Maurice Ambler, in Crowle, *Moira Shearer*, 56.

29. See Powell, *A Life in Movies*, 610–611.

30. Jack Cardiff, "'The Red Shoes' and Ciné-Choreography," in *Ballet Annual*, vol. 3, ed. Arnold Haskell (London: Adam and Charles Black, 1948), 56.

31. Powell, *A Life in Movies*, 629.

32. Ibid., 584.

33. All here is from Herb Lightman, "*The Red Shoes:* The Ultimate in Choreophotography Done in Technicolor by Jack Cardiff, A.S.C.," *American Cinematographer* 30 (March 1949): 82–83.

34. C. A. Lejeune, "London Begins a Busy Summer Film Schedule," *New York Times*, June 1, 1947; the word *surrealist* was repeated in her "Communiqués from the London Film Front," *New York Times*, June 29, 1947. The later article is C. A. Lejeune, "British Movie Memos," *New York Times*, July 27, 1947.

35. C. A. Lejeune, "The Bustling British Studios," *New York Times*, Dec. 7, 1947.

36. Gibbon, *The Red Shoes Ballet*, 76.

37. Paul Tassovin, "Ballet Film," *Dance Observer*, Nov. 1948, 125.

38. Elizabeth Salter, *Helpmann* (New York: Universe, 1978), 139.

39. See, e.g., Gibbon, *The Red Shoes Ballet*, 30.

40. Cardiff, "'The Red Shoes' and Ciné-Choreography," 60; W. A. Wilcox, "Well, the Ballet's Good," *Sunday Dispatch*, July 25, 1948.

41. Description from Croce, "Dance in Film," 439.

42. Karen Backstein, "A Second Look: *The Red Shoes*," *Cineaste* 20 (Oct. 1994): 42.

43. See chapters 2 and 3 of this book.

44. Ian Christie, *Arrows of Desire: The Films of Michael Powell and Emeric Pressburger* (London: Waterstone, 1985), 7.

45. Ibid., 111; Petley's comment is in Peter Wollen, "Tinsel and Realism," in *Hollywood and Europe: Economics, Culture, National Identity*, ed. Geoffrey Nowell-Smith and Steven Ricci (London: BFI, 1998), 131.

46. Christie, *Arrows of Desire*, 114.

47. Ibid., 110.

48. Ibid., 111.

49. Arnold Haskell, ed. *Ballet Annual*, vol. 3 (London: Adam and Charles Black, 1949), 39.

50. Arnold L. Haskell, *In His True Centre: An Interim Autobiography* (London: Adam and Charles Black, 1951), 165.

51. Arnold L. Haskell, *How to Enjoy Ballet* (New York: Morrow, 1951), 113–114.

52. All quotations here are from A. H. Franks, *Ballet for Film and Television* (London: Pitman, 1950), 5–6.

53. See also the opinions of various dance critics in *Ballet* 5 (Aug.-Sept. 1948): "This film wins my Oscar as the Biggest and Loudest and Technicoloredest film-about-ballet-which-doesn't-quite-get-there to date" (A. V. Coton); "So much of the film is so easy to criticize from every possible angle, and Miss Shearer is so easy to praise. . . . The mixture of fact and fantasy is far too confusing" (Roger Wood); "*The Red Shoes* is a long and boring film; I suppose it had to be long in order to cram in as many *clichés* as possible" (Richard Buckle). Reprinted at www.powell-pressburger.org/Reviews/48_TRS/Critics.html (accessed July 16, 2007).

54. Review of *The Red Shoes*, dir. Michael Powell and Emeric Pressburger, *Variety*, July 27, 1948.

55. Anthony Bower, review of *The Red Shoes*, dir. Michael Powell and Emeric Pressburger, *The Nation*, Nov. 6, 1948, 529.

56. *Variety*, July 27, 1948.

57. All here is from "Ballet Shoes," *Newsweek*, Oct. 25, 1948, 101.

58. "The Mysterious Box Office," *Time*, Oct. 25, 1948, 102.

59. John McCarten, "Dancers and Gangsters," review of *The Red Shoes*, dir. Michael Powell and Emeric Pressburger, *New Yorker*, Oct. 23, 1948, 107.

60. Arlene Croce, *The Fred Astaire and Ginger Rogers Book* (New York: Galahad Books, 1972), 171.

61. Arthur Hopkins, "Red Shoes," *Theatre Arts*, Jan. 1949, 52.

62. Review of *The Red Shoes*, dir. Michael Powell and Emeric Pressburger, *New Republic*, Oct. 25, 1948, 28.

63. Powell, *A Life in Movies*, 168.

64. A short 2000 documentary called *A Profile of "The Red Shoes"* (written and produced by David Lemon) includes British ballerina Darcy Bussell talking about the film's effects on her. See also Doris Perlman, "50 Years After, *The Red Shoes* Dance On and On," *Dance Magazine*, Dec. 1998, 66, in which she quotes a number of people who were influenced by the film.

65. See, e.g., "'Red Shoes' Moira Criticises Own Film," *Daily Express*, Jan. 17, 1949; or her interview with Clive Barnes, "Moira Shearer Today," *Dance Magazine*, May 1962, 48 (in which Barnes calls Shearer "the ballerina Britain somehow lost on the way"); or the 1994 interview in Brian McFarlane, *An Autobiography of British Cinema* (London: BFI, 1997), 532–535: "The whole story of Victoria Page is such nonsense from the point of view of any real person . . ." (repr. at www.powell-pressburger.org/Reviews/48_TRS/TRS01.html (accessed July 16, 2007).

66. Powell, *A Life in Movies*, 652.

67. Press book for *The Unfinished Dance*, Cinema-Television Library, University of Southern California (USC), Los Angeles.

68. The exterior shot of the Mercury Theatre was real, the interior a set; Shearer told me she had never been inside the theater itself.

69. Alexander Doty, "The Queer Aesthete, the Diva, and *The Red Shoes*," in *Flaming Classics: Queering the Film Canon* (New York: Routledge, 2000), 105–130.

70. Quoted in ibid., 109.

71. Ibid., 109, 111.

72. Ibid., 114.

73. Powell, *A Life in Movies,* 653, 660.

74. Quotations here and in the next sentence are from Doty, "The Queer Aesthete," 116.

75. Press books for *The Red Shoes* at British Film Institute, London; and Cinema-Television Library, USC.

76. George Balanchine apparently agreed. As reported by Maria Tallchief, when she and then-husband Balanchine saw the film in London, Balanchine kept mumbling, "Is ridiculous. . . . Impresario should be happy if ballerina and musician fall in love. Is ideal, the best situation. He's there, she's there. Diaghilev would have been very happy with such a situation" (Maria Tallchief, with Larry Kaplan, *Maria Tallchief: America's Prima Ballerina* [Gainesville: University Press of Florida, 2005], 147). Of course, Diaghilev was *not* happy when the "he" was his lover, Nijinsky.

77. Suzanne Gordon, *Off Balance: The Real World of Ballet* (New York: Pantheon, 1983), 45.

78. See U.S. press book for *The Red Shoes,* Cinema-Television Library, USC.

79. See, e.g., Cyd Charisse's legs as featured in the advertising campaign for *The Band Wagon* in 1953. The 2005 DVD of *The Turning Point* (1977) features a cover photograph of similar long legs rather than the artwork on the film's original poster.

80. Clive Hirschhorn, *Gene Kelly* (Chicago: Regnery, 1974), 202.

81. Powell, *A Life in Movies,* 661.

82. Quoted in Donald Knox, ed., *The Magic Factory: How MGM Made "An American in Paris"* (New York: Praeger, 1973), 44.

83. See, e.g., John McCarten, "Those Anglo-Indian Blues," *New Yorker,* June 2, 1956, 131 ("[The dancers] are agile enough, but the ideas they are so muscularly trying to convey seem hardly worth their trouble"); Arthur Knight, "*Invitation to the Dance,*" *Dance Magazine,* June 1956, 14–17, 80 ("The ironic thing . . . is that the artistic pretensions of this *Invitation to the Dance* are its weakest aspect"). See also chapter 6 of this book.

84. Moira Shearer to the author, July 13, 1987.

85. Raymond Durgnat, *A Mirror for England: British Movies from Austerity to Affluence* (London: Faber and Faber, 1970), 210.

86. Peter Brooks, "Melodrama, Body, Revolution," in *Melodrama: Stage, Picture, Screen,* ed. Jacky Bratton, Jim Cook, and Christine Gledhill (London: BFI, 1994), 18.

87. Ben Singer, *Melodrama and Modernity: Early Sensational Cinema and Its Contexts* (New York: Columbia University Press, 2001), 137, 40.

88. See, e.g., David N. Rodowick, "Madness, Authority, and Ideology: The Domestic Melodrama of the 1950s," in *Home Is Where the Heart Is: Studies in Melodrama and the Woman's Film,* ed. Christine Gledhill (London: BFI, 1987), 268–280.

89. Ibid., 275.

90. Croce, "Dance in Film," 439.

91. Ibid., 441.

CHAPTER 5   THE SECOND ACT WILL BE *QUITE* DIFFERENT

1. Mary Clarke, *The Sadler's Wells Ballet* (London: Adam and Charles Black, 1955), 244. For a vivid description of the company's New York debut see 236–246.

2. Ibid., 244.

3. Ibid., 237.

4. John Hart, Shearer's longtime ballet partner, recalled that in New York on the first tour the police arrived on opening night to protect the movie star, disappearing when they found the star was not the headliner, and that in Chicago audiences returned first-night tickets for second-night ones when they found out that Shearer was not dancing the opening (personal communication).

5. Clarke, *The Sadler's Wells,* 238.

6. For Shearer's first appearance in New York, Ninette de Valois assigned her a pas de deux that she had never before appeared in; Shearer was also excluded from several press conferences (personal communication).

7. The second Sadler's Wells U.S. tour is the subject of its own book, Franklin White's *Sadler's Wells Ballet Goes Abroad* (London: Faber and Faber, 1951).

8. "Ballerina Margot Fonteyn (For Sleeping Beauty, an Awakened Audience)," *Time,* Nov. 14, 1949, 70–75. Fonteyn appeared on the cover of *Newsweek* a year later, Nov. 13, 1950 (story 88–90).

9. Here and below are from Meredith Daneman, *Margot Fonteyn: A Life* (New York: Viking, 2004), 202.

10. Ibid., 202–203. De Valois' tactics worked quite well; Shearer told me that the amount of applause that greeted her *appearance* onstage in the third act was far greater than that which followed her performance (personal communication), and although Elizabeth Frank, in *Margot Fonteyn* (London: Chatto and Windus, 1958), writes that in "her solo in 'The Blue Bird' Shearer held up the show" (77), John Martin in the *New York Times* termed it an "adequate though not a world-beating 'Blue Bird,'" mentioning at the same time that Shearer was "laboring under the handicap of too much extraneous publicity from the movie, 'Red Shoes'" ("Sadler's Wells Makes U.S. Debut," Monday, Oct. 10, 1949). When the Sadler's Wells returned to the U.S. in 1950, it was the "better part of a week" (six days), Martin noted, before Shearer was allowed to make her first appearance onstage.

11. Cover reproduced in Lynn Garafola, ed., with Eric Foner, *Dance for a City: Fifty Years of the New York City Ballet* (New York: Columbia University Press, 1999), n.p. All other information here from 1.

12. Jennifer Fisher, *"Nutcracker" Nation: How an Old World Ballet Became a Christmas Tradition in the New World* (New Haven, Conn.: Yale University Press, 2003), 28. It would be a few years more before a television *Nutcracker* became an annual seasonal event.

13. Ibid., 3–4.

14. Cecilia Elizabeth O'Leary, *To Die For: The Paradox of American Patriotism* (Princeton, N.J.: Princeton University Press, 1999), 239–242.

15. Ibid., 240.

16. Michael Rogin, *Ronald Reagan, the Movie: And Other Episodes in Political Demonology* (Berkeley: University of California Press, 1987), 259.

17. Quoted in Peter Filene, "'Cold War Culture' Doesn't Say It All," in *Rethinking Cold War Culture,* ed. Peter J. Kuznick and James Gilbert (Washington: Smithsonian Institution Press, 2001), 156.

18. All here from Naima Prevots, *Dance for Export: Cultural Diplomacy and the Cold War* (Hanover, N.H.: Wesleyan University Press, 1998), esp. 7–14, 69–91. The "gum-chewing" quotation is from Eric Foner's introduction, 3.

19. Joanne Meyerowitz, ed., *Not June Cleaver: Women and Gender in Postwar America, 1945–1960* (Philadelphia: Temple University Press, 1994); Filene, "'Cold War Culture.'" See also the essays contained in Joel Foreman, ed., *The Other Fifties: Interrogating Midcentury American Icons* (Urbana: University of Illinois Press, 1997), which aim to locate "struggle, resistance, instability, and transformation in what is for many the least likely place: mass media popular culture" (6).

20. Quotations here from Filene, "'Cold War Culture,'" 157, 169–170.

21. Jane Feuer, *The Hollywood Musical,* 2nd ed. (Bloomington: Indiana University Press, 1993); Jerome Delamater, *Dance in the Hollywood Musical* (Ann Arbor, Mich.: UMI, 1981); Rick Altman, *The American Film Musical* (Bloomington: Indiana University Press, 1987).

22. Walter Terry, "Ballet Isn't Highbrow Anymore," *Look,* undated clipping (ca. 1950), 25–26; Sol Hurok, *S. Hurok Presents . . . The World of Ballet* (London: Robert Hale, 1955), 296.

23. Olga Maynard, *The American Ballet* (Philadelphia: Macrae Smith, 1959), 321.

24. See, e.g., David K. Johnson, *The Lavender Scare: The Cold War Persecution of Gays and Lesbians in the Federal Government* (Chicago: University of Chicago Press, 2004), esp. chap. 6, "'Let's Clean House': The Eisenhower Security Program."

25. Arlene Croce, "Dance in Film," in *Afterimages* (New York: Random House, 1977), 441.

26. The information in this and subsequent paragraphs can be found in any number of standard film sources; see, e.g., Robert Sklar, *Movie-Made America: A Cultural History of American Movies,* 2nd ed. (New York: Vintage, 1994), esp. chaps. 11–17. See also Murray Pomerance, ed., *American Cinema of the 1950s: Themes and Variations* (New Brunswick, N.J.: Rutgers University Press, 2005).

27. Thomas Doherty, *Teenagers and Teenpics: The Juvenilization of American Movies in the 1950s* (Boston: Unwin Hyman, 1988), 182–184.

28. Croce, "Dance in Film," 441.

29. A quite weird parody of *Swan Lake* appears in Betty Grable's last big musical, *Three for the Show* (1955), with Jack Lemmon and Marge and Gower Champion and choreography by Jack Cole. According to Gower Champion's biographer, Cole met Columbia studio head Harry Cohn one morning "after his first ballet, a production of *Swan Lake.* Cohn, completely transfixed by the performance, was still clearly in a state of childlike wonder. Ebullience unrestrained, he declared to Cole, 'That music was sensational! You've just got to use it in the new Grable film!'" Although Cole was horrified, Cohn insisted; and Cole got his "revenge" by combining Tchaikovsky's music with visuals drawn from a "popular perfume advertisement." The resulting dream ballet combines women with guns, footmen bearing candelabra, and Grable, Lemmon, and the Champions dueling and dancing. John Anthony Gilvey, *Before the Parade Passes By: Gower Champion and the Glorious American Musical* (New York: St. Martin's, 2005), 58–59. Cole's biographer mentions the number,

too, but as a tremendous disappointment to Cole because the whole thing had been made, by editing and cutting, into something "'serious,' which is not what he wanted at all" (Glenn Loney, *Unsung Genius: The Passion of Dancer-Choreographer Jack Cole* [New York: Franklin Watts, 1984], 212).

30. A similar use is made by *The Red Danube* (1949), in which Janet Leigh plays a Russian ballet dancer in Vienna with whom a soldier (Peter Lawford) falls in love when he catches sight of her dancing in a rehearsal early in the film. Leigh's status as a "great artist" is referred to in dialogue, but we never see ballet again; she kills herself at the end rather than allowing herself to be deported back to Moscow.

31. *Never Let Me Go,* MGM Collection, Cinema-Television Library, University of Southern California (USC), Los Angeles.

32. Press book for *Never Let Me Go,* Cinema-Television Library, USC.

33. Tallchief describes the experience of filming *The Dying Swan,* to which she was asked to add steps from *The Firebird* to "make it a lot livelier," in Maria Tallchief, with Larry Kaplan, *Maria Tallchief: America's Prima Ballerina* (Gainesville: University Press of Florida, 2005), 163–167.

34. Review of *The Man Who Loved Redheads,* dir. Harold French, *New York Times,* July 26, 1955.

35. Review of *The Man Who Loved Redheads,* dir. Harold French, *Time,* Aug. 8, 1955, 82, 85.

36. See, e.g., David Caute, *The Dancer Defects: The Struggle for Cultural Supremacy during the Cold War* (New York: Oxford University Press, 2003), esp. chap. 9, "Passports for Paintings: Abstract Expressionism and the CIA."

37. As one congressman quoted by Naima Prevots put it, "I wonder where in the Constitution you can find anything that gives me the right to spend the taxpayers' money for projects of this sort. . . . I simply cannot find the justification to take [money] away from the people. I am out of sympathy with it" (Prevots, *Dance for Export,* 30).

38. Maynard, *The American Ballet,* 321.

39. Prevots, *Dance for Export,* 8.

40. From Steven Cohan, "Dancing with Balls: Sissies, Sailors, and the Camp Masculinity of Gene Kelly," in *Incongruous Entertainment: Camp, Cultural Value, and the MGM Musical* (Durham, N.C.: Duke University Press, 2005), 149–199.

41. Lincoln Kirstein, *What Ballet Is About: An American Glossary* (New York: Dance Perspectives, 1959), 47.

42. All quotations here and in the next paragraph are from Jane Feuer, "The Self-Reflexive Musical and the Myth of Entertainment," in *Film Genre Reader,* ed. Barry Keith Grant (Austin: University of Texas Press, 1986), 332–335, 361.

43. I have reworked Feuer's formulation in relation to noncanonical musicals elsewhere as well; indeed, I find the exercise to be extremely useful in understanding not only how the myth of entertainment works but how and why and when it does not. See Adrienne L. McLean, *Being Rita Hayworth: Labor, Identity, and Hollywood Stardom* (New Brunswick, N.J.: Rutgers University Press, 2004), 140–143, in which I explore the myth of entertainment in relation to *Down to Earth* (1947), a "women's musical" that also fails to manage the demystification of art and the valorization of spontaneity.

44. Script collection, *The Story of Three Loves*, Margaret Herrick Library, Academy of Motion Picture Arts and Sciences, Los Angeles.

45. Elisabeth Bronfen, *Over Her Dead Body: Death, Femininity, and the Aesthetic* (New York: Routledge, 1992), xi.

46. Susan Felleman, *Art in the Cinematic Imagination* (Austin: University of Texas Press, 2006), 157.

47. John McCarten, "A Touch of Mal de Mer," review of *The Story of Three Loves*, dir. Vincent Minnelli and Gottfried Reinhardt, *New Yorker*, March 14, 1953, 70.

48. Review of *The Story of Three Loves*, dir. Vincent Minnelli and Gottfried Reinhardt, *Commonweal*, March 20, 1953, 602.

49. Review of *The Story of Three Loves*, dir. Vincent Minnelli and Gottfried Reinhardt, *Newsweek*, March 16, 1953, 103.

50. Parker Tyler, "A Dance, a Dream and a Flying Trapeze," *Theatre Arts*, May 1953, 81.

51. All here is from McCarten, "A Touch of Mal de Mer," 70.

52. Review of *Dance Little Lady*, dir. Val Guest, *Variety*, July 29, 1954.

53. All here is from David N. Rodowick, "Madness, Authority, and Ideology: The Domestic Melodrama of the 1950s," in *Home Is Where the Heart Is: Studies in Melodrama and the Woman's Film*, ed. Christine Gledhill (London: BFI, 1987), 268–280.

54. Review of *Dance Little Lady*, dir. Val Guest, *Spectator*, July 9, 1954.

55. Press book for *Gaby*, Cinema-Television Library, USC.

56. PCA files, *Gaby*, Margaret Herrick Library, Academy of Motion Picture Arts and Sciences, Los Angeles; *Gaby*, MGM Collection, Cinema-Television Library, USC.

57. According to its press book, *Gaby* is a colorful love story about "tender, laughing, fleeting hours," Leslie Caron is "even more adorable" than in her earlier films (and is especially adorable in the "jitterbug sequence"), *and* it is an adult film about an "embittered" Gaby who "offers what happiness she can to other boys who may never come back from the fighting."

58. Mary Ann Doane, *The Desire to Desire: The Woman's Film of the 1940s* (Bloomington: Indiana University Press, 1987), 119.

59. Caute, *The Dancer Defects*, 468.

60. Feuer, *The Hollywood Musical*, 8.

61. Delamater, *Dance in the Hollywood Musical*, 98 (italics mine).

62. All here is from ibid.

63. Review of *Invitation to the Dance*, dir. Gene Kelly, *Time*, June 11, 1956, 105.

64. Arthur Knight, "*Invitation to the Dance*," *Dance Magazine*, June 1956, 14.

65. Delamater, *Dance in the Hollywood Musical*, 74. As Martin Rubin's work on the "aggregate musical" makes clear, "thirties musical" is a misnomer; many musicals throughout the 1940s and 1950s were not integrated, nor were they trying to be (see Martin Rubin, *Showstoppers: Busby Berkeley and the Tradition of Spectacle* [New York: Columbia University Press, 1993]).

66. Press book for *Meet Me in Las Vegas*, Cinema-Television Library, USC.

67. John McCarten, "Pretty Good Deal," review of *Meet Me in Las Vegas*, dir. Roy Rowland, *New Yorker*, March 24, 1956, 126.

68. Delamater, *Dance in the Hollywood Musical*, 164.

CHAPTER 6   TURNING POINTS

1. Quotations here and in the following two paragraphs are from *Time*, April 16, 1965, 48–52; and March 15, 1968, 44–48. The 1965 article is in the "Music" section, the second in "The Theater." Both have accompanying color photo spreads. For more on the defections of the Soviet dancers, see David Caute, *The Dancer Defects: The Struggle for Cultural Supremacy during the Cold War* (New York: Oxford University Press, 2003), chap. 17.

2. The solidification of ballet's status as the best-known and best-funded American theatrical dance art arises from a complex concatenation of factors, among them ballet's inherited but stable vocabulary and technique, as opposed to modern dance's more personal, idiosyncratic, and variable forms and modes; the rise to prominence of American art generally after World War II, with New York City becoming the international "capital" of dance as it had of visual art; and, concomitant to these, the incorporation of ballet companies and, as mentioned, the financial support put in place for them—with large amounts for a few big companies rather than smaller amounts spread among many different dance groups—by the Ford Foundation and the National Endowment for the Arts. I would also add—indeed, the thrust of this project has been to argue—that ballet had become more famous as art because it was also more popular as entertainment, at least in part because of its ubiquity in American commercial cinema.

3. All here comes from the "Dance" section of *Time*, Jan. 27, 1975, page number unknown.

4. Quoted in Caute, *The Dancer Defects*, 497.

5. Lynn Garafola, ed., with Eric Foner, *Dance for a City: Fifty Years of the New York City Ballet* (New York: Columbia University Press, 1999), 29.

6. In *All That Jazz* (1979), director/choreographer Bob Fosse's take on his own life and career through the character of Joe Gideon (played by Roy Scheider), Fosse could not only show his own open heart surgery in graphic detail, but Joe could ask of Kate (Ann Reinking, one of Fosse's real-life girlfriends) whether the male ballet dancer to whom she had just talked on the phone was "straight or gay"—and further, when the dancer turns out to be straight, yell at her for daring to use his phone to "call someone who is not gay."

7. Jane Feuer, *The Hollywood Musical*, 2nd ed. (Bloomington: Indiana University Press, 1993), 62.

8. Wendy Buonaventura, *Something in the Way She Moves: Dancing Women from Salome to Madonna* (Cambridge, Mass.: Da Capo Press, 2003), 233. See also Helen Thomas, *The Body, Dance and Cultural Theory* (London: Palgrave, 2003), for a discussion of the return to prominence, contra the "*Swan Lake* and *Giselle* are gone forever" claim quoted in *Time* in 1968, of romantic ballets: "a brief glance at the repertoires of the major national ballet companies shows that the hegemonic draw of 'classic' ballets like *Swan Lake* and *The Nutcracker*, which stem from the nineteenth century, remains intact. Even the iconoclastic versions . . . pay tribute to the staying power of the form" (109). In *Attitude: Eight Young Dancers Come of Age at the Ailey School* (New York: Tarcher/Penguin, 2004), Katharine Davis Fishman describes ballet's hegemony even in the daily life of a "modern dance company": "Students learn one modern technique at a time . . . but they are in ballet class every day they're at Ailey." Fishman notes the "irony here," that the founders of modern

dance in America "sought to free dancers from the strict postures and fairy-tale plots of European classical ballet. But lately, American audiences have again become smitten with the ballet aesthetic" (14).

9. Although I am concentrating most on English-language films, Pedro Almodóvar's *Talk to Her* (*Hable con ella*, 2002) also features a ballet-student character, desired *because* she is a budding ballerina by one of the film's two male protagonists; for most of the film she is literally a beautiful body in a coma. Whatever else is wonderful about *Talk to Her*, the ballet dancer is by far the most stereotypical and least developed character in the film.

10. Nancy Reynolds and Malcolm McCormick, *No Fixed Points: Dance in the Twentieth Century* (New Haven, Conn.: Yale University Press, 2003), 741–742.

11. Review of *The Turning Point*, dir. Herbert Ross, *Variety*, Oct. 19, 1977.

12. Review of *The Turning Point*, dir. Herbert Ross, *New York Times*, Nov. 15, 1977.

13. *Variety*, Oct. 19, 1977.

14. *New York Times*, Nov. 15, 1977.

15. Arlene Croce, "The Godmother," *New Yorker*, Nov. 21, 1977, 185.

16. Ibid., 184.

17. *Newsweek*, Nov. 28, 1977, 97.

18. Leslie Browne disappeared even more from *The Turning Point* as time went on. The film's original poster featured images of Baryshnikov and Browne together, their names in a small "and introducing" box. The 2005 DVD sports the faces and names of Baryshnikov, Bancroft, and MacLaine only (and a pair of unattached "long legs"—see chapter 4), as though Baryshnikov is one of the film's three stars.

19. All quotations are from *New York Times*, Nov. 8, 1978.

20. Angela McRobbie, "*Fame, Flashdance*, and Fantasies of Achievement," in *Fabrications: Costume and the Female Body*, ed. Jane Gaines and Charlotte Herzog (New York: Routledge, 1990), 39–58; "Dance Narratives and Fantasies of Achievement," in *Meaning in Motion: New Cultural Studies of Dance*, ed. Jane C. Desmond (Durham, N.C.: Duke University Press, 1997), 207–231. See also Sherril Dodds's discussion of the film in her *Dance on Screen: Genres and Media from Hollywood to Experimental Art* (Basingstoke, U.K.: Palgrave, 2001), 37–44.

21. From an episode of *E! True Hollywood Stories* about *Flashdance* that aired on the E! Entertainment cable channel several times in 2005. See also the entry for the film on the Internet Movie Database (www.imdb.com), which lists the uncredited personnel.

22. See, e.g., Lydia Lane, "Vera-Ellen Tells How Dancing, Posture Keep Waist Thin and Muscles in Trim": "I was told that I was too thin but I paid no attention to anyone," *Los Angeles Times*, undated clipping from the Vera-Ellen scrapbook in the Constance McCormick Collection (CMC), Cinema-Television Library, University of Southern California (USC), Los Angeles; Lydia Lane, "Leslie Caron Tell [*sic*] Her Secrets for Slim Waist, Twinkly Toes," *Los Angeles Times*, ca. 1953–1954, Leslie Caron scrapbook, CMC; Lydia Lane, "Cyd Charisse Tells Value of Exercise," *Los Angeles Times*, ca. 1958–1959, Cyd Charisse/Tony Martin scrapbook, vol. 1, CMC: "You don't have to worry about keeping your figure if you use your body. If more people would exercise they could eat what they wanted without getting fat."

23. Leslie Caron, "Ballet Is an Adolescent Passion," *Dance Magazine,* Oct. 1963, 26–27.

24. L. M. Vincent, M.D., *Competing with the Sylph: Dancers and the Pursuit of the Ideal Body Form* (Kansas City, Kans.: Andrews and McMeel, 1979; see also 2nd ed. *Competing with the Sylph: The Quest for the Perfect Dance Body* [Princeton, N.J.: Dance Horizons, 1989]); Suzanne Gordon, *Off Balance: The Real World of Ballet* (New York: Pantheon, 1983); Gelsey Kirkland, with Greg Lawrence, *Dancing on My Grave* (New York: Doubleday, 1986). See also Keryn Lavinia Carter's discussion of the "spectral, contemporary, employable" woman dancer's body in "Constructing the Balletic Body: The 'Look,' the Sylph and the Performance of Gendered Identity," in *Reframing the Body,* ed. Nick Watson and Sarah Cunningham-Burley (London: Palgrave, 2001), 112–127. But as noted earlier, there is no mention of dance or ballet in the discussions of anorexia in Susan Bordo's *Unbearable Weight: Feminism, Western Culture, and the Body* (Berkeley: University of California Press, 1993).

25. Joseph H. Mazo, *Dance Is a Contact Sport* (New York: Dutton, 1974), 20. Certainly the ballerina's body had always been *idealized* as light, weightless, attenuated; see, e.g., lithographs from the romantic era in which impossibly tiny feet support impossibly slender women *and* men (*The Romantic Ballet from Contemporary Prints,* introduction and notes by Sacheverell Sitwell [London: Batsford, 1948]). But at this time, photographs of the same dancers show them to be of considerably different (larger) sizes and shapes.

26. Bernard Taper, *Balanchine* (New York: Times Books, 1984), 163. Quite a number of Balanchine ballerinas *have* claimed that dancing for Balanchine changed their bodies: Mary Ellen Moylan, one of Balanchine's first American ballerinas, said that "we were gorgeously thin" but also that unfortunately she "became sick and couldn't [dance]. This being very thin business is not without hazard." Maria Tallchief maintains, "If one compares various pictures of me in *Ballet Imperial* [choreographed by Balanchine first for the Ballet Russe de Monte Carlo, later in the repertoire of the New York City Ballet], it's obvious that the shape of my leg was completely different after I had begun training with Balanchine." Karin von Aroldingen feels she "did have to rearrange [her] body for him," a body that was more "sculptured" than he liked. Melissa Hayden goes further: "You make yourself a Balanchine dancer by dancing his ballets. Your legs change, your body changes." All quotations are from Robert Tracy's oral history, *Balanchine's Ballerinas* (New York: Linden Press, 1983).

27. Taper, *Balanchine,* 251.

28. Judith Lynne Hanna, *Dance, Sex, and Gender: Signs of Identity, Dominance, Defiance, and Desire* (Chicago: University of Chicago Press, 1988), 152.

29. Lincoln Kirstein, *Thirty Years: Lincoln Kirstein's The New York City Ballet* (New York: Knopf, 1978), 335–336.

30. Kirstein, *Thirty Years,* 233–235.

31. Toni Bentley, *Winter Season: A Dancer's Journal* (New York: Random House, 1982).

32. Remi Clignet, *The Structure of Artistic Revolutions* (Philadelphia: University of Pennsylvania Press, 1985), 58.

33. Although a version of *Spectre de la rose* remained in the repertoire of the Ballet Russe de Monte Carlo in the United States, it was always somewhat controversial; ballet critic Walter Terry declared in 1939 that "as a male I resent seeing a man impersonate a rose—or even the spirit of one, for that matter" (in Jack Anderson, *The One and Only: The Ballet Russe de Monte Carlo* [New York: Dance Horizons, 1981],

264–267). Moreover, photographs show that the company's version of the costume grew less and less flowery as the years went on. See chapter 1 of this book for a photo of Nijinsky dressed in the 1911 costume.

34. Quotations here and below are from "Pointeless," review of *Nijinsky*, dir. Herbert Ross, *New York Times*, March 20, 1980.

35. See again Steven Cohan's discussion of the "manly/effeminate" dynamic of the male dancer in "Dancing with Balls: Sissies, Sailors, and the Camp Masculinity of Gene Kelly," in *Incongruous Entertainment: Camp, Cultural Value, and the MGM Musical* (Durham, N.C.: Duke University Press, 2005), 149–199.

36. It was called *Indian Summer* in the U.K.

37. *Dancers* grossed $500,000 in five weeks before disappearing from theaters, which was more than *Nijinsky* had taken in; Otis Stuart cites these figures, from *Variety*, in his "*Dancers*: The Movie," *Ballet Review* 15 (fall 1987): 70–72.

38. It was well known that Baryshnikov was involved on every level with *Dancers*; see, e.g., Holly Brubach, "Lovers Leap: Behind the Scenes with Baryshnikov," *Vogue*, July 1, 1987, 220–223.

39. Maybe it was the relative success of Baryshnikov's appearance in the late–cold war thriller *White Nights* in 1985 that made it seem as though he could carry a film on his own. In *White Nights* Baryshnikov plays a great male ballet dancer who defected from the Soviet Union and after a plane crash finds himself there again, forced to remain and made a prisoner in a gilded cage. But *White Nights* also starred Gregory Hines, as an American man who defected *to* the Soviet Union in search of an illusory racial justice, and Isabella Rossellini, as Hines's wife. The thrill is in the daring escape the three plan together, as well as the "impromptu" noodling-around-in-a-studio tap-ballet dance interludes with Hines and Baryshnikov performing to the decadent "jazz" music that Baryshnikov has brought with him. Baryshnikov was part of the appeal and success of *White Nights*—it was fun to watch him pretend to be in trouble for having defected but really being a big star making movies about defecting—but he was not the only draw.

40. Brubach, "Lovers Leap," 222.

41. Otis Stuart writes in his review of the film that "Baryshnikov's film career, however much it has trafficked on the specifics of his life, has established him as the only male ballet dancer ever able to sustain a full-screen close-up without loss of impact, complexity, or sexual specificity." Stuart also claims, somewhat oddly to my mind, that "the heterosexual impulse that *Dancers* celebrates . . . is one any father would approve [of]" (Stuart, "*Dancers*: The Movie," 70).

42. John Gruen, "Ferri Tales Can Come True: Giselle Goes to the Movies," *Dance Magazine*, Oct. 1987, 38.

43. Joan Acocella, for example, details the "terrible troubles" that beset Martha Graham's dance company after Graham's death in 1991 in "Happy Face: The Martha Graham Company, Contextualized," *New Yorker*, May 8, 2006, 80–81.

44. Lisa Schwarzbaum, "Agony of the Feet," *Entertainment Weekly*, May 19, 2000, 45.

45. See *Billy Elliott*, the Internet Movie Database, www.imdb.com/title/tt0249462/release info; and www.imdb.com/title/tt0249462/business (both accessed July 8, 2007).

46. *Step Up*, a cheerful 2006 teen film whose tagline is "Every second chance begins with a first step," opens with a montage that crosscuts between street dancers and ballet students taking class in a studio. In both cases the genders and races of the

dancers are mixed, and the white male protagonist, Tyler (Channing Tatum), is a working-class foster-homed mixed-up hip-hop dancer who will end up enrolled in the Maryland School of the Arts after partnering and falling in love with a female student, Nora (Jenna Dewan). Race is represented as much less of a barrier to achievement than class or gender ("Man, these rich kids have *everything*"), although the film is predictable in the horror that Tyler is made to exhibit at the thought of wearing tights (which we never see him do).

47. In the "Good and Bad Hair" challenge dance in Spike Lee's reworking of the "college musical," *School Daze* (1988), at one point the "wannabe" girls (who straighten and dye their long hair and adopt a coiffed and made-up version of dominant white femininity) perform a classical ballet *enchaînement*, signifying their cultural pretensions as against their darker "bad hair" cohort (who assertively identify as African American). Of course, most if not all of the dancers in the number demonstrate considerable ballet training and technical proficiency, and all are equally adept in jazz styles.

48. *The Company* (May 23, 2004), www.theage.com.au/articles/2004/05/19/1084917648 297.html (accessed July 16, 2007).

49. All quotations used here are from Joan Acocella, "No Bloody Toe Shoes," *New York Review of Books*, Feb. 26, 2004, 7–8.

50. Bill Nichols, *Representing Reality: Issues and Concepts in Documentary* (Bloomington: Indiana University Press, 1991), 247.

51. See David Román, *Performance in America: Contemporary U.S. Culture and the Performing Arts* (Durham, N.C.: Duke University Press, 2005): "in the early-mid 1990s . . . *performance* became the critical term of choice across the humanities. . . . To complicate matters, the terms *performance, performativity,* and *performative* were invoked interchangeably. . . . Moreover, the interest in performance did not necessarily inspire scholarship on theatre and performance itself" (22–23). Román's book is also a compelling exploration of the "suspicion of commercial theatre endemic to [cultural studies]," which constitutes a "strain of antitheatricality that is symptomatic of larger cultural anxieties about class, capital, pleasure, and the popular" (35). Although he too deals only with "the live," I believe, for the reasons explored in this book, that commercial film and its theatricalized performances also can be significant politically as well as sources of great *pleasure.*

52. Peggy Phelan, *Unmarked: The Politics of Performance* (New York: Routledge, 1993), 146.

53. All quotations here are from Philip Auslander, *From Acting to Performance: Essays in Modernism and Postmodernism* (New York: Routledge, 1997), 7.

54. All quotations here are from Cynthia Baron, Diane Carson, and Frank P. Tomasulo, "Introduction: More Than *the* Method, More Than One Method," in *More Than a Method: Trends and Traditions in Contemporary Film Performance,* ed. Cynthia Baron, Diane Carson, and Frank P. Tomasulo (Detroit, Mich.: Wayne State University Press, 2004), 11, 14.

55. Robert Knopf, introduction to *Theater and Film: A Comparative Anthology,* ed. Robert Knopf (New Haven, Conn.: Yale University Press, 2005), 1.

56. See overview in Román, *Performance in America,* 22–30.

57. Thomas Waugh, "'Acting to Play Oneself': Notes on Performance in Documentary," in *Making Visible the Invisible: An Anthology of Original Essays on Film Acting,* ed. Carole Zucker (Metuchen, N.J.: Scarecrow, 1990), 67.

58. An obvious comparative text is Frederick Wiseman's 1985 documentary *Ballet,* in which his camera and tape recorder observe and listen to classes, rehearsals, performances, business meetings, auditions, free time, and so on at American Ballet Theatre. As an example of Wiseman's interest in "direct cinema," it has no script, no voice-over narration, no talking heads. *Ballet* has received relatively little attention among Wiseman scholars, perhaps because of the ambiguity of the film's levels of performance in combination with its subject matter. There are many interesting things in *Ballet,* but because nothing is placed in any context, it is difficult for a layperson to recognize what is going on or why it matters. Michael Somes, for example, rehearsing a revival of Frederick Ashton's 1946 masterpiece *Symphonic Variations,* is not named (nor is the ballet itself), so Somes, who was in the original cast, becomes just a paunchy old man in an ill-fitting track suit and lace-up oxfords.

59. Quoted in Acocella, "No Bloody Toe Shoes," 7.

60. Ibid.

61. In Robert Gottlieb, "Altman's Love for Ballet Makes for a Serious Misstep," *New York Observer,* Jan. 4, 2004, www.observer.com/node/48580 (accessed July 8, 2007). Gottlieb asks, "Why movie and dance critics are taking *The Company* seriously, I can't imagine. Are they impressed by Altman's reputation and naïve sincerity? . . . Or are they just relieved to see a ballet movie in which the heroine neither dies *(The Red Shoes)* nor has an overnight sensational success (most of the others)?" It should be noted, too, that some of the Joffrey's ballets were being touted in the *Time* articles cited at the beginning of this chapter as examples of the "new" dance that was freeing itself from the "rules, clichés, and conventions of the past" *(Time,* March 15, 1968, 44).

62. Robert T. Self, "Resisting Reality: Acting by Design in Robert Altman's *Nashville,*" in *More Than a Method: Trends and Traditions in Contemporary Film Performance,* ed. Cynthia Baron, Diane Carson, and Frank P. Tomasulo (Detroit, Mich.: Wayne State University Press, 2004), 130.

63. Unless you have a stage mother, no one can force you to dance ballet; one does it because it feels good, because of the tremendous sense of accomplishment and joy that mastery of its difficult vocabulary can produce, because it exercises the brain as well as the body, because one loves the music, and so on and so on. See also the discussions by dancers in Helena Wulff, *Ballet across Borders: Career and Culture in the World of Dancers* (Oxford, U.K.: Berg, 1998), esp. 152–157.

64. All quotations here are from Toni Bentley, "The Master [George Balanchine]," *New York Review of Books,* March 10, 2005, 13.

65. Acocella, "No Bloody Toe Shoes," 8.

66. Self, "Resisting Reality," 142.

67. Altman's comment is from the "making of" featurette on the DVD, the rest from the film's own press kit, www.sonyclassics.com/thecompany/theCompany.pdf (accessed July 8, 2007). The section entitled "On the Dancing" consists almost entirely of dutifully laudatory comments by the Joffrey's ballet master and ballet mistress: "Neve Campbell is a beautiful and dedicated artist. Her discipline for getting back in shape after ten years off pointe was amazing and inspiring to the entire Joffrey Ballet. In class she made it her priority to take corrections from the Joffrey Ballet Masters and she achieved the Joffrey look in a relatively short time."

And "[i]n everyway [*sic*], Neve Campbell epitomized the Joffrey dancer. She is exceptionally talented physically and mentally for both classical ballet and contemporary works." This differs little from the situation pertaining to Julia Stiles in *Save the Last Dance,* but more interesting is that the comments are also very similar to those made about much older films. See, again, David Lichine's remarks about Margaret O'Brien in the press book for *The Unfinished Dance* (1946): "Margaret is one of the finest young dancers [I have] ever seen. In six months [*sic*] time she learned what most young ballet students must study years to accomplish." Or those about Gene Tierney in the press book for *Never Let Me Go* (1953): "Anton Dolin, world-famed dancer and choreographer who has discovered and trained fully as many dancers as any of his contemporaries, recently put himself on record as stating that had Hollywood's Gene Tierney not chosen a film career she might have been an outstanding ballerina. . . . [T]hrough sheer hard work, determination and enthusiasm, the actress achieved a point of perfection in her four months of ballet that many have struggled years to attain." Both press books from Cinema-Television Library, USC. See also the discussions of the films in chapters 2 and 5 of this book.

68. Waugh, "'Acting to Play Oneself,'" 68.

69. John Chapman, "The Aesthetic Interpretation of Dance History," *Dance Chronicle* 3 (1979–1980): 260.

70. Ibid.

71. From Lincoln Kirstein, *Dance: A Short History of Classical Theatrical Dancing* (New York: Dance Horizons, 1969), 151 (quoted in Chapman, "The Aesthetic Interpretation of Dance History," 261); and Alexander Bland, *A History of Ballet and Dance* (London: Hamlyn, 1963), 16 (quoted in Chapman, "The Aesthetic Interpretation of Dance History," 265–266). One of the best-known "antievolutionary" works on dance history is Selma Jeanne Cohen, *Next Week, "Swan Lake": Reflections on Dance and Dances* (Middletown, Conn.: Wesleyan University Press, 1982), which explores, among many other things, precisely how little of the dancing of "our present" would make sense in or to the past from which evolutionary scholars claim it developed in such a linear fashion.

72. Here and next sentence are from Richard Dyer, "Classical Ballet: A Bit of Uplift," in *Only Entertainment* (New York: Routledge, 1992), 41.

73. See www.imdb.com, *Sun Valley Serenade,* "user comments"; there are twenty-three postings as of this writing (July 2007).

74. See www.imdb.com, *Ice Princess,* "user comments" (sixty-seven total as of July 2007).

75. Turner Classic Movies is probably the best-known cable channel that specializes in the circulation of "old movies," but many other channels might feature one or another of them from time to time. Films once thought "lost," such as the 1931 version of *Waterloo Bridge,* or new prints of silent films, also are shown and reshown in specialized programs devoted to particular topics, stars, or, in some cases, completely arbitrary groupings (a program of films that all have the word *city* in the title, for example).

76. Lincoln Kirstein, *What Ballet Is About,* 51.

FILMOGRAPHY

For more information on the casts (here people who play dance artists of some kind are favored) and production personnel of these films, see the Internet Movie Database (www.imdb.com).

An American in Paris (MGM, 1951). Gene Kelly, Leslie Caron, Oscar Levant, Georges Guetary, Nina Foch. Director Vincente Minnelli. Writer Alan Jay Lerner. Choreography Gene Kelly.

The Ballet Girl (William A. Brady Picture Plays, 1916). Alice Brady, Holbrook Blinn, Robert Frazer. Director George Irving. Based on Compton Mackenzie's novel *Carnival.*

The Band Wagon (MGM, 1953). Fred Astaire, Cyd Charisse, Jack Buchanan, Oscar Levant, Nanette Fabray, James Mitchell. Director Vincente Minnelli. Writers Betty Comden and Adolph Green. Choreography Michael Kidd.

Bathing Beauty (MGM, 1944). Red Skelton, Esther Williams. Director George Sidney. Writers Dorothy Kingsley, Allen Boretz, Frank Waldman. Choreography Robert Alton and Jack Donohue; water ballet John Murray Anderson.

Billy Elliot (Arts Council of England/BBC Films/Studio Canal/Tiger Aspect Pictures/WT2 Productions/Working Title Films, 2000). Jamie Bell, Jamie Draven, Gary Lewis, Julie Walters. Director Stephen Daldry. Writer Lee Hall. Choreography Peter Darling. *Swan Lake* courtesy of Matthew Bourne.

Black Tights (Talma Films, 1962 [U.S.]). Zizi Jeanmaire, Cyd Charisse, Roland Petit, Moira Shearer, Dirk Sanders, George Reich, Josette Clavier, Hans von Manen. Director Terence Young. Choreography Roland Petit.

Bobbie of the Ballet (Universal, 1916). Louise Lovely, Lon Chaney. Director Joseph De Grasse. Writers Grant Carpenter and Ida May Park.

Center Stage (Columbia, 2000). Amanda Schull, Zoe Saldana, Susan May Pratt, Peter Gallagher, Donna Murphy, Ethan Stiefel, Sascha Radetsky, Julie Kent, Ilya Kulik. Director Nicholas Hytner. Writer Carol Heikkinen. Choreography Susan Stroman. Additional choreography Christopher Wheeldon.

The Company (Sony Pictures Classics, 2003). Neve Campbell, Malcolm McDowell, James Franco, Marilyn Dodds Frank, Deborah Dawn, Suzanne L. Prisco, Domingo Rubio, Maia Wilkins, Sam Franke, Trinity Hamilton, Julianne Kepley, Lar Lubovitch, Robert Desrosiers, Charthel Arthur, Cameron Basden, Mark Goldweber, Pierre Lockett, Adam Sklute (and other members of the Joffrey Ballet). Director Robert Altman. Writers Neve Campbell and Barbara Turner (story); Barbara Turner (screenplay). Choreography Lar Lubovitch, Robert Desrosiers, Gerald Arpino, Robert Joffrey.

Dance, Girl, Dance (RKO-Radio, 1940). Maureen O'Hara, Lucille Ball, Marie Ouspenskaya, Ralph Bellamy, Katherine Alexander, Louis Hayward, Virginia Field, Vivian Fay. Director Dorothy Arzner. Writers Vicki Baum (story), Frank Davis, Tess Slesinger. Choreography Ernst Matray.

Dance Little Lady (Alderdale, 1955). Mai Zetterling, Terence Morgan, Guy Rolfe, Mandy Miller. Director Val Guest. Story R. Howard Alexander, Alfred Dunning, Val Guest, Doreen Montgomery. Dancers [uncredited] Harold Lang, Maryon Lane, David Poole.

Dance Pretty Lady (British Instructional Films, 1932). Ann Casson, Carl Harbord, Michael Hogan, Norman Claridge, Marie Rambert's Dancers. Director Anthony Asquith. Writing credits Anthony Asquith and Compton Mackenzie. Choreography Frederick Ashton.

Dancers (Golan-Globus and Hera/Baryshnikov Productions, 1987). Mikhail Baryshnikov, Alessandra Ferri, Leslie Browne, Tommy Rall, Lynn Seymour, Victor Barbee, Julie Kent. Director Herbert Ross. Writer Sarah Kernochan. Ballet sequences Mikhail Baryshnikov.

The Dancer's Peril (World, 1917). Alice Brady, Philip Hahn, Harry Benham, Montagu Love, Alexis Kosloff. Director Travers Vale. Story Harriet Morris. Dances staged Alexis Kosloff.

The Dancing Masters (Twentieth Century–Fox, 1943). Stan Laurel, Oliver Hardy, Trudy Marshall, Robert Bailey, Margaret Dumont. Director Malcolm [Mal] St. Clair. Writers George Bricker (story); W. Scott Darling (screenplay).

Days of Glory (RKO-Radio, 1944). Gregory Peck, Tamara Toumanova, Alan Reed, Maria Palmer, Lowell Gilmore, Hugo Haas, Glenn Vernon, Dena Penn. Director Jacques Tourneur. Writers Melchior Lengyel (story); Casey Robinson (screenplay).

The Dumb Girl of Portici (Universal, 1916). Anna Pavlova, Rupert Julian, Wadsworth Harris, Douglas Gerrard. Directors Phillips Smalley, Lois Weber. Writer Lois Weber (opera Germain Delavigna and Eugène Scribe).

Fame (MGM, 1980). Irene Cara, Laura Dean, Antonia Franceschi, Boyd Gaines, Paul McCrane, Gene Anthony Ray, Maureen Teefy, Anne Meara, Debbie Allen. Director Alan Parker. Writer Christopher Gore. Choreography Louis Falco.

Flashdance (Paramount, 1983). Jennifer Beals, Michael Nouri, Lilia Skala, Marine Jahan [uncredited], Sharon Shapiro [uncredited], Crazy Legs [uncredited]. Director Adrian Lyne. Writers Tom Hedley (story); Tom Hedley and Joe Eszterhas (screenplay). Choreography Jeffrey Hornaday.

Gaby (MGM, 1956). Leslie Caron, John Kerr, Taina Elg, Cedric Hardwicke, Margalo Gillmore. Director Curtis Bernhardt. Writers Robert E. Sherwood (play); S. N. Behrman, Paul. H. Rameau, George Froeschel (earlier screenplay); Albert Hackett, Frances Goodrich, Charles Lederer (screenplay). Choreography Michael [Michel] Panaieff.

Gold Diggers in Paris (Warner Bros., 1938). Rudy Vallee, Rosemary Lane, Hugh Herbert, Allen Jenkins, Curt Bois. Director Ray Enright. Writers Jerry Wald, Richard Macaulay, Maurice Leo (story); Earl Baldwin and Warren Duff (screenplay). Musical numbers Busby Berkeley.

The Goldwyn Follies (Samuel Goldwyn, 1938). Vera Zorina, Adolphe Menjou, Kenny Baker, Andrea Leeds, the American Ballet of the Metropolitan Opera. Directors George Marshall, H. C. Potter. Writers Ray Golden, Ben Hecht, Sid Kuller, Sam Perrin, Arthur Phillips. Ballet choreography George Balanchine.

Grand Hotel (MGM, 1932). Greta Garbo, John Barrymore, Joan Crawford, Wallace Beery, Lionel Barrymore, Lewis Stone. Director Edmund Goulding. Writers Vicki Baum (novel, play); William A. Drake (play).

Hans Christian Andersen (Samuel Goldwyn, 1952). Danny Kaye, Farley Granger, [Zizi] Jeanmaire, Joey Walsh, Erik Bruhn, Roland Petit. Director Charles Vidor. Writers Myles Connolly (story); Moss Hart (screenplay). Choreography Roland Petit.

Honey (Universal, 2003). Jessica Alba, Lil' Romeo, Mekhi Phifer, Missy Elliott, Lonette McKee, Michael Ellis. Director Billie Woodruff. Writers Alonzo Brown and Kim Watson. Choreography Luther A. Brown.

Invitation to the Dance (MGM, 1956). Gene Kelly, Tamara Toumanova, Igor Youskevitch, Belita, Diana Adams, Claude Bessy, Daphne Dale, Carol Haney, David Paltenghi, Tommy Rall, Claire Sombert. Director Gene Kelly. Writer Gene Kelly. Choreography Gene Kelly.

I Was an Adventuress (Twentieth Century–Fox, 1940). Vera Zorina, Richard Greene, Erich von Stroheim, Peter Lorre, Sig Ruman, George Balanchine [uncredited], Lew Christensen [uncredited], Charles Laskey [uncredited]. Director Gregory Ratoff. Writers Jacques Companéez, Herbert Juttke, Hans Jacoby, Michel Duran, Karl Tunberg, Don Ettlinger, John O'Hara. Ballet choreography George Balanchine.

The Jazz Singer (Warner Bros., 1927). Al Jolson, May McAvoy, Warner Oland, Eugenie Besserer. Director Alan Crosland. Writers Samson Raphaelson, Alfred A. Cohn, Jack Jarmuth (titles). Choreography [uncredited] Ernest Belcher.

Knock on Wood (Paramount, 1954). Danny Kaye, Mai Zetterling, Torin Thatcher, Diana Adams, Alex Goudavich [uncredited]. Directors Melvin Frank and Norman Panama. Writers Norman Panama and Melvin Frank. Choreography Michael Kidd.

La Mort du cygne (Ballerina) (Cineatlantica, 1938). Yvette Chauviré, Mia Slavenska, Janine Charrat, Mady Berry. Director Jean Benôit-Lévy. Writers Paul Morand (novella); Jean Benôit-Lévy and Marie Epstein (screenplay). Choreography Serge Lifar; assistant choreographer Léone Mail.

Limelight (United Artists, 1952). Charles Chaplin, Claire Bloom, Nigel Bruce, Sydney Chaplin, Buster Keaton, Andre Eglevsky, Melissa Hayden. Director Charles Chaplin. Writer Charles Chaplin. Choreography Charles Chaplin and Andre Eglevsky.

The Little Ballerina (GB Instructional Films, 1948). Yvonne Marsh, Marian Chapman, Doreen Richards, Margot Fonteyn, Michael Somes [uncredited]. Director Lewis Gilbert. Writers Michael Barringer, Mary Cathcart Borer, Lewis Gilbert. Choreography [uncredited] Michel Fokine.

The Mad Genius (Warner Bros., 1931). John Barrymore, Marian Marsh, Charles Butterworth, Donald Cook, Luis Alberni. Director Michael Curtiz. Writers Martin Brown (play); J. Grubb Alexander and Harvey Thew (screenplay). Choreography Adolph Bolm.

The Man Who Loved Redheads (British Lion/London Films, 1955). Moira Shearer, John Justin, Roland Culver, Gladys Cooper, Denholm Elliot, Moyra Fraser, John Hart. Director Harold French. Writer Terence Rattigan. Choreography Alan Carter.

Meet Me in Las Vegas (MGM, 1956). Cyd Charisse, Dan Dailey, Agnes Moorehead, Lili Darvas, Paul Henreid, John Bracia, Liliane Montevecchi. Director Roy Rowland. Writer Isobel Lennart. Choreography Hermes Pan and Eugene Loring.

The Men in Her Life (Columbia, 1941). Loretta Young, Conrad Veidt, Dean Jagger, Eugenie Leontovich, Ann Todd, Ludmila Toretzka, Tommy Ladd. Director Gregory Ratoff. Writers Eleanor Smith (novel); Frederick Kohner, Paul Trivers, Michael Wilson. Choreography Adolph Bolm.

The Midnight Sun (Universal, 1926). Laura La Plante, Pat O'Malley, Raymond Keane, Earl Metcalf. Director Dimitri Buchewetzki. Writers Pierre Benôit (novel); A. P. Younger (screenplay).

Million Dollar Mermaid (MGM, 1952). Esther Williams, Victor Mature, Walter Pidgeon, Maria Tallchief. Director Mervyn LeRoy. Writer Everett Freeman. Choreography Busby Berkeley and Audrene Brier; Tallchief's choreography [uncredited] Michel Fokine and George Balanchine.

Mission to Moscow (Warner Bros., 1943). Walter Huston, Ann Harding, Eleanor Parker, Lily Norwood [Cyd Charisse] [uncredited], Michel Panaieff [uncredited]. Director Michael Curtiz. Writers Joseph E. Davies (book); Howard Koch (screenplay). Ballet choreography [uncredited] Michel Panaieff, staged Leroy Prinz.

Never Let Me Go (MGM, 1953). Clark Gable, Gene Tierney, Belita, Richard Haydn, Kenneth More, Anna Valentina. Director Delmer Daves. Writers Roger Bax, George Froeschel, Ronald Millar. Ballet scenes danced by the London Festival Ballet Company [uncredited]; Tierney's dance double [uncredited] Violetta Elvin, Tierney's partner [uncredited] Anton Dolin.

Nijinsky (Hera Productions, 1980). Alan Bates, George de la Peña, Leslie Browne, Carla Fracci, Alan Badel, Ronald Pickup, Jeremy Irons, Anton Dolin. Director Herbert Ross. Writers Romola Nijinsky and Hugh Wheeler.

Oklahoma! (Magna/Rodgers & Hammerstein Productions, 1955). Shirley Jones, Gordon MacRae, Gloria Grahame, Gene Nelson, Charlotte Greenwood, Rod Steiger, James Mitchell, Bambi Lynn. Director Fred Zinnemann. Writers Lynn Riggs (play); Oscar Hammerstein II (play); Sonya Levien and William Ludwig. Choreography Agnes de Mille.

On Your Toes (Warner Bros./First National, 1939). Vera Zorina, Eddie Albert, Alan Hale, Frank McHugh, James Gleason, Leonid Kinskey, Charles Laskey. Director Ray Enright. Writers George Abbott, Lorenz Hart, Richard Rodgers (play); Hugh Cummings, Sig Herzig, Richard Macaulay, Lawrence Riley, Jerry Wald. Choreography George Balanchine.

The Philadelphia Story (MGM, 1940). Katharine Hepburn, Cary Grant, James Stewart, Virginia Weidler, Ruth Hussey, John Howard. Director George Cukor. Writers Philip Barry (play); Donald Ogden Stewart (screenplay).

The Red Danube (MGM, 1949). Janet Leigh, Peter Lawford, Angela Lansbury, Walter Pidgeon, Ethel Barrymore. Director George Sidney. Writers Bruce Marshall (novel); Gina Kaus and Arthur Wimperis (screenplay).

The Red Shoes (The Archers, 1948). Moira Shearer, Marius Goring, Anton Walbrook, Albert Bassermann, Ludmilla Tcherina, Robert Helpmann, Leonide Massine, Esmond Knight, Marie Rambert. Directors Michael Powell and Emeric Pressburger. Writers Hans Christian Andersen (fairy tale); Michael Powell and Emeric Pressburger. Choreography Robert Helpmann and Leonide Massine.

Save the Last Dance (Cort/Madden Productions/MTV Films, 2001). Julia Stiles, Sean Patrick Thomas, Kerry Washington. Director Thomas Carter. Writers Duane Adler (story); Duane Adler and Cheryl Edwards (screenplay). Ballet choreography Randy Duncan, hip-hop choreography Fatima.

Shall We Dance (RKO-Radio, 1937). Fred Astaire, Ginger Rogers, Ketti Gallian, Edward Everett Horton, Jerome Cowan, Harriet Hoctor. Director Mark Sandrich. Writers Harold Buchman and Lee Loeb (story); Ernest Pagano, Allan Scott, P. J. Wolfson (screenplay). Choreography Hermes Pan, ballet staging Harry Losee.

Silk Stockings (MGM, 1957). Fred Astaire, Cyd Charisse, Janis Paige, Peter Lorre, Jules Munshin, George Tobias, Belita. Director Rouben Mamoulian. Writers Abe Burrows,

George S. Kaufman, Leueen MacGrath (play); Leonard Gershe and Leonard Spigelgass (screenplay). Choreography Eugene Loring and Hermes Pan.

Six Weeks (Polygram/Universal, 1982). Dudley Moore, Mary Tyler Moore, Katherine Healy, Michael Ensign, Anne Ditchburn, Jennifer Adams. Director Tony Bill. Writers Fred Mustard Stewart (novel); David Seltzer (screenplay). Choreography Willem F. Christensen and Anne Ditchburn.

Slow Dancing in the Big City (CIP, 1978). Paul Sorvino, Anne Ditchburn. Director John G. Avildsen. Writer Barra Grant. Choreography Anne Ditchburn and Robert North.

Something in the Wind (Universal International, 1947). Donald O'Connor, Deanna Durbin, John Dall, Jan Peerce. Director Irving Pichel. Writers Charles O'Neal and Fritz Rotter (story); William Bowers and Harry Kurnitz (screenplay). Choreography Eugene Loring.

Specter of the Rose (Republic, 1946). Ivan Kirov, Viola Essen, Judith Anderson, Michael Chekhov, Lionel Stander. Director Ben Hecht. Writer Ben Hecht. Choreography Tamara Geva.

Stage Madness (Fox, 1927). Virginia Valli, Tullio Carminati, Virginia Bradford, Lou Telegen, Richard Walling. Director Victor Schertzinger. Writers Polan Banks and Randall H. Faye.

Step Up (Eketahuna/Summit/Touchstone, 2006). Channing Tatum, Jenna Dewan, Damaine Radcliff, De'Shawn Washington. Director Anne Fletcher. Writers Duane Adler and Melissa Rosenberg. Choreography Anne Fletcher.

The Story of Three Loves (MGM, 1953), "The Jealous Lover." Moira Shearer, James Mason, Agnes Moorehead. Director Gottfried Reinhardt. Writer John Collier. Choreography Frederick Ashton.

Tonight We Sing (Twentieth Century–Fox, 1953). David Wayne, Ezio Pinza, Roberta Peters, Anne Bancroft, Tamara Toumanova, Isaac Stern, Jan Peerce. Director Mitchell Leisen. Writers Ruth Goode, Sol Hurok, Harry Kurnitz, George Oppenheimer. Choreography David Lichine and Michel Fokine [uncredited].

The Turning Point (Hera/Twentieth Century–Fox, 1977). Anne Bancroft, Shirley MacLaine, Leslie Browne, Mikhail Baryshnikov, Tom Skerritt, Martha Scott, Alexandra Danilova, James Mitchell, Antoinette Sibley. Director Herbert Ross. Writer Arthur Laurents. Choreography Alvin Ailey, Frederick Ashton, George Balanchine, Jean Coralli, John Cranko, Michel Fokine, Lev Ivanov, Harald Lander, Kenneth MacMillan, Alexander Minz, Dennis Nahat, Jules Perrot, Marius Petipa.

The Unfinished Dance (MGM, 1947). Margaret O'Brien, Cyd Charisse, Karin Booth, Danny Thomas, George Zoritch [uncredited]. Director Henry Koster. Writers Paul Morand (story); Myles Connolly (screenplay). Choreography David Lichine.

Valentino (Anglo-EMI/United Artists, 1977). Rudolf Nureyev, Leslie Caron, Michelle Phillips, Carol Kane, Anthony Dowell. Director Ken Russell. Writers Chaw Mank and Brad Steiger (novel); Mardik Martin and Ken Russell (screenplay). Choreography Gillian Gregory.

Waterloo Bridge (MGM, 1940). Vivien Leigh, Robert Taylor, Virginia Field, Maria Ouspenskaya, Lucile Watson, C. Aubrey Smith. Director Mervyn LeRoy. Writers Robert E. Sherwood (play); S. N. Behrman, Hans Rameau, George Froeschel (screenplay). Choreography Ernst Matray.

White Nights (Columbia/Delphi IV/New Visions, 1985). Mikhail Baryshnikov, Gregory Hines, Isabella Rossellini, Helen Mirren. Director Taylor Hackford. Writers James Goldman (story); Eric Hughes and James Goldman (screenplay). Choreography Twyla Tharp, Roland Petit, Gregory Hines.

A Woman's Way (Columbia, 1928). Margaret Livingston, Warner Baxter, Armand Kaliz, Mathilde Comont. Director Edmund Mortimer. Writers Izola Forrester (story); Elmer Harris and Will M. Ritchey (screenplay).

Yolanda and the Thief (MGM, 1945). Fred Astaire, Lucille Bremer, Frank Morgan, Mildred Natwick, Leon Ames. Director Vincente Minnelli. Writers Ludwig Bemelmans (story); Irving Brecher and Jacques Théry (screenplay). Choreography Eugene Loring.

You Can't Take It with You (Columbia, 1938). Jean Arthur, Lionel Barrymore, James Stewart, Edward Arnold, Mischa Auer, Ann Miller, Spring Byington, Dub Taylor, Lillian Yarbo, Eddie Anderson. Director Frank Capra. Writers George S. Kaufman and Moss Hart (play); Robert Riskin (screenplay).

INDEX

ABOUT THE AUTHOR

ADRIENNE L. McLEAN obtained her M.F.A. in Dance as a Meadows Fellow at Southern Methodist University in 1981 and, after an interval of "normal" life, returned to school and acquired an interdisciplinary Ph.D. in Film Studies and American Studies from Emory University in 1994. She is currently a professor of Film and Aesthetic Studies at the University of Texas at Dallas and the author of *Being Rita Hayworth: Labor, Identity, and Hollywood Stardom* (Rutgers University Press, 2004), as well as the coeditor of *Headline Hollywood: A Century of Film Scandal* (Rutgers University Press, 2001). With Murray Pomerance she is currently editing the Rutgers book series Star Decades: American Culture/American Cinema. In addition to publishing in film journals such as *Cinema Journal, Film Quarterly,* and the *Journal of Film and Video,* she has also written for *Dance Chronicle, The Dancing Times,* and *The International Dictionary of Ballet* (St. James Press, 1992).